T0342461

THE INDUSTRIALISTS

Politics and Society in Modern America

William H. Chafe, Gary Gerstle, Linda Gordon, and Julian E. Zelizer, Series Editors

The Industrialists: How the National Association of Manufacturers Shaped American Capitalism, Jennifer Delton

Gateway State: Hawai'i and the Cultural Transformation of American Empire, Sarah Miller-Davenport

Getting Tough: Welfare and Imprisonment in 1970s America, Julilly Kohler-Hausmann

The Rise of a Prairie Statesman: The Life and Times of George McGovern, Thomas J. Knock

The Great Exception: The New Deal and the Limits of American Politics, Jefferson Cowie

The Good Immigrants: How the Yellow Peril Became the Model Minority, Madeline Y. Hsu

A Class by Herself: Protective Laws for Women Workers, 1890s–1990s, Nancy Woloch

The Loneliness of the Black Republican: Pragmatic Politics and the Pursuit of Power, Leah Wright Rigueur

Don't Blame Us: Suburban Liberals and the Transformation of the Democratic Party, Lily Geismer

Relentless Reformer: Josephine Roche and Progressivism in Twentieth-Century America, Robyn Muncy

For a full list of books in this series see: http://press.princeton .edu/series/politics-and-society-in-modern-america

The Industrialists

How the National Association of Manufacturers Shaped American Capitalism

Jennifer A. Delton

PRINCETON UNIVERSITY PRESS

PRINCETON AND OXFORD

Requests for permission to reproduce material from this work
should be sent to permissions@press.princeton.edu

Published by Princeton University Press
41 William Street, Princeton, New Jersey 08540
6 Oxford Street, Woodstock, Oxfordshire OX20 1TR

press.princeton.edu

Library of Congress Control Number 2019956216
ISBN 978-0-691-16786-2
ISBN (e-book) 978-0-691-20332-4

British Library Cataloging-in-Publication Data is available

Editorial: Eric Crahan and Thalia Leaf
Production Editorial: Jill Harris
Jacket Design: Chris Ferrante
Production: Jacqueline Poirier
Publicity: Alyssa Sanford and Kate Farquhar-Thomson
Copyeditor: Cynthia Buck

Jacket image: *Business Screen Magazine*, issue 4, vol. 9 (May 1948).
Courtesy of Hagley Digital Archives, Hagley Library, Wilmington, DE

This book has been composed in Adobe Text and Gotham

Printed on acid-free paper. ∞

Printed in the United States of America

10 9 8 7 6 5 4 3 2 1

For Ed

The bourgeoisie has through its exploitation of the world market given a cosmopolitan character to production and consumption in every country. To the great chagrin of Reactionists, it has drawn from under the feet of industry the national ground on which it stood. All old-established national industries have been destroyed or are daily being destroyed.

—MARX AND ENGELS, 1848

I am filled with the spirit of the export trade. I love to do business with the big importing houses of the world . . . and I know that when the day comes when we can better understand one another and realize that, after all, the race is one, with fundamental interests identical, we will usher in the millennium.

—ATTENDEE AT INTERNATIONAL TRADE CONFERENCE, 1915

CONTENTS

ILLUSTRATIONS

THE INDUSTRIALISTS

Introduction

American companies used to make things. In the United States. With American workers. Manufacturing drove economic growth in the twentieth century. It made the United States the most powerful nation in the world and paved the way for the American-styled global capitalism of the twenty-first century. Manufacturing gave birth to industrial unions, shaped US politics, and, at its height, employed one in four American workers. When it declined in the late twentieth century, it took organized labor and the Democrats' New Deal coalition down with it. Manufacturing still exists in the United States, of course, but it is now a mere economic sector, no longer the central measure of growth, and no longer a major source of employment.

This is the story of manufacturing's main lobbyist and trade association, the National Association of Manufacturers, more commonly known as NAM.[1] Founded in 1895 to expand foreign trade, it became known for its staunch, at times extreme conservatism, expressed in its ardent defense of "free enterprise" and unending battle against unions and government regulation. The industrialists who led NAM were proud capitalists. They nurtured and defended capitalism, extolled its virtues, fought its enemies, and built its institutions. NAM was thus front and center in all of the major political struggles over the shape of the US political economy. It battled organized labor, defended employers' rights, opposed the New Deal, and staked out positions in myriad contests over taxation, trade, patents, and government

---

1. I refer to it throughout as "NAM." Elsewhere the acronym is sometimes preceded by "the" ("the NAM") or, when spoken, sometimes spelled out ("N-A-M").

regulations. Its members were soldiers for the conservative movement that gave us Barry Goldwater and later Ronald Reagan. Thus, political scientists and historians have written extensively about NAM, mostly in the context of lobbying, labor, and US conservatism, and mostly from the perspective of its many critics.

But NAM was also liberal and progressive. It promoted international trade, encouraged intercultural understanding and education, and welcomed women and the disabled into the workforce. It supported the United Nations (UN) and the Marshall Plan and called for an end to trade barriers. NAM encouraged companies to modernize and adopt innovations such as safety standards, workmen's compensation, and affirmative action. It published "best practices" guidelines and informed employers of the latest research on management, trade, and regulatory standards. In other words, while conservative, NAM was also forward-looking, innovative, and progressive—much like capitalism itself.[2]

This book examines NAM in the context of US manufacturing and twentieth-century capitalism. It traces NAM's role in the development of industrial capitalism, freer trade, and global economic integration, highlighting the organization's progressive, modernizing impulses as much as its conservative reflexes. By "progressive," I mean its role in crafting a variety of reforms and policies—such as tariff reform, more open borders, and affirmative action—that changed the national landscape and helped manufacturers adapt to new circumstances and opportunities. These types of reform "moved history forward" and were surprisingly compatible with NAM's anti-unionism. Although not as powerful as its enemies believed, nor as effective as it hoped, NAM nonetheless worked in concert with the US government and international institutions to shape twentieth-century capitalism in the United States and the world.

This globalizing impulse was not without consequence: a large part of this story is about how NAM's support for the free flow of goods, services, and currency across national boundaries not only divided the organization but also contributed to deindustrialization and the closing of thousands of US factories, many of them NAM members. The post-industrial, global, finance- and tech-based economy we live in today is partly the result of NAM's

---

2. Many people have argued that capitalism is progressive, including Karl Marx, but more recently see Joyce Appleby, *The Relentless Revolution: A History of Capitalism* (New York: W. W. Norton, 2010), and Edmund Fawcett, *Liberalism: The Life of an Idea* (Princeton, NJ: Princeton University Press, 2014).

century-long promotion of trade expansion and economic integration.[3] The great irony here is that in shaping trade and economic policies to fit their global interests and ambitions, the industrialists who led NAM undermined their own political and economic power. Did they know this? Could they have anticipated it? These questions and others will be addressed in the chapters ahead, which offer both an examination of how NAM worked (and didn't work) and an argument about NAM as a capitalist modernizer.

NAM as Capitalist Modernizer

Historians and political scientists have examined NAM first and foremost as a lobbyist for corporate capitalism and have thus focused overwhelmingly on its role in US politics, in which it represented the conservative opposition to the labor movement, liberals, environmentalists, and government regulations.[4] I have no quibble with these analyses. NAM *was* conservative, especially in its political activity, and I will be examining the forms its conservatism took throughout this book. But the question I am asking is different: What did NAM do for the manufacturers it represented? And given the centrality of manufacturing to the US economy, how did NAM's efforts shape capitalism? In addressing these questions, the more progressive side of the organization necessarily comes into focus. Recognizing these progressive tendencies not only provides a more textured understanding of this particular organization but also helps explain US manufacturing's rise and unlikely survival in a post-industrial age.

To understand how a conservative, anti-union organization can also be seen as progressive, it helps to remember how unorganized and chaotic US capitalism was at the end of the nineteenth century, when NAM was founded. Imagine investing money or producing goods in an economy with

3. In this regard, this book draws from and contributes to the recent literature on the history of twentieth-century capitalism, which includes works like Gerald F. Davis, *Managed by the Markets: How Finance Reshaped America* (New York: Oxford University Press, 2009), Louis Hyman, *Debtor Nation: The History of America in Red Ink* (Princeton, NJ: Princeton University Press, 2011); Quinn Slobodian, *Globalists: The End of Empire and the Birth of Neoliberalism* (Cambridge, MA: Harvard University Press, 2018); Youn Ki, "Large Industrial Firms and the Rise of Finance in Late Twentieth-Century America," *Enterprise and Society* 19, no. 4 (2018): 903–45.

4. Most recently, see Kim Phillips-Fein *Invisible Hands: The Making of the Conservative Movement from the New Deal to Reagan* (New York: W. W. Norton, 2009), Kevin Kruse, *One Nation under God: How Corporate America Invented Christian America* (New York: Basic Books, 2015), and Allan J. Lichtman, *White Protestant Nation: The Rise of the American Conservative Movement* (New York: Grove Press, 2008).

no centrally regulated currency, with no standardized measures or weights, and with laws preventing the sharing of information about pricing, wages, and technical innovation. Imagine proposing economic policies when most people saw the economy as a simple interaction between competing individuals, rather than as a system that could be understood, coordinated, and rationalized. Historians often characterize nineteenth-century American capitalism as unregulated, but that is not entirely true. Individual states regulated enterprises and trade, creating a patchwork of legal hurdles to interstate trade, akin to international trade barriers. To fulfill its promise nationally capitalism had to be reorganized and reformed. This was the work NAM took up.

NAM was not alone in this endeavor. In the early 1900s, all of the major players—manufacturers, workers, local and state government officials, wholesalers, retailers, transporters, and the US government—formed associations, unions, or agencies to bring order to the economic chaos, to standardize and regulate practices, and to coordinate and rationalize economic activity. Historians have since dubbed this activity "progressive," in that it was reform that defined in part the Progressive Era, but also because these initiatives helped Americans adapt their political and economic systems to new innovations and realities, which were generally seen as "progress" in that they bettered humans' material existence.[5] In twists and turns, this activity led to what historian Martin Sklar has called "the corporate reconstruction of capitalism," by which a new, cooperative, corporate form of capitalism, based on large conglomerations, information-sharing, and long-term planning, supplanted an older, proprietary, competitive form of capitalism in the early twentieth century.[6]

5. See especially Robert Wiebe, *The Search for Order, 1877–1920* (New York: Hill and Wang, 1966). I see no need to go over the scholarly debates about the Progressive Era, but on the concept of progress in US history, see Christopher Lasch, *The True and Only Heaven: Progress and Its Critics* (New York: W. W. Norton, 1991).

6. A large body of literature is devoted to this transformation in American capitalism. I have relied mostly on Martin Sklar, *The Corporate Reconstruction of American Capitalism* (New York: Cambridge University Press, 1988), but the transition was identified earlier by Adolph Berle and Gardiner Means, *The Modern Corporation and Private Property* (1932; New York: Harcourt, Brace and World, 1967); James Burnham, *The Managerial Revolution* (New York: John Day Co., 1941); and William Appleman Williams, *The Contours of American History* (New York: World Publishing Co., 1961). The transition was finally fully elaborated as a historical phenomenon by Alfred Chandler Jr., *The Visible Hand* (Cambridge, MA: Harvard University Press, 1977), and Stephen Skowronek, *Building a New American State* (New York: Cambridge University Press, 1983), among others.

In this new economy, organization and cooperation replaced "rugged individualism," a concept that continued as myth but no longer defined economic actors, if it ever had. The main economic actors were now large corporations presided over by a phalanx of managers and boards of directors and driven more by data and policy than by character or luck.[7] Economists, trade associations, and government officials tracked economic activity, collecting trade and labor statistics in an attempt to coordinate and shape the national economy. The New Deal and World War II furthered these centralizing tendencies, naturalizing the large corporation as an economic inevitability. In 1950, management guru Peter Drucker declared individualism irrelevant: "it is not individuals who produce but a human organization," that is, the professionally managed, multidivisional, multinational corporation.[8] While NAM vigorously defended American individualism, its leaders represented the large multi-unit corporations that had snuffed out individualism and welcomed corporate-friendly government policies.

International trade was likewise in need of rationalization and standardization, beginning with transportation, legal protections, and payment collection. Those who were charting a truly global economy in the wake of the Great Depression hoped to develop internationally agreed upon laws of property and contract that would loosen trade restrictions and protect foreign investments.[9] Here, too, NAM stepped up, working with international organizations, such as the International Chamber of Commerce (ICC), the Inter-American Council, and the United Nations, as well as the US State Department, in setting up international trade regulations and selecting representatives for the International Labor Organization (ILO). It also participated in the development of the General Agreement on Tariffs and Trade (GATT), the North American Free Trade Agreement (NAFTA), and the World Trade Organization (WTO). Its international programs and activism helped acclimate a largely parochial and protectionist membership to the ideas of reciprocity, freer trade, and international cooperation.

In trying to bring order to capitalism both at home and internationally, NAM worked closely with the government, especially the US Commerce

7. On this organization-centric economy and its "social responsibility" ethos, see Peter Drucker, *The New Society* (1950; New York: Harper & Row, 1962), and Davis, *Managed by the Markets*, chap. 1.

8. Drucker, *The New Society*, 207.

9. This characterization is from the Austrian School economist Lionel Robbins; see Slobodian, *Globalists*, chap. 3, which examines the Austrian School economists as early "neoliberals." For a more positive view of this endeavor, see Mark Mazower, *Governing the World: The History of an Idea* (New York: Penguin, 2012).

and State Departments. Although NAM claimed to act in the name of "free enterprise" and against "government interference," a totally "free" market such as existed in its rhetoric was the last thing it actually wanted. From the start, NAM was dedicated to supporting legal arrangements and institutions that insulated the market from the vagaries of politics and greed, otherwise known as democracy and competition. It put its trust not in "the market," but in experts and bureaus that collected statistics for use in business planning, in laws and regulations that protected corporate autonomy and private property, and in international institutions that stabilized currency and underwrote credit.

Despite its largely Republican and protectionist membership, NAM's economic aims were very much in line with the liberal internationalism of the Democratic Party, as represented by Woodrow Wilson, Franklin Roosevelt, John F. Kennedy, and Bill Clinton. Like NAM, liberal Democrats sought to spread American influence abroad and make the world safe for American-style capitalism. NAM raised nary a peep as Democratic administrations transferred trade authority from Congress (which represented sectional and local interests) to the executive branch (which represented national interests) and finally to the WTO (which represented the interests of international business). It is not without significance that the first sitting president to speak at NAM was the liberal Democrat John Kennedy. Still, trade expansion was always a divisive issue for NAM, a large portion of whose members supported protection. Accordingly, NAM globalists pulled their punches until the 1960s, treading carefully so as to avoid a blowup. Nonetheless, NAM's leadership consistently, if quietly, favored Democratic policies in the area of trade expansion. The last two NAM presidents of the twentieth century were Democrats.

Finally, to the extent that capitalism is a driver of change, NAM acted to help its members accept change, with respect to both technological and social innovations. As an ideology and an economic system, capitalism directs its adherents to find the next new thing—the next new invention, market, product, labor source—that can be exploited to make a fortune. In seeking innovation and newness, capitalists embrace change, even when it challenges social custom and their own preconceptions.[10] While manufacturers in NAM harbored the common race, gender, and cultural prejudices

---

10. This perspective was articulated most famously by Friedrich Hayek's "Why I Am Not a Conservative," published in his book *The Constitution of Liberty* (1960) and available at: https://www.press.uchicago.edu/books/excerpt/2011/hayek_constitution.html.

of the twentieth century, some were quick to overcome these if there was a profit to be made or a regulation to be sidestepped. Thus, NAM promoted intercultural understanding in part to exploit markets abroad. It welcomed the immigrants its members needed to keep unions out and wages low. It advocated the hiring of women in part to get around unions. During the civil rights era, NAM encouraged its members to integrate their factories—and instructed them in how to do so—to avoid further legislation. Its motives may have been selfish, but the net result helped change attitudes and policies.

NAM as an Organization

In addition to examining NAM's role in organizing and globalizing capitalism, I explore how it worked, who it represented, and how effective it was as a lobbyist. I also identify its many internal tensions. As a workplace and a (nonprofit) business, NAM was shaped as much by concerns over membership and morale as it was by politics and ideology. Its modernizing, developmental, free-trade impulses exacerbated fissures within the organization—fissures between protectionists and free-traders, pragmatists and ideologues, small concerns and large corporations, staff members and board leaders, anticommunists and those interested in trading with communists. While its enemies saw NAM as a powerful, unified lobby, NAM leaders fretted about how to keep the divided organization afloat. So split was NAM on the tariff issue, for instance, that it took no official position on it, which made it a poor lobbyist for 100 percent of its membership.

From the start, small and medium-sized companies of fewer than 500 employees made up the majority (around 80 to 85 percent) of NAM members, simply because smaller companies represented the majority of manufacturing concerns in general. NAM's programs, data, and services helped them become more modern and efficient, while its pro-industry, anti-union lobbying formed a community of interests and networks for them. NAM needed its small members to bolster its numbers and legitimacy, but it depended on large corporations for financial support, and in the end those were the interests it most fully served.

NAM was governed by a board of directors, made up of representatives from member companies. Eventually numbering over 200, the board of directors elected a president, officers, and a vice president from each state in which it had members; these officers in turn also sat on the board. Members sat on policy committees, formulating policies on such topics as conservation, taxation, patents, and international relations, which were then

TABLE I.1. NAM Presidents, 1895–2004

Year	President	Company	Product/industry	Location
1895	Thomas Dolan	Thomas Dolan & Company	Wool	Philadelphia, PA
1896–1901	Theodore Search	John B. Stetson Company	Wool, hats	Philadelphia, PA
1902–1905	David Parry	Parry Manufacturing Company	Carriages, pipe-fittings	Indianapolis, IN
1906–1908	James Van Cleave	Buck's Stove and Range Company	Stoves	St. Louis, MO
1909–1912	John Kirby Jr.	Dayton Manufacturing Company	Railroad equipment	Dayton, OH
1913–1917	George Pope	Pope Manufacturing Company	Bicycles	Hartford, CT
1918–1920	Stephen Mason	McConway and Torley Company	Railroad equipment	Pittsburgh, PA
1921–1931	John Edgerton	Lebanon Woolen Mills	Textiles	Lebanon, TN
1932–1933	Robert Lund	Lambert Pharmaceutical Company	Listerine, toothpaste	St. Louis, MO
1934–1935	Clinton L. Bardo	New York Shipbuilding Corporation	Shipbuilding	Camden, NJ
1936	Colby M. Chester	General Foods, Inc.	Food products	New York, NY
1937	W. B. Warner	McCall Corporation	Publishing	New York, NY
1938	Charles R. Hook	American Rolling Mill Company, Inc.	Steel	Columbus, OH
1939	Howard Coonley	Walworth Company	Valves, pipe-fittings	New York, NY
1940	H. W. Prentiss Jr.	Armstrong Cork Company	Linoleum, floor coverings	Lancaster, PA
1941	Walter Fuller	Curtis Publishing Company	Magazines	Philadelphia, PA
1942	William Witherow	Blaw-Knox Company	Road paving equipment	Blaw-Knox, PA
1943	Frederick Crawford	Thompson Product Company	Steel products	Euclid, OH
1944	Robert Gaylord	Ingersoll Milling Machine Company	Machine tools	Rockford, IL
1945	Ira Mosher	Russell Harrington	Cutlery	Southbridge, MA
1946	Robert R. Wason	Manning, Maxwell, and Moore	Valves, cranes, hoists	Stratford, CT

Year	Name	Company	Industry	Location
1947	Earl Bunting	O'Sullivan Rubber	Rubber heels, plastics	Winchester, VA
1948	Morris Sayre	Corn Products Refining Company	Starch, sugar, syrup	Illinois
1949	Wallace Bennett	Bennett's Paint Company	Paint	Salt Lake City, UT
1950	Claude A. Putnam	Markhem Machine	Packaging machinery	Keene, NH
1951	William H. Ruffin	Erwin Mills, Inc.	Textiles	Durham, NC
1952	William J. Grede	Grede Foundries, Inc.	Steel casings	Milwaukee, WI
1953	Charles R. Sligh Jr.	Sligh Furniture Companies	Furniture	Grand Rapids, MI
1954	Harold McClellan	Old Colony Paint and Chemical Company	Paint, chemicals	Los Angeles, CA
1955	Harry Riter	Thomas A. Edison, Inc.	Electronics	West Orange, NJ
1956	Cola Parker	Kimberly Clark, Inc.	Paper, sanitary products	Neenah, WI
1957	Ernie Swigert	Hyster Company	Forklifts, earth-moving equipment	Portland, OR
1958	Milton Lightner	The Singer Manufacturing Company	Appliances	Elizabeth, NJ
1959	Stanley Hope	Esso Standard Oil (former president); SoundScriber Corporation	Oil; dictation equipment	New Haven, CT
1960	Rudy Bannow	Bridgeport Machines, Inc.	Machine tools	Bridgeport, CT
1961	Jack McGovern	US Rubber Company	Rubber, tires	New York, NY
1962	Donald J. Hardenbrook	American Creosoting Corporation	Paper, boxes, cardboard	New York, NY
1963–1972	Werner P. Gullander	General Dynamics, Inc.	Aerospace	Fort Worth, TX
1973–1976	E. Douglas Kenna	Carrier Corporation	Air conditioning	Syracuse, NY
1977–1979	Heath Larry	US Steel Corporation	Steel	Pittsburgh, PA
1980–1989	Alexander Trowbridge	Allied Chemical Corporation	Chemicals, oil, gas	Morristown, NJ
1990–2004	Jerry Jasinowski	US Department of Commerce	Public policy	Washington, DC

Source: Author's compilation from NAM annual reports.

submitted for final approval by the board of directors and, if approved, executed by NAM staff.

A few generalizations can be made about NAM presidents over time. They overwhelmingly came from the industrial states of the Northeast and Midwest. Until the 1960s, they also tended to come from large companies, but not the largest corporations. Some of these companies, however, such as Armstrong Cork Company and Walworth Company, were very large multinational corporations that employed thousands in the United States and abroad. Others were considerably smaller. Executives from the largest US corporations, such as General Electric, General Motors, IBM, Standard Oil, and DuPont, were active and influential on the board of directors and on NAM committees, but their leaders never served as president. Beginning in 1961, NAM presidents were uniformly from large multinational corporations, and after 1990, they tended to come from government or other lobbying firms.

NAM's fortunes rose and fell with those of manufacturing, as indicated in its membership rates, which track the dramatic rise of manufacturing after the Great Depression, the onset of deindustrialization beginning in the 1960s, and the relative stasis since the 1970s. NAM's membership peaked in 1956–1957, when it reached 21,600 (or 22,000 according to NAM press releases).[11] NAM's membership was typically much lower than that of its main ally and rival, the US Chamber of Commerce, which included retailers, bankers, and service industries, as well as manufacturers. In 1976, when NAM considered a possible merger with the Chamber, its membership stood at thirteen thousand compared to the Chamber's robust membership of sixty thousand, and the Chamber's membership has only increased since then. Mergers, recession, and deindustrialization all contributed to high rates of attrition in NAM membership.

Liberals, Conservatives, and Neoliberals

Identifying the economic, ideological, and institutional concerns that drove NAM actors offers insight into the evolving political taxonomies of our own day. So let me define my terms and connect NAM's story to an idea with

11. Membership data collected from NAM annual reports; proceedings of annual conventions; "Memberships and Resignations, 1949–1967," series 8, box 148, "Membership" folder, accession 1411, National Association of Manufacturers Records, Hagley Library and Museum, Wilmington, DE (hereafter cited as NAMR); "Membership Change Summaries, 1979–1997," in board of directors meeting minutes, series 13, NAMR.

FIGURE I.1. NAM Membership, 1895–2000. *Source*: Author's compilation from NAM annual reports and other sources.

growing relevance: neoliberalism. Let's begin with "liberalism," a notoriously slippery concept with a variety of changing meanings in the context of US politics and global capitalism over the course of the twentieth century. Most broadly, a strain of what I call "philosophical liberalism" shares a historical heritage with capitalism in terms of disrupting traditional hierarchies and customs, embracing change, prizing individual liberty, overturning barriers, promoting tolerance, crossing borders, valuing diversity, seeking peace, and defining progress as material improvement. This version of liberalism has been embraced by people around the world and is generally associated with progress, openness, and modernity.[12]

Relatedly, there is the liberalism of the "American liberal tradition," which is associated with "rugged individualism," John Locke, and Americans' deep fear of overcentralized state power.[13] Sometimes called "classical liberalism," this version of liberalism has defined US political conservatism since the early twentieth century. NAM leaders always championed this version of individualistic liberalism, even as they presided over impersonal mega-organizations and favored policies that expanded the government's economic role.

12. Elements of this generic, baseline liberalism could, arguably, describe people as diverse as Voltaire, Mary Wollstonecraft, George Orwell, Elizabeth Cady Stanton, Andrew Carnegie, Walter Reuther, Martin Luther King Jr., Gloria Steinem, Steve Jobs, and current-day trans activists, although it would not describe any of them completely. See Karl Marx's *Communist Manifesto* for an analysis of capitalism/liberalism as disruptive progress, and more recently, Fawcett, *Liberalism*, 1–26.

13. See Louis Hartz, *The Liberal Tradition in America* (New York: Harcourt, Brace, 1955).

In twentieth-century US politics, liberals were those people who embraced philosophical liberalism, as described here, but also wanted to regulate capitalism to stabilize its catastrophic boom-and-bust cycles and better distribute its progressive benefits in order to end poverty and "raise all ships." Like all liberals, modern US liberals opposed concentration of power, which they saw in the monopoly power of large corporations, such as those that led NAM. They believed that labor unions and the state could be a check on large corporations. The crisis of the Great Depression enabled liberals to build a political coalition in the Democratic Party that strengthened both unions and what became the New Deal state.[14] Unions and the New Deal state thus became the cutting edge of progress and the liberal future; to oppose either—and NAM opposed both—would be to oppose progress, to be conservative.[15]

The New Deal state was nonetheless friendly to large corporations, who welcomed economic stabilization, as well as the expansion of international trade. The Democrats' liberal internationalism affirmed the philosophical form of liberalism and also required a stronger state and a more active foreign policy, both of which were opposed by the Republican Party and traditional conservatives, but supported by large multinational corporations.[16] Democrats' political rhetoric was geared toward capturing the votes of workers and liberals and thus downplayed the ways in which large corporations benefited from Democratic liberal internationalism.[17]

Although I am loath to wade into what I know is a quagmire, it cannot be ignored the extent to which Democratic liberal internationalism laid

14. For a description of US liberals, see Eric Alterman, *Why We're Liberals* (New York: Viking, 2008), and Paul Krugman, *The Conscience of a Liberal* (New York: W. W. Norton, 2007). The best new work on New Deal liberalism is Jefferson Cowie, *The Great Exception: The New Deal and the Limits of American Politics* (Princeton, NJ: Princeton University Press, 2016).

15. Unless one was opposing unions and the New Deal from the left.

16. On the New Deal's liberal internationalism, see Thomas Ferguson, "Industrial Conflict and the Coming of the New Deal," in Gary Gerstle and Steve Fraser, eds., *The Rise and Fall of the New Deal Order* (Princeton, NJ: Princeton University Press, 1989), 3–31.

17. Until, that is, the 1960s, when revisionist historians reminded Democrats that their policies had led to the Vietnam War. New Left revisionists saw the liberal internationalism of FDR and Truman as conservative, ignoring the fact that politically it was part of the New Deal, although some saw the New Deal as tainted by imperialism. See, for instance, William Appleman Williams, *The Tragedy of American Diplomacy* (1959; New York: W. W. Norton, 2009), chaps. 6–8; Lloyd Gardner, *Imperial America: American Foreign Policy since 1898* (New York: Harcourt, Brace, Jovanovich, 1976); and, more recently, Leo Panitch and Sam Gindin, *The Making of Global Capitalism: The Political Economy of American Empire* (New York: Verso, 2013). In contrast, Ferguson ("Industrial Conflict and the Coming of the New Deal") offers a perspective similar to my own.

the groundwork for what many today call neoliberalism. "Neoliberalism" is a politicized term still very much in flux. Once an ideological accusation hurled at the ruling class, it has come to be used more historically to describe the global movement of goods, services, and capital that began to accelerate in the 1980s, accompanied by the simultaneous curtailment of national welfare states, regulation, and unions. Think Ronald Reagan and Margaret Thatcher.[18] In this definition, neoliberalism refers to the revival of classical liberal ideas, which in the United States were typically called "conservative."

In US politics, "neoliberal" was also used to describe the "New Democrats" of the 1970s and 1980s—those like Paul Tsongas, Gary Hart, and eventually Bill Clinton who sought to shift the Democratic Party away from unions and welfare to the new economy of tech and trade.[19] In this case, the "neo" of "neoliberalism" described the updating of US liberalism in the Democratic Party. Since this happened alongside the Reagan Revolution, historians have seen it as part of a larger "turn to the right," which the rest of the world called "neoliberal." So what is known as neoliberalism internationally is examined in US historiography in the context of US conservatism.

But US conservatism was not historically the same thing as neoliberalism. A large part of what the rest of the world sees as neoliberalism—globalism and US interventionism—was not part of American conservatism, which was historically isolationist and protectionist, but instead was a characteristic of liberal democratic internationalism and tied to the liberal, New Deal, freer-trade Democratic Party. Yes, Republicans eventually got on board during (and because of) the Cold War, and even more so after the election of Ronald Reagan, but the institutional framework that allowed for the globalization of American capitalism was built by Democratic administrations.

Because analyses of neoliberalism are invariably critiques, they tend to underplay or ignore altogether the cosmopolitan openness of late-twentieth-century "neoliberalism" to immigration, diversity, and changing conceptions of gender and sexuality. Neoliberalism's openness to these issues separates

18. See Manfred B. Steger and Ravi Roy, *Neoliberalism: A Very Short Introduction* (New York: Oxford University Press, 2010); Panitch and Gindin, *The Making of Global Capitalism*, 14–17; and David Harvey, *A Brief History of Neoliberalism* (New York: Oxford University Press, 2005). The literature of neoliberalism is transnational and global, more concerned with NGOs and the World Bank than the American political economy per se; see Alfredo Saad-Fihlo and Deborah Johnston, eds., *Neoliberalism: A Critical Reader* (London: Pluto Press, 2005), and Philip Mirowski and Dieter Plehwe, eds., *The Road from Mont Pelerin: The Making of the Neoliberal Thought Collective* (Cambridge, MA: Harvard University Press, 2009).

19. Randall Rothenberg, *The Neoliberals: Creating the New American Politics* (New York: Simon & Schuster, 1984).

it from traditional conservatism and reflects its etymological origins in philosophical liberalism.[20] With the international resurgence of nationalism, including the rise of Trumpism in the United States, we can see more clearly the ways in which neoliberalism represents a cosmopolitan appreciation for diversity, even as it has created deeper economic and class inequality.

My understanding of neoliberalism has been influenced by Quinn Slobodian's recent book *Globalists*, which examines the internationalist perspective of European economists of the Geneva School, including Friedrich Hayek and the Mont Pelerin Society (MPS), regarded by Slobodian and others as one of the founding institutions of neoliberalism. Slobodian argues that neoliberalism has been less about "free trade" or "market fundamentalism" than about a search for international institutions to protect private capital and regulate trade after decolonization. Think GATT and WTO. Neoliberalism began not in the Reagan-Thatcher era, argues Slobodian, but rather earlier in the wake of European imperialism's collapse after World War I, as economists sought to reconstruct a worldwide capitalist economy in the face of rising democracy and decolonization.[21] I will be drawing on Slobodian's earlier timeline to argue that liberal internationalism, sometimes called "Wilsonianism," can be seen as a crucial step toward the sort of international institutions that post–World War II European neoliberals were calling for. With its promises of democracy and self-determination of nations, Wilsonianism was a powerful idea that put in motion exactly the democratic chaos that Hayek and other so-called neoliberals feared. But Wilsonians also advocated for capitalism, free trade, and, most of all, international institutions, all components of neoliberals' globalist vision. Inspired by Wilson, liberal internationalists of many nationalities helped create the international institutions and agreements that would eventually allow for the freer movement of capital, goods, and services, as well as the protection of capital and property. They did not see themselves as conservative, but rather as peacemakers and idealists.[22]

Historians are just beginning to piece together and explain neoliberalism, and this book hopes to contribute to that project. Much of that work

20. Indeed, the literature on neoliberalism emphasizes its racism with regard to underdeveloped nations; see works cited in note 18. One recent book on liberalism that understands neoliberalism as cosmopolitan and liberal is Fawcett, *Liberalism*, 17–17, 276–78.

21. Slobodian, *Globalists*.

22. See Mazower, *Governing the World*, chaps. 5–7, 10. For a definition of liberal internationalism, see Anthony Smith, *America's Mission: The United States and the Worldwide Struggle for Democracy* (Princeton, NJ: Princeton University Press, 1994). Neither Mazower nor Smith would equate liberal internationalism with neoliberalism, which is still regarded as pejorative.

has been done at the theoretical and transnational level; I attempt here to understand how the globalizing impulse of neoliberalism played out historically in twentieth-century US politics—or more specifically, how liberal internationalist ideas that were promoted by Democrats and antithetical to traditional US political conservatism came to be espoused by the Republican Party. This is especially relevant now, as the current head of the Republican Party seems to be undoing the work of neoliberals and liberal internationalists alike. NAM's history helps explain the bipartisan support for economic internationalism, freer trade, and what would later be called neoliberalism, even before the Cold War and Reagan, and even as voters (and Congress) remained extremely divided about these issues.

What to Expect

This is the first complete history of NAM, from its birth in 1895, through manufacturing's heyday in the mid-twentieth century, to deindustrialization and its survival in our present post-industrial age. All histories are stories, and like all authors, historians are forced to make choices. In making these choices, I have tried to balance detail and readability, depth and breadth, and competing perspectives, both those outside NAM and those within it. It is by no means a comprehensive history of all of NAM's policy positions or political activities, but it captures a story about manufacturing's role in the development of twentieth-century capitalism at home and abroad.

I focus on the themes and argument outlined in this introduction, tracing their development over time while also emphasizing colorful personalities and unexpected contradictions. Highlights of the story I tell include NAM's support for trade with the Soviet Union and other communist countries; congressional investigations and changing lobbying laws; a history of tariff legislation and protectionism; women in industry and NAM; the evolution of the Export-Import Bank and other government subsidies; NAM's membership quandaries; and a new interpretation of NAM in the Reagan Era. Based mainly on materials from the NAM archives, the book also draws on congressional hearings, newspaper accounts, trade journals, and a wide array of secondary sources.

I have organized the story chronologically according to three overlapping phases of industrial manufacturing since the 1890s. The first phase is the ascent and reorganization of industrial manufacturing from the 1890s to 1940. The second phase, from 1941 to 1980, marked manufacturing's dominance in US society and the world as the United States lowered tariffs and pursued freer trade. Manufacturing's share of the GDP peaked in 1953, when it represented 25.8 percent of domestic production. Despite its economic centrality well into the 1980s, US manufacturing began to decline in the 1960s; the third phase, from 1960 to 2004, featured deindustrialization, globalization, and the disintegration of the large multidivisional corporation in the 1990s. This process resulted in a new sleek, high-tech, down-sized manufacturing sector, integrated into global supply chains and more productive than ever before.

Manufacturing is still a substantial part of the US economy, holding steady at 11 to 12 percent of GDP. Indeed, the United States, after China, is still the leading producer of manufactured goods.[23] But the industrial capitalism that NAM helped shape and rationalize in the twentieth century is no longer the coin of the realm. It has been replaced by what Gerald Davis has called "shareholder capitalism," which is organized around tech-enhanced finance markets rather than a manufactured-goods market.[24] Thus, manufacturers (and NAM) no longer occupy the uppermost echelons of power. That role has been assumed by the heads of the finance sector and the tech industries, whose goods are of indeterminate materiality and international origin. Nor, of course, is manufacturing a major employer. After a century of fighting unions, NAM only really "won" when US manufacturers shut down their large multidivisional plants. Unions' demise went hand in hand with manufacturers' own diminished political significance and the passing of the industrial capitalism that NAM had done so much to nurture and shape.

Were NAM's leaders simply short-sighted individuals who destroyed the sector they were supposed to advance? Or were they an economic class struggling to stay ahead of changes they had little control over? Did they get what they wanted? Or did they miscalculate? Did short-term profits for some manufacturers consign others to failure and obsolescence? In raising these questions, this book aims to capture how NAM's leaders were both actors in and entangled by history.

23. Martin Neil Baily and Barry Bosworth, "US Manufacturing: Understanding Its Past and Potential Future," *Journal of Economic Perspectives* 28, no. 1 (Winter 2014): 2–26.

24. See Davis, *Managed by the Markets*, chaps. 2–3; Hyman, *Debtor Nation*; and Nicholas Lemann, *Transaction Man: The Rise of the Deal and the Decline of the American Dream* (New York: Farrar, Straus and Giroux, 2019).

PART I

Ascent, 1895–1940

Manufacturing skyrocketed in the United States after the Civil War, driven by the development of steel and the new electrical industry, which together produced the materials to build a national industrial infrastructure: railroad tracks and cars, bridges, girders, machine tools, and other foundational necessities for the industrialization of American manufacturing. By the 1890s, the largest companies had become vertically integrated, multi-unit corporations, overseeing the attainment of raw materials, their transformation into products, and the distribution of those products to buyers—all in one plant or factory complex. The rise of these heavily capitalized enterprises led to a concentration of production and distribution, also known as "monopolies."

These changes created numerous economic depressions, a flood of immigrants, a crisis for America's individualist tradition, and open class conflict. In other words, the rise of industrial capitalism was as destructive as it was creative, as terrifying as it was clarifying. In an attempt to bring order to the chaos, organizations like the National Association of Manufacturers were formed, as were the American Federation of Labor, the US Department of Labor and Commerce, and the Federal Reserve. Manufacturing output and employment increased steadily in the first quarter of the twentieth century under the stabilizing effect of such institutions, until it all came hurtling down in the Great Depression.

1

Improving Industry

When a group of six hundred manufacturers met in Cincinnati in January 1895 to form a national organization to promote and defend their interests, their efforts were met with some alarm. Farmers had organized, so had workers. But why would thoroughly enfranchised and prosperous businessmen need to organize? Their interests were on the rise, after all. Never had manufacturing produced so much, and never had its factories been so large. Armed with technological advances and organizational innovations, the largest US corporations were outproducing entire nations in steel, pig iron, farm equipment, railroad tracks, and refined oil. Manufacturers were hardly in need of organization. In fact, their existing organization—in the form of gigantic trusts and interconnected directorships—was reason for other more vulnerable groups to organize.

The 1890s, however, were years of deep depression, falling prices, and cutthroat competition, and manufacturers were subsumed by problems unleashed by their own advances. New machinery and the introduction of electricity had increased production, leading to greater supply, as more manufacturers mechanized their plants to compete. In the past, producers stopped producing when demand was low and supply high, waiting for more advantageous conditions before powering back up. But the new machinery came with greater fixed costs, which made it difficult to stop production even if demand was low. Forced to keep up production, producers could compete only by slashing prices, which led to more falling prices. This cycle contributed to factory closures, bankruptcy, and the consolidation of industries, otherwise known as "horizontal integration." Between 1895 and 1904, more than 1,800 firms merged into 157 consolidated corporations. As historian Naomi Lamoreaux has argued, this merger wave was one solution to low prices and cutthroat competition.[1]

Manufacturers saw overproduction as the primary cause of their woes and had two responses to it. First, they turned to the promise of foreign markets, both to off-load surpluses and find new markets. And second, they tried to find ways to subvert the debilitating effects of competition through cooperation and planning, first in the form of unworkable "pools" and "gentlemen's agreements" and eventually, more legitimately, in the form of trade associations. The manufacturers who met in Cincinnati that January were creating an organization that would pursue both strategies, thereby facilitating the modernization of American industry and government. The result was what historian Martin Sklar has called the "corporate reconstruction of capitalism": a new form of capitalism based on cooperation, rationality, and long-term planning superseded a nineteenth-century proprietary capitalism based on competition, "rugged individualism," and decentralized government.[2] Trade associations like NAM were key to this transition.

The Trade Association Idea

Trade associations arose in the late nineteenth century to help their members deal with the chaotic effects of unregulated capitalism and uncoordinated growth.[3] At the time and even after, they were regarded by many

1. Albert K. Steigerwalt, *The National Association of Manufacturers: A Study in Business Leadership* (Ann Arbor: University of Michigan, Graduate School of Business Administration, Bureau of Business Research, 1964), 8–9; Naomi Lamoreaux, *The Great Merger Movement in American Business, 1895–1904* (New York: Cambridge University Press, 1985), chap. 1.

2. Sklar, *The Corporate Reconstruction of Capitalism*. This transition was identified earlier by Berle and Means, *The Modern Corporation and Private Property* (1932; New York: Harcourt, Brace and World, 1967), James Burnham, *The Managerial Revolution* (New York: John Day Co., 1941), and Peter Drucker, *The New Society* (1950), and fully elaborated as a historical phenomenon by Chandler in *The Visible Hand* (1977). The accompanying governmental change is examined in Skowronek, *Building a New American State* (1983).

3. Though there are different schools of thought regarding the emergence of the administrative state and the rise of corporate capitalism, historians identify trade associations as playing an important and positive role in stabilizing and transforming American capitalism. See Gerald Berk, *Louis D. Brandeis and the Making of Regulated Competition, 1900–1932* (New York: Cambridge University Press, 2009); Robert F. Himmelberg, *The Origins of the National Recovery Administration: Business, Government, and the Trade Association Issue* (New York: Fordham University Press, 1993); and Louis Galambos, *Cooperation and Competition: The Emergence of a National Trade Organization* (Baltimore: Johns Hopkins University Press, 1966).

as unscrupulous conspirators, powerful lobbyists beholden to greed. That individual businesses were banding together to share information, set price structures, support legislation, or otherwise cooperate went against the idea of free competition, which was the principle upon which free-market capitalism was allegedly based. For many, including the courts, these kinds of "cooperative" practices were collusive and anticompetitive, exactly what the Sherman Antitrust Act (1890) had banned.[4] So prevalent was this attitude that a lawyer named Arthur Jerome Eddy wrote a book condemning it, arguing that "competition" as traditionally understood was a dangerous fetish that stood in the way of transparent business practices, lower prices, and fair play. Published in 1912, *The New Competition* bore a subtitle that stated its argument: *An examination of the conditions underlying the radical change that is taking place in the commercial and industrial world—the change from a competitive to a cooperative basis.*[5]

Like many social scientists of the time, Eddy argued that the old ideals of "individualism" and "competition" were no longer useful in an increasingly interdependent, technologically advanced, modern society. Competition was war, he wrote, and war divided societies, preventing the kind of cooperation that led to social progress. Technological and organizational progress would not be realized if individual companies hoarded their secrets. Instead, Eddy proposed the sharing of information—information on prices, wages, costs, accounting practices, safety appliances, provisions for injuries—to help all companies run more efficiently and profitably. To compete, a company owner had to know the norms and standards of his market. What exactly did it cost to do business, to manufacture a product? How would individual business owners know if they were allocating resources efficiently, making a bad deal, or getting the best deal? In an effort to counter antitrust laws that prohibited collusion, Eddy promoted what he called "open price associations," which would make price information available and transparent to all. Information-sharing, or "cooperation," would be most helpful to the small producer, who did not have the wherewithal to collect the kind of data used by larger corporations to make decisions and plan ahead.[6]

Such thinking sought to standardize and stabilize market processes in ways that would benefit not just companies but employees and consumers as well. By sharing information instead of hiding it, companies would

---

4. For discussion of these attitudes, see Himmelberg, *The Origins of the National Recovery Administration*, chap. 1, and Galambos, *Cooperation and Competition*.

5. Arthur Jerome Eddy, *The New Competition* (Chicago: McClurg & Co., 1914).

6. Ibid., 82–121.

contribute to the stock of organizational knowledge, developing what we now call "best practices." "Cooperation is the watchword of the day," said the new head of the Federal Trade Commission (FTC) in 1916, adding, "We protect ourselves from competition by helping our competitor become more efficient."[7]

Proponents of "cooperative competition" saw the maligned trade organization as the proper institution for the kind of information-sharing and coordination they envisioned. Trade associations were "agencies of efficient industry," enablers of progress, organized, as President Wilson observed, "for the purpose of improving conditions in their particular industry."[8] A *Saturday Evening Post* article highlighted the valuable information provided by trade associations in the story of a paper manufacturer who, after being shown data about South American markets, the correlation between rainfall and pulp costs, and the average monthly cost of producing a ream of paper, exclaimed that he now felt like a ship captain who'd just discovered a chart and compass: "No more groping about in the dark for me—not when I can get the benefit of the kind of facts you've spread out here before me in black and white!"[9]

In helping to create the FTC in 1914, lawyer Louis Brandeis, serving as an adviser to President Wilson, hoped it would not just monitor illegal trusts but also identify and encourage "constructive cooperation," which would facilitate trade, as something different from collusion, which restrained trade.[10] Like Eddy, Brandeis saw trade associations as organizations "for mutual benefit, which substitute knowledge for ignorance, rumor, guess, and suspicion," replacing "gambling and piracy" with "research and reasoning."[11] By the 1920s, trade associations were not only legitimate organizations, but also the basis of Herbert Hoover's "associative state"—the idea that private trade associations could promote and regulate industry and commerce so that the

7. Edward Hurley, *Awakening of Business* (Garden City, NY: Doubleday, 1917), 43.

8. Hurley, *Awakening of Business*, 43; Woodrow Wilson to Edward Hurley, May 12, 1916, as cited in Hurley, *Awakening of Business*, preface.

9. Forrest Crissey, "Teamwork in Tradebuilding," *Saturday Evening Post* 136 (March 1914). The left remained critical of the kind of collusion advocated by Hurley and others, especially as practiced by the NAM; see Robert Brady, *Business as a System of Power* (New York: Columbia University Press, 1943), chaps. 1 and 6.

10. See Berk, *Louis D. Brandeis and the Making of Regulated Competition*, 27–28; Laura Phillips Sawyer, *American Fair Trade: Proprietary Capitalism, Corporatism, and the New Competition* (New York: Cambridge University Press, 2018), chap. 3.

11. From Brandeis's dissent in *American Column Lumber Company vs. the United States* (1921), (discussed later in the chapter), quoted in Jeffrey Rosen, *Louis D. Brandeis: American Prophet* (New Haven, CT: Yale University Press, 2016), 107.

state would not have to.[12] Suspicions of trade associations would remain, of course, especially with regard to lobbying. But the educational, standardization, and coordination efforts of organizations like NAM operationalized the "new competition" as outlined by Eddy and Brandeis and thereby helped bring about the new interdependent world of managed capitalism and the administrative state.

The New Organization

The idea for a national manufacturers association came in the aftermath of the 1893 depression. An editor of a Southern trade paper called the *Dixie Manufacturer* was trying to drum up participation for a manufacturing exposition in Mexico City and suggested that manufacturers form a national association to help promote foreign trade and their collective interests. The suggestion caught the eye of Thomas Egan, president of the J. A. Fay and Egan Company in Cincinnati, Ohio; having won several international awards in the 1890s for its machines, this manufacturer of woodworking machinery had a stake in international markets.[13] Egan and his buddies at the Cincinnati and Hamilton County Manufacturers Association put out a national call for manufacturers to meet in Cincinnati on January 22, 1895, for the purpose of organizing a permanent national association. The invitation noted that the new organization would be nonpolitical, nonsectional, and nonpartisan, and dedicated to expanding foreign trade and considering questions of national interest to manufacturers as a group.

More than six hundred manufacturers answered the call and attended the founding convention.[14] The keynote speaker was William McKinley, then the Republican governor of Ohio, who spoke about the importance of foreign markets for surplus goods. Others spoke on the need for a Nicaraguan canal and merchant marine. Many in attendance were already members of industry-specific trade associations, such as the National Stove

12. See Himmelberg, *The Origins of the National Recovery Administration*; Ellis Hawley, "Herbert Hoover, the Commerce Secretariat, and the 'Associative State,' 1921–1928," *Journal of American History* 61, no. 1 (1974): 116–40.

13. This account of the founding is taken from Steigerwalt, *The National Association of Manufacturers*, 17–19, and Vada Horsch, "NAM Past and Present," September 4, 1951, updated June 10, 1963, as found in series 1, box 43, NAMR. Horsch was assistant secretary of the NAM and compiled this short history in 1951.

14. Steigerwalt, *The National Association of Manufacturers*, 18. Three hundred attended, according to the *New York Times*, January 23, 1895, p. 5. Vada Horsch ("NAM Past and Present," 2) cites the figure of 583.

Manufacturers Association and the American Iron and Steel Institute. This new organization was originally supposed to be a federation, uniting all these industry-specific associations under the big umbrella of manufacturing. Membership was to be based on these associations, rather than individual companies. But that proved financially inadequate, and within two years the membership was changed to consist of individual dues-paying companies. The first president was Thomas Dolan of Philadelphia, a wool manufacturer, president of the Crampton Shipyards, and an art collector.

The men in attendance drew up and voted on a constitution, thereby creating a permanent new national organization that would seek to influence legislation on behalf of all manufacturing interests in the United States. Its voice would be so potent, said one of the constitution's authors, "that there is no legislature, no Congress, no organization of any kind that will not listen to that voice, provided that its demands be according to reason and justice."[15] Thus, from the start, the organization was openly a lobbying organization that hoped to influence legislatures on a variety of issues. Soon enough, its enemies would accuse it of trying to influence Congress, as if that were illegal. This accusation baffled NAM officials, who responded that yes, one of the purposes of their organization was to influence legislation.[16] If only they were better at it. Divisions among its members, as well as their adherence to Republican Party shibboleths, often prevented NAM from taking a strong position on important issues, such as the tariff, diminishing its influence as a lobbyist.

In 1908, the organization established its headquarters in Manhattan, where it remained until 1973, when it moved to Washington, DC. Though its governance structure would change over time, early constitutions put in place a few basic elements. The officers included a president, a vice president from each state in which NAM had members, a treasurer, and a secretary. These officers were initially elected by the membership and then, after 1913, by the board of directors.[17] Standing committees on such topics as the tariff, uniform state laws, patents, safety, and international trade allowed members with particular interests or expertise to formulate policy recommendations, which were then submitted for approval to the board of directors.[18] Over

---

15. Quoted in Steigerwalt, *The National Association of Manufacturers*, 27.

16. NAM's position would change in response to the Federal Regulation of Lobbying Act of 1946, when it would claim that its primary aim was service, not lobbying (see chapter 6).

17. See early constitutions reprinted in Steigerwalt, *The National Association of Manufacturers*, 184–202.

18. Ibid., 159.

the years, the board's failure to approve many committee recommendations would leave NAM with no official position on important issues, and
thus not in a position to lobby. The officers, board directors, and members
of the standing committees were representatives from individual member
companies. As the organization expanded its services, it also developed a
paid staff to manage the business of the organization, conduct research for
committees, recruit members, produce publications, and organize conferences and workshops. By 1922, there were sixty staff members in the New
York office.[19]

NAM members manufactured a wide array of goods, from anvils,
engines, steel, locomotives, and elevators to cereal, velocipedes, bags,
boxes, preserves and jellies, tile flooring, conveyor belts, pulleys, lathes,
textiles, fruit jars, buttons, stoves, gloves, and elixirs. They included coal
companies and wheat mills, dam-builders and garment-makers, pharmaceuticals and confectioneries. NAM was not the sort of trade association
that sought to monopolize, or "organize," a specific industry. Nonetheless,
contemporaries and historians were wary of its "commanding position" in
the new economic landscape. As one historian put it: "It was the peculiar
role of the NAM to undertake the coordination of the efforts of all business
associations—existing, subsequently organized, and special-purpose—in
the entirety of manufacturing industries of the whole United States."[20] Its
industrial diversity, however, as we will see, made it less effective as a lobbyist because the range of perspectives made it difficult for the organization
to come to agreement on specific issues.

Most of NAM's members were from New England and the Midwest. In
1899, more than half the membership came from Pennsylvania, New York,
Illinois, and Ohio, although companies from twenty-six other states, including the South, were also represented.[21] Since the organization's leadership
came from the twelve largest industrialist states, it was dominated by Midwestern and New England members, who were staunch Republicans.

NAM's claim of nonpartisanship rested in large part on "New South"
manufacturers, who were Democrats. This made the new organization an
experiment in transcending the sectionalism that had defined the US political economy since before the Civil War. NAM was an economic group based
not on sectional interests but on class interests, which brought it closer to

19. Clarence Elmore Bonnett, *Employers' Associations in the United States: A Study of Typical
Associations* (New York: Macmillan, 1922), 294–95.
20. Brady, *Business as a System of Power*, 191.
21. Steigerwalt, *The National Association of Manufacturers*, 40.

what existed in Europe and was indicative of the nationalization of the US economy. A year after NAM's founding, the *Atlanta Constitution* featured an interview with T. H. Martin, the *Dixie* editor who originally suggested the creation of a national organization of manufacturers. The paper wanted to know: Did the South get credit for originating the idea? What influence would it have on the South? Martin reported that yes, there was a resolution recognizing the *Dixie Manufacturer*. Then he assured readers that the new organization was strictly national in scope and would not be interfering in regional questions (that is, Jim Crow), and that the South stood to benefit from its participation in a national manufacturing group whose purpose was "united action for mutual benefit."[22] Like many New South enthusiasts, Martin was hoping to develop Southern industry, attract branch plants to Southern cities, and open foreign markets for Southern cotton.[23]

The new organization's leadership was likewise interested in Southern manufacturers, mostly because of their connections to congressional Democrats. Connections to Southern Democrats initially gave the overwhelmingly Republican NAM an additional "in" in Congress that helped them avoid relying solely on Northern Republicans, who were increasingly pressured by unions and working-class voters. NAM officials corresponded regularly with Southern industrialists, requesting that they telegram a (Democratic) congressman or a judge to prevent a bill from reaching the floor or to keep an item off the Democratic platform.[24] It was testimony to the South's importance to NAM that the organization held its 1903 and 1905 conventions in New Orleans and Atlanta, respectively, despite a shortage of hotel rooms and the inconvenience of travel.[25] The attempt to overcome sectional politics was the beginning of a bipartisan alliance between conservative Republicans and Southern Democrats in the twentieth century that would contribute to an unusual degree of bipartisanship and cooperation.[26]

22. "The Cincinnati Convention," *Atlanta Constitution*, January 27, 1896.

23. See, for instance, "Atlanta's Vital Opportunity," *Atlanta Constitution*, February 26, 1905.

24. See, for instance, Cushing to Gordon, January 25, 1905, January 17, 1905, and May 2, 1904, in series 1, box 43, "Corporate Records, 1903–1905" file, NAMR.

25. See Cushing to Gordon, April 10, 1905, and April 19, 1905, in series 1, box 43, "Corporate Records, 1903–1905" file, NAMR. The Piedmont Hotel double-charged for all rooms, assuming that the businessmen would double up because of the shortage of rooms.

26. Cathie Jo Martin has suggested that NAM's founding was a Republican ploy to "overcome the incapacities of a sectional two-party system" and reach out to Southern businessmen otherwise trapped in the Democratic Party. She does not supply much evidence for this hypothesis other than NAM leadership's close relationship with McKinley. But it supports the idea that both Republicans and NAM were looking for ways to bring in Southern businessmen. Cathie Jo Martin and Duane

It is difficult to determine the typical size of member companies in NAM's first decades. NAM claimed to serve the "average" manufacturer. And indeed, one of the main functions of trade associations during this time was to serve the needs and interests of smaller companies, which, unlike large corporations, lacked the resources for lobbying and research. An examination of the member companies at this time, however, suggests that there was a preponderance of large companies in NAM, if by "large" we mean market-dominating companies with multiple plants and offices across the United States and Canada, foreign agents or offices, and over two thousand employees.[27] NAM's members in 1906 included such aspiring trusts as the Otis Elevator Company, American Rolling Mill Company, Inland Steel, Weyerhauser Timber, Union Carbide, Merck, National Cash Register, Pillsbury, Eli Lilly, Scott Paper, Anheuser-Busch, H. J. Heinz, Bristol-Myers, and B. F. Goodrich. Also numbering among NAM members were already mammoth corporations such as General Electric, Armour & Company, Goodyear Tire and Rubber, Bethlehem Steel, and International Harvester. Although NAM claimed to represent the "average" manufacturer, it also tried to build legitimacy by trumpeting that its members included some of the largest corporations in the nation. Indeed, some of these very large corporations would eventually acquire or merge with other NAM companies to become even larger.

Historians Robert Wiebe and James Weinstein have contended that NAM was led by the owners of small and medium-sized companies who were at odds with the large trusts of the era.[28] Writing in 1922, however, industrial relations specialist Clarence Bonnett claimed that the NAM of 1904 and "still today" (1922) was made up of "mostly large manufacturers, some trusts, and a few small manufacturers," but the "great combinations," he added, did not participate in leadership: "The life of the Association is upon the average man."[29] Nevertheless, here, too, it is not clear that the leadership was from small companies. David Parry, who was NAM president from 1902 to 1905, owned the country's largest carriage manufacturing plant, which covered six city blocks in Indianapolis and employed 2,800 men in 1906. In addition, he owned and directed other companies, such

Swank, *The Political Construction of Business Interests: Coordination, Growth, and Equality* (New York: Cambridge University Press, 2012), 92–99.

27. National Association of Manufacturers, *American Trade Index*, 1906.

28. Robert Wiebe, *Businessmen and Reform* (Cambridge, MA: Harvard University Press, 1962), and James Weinstein, *The Corporate Ideal in the Liberal State* (Boston: Beacon Press, 1968).

29. Bonnett, *Employers' Associations in the United States*, 291.

as Overland Automobile. James Van Cleave, NAM president from 1906 to 1908, was the owner of Buck's Stove and Range Company in St. Louis; his company employed over 700 men and was described as one of the largest stove manufacturers in the United States. John Kirby, president from 1909 to 1912, headed the Dayton Manufacturing Company of Dayton, Ohio, "a large concern making steel railroad supplies" that did business in Canada, Australia, and South America.[30] Daniel A. Tompkins, who was active in a number of leadership positions in the organization, was head of the Southern Cotton Oil Company, a large trust, and the D. A. Tomkins Company, a Charlotte, North Carolina, engineering firm that built mills and electric plants, as well as several other concerns.[31] NAM leader C. W. Post had the beginnings of a cereal and real estate empire. These substantial enterprises may not have been General Electric or International Harvester, but they would have been seen at the time as "big business."

NAM's membership grew steadily but not spectacularly in its first years, reaching 1,000 members by 1899 and 3,000 by 1904. By 1914, however, it was still only at 3,400. In 1922, it reached 5,350 companies.[32] It was not until World War II that its membership reached 10,000. NAM's creation in the first decades of the twentieth century of auxiliary organizations and ad hoc groups, such as the National Council for Industrial Defense (NCID) and the National Industrial Conference Board (NICB), suggests that its influence was wider than its official membership numbers. The NCID's 253 member organizations at the state, local, and national levels, for instance, gave NAM access to a much wider constituency and audience than its own membership figures indicate.[33] NAM's membership figures also hide the constant attrition

30. Dayton Manufacturing Company described in "Classes Roosevelt with Conspirators," *New York Times*, May 19, 1908, p. 12, and "Dayton Manufacturing Company," Wright State University, Department of Special Collections and Archives. On Parry, see Steigerwalt, *The National Association of Manufacturers*, 108; David Parry, *The Scarlet Empire*, edited by Jerome Clubb and Howard W. Allen (1906; Carbondale: Southern Illinois University Press, 2001), introduction; and "The Man of Millions, the Packhorse of the Masses," *New York Times*, June 3, 1906, p. x6. On Van Cleave, see *The National Cyclopaedia of American Biography*, vol. 14 (J. T. White Co., 1910), p. 372.

31. Brenda Marks Eagle, "Daniel Augustus Tompkins, 1851–1914," *Documenting the American South* (website), http://docsouth.unc.edu/nc/tompkins/bio.html.

32. For the 1922 figure, see See Richard S. Tedlow, "The National Association of Manufacturers and Public Relations during the New Deal," *Business History Review* 50, no. 1 (Spring 1976): 25–45; and Bonnett, *Employers' Associations in the United States*, 291, which records NAM's 1922 membership as 5,700; other figures are from William H. Becker, *The Dynamics of Business and Government Relations, Industry, and Exports, 1893–1921* (Chicago: University of Chicago Press, 1981); and *NAM Annual Report*, 1902, 65.

33. See Brady, *Business as a System of Power*, 199–201; see also chapter 3.

as companies died, merged, or withdrew in a huff, only to be replaced by new recruitments. The organization's increasing dependency on membership fees as it increased its staff and services resulted in a constant attention to recruitment and retention that would shape both its policies and influence.

One area that historians have identified as having a positive effect on membership was NAM's anti-union activity, which was not one of its original stated aims. It was not until 1902, in the wake of increasing union activity, that NAM became interested in labor relations and elected as its president David Parry, head of Parry Manufacturing Company of Indianapolis and a leader in the "open-shop" movement.[34] Parry pushed an anti-union agenda to the fore of NAM's activities, and some historians have argued that it led to an increase in membership. Many issues divided manufacturers, but most of them found agreement in their opposition to the AFL.[35] NAM's anti-union activities may indeed have attracted more members, but it also alienated others, so the net effect on membership is difficult to ascertain.

What is certain is that in the first decade of the twentieth century, just as NAM was establishing itself as a voice for manufacturers, it was led by a succession of extremely vocal open-shop presidents from the Midwest who vigorously opposed the eight-hour day, anti-injunction legislation, and the American Federation of Labor. They promised to "conduct propaganda along the lines of truth and justice" to counter labor's "malicious lies" in the court of public opinion.[36] This was what *employers'* associations did. And so NAM, which had begun as a trade association, uniting manufacturers *for* trade expansion and industrial improvement, became also an employers' association when it organized manufacturers *against* labor unions.

It was an awkward pairing, combining the modernizing function of the trade association with what was seen as a reactionary assault on unions. Unions, after all, were part of the same historical transformation of capitalism that had given birth to trade associations. Part of adjusting to the new corporate capitalism was the acceptance of unions as a political and economic reality, or at least that was the opinion of the new corporate elite. The modern capitalist didn't have to love unions and could even continue

---

34. Steigerwalt, *The National Association of Manufacturers*, 108; Horsch, "NAM Past and Present," 4; Bonnett, *Employers' Associations in the United States*, 301–9.

35. Steigerwalt, *The National Association of Manufacturers*, 110–11; Julie Greene, *Pure and Simple Politics: The American Federation of Labor and Political Activism, 1881–1917* (New York: Cambridge University Press, 1994), 91–93.

36. David Parry, presidential address, *Proceedings of the Eighth Annual Convention of the National Association of Manufacturers* (hereafter *NAM Proceedings*), New Orleans, April 14–16, 1903, p. 58.

to thwart them, but he had at the very least to see them as legitimate groups in a modern democracy. While these early NAM leaders could accept—and indeed embraced—such innovations as a centralized banking system, women in the workplace, a bureaucratic administrative state, unrestricted immigration, and an international cosmopolitanism, they could not accept unions as anything other than criminal organizations. Nevertheless, they saw no contradiction in NAM's purposes. Parry, Van Cleave, and Kirby were internationalist trade expansionists, as well as reformers seeking to rationalize business practices. Their contest with labor was over who would control the future; in this sense their anti-unionism was consistent with their modernizing impulse.

Still, the outside world tended to see the organization as reactionary, conservative, and anti-union. Decades later, in the 1950s, that reputation was more ingrained than ever, and the organization's executive assistant secretary, Vada Horsch, lamented that no one ever paid attention to NAM's progressive work, especially in safety improvement and international trade. She attributed this neglect to what we would call today "the liberal media" and took it upon herself to write NAM's "real" history, in which anti-unionism played a smaller role. But to some extent, NAM itself had created this rupture in its reputation. As a trade association, NAM advocated for many progressive policies. But other organizations did as well, and they did so without being so explicitly anti-union. Indeed, the National Civic Federation (NCF), a group of wealthy businessmen working for many of the same reforms as NAM during the Progressive Era, included union leaders in its leadership and thus was regarded by journalists and historians as the "progressive" business group—the opposite of the "conservative" NAM. Similarly, in the field of international trade, various other groups arose that had no anti-union agenda, such as the National Foreign Trade Council, and they were more successful lobbyists than NAM. NAM's protectionist Republican membership made it a poor lobbyist for its progressive, internationalist goals, and its greater success in its war on labor unions was another reason why contemporaries, journalists, and historians saw it as primarily conservative. Nonetheless, what made it a trade association was its dedication to industrial improvement and standardization, and its activities in this area were not insignificant.

Improving Industrial Practices

NAM's cooperative, developmental character can be seen in its efforts to improve industry at home through standardization, information-sharing, and education. The goal was to make all of industry more efficient, safer, and hence more profitable. NAM's work in industrial improvement would knit together an economically fragmented nation. Through its efforts, it would bring about a greater uniformity in units of measurement, freight rates, and state laws and reshape standard practices in industrial safety, workmen's compensation, and dozens of other policy areas.

STANDARDIZATION

It is accepted historical wisdom that the railroad tracks crisscrossing the nation by the end of the nineteenth century played a significant role in creating national markets. But a national market required not just the ability to transport goods to all parts of the nation, but also, as importantly, some uniformity across state lines in sales contracts, freight rates, bankruptcy laws, commercial regulations, product specifications, and weights and measurements. These developed more slowly than one might assume; moreover, initiatives to achieve greater uniformity and create standards in commercial practices did not come from the federal government, but rather from trade associations and other organizations working together.[37]

A few examples should suffice to illustrate NAM's involvement in this work. Varying freight rates were a problem for manufacturers shipping raw materials to their plants and finished products from them. Freight rates were based on the classification of the item being transported. Classifications were determined by weight, length, density, difficulty of handling, liability, and value, and they were set up by state railroad commissions. Railroad companies had instituted some uniformity by developing over time three regional classification systems: Official (the East and Midwest), Western, and Southern. The use of three separate classification systems, however, made planning difficult and rates unfair. A witness testifying in 1900 before the US Industrial Commission (formed in part to deal with the issue) explained that the classification system made his product cost 50 percent more than that of a competitor shipping the same distance to the same market but from a different region.[38] Moreover, railroads maintained control of the rates and changed them in ways that appeared arbitrary and unfair. NAM took up the drive for one uniform national classification system and endorsed a strengthened Interstate Commerce Commission (ICC) to implement it. The problem turned out to be more complicated, however, than the various

37. For a description of these efforts, see *The Memoirs of Herbert Hoover: The Cabinet and the Presidency, 1920–1933* (New York: Macmillan, 1952), 66–73.

38. Cited in Steigerwalt, *The National Association of Manufacturers*, 88.

organizations working on it had realized. For instance, NAM members who benefited from the uneven classification structure opposed changing it. As late as 1942, there were still three different areas. But NAM was part of the ongoing conversation, updating members on small changes along the way.[39]

Manufacturers also faced a bewildering array of state laws regarding employment conditions, bankruptcy, stock certificates, and bills of lading. States imposed different fees, taxes, and restrictions on "foreign companies," meaning companies from other *states*. Laws regarding "foreign companies" varied widely, from having to register or obtain a license to do business in a particular state to having to pay a tax based on the capitalization of one's company.[40] Not only was it difficult for a company to keep track of these laws, but it could also be costly to sell one's product in adjoining states, let alone attempt to reach anything resembling a national market. Some companies had successfully challenged these taxes in court as impediments to trade, but such challenges were expensive and time-consuming for the average manufacturer. NAM's Legal Department helped the average manufacturer navigate the maze of state laws; it also worked to repeal and prevent state laws that imposed taxes or restrictions on businesses not domiciled in the state.[41] In 1908, NAM's Committee on Uniform State Laws suggested that NAM work with the Commissioners on Uniform State Laws to bring about the desired reforms. That national organization was getting around American federalism by crafting uniform laws, which it then introduced into state legislatures. NAM representatives participated in crafting these laws and alerted its members to lobby for them in their state legislatures. They were able to get the Uniform Warehouse Receipts Act passed in eighteen states and the Uniform Negotiable Instruments Act passed in thirty-eight states.[42] It was a similar story for a host of other issues, including bankruptcy, contract, and sales laws. This work would be taken up by New Deal

---

39. Ibid., 156–57; see also "The Movement for Better Freight Packing," *American Industries* (July 1, 1909): 15; and Frank Barton, "Uniform Freight Classification and the Interstate Commerce Commission," *Journal of Land and Public Utility Economics* 18, no. 3 (August 1942): 312–22.

40. For a description of these practices, see US Department of Commerce, "Report on the Commission of Corporations on State Laws Concerning Foreign Corporation" (Washington, DC: US Government Printing Office, 1915).

41. Steigerwalt, *The National Association of Manufacturers*, 91–92.

42. Ibid., 156–57; see also A. Parker Nevin, "Uniform Bill of Lading," *American Industries* (November 15, 1908): 25; A. Parker Nevin, "A Movement for Uniform State Laws," *American Industries* (August 15, 1909): 15; and Edwin Krauthoff, "The Need for Uniform State Laws," *American Industries* (June 1918): 20.

administrators and eventually led to the adoption of the Uniform Commercial Code in 1952.

SAFETY AND WORKMEN'S COMPENSATION

Work in industrial America was dangerous. One estimate indicated that between twenty-five thousand and thirty-five thousand workers died and over two million were seriously injured annually in American industries in the first decade of the twentieth century. Another summary showed that over a five-year period the United States had almost three times the number of mining deaths as France, Belgium, and Great Britain.[43] US rates of industrial deaths, fires, injuries, and accidents were higher than anywhere else in the industrial world.[44] Many companies paid only a token amount to victims' families. If the families of those injured or killed wanted real compensation, they had to seek it in the courts; this was a costly process, and only 15 percent of those who tried actually received compensation. Employers had good lawyers and three common law defenses: the worker was at fault, the workers' buddies were at fault, or the worker had assumed the risk of the job. When reformers mobilized to tackle what looked to many like a public health crisis, industrialists surprisingly fell in line.

From the industrialists' perspective, accidents and deaths represented waste. Though saddened by the "human cost," employers saw primarily the dollar cost to them, not just in potential liability but also in property damage. In 1908, US Steel Corporation became the first company to inaugurate a safety program and invest in safety equipment for its workers and factories. US Steel head Elbert Gary told stockholders that no expense should be spared when it came to keeping workers safe and preventing accidents.[45] In 1910, the steelmaker instituted an accident relief plan for workers. Not only was this the right thing to do, but it was also profitable. The old liability system was becoming a liability for employers. Owing in part to reformers' efforts, courts were narrowing employers' traditional advantages and pressuring them to pay ever greater liabilities. Some kind of insurance or

43. David Brian Robertson, *Capital, Labor, and State: The Battle for American Labor Markets from the Civil War to the New Deal* (Lanham, MD: Rowman and Littlefield, 2000), 232; Fred. C. Schwedtman, "The National Association of Manufacturers' Attitude toward the Injured Members of the Industrial Army," *American Industries* (May 1910): 18–22.

44. James Weinstein, "Big Business and the Origins of Workmen's Compensation," *Labor History* 8, no. 2 (Spring 1967): 156–74.

45. Mark Aldrich, *Safety First: Technology, Labor, and Business in the Building of the American Work Safety* (Baltimore: Johns Hopkins University Press, 1997), 91–92.

public compensation plan for workers seemed a safer bet. Instead of setting aside money for lawyers and liability payments, employers could put that money toward compensation to injured workers. Instead of casting blame on individuals, society was starting to see accidents as a systemic problem of industrial society. Under workmen's compensation plans, workers would not have to sue, and employers would benefit from more predictable costs, enjoy smoother labor relations, and get relief from bad publicity.[46] These plans also incentivized investment in safety and safety equipment, since contributions to a public compensation fund would be based on a company's safety record.

Organized labor initially opposed the turn toward workmen's compensation. Unions wanted employers to be held accountable for safety conditions in their factories and wanted the courts to make it easier for workers to recover damages. Reluctant to give up the right to sue employers for accidents and death, unions believed that they could get higher rates of compensation through the courts than through insurance or compensation plans set up by companies or the state.[47] Labor's suspicion of workmen's compensation plans may have contributed to NAM's support for them, since it typically supported anything opposed by the AFL.

In early 1910, NAM president John Kirby appointed a committee to study the problem of industrial liability with the aim of moving toward some kind of voluntary insurance program to which both employers and employees would contribute. It also adopted a resolution stating dissatisfaction with the current system and tentatively supporting state legislation, provided it was "based on sound economic principles and mutuality."[48] NAM members were overwhelmingly in favor of some sort of change, although 78 percent of NAM member companies had "no systematic relief provisions" for injured workers.[49] Unlike US Steel, these small to medium-sized companies could not afford a compensation program. What they favored, by 67 percent, was some kind of voluntary mutual insurance program for NAM members. Taking this under advisement, the NAM board adopted the committee's recommendations supporting some "constructive" state laws that provided

46. Roy Lubove, "Workman's Compensation and the Prerogatives of Voluntarism," *Labor History* 8, no. 3 (Fall 1967): 254–79.

47. Weinstein, "Big Business and the Origins of Workmen's Compensation," 159–60; see also Robertson, *Capital, Labor, and State,* chap. 9.

48. "The Problem of Industrial Liability," resolution adopted by the NAM board of directors, February 25, 1910, in *American Industries* 10, no. 8 (March 1910): 10; see also Steigerwalt, *The National Association of Manufacturers,* 160–62.

49. Almost 20 percent had "some [undefined] kind of relief association"; see "Report of the Committee on Industrial Indemnity Insurance," *American Industries* (June 1910): 26–30, 26.

for equitable compensation insurance, a mutual insurance program, and an industrial accident prevention department, but also affirming NAM opposition to certain compulsory programs.[50] Then they sent engineer and NAM consultant Ferdinand Schwedtman and legal counsel James Emery abroad to research European programs.

When they returned, NAM changed its tune and accepted the idea of workmen's compensation legislation that would compel employers to contribute to a public compensation fund. Based on their European excursion, Schwedtman and Emery coauthored *Accident Prevention and Relief,* a book published by NAM in 1911 in which they concluded that legislation was the fairest, most efficient way to provide quick and basic relief for victims of accidents and fatalities. Compulsion would force "reactionary employers" to do their fair share, while those employers who wanted to offer more comprehensive relief were free to do so through voluntary programs.[51] Given the federal tradition of the United States, these laws would be enacted at the state level, and those states with the most effective laws would be copied by the others—or so Schwedtman hoped. In 1912, NAM adopted resolutions to create a new committee on accident prevention and workmen's compensation that would work with state and federal legislators and commissions engaged in drafting workmen's compensation laws. It would also work closely with organizations seeking to develop more comprehensive voluntary schemes for injured workers and encourage members to collect statistics on accidents and relief.[52] Gone was NAM's traditional opposition to compulsory legislation; in its stead was cooperation with state and federal lawmakers and a pronounced campaign for accident prevention. Most apparent in the pages of NAM's official organ, the biweekly journal *American Industries,* the campaign focused on new safety devices, training programs, and voluntary relief plans.[53]

50. Ibid., 26, 30; see also the summary of NAM's workmen's compensation activity, as compiled by NAM staff member Sybyl Siegal, in a letter to H. M. Taliaferro, May 19, 1941, in series 1, box 42, NAMR.

51. Ferdinand Schwedtman, "Relief Tendencies in the United States," *American Industries* 12 (August 1911): 19–21. See also Schwedtman and Emery, *Accident Prevention and Relief* (New York: NAM, 1911), 263–66; and Robertson, *Capital, Labor, and State,* 234–36.

52. "Resolutions Adopted," *American Industries* (June 1912): 8. See also James Emery's recollection of these events in "Industrial Pioneering in Accident Prevention and Relief," series XII, box 192, NAMR.

53. See the heading for NAM's 1912 convention, for instance, advertising lessons in accident and fire prevention, in *American Industries* (May 1912): 7.

Historians like James Weinstein and Roy Lubove believe that workmen's compensation laws favored the economic interests of employers and thus were ultimately conservative. From NAM's perspective, however, these laws were progressive, and their mission was to convince conservative manufacturers to get on board with them. You can see this in Schwedtman's attempts to distinguish "progressive," which he sees as scientific, rational, and desirable, from "radicalism," which he sees as idealistic, uninformed, and undesirable. His vilification of the "reactionary employer" connects progress and reform with profits, and conservative reaction with bad economic choices.[54] Understanding that their recommendations on this issue seemed to go against their normal defense of "individualism," NAM leaders used up a lot of print justifying such a departure with evidence and arguments about efficiency. This was the work of a trade association. Organized labor ended up supporting state workmen's compensation plans; it had no alternative.

INDUSTRIAL EDUCATION

One of NAM's most active committees was the Industrial Education Committee, which kept members apprised of commercial and industrial training programs and opportunities. It developed training policies based on research and a systemic understanding of the changing labor market. Given that large companies like General Electric were able to set up their own training schools, NAM advocated for public trade schools to give smaller companies access to trained workers. In some ways, its support for public trade schools was a jab at the AFL's attempts to control apprenticeships. Unions were interested in preserving control over skilled labor and initially opposed public trade schools, which they saw as schools for "strikebreakers," or "scab hatcheries."[55] The Education Committee, in turn, stated that it was "the right of every individual, whether native or foreign born, to learn a trade and earn what he can by working at it"—language that mirrored open-shop arguments.[56] In 1912, however, NAM's Industrial Education Committee discovered that the United States was doing a poor job with *any* kind of

---

54. See for instance, Schwedtman and Emery, *Accident Prevention and Relief*; and F. C. Schwedtman, "Principles of Sound Employers' Liability Legislation," *Annals of the American Academy of Political and Social Sciences* 38, np. 1 (July 1911): 202–4.

55. Steigerwalt, *The National Association of Manufacturers*, 158; see also Philip Taft, *The AFL in the Time of Gompers* (New York: Harper & Row, 1957), 353–54; and Paul Moreno, *Black Americans and Organized Labor* (Baton Rouge: Louisiana State University Press, 2006).

56. Steigerwalt, *The National Association of Manufacturers*, 158.

education and refocused its efforts on compulsory general education and away from fighting the AFL over apprenticeship programs.

NAM's push for compulsory high school education was part of a larger industry effort to align the public schools with the needs of industry.[57] The Industrial Education Committee reported several findings: at least half of American children never made it past the sixth grade; truancy and absence rates in US schools were excessive; illiteracy rates were higher among American children than European children; and illiteracy was four times more common among white native-born kids than among immigrants. Other industrialized countries—otherwise known as competitors—invested resources in training their workforces; the United States, the committee recommended, should do the same. The committee called for compulsory school attendance to the age of seventeen and a less "abstract," more practical and creative school curriculum.[58] Adopting these recommendations, NAM also urged its members to support a bill sponsored by Vermont senator Carroll Page in 1912 to provide federal grants to states for industrial training.[59] In a rare moment of agreement, both NAM and the AFL supported the legislation. Pointing to Germany and Austria, NAM member and industrialist H. E. Miles argued for "compulsory part-time school attendance for young workers during working hours," as a social recognition of every child's right "to efficient, vital training in the pathways of life which each must tread."[60] Under pressure of war, a version of this bill eventually passed in 1917 as the Smith-Hughes Vocational Education Act. Not for the last time, the threat of foreign competition persuaded NAM members to become more like their European rivals and support federal subsidies.[61] Together with the AFL, NAM lobbied to pass this piece of legislation, which, along with NAM's many reports and publications on industrial education around the world,

57. See David Noble, *America by Design* (New York: Oxford University Press, 1997), chap. 8.

58. Steigerwalt, *The National Association of Manufacturers*, 159; see also David Nasaw, *Schooled to Order* (New York: Oxford University Press, 1981), 121–24, which is critical of American industry for its role in shaping education.

59. "Vocational Training," *American Industries* (April 1912): 8; Robertson, *Capital, Labor, and State*, 214.

60. H. E. Miles, "Federal Aid for Vocational Education," *American Industries* (April 1916): 20–21.

61. See J. C. Monaghan, "Industrial Education," *American Industries* (September 15, 1908): 21–22; H. E. Miles, "Federal Aid for Vocational Education." By 1929, almost half a million young workers (ages fourteen to eighteen) had benefited from the act, although it was a far cry from European sponsorship of education; see Robertson, *Capital, Labor, and State*, 212–15.

helped industrialists understand the importance of social infrastructure like education to the success of their enterprises.

Over time NAM developed working committees ranging from conservation and natural resources to women workers, patents, banking and currency, immigration, and internal improvements (infrastructure). *American Industries* regularly ran articles and symposia that educated members about the work of these committees and other issues of interest. Often, as was the case with workmen's compensation, the best possible outcome for industry required a new attitude toward government's role. NAM's many publications and conferences helped its members make that accommodation. One area where NAM members eagerly sought government cooperation was international trade, the topic of the next chapter.

2

Expanding Trade

In the 1885 novel *The Rise of Silas Lapham,* the eponymous protagonist, a paint manufacturer, considers joining the mad rush of American manufacturers selling their products abroad:

> There's an overstock in everything, and we've got to get rid of it, or we've got to shut down till the home demand begins again. We've had two or three such flurries before now, and they didn't amount to much. They say we can't extend our commerce under the high tariff system we've got now because there ain't any reciprocity on our side,—and the English have got the advantage of us every time.[1]

Lapham's attempts to sell paint abroad led to his downfall. NAM worked to make sure that did not happen to other enterprising would-be exporters.

The expansion of foreign trade was the original impetus for NAM's creation in 1895 and would remain a critical focus of the organization's activities throughout the twentieth century. NAM's efforts in this area contributed significantly to the development of international capitalism, or what we now know as "globalization." But it was not smooth sailing. Many NAM members relied on the protective tariff and opposed any kind of reform to it, which they regarded as a "slippery slope" to free trade. Nor was the Republican Party, with which NAM had the most influence, interested in tariff reform. NAM leadership fully supported tariffs, but it also advocated tariff reforms designed to encourage

1. William Dean Howells, *The Rise of Silas Lapham* (Boston: Houghton Mifflin Company, 1912), 125.

trade, and in this regard it was uncomfortably in alignment with the Democratic Party, which had long been the party of free trade and lower tariffs. So NAM's work in this area was significant less for its influence on government, which was negligible, and more for introducing and acclimating its members to the new norms and values of multinational, internationalist capitalism, thus bringing a largely conservative and parochial clientele into the modern political economy. A forgotten by-product of its efforts was the promotion of and appreciation for cultural diversity and international cooperation.

Getting Started

There was strong consensus among US policymakers and industrialists in the late nineteenth century that the solution to depression and overproduction was foreign markets, but how did a mill owner from Columbus, Georgia, or a machine maker from Pittsburgh, Pennsylvania, even begin the process of finding potential customers in Chile or Argentina or Germany? How did a small to midsized US manufacturer, unfamiliar with the language, customs, laws, and currencies of foreign nations, establish the sort of trust and credit necessary for trade relations? How did he alert foreign buyers to the existence of his product? And if he managed somehow to find a foreign buyer, how did he transport his goods safely, reliably, and at a cost that allowed him to make the venture worthwhile?

For decades, American manufacturers had prospered selling their products in a protected and expanding domestic market and had never had to think about these vexing questions of foreign trade. Large corporations with a unique, patented product, such as General Electric or Kodak, had no trouble finding foreign customers, and they had the resources to support foreign offices.[2] But the process was daunting for hundreds of manufacturers of undifferentiated goods (such as shoes, ball bearings, or paper) competing directly with European manufacturers making the same undifferentiated goods. In addition, few countries were willing to trade with the United States because of its high tariffs and unregulated, unstable currency. In other words, there was simply no financial, political, or material infrastructure in place to facilitate trade. NAM's main focus its first decade of existence was on

---

2. See Mira Wilkins, *The Emergence of Multinational Enterprise: American Business Abroad from the Colonial Era to 1914* (Cambridge, MA: Harvard University Press, 1970), and Becker, *The Dynamics of Business and Government Relations, Industry, and Exports*, chaps. 1–2.

developing this infrastructure, and it pursued this goal along two paths: providing services to its members and lobbying for specific government policies.

MEMBER SERVICES

In the absence of governmental infrastructure for foreign trade, NAM's Foreign Department provided assistance to manufacturers seeking to sell goods abroad, translating business correspondence and official documents and supplying letters of introduction to potential buyers. It arranged for insurance, the collection of invoices, the registration of trademarks, and the shipment of goods to international exhibitions.[3] NAM also offered members specific information, such as credit reports on foreign firms, foreign tariff rates, exchange rates, customs regulations, cost-of-landing charges, shipping options, trade conditions, and transport rates from ports to inland cities. The department maintained a team of correspondents in Europe, Asia, Africa, Australia, Canada, and Latin America; in 1912, that team numbered 1,400, twice the number of US consuls employed by the federal government.[4] It set up two exhibition warehouses for American producers to store and show products abroad, one in Caracas in 1898 and the other in Shanghai in 1900. Neither lasted more than a few years, but they illustrate what trade expansion efforts looked like.

More successfully, NAM's international freight bureau helped arrange members' shipments to various countries. Operating much like a shipping agent, it was able to secure lower customs and shipping rates for members by combining their cargo shipments to certain countries. In 1905, it handled the shipments of one thousand NAM members. The steady business it received led the NAM to sell the bureau to a freight-forwarding firm.[5] Large corporations were able to set up sales branches abroad to do this sort of work. For the smaller producer, however, NAM was the best way to participate in foreign markets.

In addition to these services, NAM also provided communication platforms between its members and foreign traders. The *American Trade Index*,

---

3. Becker, *The Dynamics of Business and Government Relations, Industry, and Exports*, 61–64; Steigerwalt, *The National Association of Manufacturers*, 44–52, 153–56.

4. Steigerwalt, *The National Association of Manufacturers*, 47–51, 153–54; see also Becker, *The Dynamics of Business and Government Relations, Industry, and Exports*, 60–64.

5. Becker, *The Dynamics of Business and Government Relations, Industry, and Exports*, 63, citing *NAM Proceedings*, 1908; Steigerwalt, *The National Association of Manufacturers*, 48–49; "In the Business World," *New York Times*, January 10, 1904, p. 25.

published in four languages and distributed on six continents, advertised its members' wares to international buyers. NAM's biweekly journal *American Industries* likewise informed foreign buyers about what American manufacturers were selling, while also apprising American manufacturers of opportunities and market conditions abroad. Circulation for these publications was around twelve thousand between 1905 and 1912.[6] Foreign traders identified NAM as a source of information on the American market and began sending it various queries about American goods, which NAM then published in its *Confidential Bulletin*, available only to members. NAM also organized lectures and conferences for its members, featuring foreign trade representatives or dignitaries. It hosted tours of local factories and businesses for foreign trade delegations and sent its own delegations abroad to investigate market conditions.[7] These tours and conferences were not just about previewing the latest gadgets or management technique, but also about establishing contacts and networks with foreign representatives and governments.

After World War I, as the US government began to dedicate more resources to trade infrastructure and information-gathering, NAM offered fewer and fewer specific trade services. But it would continue educating its members about foreign trade opportunities, hosting foreign trade delegations and conferences, and cultivating trade networks abroad.

GOVERNMENT POLICIES

The services and information that NAM offered its members were valuable, but they were a drop in the bucket compared to the deeper, more structural, more *political* problems that needed to be addressed if American manufacturers were to compete in the global marketplace. The US tariff system and British control of finances, shipping, and trade routes were two serious impediments to trade expansion that no amount of "services" and information could overcome. NAM lobbied for policies that would address these realties, but such policies were not always popular with its conservative, protectionist membership, which was largely Republican.

At this time, NAM supported protective tariffs and opposed Democratic attempts to lower them. But to get around tariffs' trade-dampening effects,

6. Becker, *The Dynamics of Business and Government Relations, Industry, and Exports*, 60–61, Steigerwalt, *The National Association of Manufacturers*, 154–55.

7. "Welcome for Merchants," *New York Times*, August 1, 1896, p. 7.

NAM also supported a policy of *reciprocity*. Reciprocity offered a few countries reduced tariffs on a few particular imports in exchange for opening their markets to US manufactured goods.[8] It was a way to keep high tariffs in general but offer deals to certain nations on certain, limited imports, such as the raw materials that went into manufactured goods. At NAM's founding meeting, then-Governor McKinley endorsed reciprocity, which he saw as completely compatible with the protection of the home market:

> We want our own markets for our manufacturers and agricultural products; we want a foreign market for our surplus products. . . . We want a reciprocity which will give us foreign markets for our surplus products and in turn that will open our markets to foreigners for those products which they produce and we do not.[9]

Another speaker affirmed that the protective tariff actually helped exports because the higher prices paid by US consumers subsidized the loss that came with selling surplus goods abroad at lower prices than their European competitors, a practice otherwise known as "dumping."[10]

NAM and other business groups lobbied for the creation of a nonpartisan, independent commission to study reciprocity and make recommendations based on objective fact and economic efficacy rather than politics. To the extent that proponents of reciprocity sought changes to the way "things were done," they were reformers, and like other reformers working to adjust American politics to the new corporate capitalism, they needed to overcome Congress's power. The goal behind their support for commissions and government agencies was not to expand the power of the federal government, but rather to remove issues like the tariff from the inefficiencies and divisiveness of congressional battles.[11]

Reciprocity was a tricky issue for NAM. Some members felt that this policy was a slippery slope to "free trade." Reciprocity was opposed for this reason by, for instance, the American Protective Tariff League, wool manufacturers, and the American Iron and Steel Institute (whose membership

---

8. For a discussion of reciprocity, see Emily Rosenberg, *Spreading the American Dream: American Economic and Cultural Expansion, 1890–1945* (New York: Hill and Wang, 1982), 51–53; on reciprocity with regard to NAM, see Becker, *The Dynamics of Business and Government Relations, Industry, and Exports*, chaps. 2–4.

9. Quoted in Steigerwalt, *The National Association of Manufacturers*, 19.

10. Ibid., 23.

11. See Becker, *The Dynamics of Business and Government Relations, Industry, and Exports*, chap. 4; Skowronek, *Building a New American State*; and Sidney Milkis, *The President and the Parties* (New York: Oxford University Press, 1993).

overlapped with NAM's). They opposed any attempt to even set up an independent tariff commission.[12] NAM secretary Marshall Cushing felt that reciprocity risked further alienating labor, whose jobs were protected by tariffs. He was asked to resign his position.[13] Free-trade editorialists affirmed the fears of protectionists when they called NAM's position "nonsensical" and argued that if manufacturers were really interested in expanding foreign trade, they would support lower tariffs and free trade.[14] Even NAM's in-house historian, writing in 1951, admitted that there was "something of conflict" between the organization's desire to protect American industry from competition and the "broad expansion of American products in foreign countries."[15]

Tariff reform was a divisive issue for Republicans as well. President Roosevelt had avoided it during his presidency, but by 1907 financial crisis and widespread reaction against the Dingley tariff—enacted during the first year of the McKinley administration—had increased support for a commission to study tariff reform. NAM president James Van Cleave, a stove manufacturer, helped lead the effort. To chair NAM's Tariff Committee he appointed a carriage manufacturer from Racine, Wisconsin, named Herbert Miles, who was also involved in other reciprocity-supporting organizations. Together, they committed NAM to a position of official support for an independent tariff commission. As Miles told the *New York Times*, "The tariff is an economic question not a political one, and it requires the work of a nonpartisan expert, sane commission to say what schedules should be reduced and what increased."[16] A critic of high tariffs, the *Times* reported favorably on NAM's enlightened position. Van Cleave and Miles persuaded Indiana senator Albert Beveridge, a progressive Republican (and famous imperialist), to sponsor a bill for an independent, scientific commission to consider tariff revision. Demonstrating the trend toward cooperation, Miles organized a large number of like-minded trade associations into the National Tariff Commission Association, which launched a coordinated lobbying effort in support of the

12. Becker, *The Dynamics of Business and Government Relations, Industry, and Exports*, chap. 4; see also Secretary to H. E. Miles, January 11, 1908, and Boudinot to Miles, January 13, 1908, in US Senate Judiciary Committee, *Maintenance of a Lobby to Influence Legislation*, 4 vols. (Washington, DC: US Government Printing Office, 1913), vol. 2, appendix, pp. 1273–74 and 1286–87, respectively.

13. "Low-Tariff Men Push Cushing Out," *New York Times*, June 1, 1907, p. 6. Cushing went on to open an anti-union detective firm (see chapter 3).

14. See, for instance, "Too Much Protection," *New York Times*, January 29, 1898, p. 6; and "The Hill of Difficulty," *New York Times*, January 28, 1898, p. 8.

15. Horsch, "NAM Past and Present," p. 3.

16. "A Political Question," *New York Times*, August 31, 1907, p. 6.

bill. The forces of protection were fierce, however, and combined with the natural inertia against possibly destabilizing change, Beveridge's bill was abandoned, superseded by the Payne-Aldrich Tariff (1909), which maintained high overall tariffs, while lowering duties on a few specific items. Taft did appoint a tariff board, although historians have seen it as weak and insubstantial and NAM was unable to influence its makeup.[17]

NAM's involvement in this debacle brought forth a hail of vindictive insults from protectionists, many of them NAM members. The Home Market Club called NAM, "the National Association of (Free Trade) Manufacturers" and put out hostile circulars to deter attendance at NAM's 1909 tariff convention in Indianapolis.[18] They alleged that NAM had lost seven hundred to eight hundred members as a result of its tariff position; this figure was hugely exaggerated, although there had been some resignations among the steel and wool men.[19] Unions reprinted the resignation letters, mocking Van Cleave's incompetence and unpopularity even among capitalists.[20] So vigorous was the backlash that Van Cleave softened his approach, declaring repeatedly that NAM was "Unequivocally and Absolutely Devoted to the Principle of Ample PROTECTION to All American Industries."[21] Privately, Van Cleave and Miles regretted having listed steel and wool as examples of unreasonable tariffs and agreed to limit their public statements on tariff reform to "generalities" so as to avoid antagonizing members.[22]

The controversy continued at a NAM banquet, when a protectionist loudly interrupted a German trade envoy who spoke on the "mutuality of foreign trade." The envoy apologized but wondered out loud why he had been invited if the organization did not in fact support "mutuality of trade."[23] NAM thereafter sought to sidestep the divisive issue by affirming its vigorous support

---

17. Wiebe, *Businessmen and Reform*, 90–91; Becker, *The Dynamics of Business and Government Relations, Industry, and Exports*, 81–82; "NAM Sought to Influence Tariff," *Chicago Tribune*, July 19, 1913, p. 2.

18. Wiebe, *Businessmen and Reform*, 93–94. See also "Manufacturers in a Tariff Wrangle," *New York Times*, May 19, 1908, p. 12, "Sharp Fight on Tariff," *New York Tribune*, May 19, 1909, 3; and Becker, *The Dynamics of Business and Government Relations, Industry, and Exports*, chap. 4.

19. Miles to Schwedtman, January 11, 1908, in US Senate Judiciary Committee, *Maintenance of a Lobby*, vol. 2, appendix, 1275.

20. "Van Cleave a Failure as President," *Our Journal* 17, no. 2 (February 1908): 14. This was the journal of the Metal Polishers, Buffers, Platers' Union, AFL, who were boycotting Van Cleave's company.

21. Quoted in Wiebe, *Businessmen and Reform*, 94.

22. Secretary to Miles, January 11, 1908, in US Senate Judiciary Committee, *Maintenance of a Lobby*, vol. 2, appendix, 1273.

23. "Fowler Disagrees with German Envoy," *New York Times*, May 20, 1909, p. 18.

for both protection *and* a permanent nonpolitical tariff commission, which was akin to taking no position.[24] Those NAM manufacturers who favored reciprocity and a tariff commission had to wait for Democratic administrations to get a Tariff Commission (under Wilson in 1916) and a Reciprocal Trade Act (under Franklin Roosevelt in 1934).

It is difficult to draw a map of which NAM members supported or opposed tariff reforms, since positions varied even within industries and changed over time. Some supported more moderate tariffs, while not necessarily wanting a tariff commission; others favored higher tariffs, but liked the idea of reciprocity. In general, however, the most ardent supporters of reciprocity and tariff reform were smaller producers of specialized machines and undifferentiated goods, who saw foreign trade as a way out of the price wars. Larger corporations, such as International Harvester and Singer Manufacturing (sewing machines) were able to build plants abroad and sidestep the tariff issue altogether. Iron, steel, chemical, and textile producers were reliably protectionist, unless they sought foreign markets, in which case they might support reciprocity and tariff reform.[25]

Other policies for improving the foreign trade infrastructure were only slightly less controversial, since they too involved revising the status quo. Take the rehabilitation of the merchant marine. British control of all shipping and all shipping lanes put the Americans at a severe competitive disadvantage, because American manufacturers who managed to find buyers in Brazil or Peru had to ship their products by way of Liverpool. In 1904, over 95 percent of US exports were transported in foreign-built vessels.[26] The US shipbuilding industry had few investors because trade occurred primarily in home markets and US shipbuilders could not compete against the subsidized shipping industries of other countries. Some kind of government subsidy was necessary to, as one supporter put it, "induce practical businessmen to enter this hazardous business." Without a merchant marine, "a nation is helpless in the world race for trade."[27] For these reasons, NAM endorsed government subsidies for an American merchant marine.[28]

24. See "Chronological Documentation of the NAM Positions on the Tariff and Reciprocity Agreements Since 1895," in series 1, box 105, NAMR.

25. See Becker, *The Dynamics of Business and Government Relations, Industry, and Exports,* 40–46, 69–90, and throughout.

26. *NAM Proceedings,* 1905, 185.

27. Charles H. Winter, "President Harding and Our Ships," *American Industries* (July 1922): 13–15, 13.

28. Steigerwalt, *The National Association of Manufacturers,* 22; James Ewell, "American Ships and American Banks Abroad," *American Industries* (June 1, 1909): 27; James Watson, "A Great National Crime," *American Industries* (July 15, 1909): 9–12.

Just as Britain dominated shipping, it also controlled international banking. Because the pound served as the world's international currency, American manufacturers, forced to rely on British banks for financing these ventures, lost money in exchange rates and fees and had to share confidential information with their competitors. Thus, NAM supported the creation of a central bank for the United States, which would practice sound money policies, offer international loans, and uphold the integrity of the dollar.[29] There was also support for a US-chartered inter-American bank with branches in South America that would provide credit to buyers and collect payments for exporters. Either way, NAM looked to the federal government to create centralized financial institutions to facilitate trade. Britain had done the same for its manufacturers, reinforcing their continued competitive advantage.

Not surprisingly, NAM championed the government's expansionist impulses. Joining the chorus of those roused by Chinese markets, it called on the government to ensure "freedom of trade and equality of privilege" in China: "the struggle for markets should be open to all," it exhorted, endorsing what would be become the "open door" policy.[30] *American Industries* touted Chinese trade, and the organization opened a warehouse in Shanghai in 1900 for display of American goods for export.[31] The China market spurred NAM to call on the government to build a Nicaraguan canal, which would also open new markets on the west coast of South America. This demand was happily realized when President Roosevelt outmaneuvered a resistant Senate and built the Panama Canal.[32]

So important was China in NAM's imagination that it lobbied the government to loosen restrictions on Chinese immigration (enacted by the 1882 Chinese Exclusion Act) and "restore friendly relations with China."[33] In 1900, Chinese minister Wu Ting Fang spoke before NAM about the importance of Chinese-US trade relations. He criticized the "hostile legislation" of the United States, noting that trade could not happen without Chinese merchants in the United States to facilitate it: "If you wish to increase your

29. Steigerwalt, *The National Association of Manufacturers*, 24–25; "Must Find New Markets," *New York Times*, January 24, 1896, p. 5, reporting on the second NAM meeting in Chicago.

30. Quoted in Steigerwalt, *The National Association of Manufacturers*, 57.

31. See, for instance, His Excellency, Wu Ting-Fang, "American Industries and Chinese Trade," and "The Tariff in the Philippines," both in *American Industries* 7 (June 1, 1908): 18, 13; Steigerwalt, *The National Association of Manufacturers*, 59. The warehouse lasted about a year before succumbing to the Boxer Rebellion.

32. The Senate took Roosevelt to task for what it said was his unconstitutional activities that led to US control of part of Panama. See Walter LaFeber, *The Panama Canal: The Crisis in Historical Perspective* (New York: Oxford University Press, 1990).

33. "Blames Our Labor Unions," *New York Times*, February 19, 1906, p. 5.

Ying Kuo Sheng Pao
Chinese Edition
OF THE
British Trade Journal
PRINTED AND PUBLISHED IN SHANGHAI

Eikoku Shogyo Zasshi
Japanese Edition
OF THE
British Trade Journal
PRINTED AND PUBLISHED IN TOKYO

ORIENTAL TRADE

The British Trade Journal

...IN...

JAPANESE AND CHINESE

REACHES THE WORLD'S GREATEST MARKET

THE FAR EAST

THE OPPORTUNITIES
THE REMARKABLE PROGRESS
OF *JAPAN*
THE AWAKENING OF *CHINA*
AND THE OPENING OF *MANCHURIA*
PRESENT TO THE AMERICAN MANUFACTURER

Fac-Simile title page new pamphlet—write for copy

THE BRITISH TRADE JOURNAL
29 BROADWAY, NEW YORK CITY

LONDON   TOKIO   SHANGHAI

FIGURE 2.1. Advertisement for trade opportunities in Asia, 1908. *Source*: NAM's journal *American Industries*, September 1, 1908, p. 2. Copyright © National Association of Manufacturers; courtesy of Hagley Library and Museum.

trade with China every obstacle in the way of free intercourse between the two countries should be removed."[34] NAM's president David Parry blamed unions (of course), but he was adamant that the exclusionary laws had destroyed trade and were "a disgrace to a civilized nation."[35]

NAM also sought the expansion and professionalization of the US Consular Service. Market-seeking businessmen needed information on foreign economic conditions, currency exchange, visas, business practices, and local customs and needs. This information was typically supplied by US consuls posted in a variety of nations, but consuls, who were patronage-appointees, were not trained to collect this information in any systematic way. NAM joined Progressive Era reformers in their calls to reform the consulate, pulling it out of the patronage system and making it a professional agency with a more commercial focus.[36]

Finally, NAM supported the creation of government agencies or commissions that would encourage coordination between government policies and market-expanding manufacturers. NAM supported the Far Eastern Commission to study markets in Asia, as well as the US Industrial Commission (1898–1902), created by the McKinley administration to investigate railroad pricing, trusts, and labor issues. NAM endorsed the Industrial Commission's call for the government to take a more active role in facilitating trade abroad. It promoted—and claimed a role in—the creation of a commerce department to coordinate the domestic economy and foreign trade. This was achieved in 1903 when Roosevelt created the US Department of Commerce and Labor (which became the US Department of Commerce in 1913, when the separate US Department of Labor was formed).[37]

These reforms and commissions were intended to build a trade infrastructure to encourage American exports. They were all eventually enacted or realized, but they were most fully enacted under Democratic administrations with progressive, internationalist aspirations. NAM was nonpartisan, as its leaders repeatedly said, but the hostility within NAM to tariff reform and Democrats was obvious and may be one reason for the appearance of

34. "American Trade in China," *Los Angeles Times*, April 28, 1900, p. III3. The act banned only Chinese labor, but made it difficult for other Chinese immigrants to verify that they were not laborers.

35. "Blames Our Labor Unions," *New York Times*, February 19, 1906, p. 5.

36. Becker, *The Dynamics of Business and Government Relations, Industry, and Exports*, 91–96; Richard Harlan, "A Consular Training School," *American Industries* (August 15, 1908): 18–21.

37. Steigerwalt, *The National Association of Manufacturers*, 81, 83–86; Horsch, "NAM Past and Present," 4, 16; "Proceedings of the International Trade Conference Held under the Auspices of the NAM," December 6–8, 1915 (New York: NAM, 1915), p. ix.

competing associations, such as the American Manufacturers' Export Association (AMEA) in 1909 and the National Foreign Trade Council (NFTC) in 1914. Republicans Roosevelt and Taft made some progress in expanding trade, especially in terms of US influence in Latin America and Asia, consular reform, and the creation of information-gathering agencies. But they did little to weaken the most significant barriers: the high tariff, unstable currency, and British dominance of the seas and banking. Real progress in those areas would not happen until there was a Democrat in office and a war in Europe.

Wilson, World War I, and the 1920s

Perhaps more than any other president, Woodrow Wilson's name and reputation is tied to economic internationalism. Indeed, "Wilsonianism" describes the liberal democratic global economic integration that would become the goal of American foreign economic policy beginning in the 1920s.[38] Wilson believed that nations that traded with each other did not go to war and that free trade would topple imperialism and free colonial peoples. He also understood that the United States was uniquely positioned to take advantage of economic integration.

Even before war destroyed Britain's monopoly in international finance and Latin American markets, Wilson's Democratic administration sought to improve the US international trade position and thereby brought about some of NAM's longtime demands. Perhaps most crucially, Wilson finally created something resembling a national bank with the capacity to establish American branch banks abroad. The Federal Reserve Act (1913) created what we now call "the Fed," a federalized system of regional banks presided over by a national board. It authorized American banks to establish branch facilities abroad and created a discount market in the United States, enabling American banks to "discount" bills drawn against foreign trades and thus freeing American exporters from British financial markets.[39] The business and banking communities argued about the bill's details and the

38. On Wilsonianism, see Smith, *America's Mission*; Walter LaFeber, *The American Age*, vol. 2 (New York: W. W. Norton, 1994).

39. Becker, *The Dynamics of Business and Government Relations, Industry, and Exports*, 136–38. Discount markets allowed foreign buyers to get cash for interim letters of credit, or promises of payment, before the goods were actually delivered and the final payment was made. Previously, the discount market had been available only in sterling. See also James Livingston, *The Origins of the Federal Reserve System* (Ithaca, NY: Cornell University Press, 1986).

Federal Reserve board's membership, but NAM was not involved. *American Industries* did, however, publish articles explaining the new bank's benefits to manufacturers, including one by financial expert William Cornwall, who called it "a new light . . . breaking over a world that had previously existed in perplexing darkness."[40]

Wilson's commerce secretary, William Redfield, a member of the AMEA, sought to increase the government's role in international trade. Key to this endeavor was the creation of the Federal Trade Commission (FTC) in 1914. Although the FTC was founded to enforce the Clayton Antitrust Act of 1914, its main proponents were most interested in having it distinguish between "bad" cooperation, like collusion, and "good" cooperation, such as trade associations. This was right up NAM's alley; the FTC legitimated NAM's work in the eyes of public opinion. Yet because many NAM members opposed its creation, trusting neither Democrats nor Wilson, NAM once again took no official position.[41] Redfield appointed Edward Hurley to head the new FTC in 1916. Hurley, a member of the Illinois Manufacturers Association as well as the recently created NFTC, was likewise committed to seeing the US government facilitate the export trade via tariff reform, a strong merchant marine, and international finance—all goals of NAM.

Both Redfield and Hurley believed that US antitrust laws hurt American companies' ability to compete with large European cartels. As Hurley pointed out in his book *Awakening of Business*, foreign governments coordinated their manufacturing, merchandising, and transportation interests into one large conglomerate, designed to compete against the conglomerates of other nations. If the United States wanted to compete internationally, it would have to "meet cooperation with cooperation."[42] Hurley easily conflates "conglomeration" with "cooperation," a term he spends the entire book legitimating. Going on to say that US antitrust laws were the major cause of the "lack of cooperation" in American business, he assured readers that antitrust laws were fine in the domestic market (he was the FTC head, after all!), but that "cooperation," that is, government-coordinated conglomeration, was necessary for American companies to compete abroad.[43]

40. William C. Cornwall, "The Currency Bill as It Affects Business," *American Industries* 14, no. 7 (February 1914): 16–18.

41. Wiebe, *Businessmen and Reform*, 140; Gabriel Kolko, *The Triumph of Conservatism* (Chicago: Quadrangle Books, 1963), 264, 273.

42. Hurley, *Awakening of Business*, 115.

43. Ibid., 117.

By the end of Wilson's second term, Redfield had managed to secure all of the reforms related to foreign trade that he had sought, beginning with the independent Tariff Commission in 1916. The war, of course, helped. A 1914 *New York Times* headline explained the situation: "European War Opens South America's Big Market to Us," and "Leading Financiers Are Already Arranging for Closer Economic Relations to Make Trading Easier with the Republics to the South of Us."[44] Ships needed to be quickly built for the war, and in 1917 Wilson put none other than Edward Hurley in charge of the newly created Shipping Board. "We are building ships not alone for the war," said Hurley with an eye toward a permanent merchant marine, "but for the future of world trade."[45] The question of how to pay for this and how much government control it entailed was highly contested in the business community and within NAM (which ostensibly supported a merchant marine). Wilson nonetheless signed the Merchant Marine (Jones) Act in 1920, creating a limited but viable merchant marine.[46] Concerns about the United States retaining its favorable trade position after the war led to the passage of the Webb-Pomerene Act (1918), which exempted US companies doing business abroad from antitrust legislation, and the Edge Act (1919), which provided short-term financing for Americans seeking to do business in postwar Europe.[47]

All of this suggests that NAM's interest in expanding trade was better served by the internationalist, free-trade Democratic Party than by isolationist, protectionist Republicans, with whom its political connections lay. NAM contributed little politically to bringing these policies about, but its many resolutions, conferences, and articles on behalf of trade expansion and internationalism affirmed and bolstered this direction of American economic and foreign policy. It fostered an internationalist subcommunity within an otherwise conservative organization that took advantage of, participated in, and ultimately helped shape American international trade, bringing manufacturers together with bankers and transportation interests and allowing

44. *New York Times*, August 23, 1914, p. SM4.

45. Quoted in Becker, *The Dynamics of Business and Government Relations, Industry, and Exports*, 149.

46. Ibid., 150–51; see also "Proceedings of the International Trade Conference Held under the Auspices of the NAM." Debates about the topic continue to this day—for example, in discussions of the US response to Hurricane Maria in Puerto Rico; see Teresa Carey, "The Jones Act, Explained (and What Waiving It Means for Puerto Rico)," *PBS NewsHour*, September 29, 2017, https://www.pbs.org/newshour/nation/jones-act-explained-waiving-means-puerto-rico.

47. Becker, *The Dynamics of Business and Government Relations, Industry, and Exports*, 142–43.

certain manufacturers to inhabit a broader, more cosmopolitan, and less partisan economic world. An example of such activities can be seen in the International Trade Conference held under NAM auspices in 1915.

Anticipating the changed trade position of the United States in the world, NAM hosted a conference attended by representatives from thirty-five countries from South America, Central America, the Caribbean, Asia, and Europe (with the exception of Germany). Also in attendance were representatives from Turkey, Persia, and Austria, which were ostensibly part of the Central Powers. Translators were provided, and discussion of the war was off-limits. The object was to facilitate international trade during the war and after, with a focus on transportation, credit, and exchange. But the subtext was very definitely the new opportunities created for the United States—if it could solve the problems of transportation, credit, and exchange. One trade dignitary after another got up to congratulate the United States on its newfound position, warn of the obstacles that stood in its way, and trumpet the wares of his own country. They were followed by experts in banking and transportation, mainly Americans stationed abroad, who offered a diversity of opinions about the pros and cons of different kinds of banks and credit, whether the government should subsidize a merchant marine, the replacement of the pound by the dollar in South America, the prognosis on reciprocity, and the current and forecasted exchange and transportation situations. It was serious information, free of the heated rhetoric that accompanied discussions of unionism and the tariff. Few pronouncements were made and no positions were staked; instead, manufacturers, bankers, and transporters engaged in international trade grappled in good faith with the issues confronting them, firm in the belief that objective information was the best tool for their resolution.

After the war, the United States became a creditor nation, and New York replaced London as the city of international banking, with foreign loans making up the bulk of the $12 billion that flowed abroad between 1919 and 1929.[48] After a brief depression in 1920–1921, the American economy took off. Between 1922 and 1928, industrial production increased by 70 percent, the gross national product by 40 percent, and per capita income by 30 percent. The overproduction that had prompted a search for markets abroad and the creation of NAM was no longer a problem. As they increased exponentially in the 1920s, American exports seemed to need no special help.

48. Warren Cohen, *Empire without Tears: America's Foreign Relations, 1921–1933* (New York: Alfred A. Knopf, 1987), 28.

Automobile industry exports increased from $34.6 million in 1914 to $541.4 million in 1929. Machinery exports went from $168 million in 1914 to $607 million in 1929. Iron and steel exports increased by 200 percent.[49] Europeans needed to rebuild (which they were able to do in large part because of loans from American banks), and Britain played a smaller role in the rest of the world, particularly in Latin America. Although the United States still lacked a comprehensive foreign trade policy and the Harding administration had adopted a high new tariff, Wilson's reforms, combined with the availability of US loans and the demand for US goods, led to increasingly smooth export pathways.

Nonetheless, large corporations continued to dominate exports, which was what led NAM to take advantage of the Webb-Pomerene Act (exempting export associations from antitrust legislation) to form a South American sales corporation in 1919. Named after its shipping code, NAMUSA, the new corporation allowed NAM members to become stockholders in the venture and to sell their goods under its name. It was incorporated under the laws of New York, and similar corporations were planned for Central America, Russia, Africa, and Europe. "The corporation will be wholly cooperative, seeking no profit," said the press release; instead, the point was to sell American goods abroad.[50] Here again was a trade association operating to benefit small and medium-sized producers by allowing them to compete, while banded together in a cooperative spirit, against the international cartels and large corporations. Participating members would have the "services of departmental salesmen operating out of the corporation's foreign offices," as well as the security of knowing there would be fair dealing and good prices.[51] About forty-nine members took advantage of the opportunity. NAMUSA, the *New York Times* reported, "provides an active, efficient, and economical organization through which American manufacturers will present a united front in world markets."[52]

The press around this experiment was positive, but the venture faltered. When its president, Phillip Bird, who was also NAM's treasurer and general manager, misled some Midwestern flour millers about the corporation's finances, a scandal erupted that led to its bankruptcy in 1921. As a result of the deception, money was exchanged and orders placed that could not be honored, which led to lawsuits against NAM and NAMUSA. NAM officers'

49. Ibid., 23–24.
50. "NAMUSA Means US Is after World Trade," *Chicago Daily Tribune*, May 21, 1919, p. 3.
51. "For Furtherance of Foreign Trade," *New York Times*, September 15, 1919, p. 19.
52. Ibid.

initial cover-up of the wrongdoing led to a rift within the organization and total confusion about who was at fault. Finally, in 1921, a third independent committee figured out what had happened.[53] Years later, in summarizing what had happened for the historical record, James Emery, NAM's legal counsel at the time, lamented the damage done to NAM's reputation and concluded: "I think it is safe to say that we will not attempt to have any brilliant ideas of that kind or launch them. We will let the businessmen conceive them themselves from now on."[54]

The "brilliant ideas" to which Emery sarcastically referred exemplify the kind of creative services that trade associations were experimenting with in this era before the federal government had a trade infrastructure in place. Although NAMUSA has the taint of an ill-advised boondoggle, it was also an attempt to bring small and medium-sized US businesses into the global future.

Emery's sour assessment marked the beginning of NAM's withdrawal from specific services and movement toward broad policy positions.[55] Yet trade expansion remained a central concern for NAM in the 1920s. It continued to hold international conferences and participate in international trade councils and called President Harding's disarmament conference, held from November 1921 to February 1922, "one of the greatest steps towards the world's industrial expansion."[56] It supported US membership in the World Court and the enlargement of the Debt Funding Commission, a precursor to what became the Dawes Committee in 1924.[57] Perhaps most tellingly, NAM was an enthusiastic supporter and facilitator of trade with the newly formed Soviet Union, a communist country that the US government refused to recognize.

Yes, despite its fiery rhetoric against the evils of socialism and communism, and despite the Bolsheviks' seizure of private property, NAM promoted trade with the Soviet Union. The Soviet demand for American

53. This information is taken from that committee's report, which it delivered in the form of a letter from the Voluntary Committee of Members of the National Association of Manufacturers to the officers, directors, and members of the NAM, May 16, 1921, series 1, box 42, "History" files, NAMR.

54. "NAMUSA," n.d., Emery's fifteen memoranda on NAM history are scattered in the history files with no dates or author information. For a list and explanation, see "NAM History Project," n.d. (c. 1950) series 12, box 192, "James Emery" file, NAMR.

55. Horsch, "NAM Past and Present," 6.

56. "Japan's Biggest Business Men Here," and "Limiting Armaments of the World," *American Industries* 22, no. 4 (November 1921): 39, 1.

57. "Significant Highlights of the Organization and History," April 1, 1948, series 12, box 194, NAMR.

engineering and heavy equipment proved too great for American dam-builders and earthmovers to resist. One subheading in *American Industries* announced optimistically to readers: "Property Rights Receiving Fresh Consideration Because Their Destruction Has Caused Much Embarrassment," adding that while the new regime was bad for the upper and middle classes, it was "not bad for peasants."[58] Because the US government refused to recognize the Soviet Union, trade had to be conducted by way of semi-illicit back channels. The organization that NAM promoted for this purpose was a Soviet purchasing agency based in New York City called Amerikanskii Torgovlaia, or Amtorg.[59] Financed in part by American banks, Amtorg purchased goods from American companies for the Soviet government. At its national conventions in 1924 and 1926, NAM invited Amtorg's director, one Dr. Isaac Sherman, to speak at panels dedicated to "the truth" about Russia. The "truth" in this case was not what many saw as Lenin's crimes against humanity, but rather the industrial opportunities awaiting the forward-looking businessman willing to extend credit to the Soviet government. And socialist planning seemed to be a good risk: "The Soviet Union is the only country in the world which has an elaborate State Plan, which not only tabulates but actually regulates the whole economic life of the country," thus ensuring repayment, reported Sherman.[60] Sherman was joined in 1926 by H. Parker Willis, the editor of the *Journal of Commerce* and an enthusiastic supporter of trade with Russia, and Hugh Lincoln Cooper, a dam-builder who directed construction of a gigantic hydroelectric dam on the Dnieper River (for which he and five other American engineers won the Order of the Red Banner of Labor).[61]

NAM claimed neutrality on what it understood was a controversial issue and presented the administration's view, which was one of skepticism about dealing with the Soviets.[62] The audience remarks included in the *Proceedings* indicate that some members were opposed to trading with communists. But on the whole, it is difficult to read the *Proceedings* and not get the impression that NAM was promoting trade with communists. Its own speakers noted that businessmen "are alive to what is going on in Russia" and commented on how much excitement the panels on Russian trade generated,

58. "Poland, Russia, and the Soviet," *American Industries* (February 1922): 39.

59. See Katharine A. S. Siegel, *Loans and Legitimacy: The Evolution of Soviet-American Relations, 1919–1933* (Lexington: University of Kentucky Press, 1996), chap. 5.

60. Sherman's speech to NAM, in *NAM Proceedings*, 1926, p. 221.

61. *NAM Proceedings*, 1926, pp. 25–39, 204–23; Siegel, *Loans and Legitimacy*, 86.

62. Siegel, *Loans and Legitimacy*, 85.

how well attended they were, and how Europeans would take advantage of these opportunities if Americans did not.[63] NAM was also involved in the newly revived American-Russian Chamber of Commerce, which would play a major role in establishing the Export-Import Bank in 1934 for the purposes of trade with the Soviet Union.

Amtorg did well. By 1930, Americans were shipping $114 million ($1.7 billion in 2018 dollars) in finished products to Russia, 85 percent of which went through Amtorg. According to the American-Russian Chamber of Commerce, Amtorg "was the largest single buyer of American agricultural and industrial equipment for export."[64] Beguiled by "Fordism" and US efficiency, Lenin and, later, Stalin favored US manufacturers, who gained a leg up in a traditionally European market. One such manufacturer was NAM member Fred Koch, whose company, Winkler-Koch Engineering, would build fifteen oil refineries for Stalin between 1929 and 1932.[65]

Internationalism and Diversity

A key part of expanding trade was promoting international understanding and respect for other cultures. Trade could not happen without trust, and to establish trust one had to show respect for those different from oneself. Building an international trade infrastructure was necessarily a cooperative project, one justified, internationalists argued, by the growing interdependence of the nations and peoples of the world. The language of cooperation and interdependence, which was so much a part of the trade association idea, also undergirded the developing ethos of cultural internationalism— the idea that intercultural understanding could help overcome the strident nationalism that led to wars.

A variety of movements and schemes were initiated at the beginning of the twentieth century to "overcome excessive parochialism," as historian Akira Iriye puts it, "with its suspicion and hatred of 'the other' and to establish more interdependent, cooperative, and mutually tolerant international community."[66] Similar movements for cultural tolerance and openness

63. Ibid., 85–86.

64. Ibid., 87.

65. See Jane Mayer, *Dark Money: The Hidden Story of the Billionaires behind the Rise of the Radical Right* (New York: Doubleday, 2016), 28–29. Koch's experience with Stalin contributed to his strong anticommunism.

66. Akira Iriye, *Cultural Internationalism and World Order* (Baltimore: Johns Hopkins University Press, 1997), 15–16.

began domestically in the United States in response to the tremendous waves of unlimited immigration that characterized the United States in the early twentieth century. Progressives like Jane Addams, Randolph Bourne, and Horace Kallen saw xenophobia and race-pride as forms of parochialism that limited democracy and led to social conflict. They advocated instead a cosmopolitan appreciation and respect for other cultures and a recognition of their dynamic contributions to national growth.[67]

In its attempts to promote trade, NAM's Foreign Trade Department likewise showed a cosmopolitan appreciation and respect for other cultures. NAM supported commercial education to train young men and women "in the cultures and languages of other nations."[68] As one NAM official told the *New York Times*, "I have noticed that Americans who get the most business abroad are those who make a study of the conditions in the country in which they are to sell their goods."[69] To help its readers along, *American Industries* recommended myriad travel books and commissioned articles by international dignitaries describing their countries' trade and attitudes toward foreigners.[70] NAM's efforts to educate manufacturers about trade opportunities took the form of culture and geography lessons that presented different nations in a positive light. To be sure, these articles can seem very condescending from today's perspective, even racist in their assumptions and in their "white man's burden" tone. But the overall message was: Get to know your trading partners! It will be profitable for you to get educated about the ways of other people![71]

The spirit of enlightened international cooperation was very much on display at the International Trade Conference of 1915, discussed earlier. "Interdependence" was the byword of the conference—the interdependence

---

67. Randolph Bourne, "Trans-National America," *Atlantic*, July 1916; Jane Addams, *Twenty Years at Hull House* (New York: Macmillan Co., 1912); Horace Kallen, "Democracy vs. the Melting Pot," *Nation*, February 25, 1915.

68. *NAM Proceedings*, 1903, 80.

69. "Aiding Our Export Trade," *New York Times*, January 10, 1904, p. 25.

70. See, for instance, Wu Ting-Fang, "American Industries and Chinese Trade," *American Industries* 7 (June 1, 1908): 18; Sajiro Tatiesh, "The Attitude of Japanese Merchants towards Foreign Manufacturers," *American Industries* 9 (April 1, 1909): 25; Carlos Manuel De Cespedes, "Cuba as Purveyor and Customer," *American Industries* (November 1920): 33, J. E. LeFevre, "Bringing the Americas Together," *American Industries* (September 1920): 33. LeFevre, the chargé d'affaires of Panama, was writing about the Pan-American College of Commerce, a new school designed to bring North and Latin America together.

71. See, for instance, Arthur K. Wing, "Porto Rico: Its Progress Our Duty," *American Industries* (September 1920); "An Intimate View of Lithuania," *American Industries* (October 1920): 36–37; "Business Candidates in Poland," *American Industries* (October 1920): 38; Consul-General of Finland, "Finland Outpost of Civilization," *American Industries* (November 1920).

of Latin America and the United States, for instance, or the interdependence of the peoples of the world. Participants called on manufacturers to travel to other lands, to learn the language, history, and culture of other nations, and to make foreign language and culture part of the secondary school curriculum. Trade was about making a profit, yes, but it required— and produced—peace, tolerance, and progress, all of which had to be cultivated to be successful in the field. As one globetrotting salesman expressed it, "I am filled with the spirit of the export trade. I love to do business with the big importing houses of the world . . . and I know that when the day comes when we can better understand one another and realize that, after all, the race is one, with fundamental interests identical, we will usher in the millennium."[72] Even the Colombians anticipated that the United States might redeem the "blot" on its name for the "unfortunate canal incident" by increasing its trade with Colombia.[73]

Writing a year after this conference, FTC head Edward Hurley celebrated the "passing of our provincialism" that would be instigated by foreign trade opportunities. His book *Awakening of American Business* cited a new acceptance of international cooperation and interdependence as one way in which American business would "awaken": "American businessmen are rapidly shaking off the exclusive, narrow national attitude and becoming cosmopolitan."[74] Like NAM, Hurley called for an educational emphasis on foreign cultures and geography. The German and French apparently had traveled to China, Turkey, Arabia, and America, learning the language and customs of the people with whom they traded; America needed to make similar educational opportunities available.[75] Condemning "national exclusiveness," Hurley looked forward to the prosperity that international cooperation and capitalism would one day bring to the United States, and indeed to the world.

The Return of the Tariff Issue

Despite the internationalism set loose by the Democrats and war, many manufacturers looked forward to a return to normalcy under the Republicans in the 1920s, as signaled by the return of new tariff legislation. The

---

72. "Proceedings of the International Trade Conference held under the Auspices of the NAM," 452.

73. After the Colombians played hardball over the projected canal, Roosevelt had fomented a revolution to get Panama to break away from Colombia. Both Colombian speeches mentioned this incident; ibid., 40, 42.

74. Hurley, *Awakening of Business*, 92.

75. Ibid., 75–77.

Fordney-McCumber Tariff of 1922 would reestablish some of the highest tariffs in US history. It was preceded by concerns that cheap German goods were "invading" American markets and threatening American jobs. In an *American Industries* article supporting the proposed tariff, the bill's coauthor, Congressman Joseph Fordney, wrote that opposition to the bill did not come from the American producer, but rather from the importer, "the man who produces or purchases abroad and the man whose chief interest is in bringing the products of cheap foreign labor into the American market."[76] Importers also tended to be immigrants concentrated in Eastern cities— tariff supporters were generally not interested in diversity.[77] In addition to raising tariff rates in general, the new tariff bill sought to establish a more scientific way to determine tariff rates on dutiable imported items.[78] It was decided that goods would be taxed on the basis of their value (*ad valorem*) as determined by the Tariff Commission. And thus the big debate around the tariff—the debate in NAM at least—was not whether to support the new high tariffs, but rather which method of determining the value on which the tax would be based: American valuation or foreign valuation. This focus is why the articles in *American Industries* in the spring of 1922 were not about the tariff per se, which continued to be divisive, but rather about valuation. NAM supported assessing value according to American costs of production rather than foreign costs, which, it argued, were unstable and difficult to determine.[79]

For those who supported international trade or sought European repayment of war debts, which many in NAM did, the new tariff was a disastrous policy. The tariff's main opponent was Democratic senator Cordell Hull, who thought it would strangle international commerce and encourage other nations to retaliate, leading to job loss and industrial decline. As US bankers began concocting the Dawes Plan, whereby the United States would loan

76. Joseph Fordney, "American Valuation vs. Importers," *American Industries* (March 1922): 7–8.

77. Raymond Bauer, Ithiel de Sola Pool, and Louis Anthony Dexter, *American Business and Public Policy: The Politics of Foreign Trade* (New York: Atherton Press, 1963), 381.

78. A new way of determining tariff rates was sought because the Revenue Act of 1913, otherwise known as the Underwood Tariff, created an income tax to provide revenue to the federal government rather than tariffs. This allowed for the lowering of tariffs without lowering revenue. The architects of the Fordney-McCumber Tariff had kept that innovation, but needed a new way to determine how imported goods should be taxed, in the absence of a revenue function; see Edward Kaplan, *American Trade Policy, 1923–1995* (Westport, CT: Greenwood Press, 1996), 1–13.

79. The debate was nonetheless testy; see "Wide Demand for US Valuation," *American Industries* 22, no. 7 (February 1922): 7–8, 41–42; and "The Urge for American Valuation," *American Industries* (March 1922): 8–9.

money to Germany so that it could pay reparations to France and Britain, which could then in turn repay their war debts to American bankers, Hull noted with irony that the same end could be achieved just by lowering tariffs and allowing Europeans to sell their goods in the United States.[80]

The connection between war debts and tariffs was not one NAM was willing to admit, since doing so might have torn the organization apart. Instead, it pursued policies that were at cross-purposes with each other, giving a bone to each constituency. NAM thus encouraged trade expansion and internationalism alongside its continued support for high tariffs and economic nationalism. It is easy to conclude that the two policies canceled each other out in the larger scheme of things. But that is not entirely correct, because globalization and freer trade was the direction in which the United States would move in the latter half of the twentieth century and ultimately NAM protectionists would fall in line. Globalization and freer trade may not have been inevitable, but it happened, and much like the rationalization of industry, it happened in part because organizations like NAM helped prepare the way for it.

80. Michael Butler, *Cautious Visionary: Cordell Hull and Trade Reform, 1933–1937* (Kent, OH: Kent State University Press, 1998), 13. In *American Trade Policy* (1996, 12), historian Edward Kaplan confirms Hull's assessment that the "bizarre" Dawes Plan would not have been necessary had the United States just lowered tariffs.

3

Fighting Unions

In 1902, NAM became an explicitly anti-union organization with the stated goal of maintaining the "open shop"—or union-free workplaces.[1] Some manufacturers were willing to accept unions as part of the modern industrial landscape, but NAM was not. From 1902 to 1912, a succession of militant open-shop activists led NAM and made it one of the most notorious anti-union organizations in the country. NAM continued to espouse cooperation, industrial improvement, and foreign trade during this period. But among labor activists and reformers, its strident anti-unionism made it a reactionary bully, the antithesis of progress, and the epitome of "the capitalist class."

NAM's chief target was the American Federation of Labor, which, like NAM, sought to bring order and standardization to the field of labor, but on workers' terms, not employers'. NAM fought the AFL using many of the same tactics the AFL deployed against employers: disciplined organization, injunctions, lobbying, and what it variously called "propaganda" or "education." The battle between NAM and the AFL was epic, conceived by both as a struggle for control of the American workplace. In Europe, that question was settled when industrialists, already banded together in cartels, chose to work with the state and negotiate with unions in order to stabilize costs and

---

1. An "open shop" was a workplace controlled by the employer; in a "closed shop," only members of a particular union could be hired; and in a "union shop," all workers hired had to join the union. Both closed shops and union shops undermined employers' control of the workplace.

prices.[2] The result was shared control of the labor market. No such agreement was reached in the United States. Instead, unions and industrialists—both wary of the state—fought one another for control. Neither the AFL nor NAM were truly representative of their alleged constituency ("workers" and "industry," respectively), but they were the organizations most fully engaged in this battle, each vilifying the other as "the enemy," both claiming to uphold American individualism.

The American Federation of Labor

By the start of the twentieth century, the AFL was the leading union organization for American workers. Its membership had grown from 280,000 workers in 1898 to 1.6 million in 1904.[3] Like NAM, it was a federation of autonomous organizations, an organization of organizations, but its members were unions, not companies. Organized by craft, or trade, it prioritized the aims of white, skilled, male workers. The rapidly growing AFL supplanted earlier national labor organizations, which had been less successful but more inclusive of the unskilled, women, and people of color. Unlike socialists or other radicals, it did not seek to bring about a revolution in the economic order, nor did it envision any kind of workers' utopia; still less did it look to the state for cradle-to-grave welfare. Although there was diversity of political and economic beliefs among AFL member unions—indeed, there were even socialists—the AFL at the national level was dedicated to what its leader, Samuel Gompers, called "pure and simple unionism."[4]

Gompers saw workers not as a class-bound proletariat with a revolutionary mission, but as hardworking men up against a rigged system. Only by banding together in unions could they hope to better their individual condition and position. In Gompers's nonpartisan AFL, union members belonged to both major political parties, which in the late nineteenth century were defined by religion, ethno-cultural identities, and local issues; there was no mainstream "workers' party." Moreover, Gompers did not trust the government to look after workers' rights. Many of unions' legislative gains won at the state level were either unenforced or invalidated by the Supreme

---

2. Robertson, *Capital, Labor, and State*, 24. A similar argument is made in Peter Swenson, *Capitalists against Markets: The Making of Labor Markets and Welfare States in the United States and Sweden* (New York: Oxford University Press, 2002).

3. Greene, *Pure and Simple Politics*, 73.

4. Ibid., chaps. 2–3; see also Taft, *The AFL in the Time of Gompers*; and Robertson, *Capital, Labor, and State*, chap. 3.

Court. Thus, Gompers urged unions to avoid politics and take their demands directly to employers.[5] Gompers sought to make the union—not the state or politicians—the progenitor of change and guarantor of working men's rights.[6] Crucial to this strategy was the union shop: new hires who had to sign up with the union and pay its dues would become enfolded into the AFL's powerbase.

Gompers's philosophy was called "volunteerism": unions were private, voluntary associations, free from state regulation and political alliances, seeking not working-class solidarity but rather specific, "pure and simple" gains for their members in the workplace. To many, this philosophy seemed very conservative, especially compared to the broad goals of socialism, the International Workers of the World (IWW), and other more class-conscious unions. But as David Brian Robertson argues, this strategy "posed a sweeping, confrontational, and credible challenge to employers' prerogatives in the labor market."[7] If successful, it would put unions in control of the workplace.

To achieve this vision the national AFL pursued a strategy of strikes, boycotts, and picketing. It was not averse to working with those employers' organizations that promoted cooperation between labor and management, such as the National Civic Federation (NCF), of which Gompers was vice president. The AFL also continued to pursue legislation, though Gompers's strategy precluded its support for reforms like universal shorter hours, which were constitutionally shaky and difficult to enforce; it focused instead on legislation to curb employers' power and improve labor's position. For instance, the AFL sought legislation prohibiting the use of injunctions against striking or boycotting workers, exempting unions from the Sherman Antitrust Act, or placing restrictions on immigration and child labor, sources of unskilled labor that lowered wages for all. In proposing an eight-hour day for government employees, which could be enforced constitutionally, Gompers hoped to set an example for other employers. The AFL also supported candidates who were friendly to labor. Thus, it did not completely abandon politics, but its political goals were in the service of a union-shop strategy, not directed toward gains that it thought should be won by unions through collective bargaining.

5. Robertson, *Capital, Labor, and State*, 15, 37–40. Greene (*Pure and Simple Politics*, 95–97) argues that the AFL maintained a political program and only dropped it after NAM's success in squashing it.
6. For this reason, the AFL leadership opposed government welfare programs, which would undercut the appeal of unions to workers.
7. Robertson, *Capital, Labor, and State*, 66.

The AFL's success was accompanied by an increase in strikes and violence, as unions pressed their demands for an eight-hour day, wage increases, and union shops. Between 1899 and 1904—the years of the AFL's greatest growth—there were 15,463 strikes, compared to 7,029 between 1893 and 1898. The number of workers involved in strikes increased to 2.6 million from the 1.7 million in the earlier period.[8] To some extent the strikes were successful in that they encouraged many employers to negotiate contracts, along the lines of what the NCF advocated. Indeed, between 1898 and 1902, a number of large employers seeking an edge over competitors negotiated with trade unions to stabilize and predict costs.[9] But the strikes (and settlements) also spurred employers to form "unions" of their own—organizations dedicated to the maintenance of the open shop.

The Open-Shop Movement

In response to the AFL's successful tactics, employers banded together to form employers' associations, local "citizens' alliances," and open-shop organizations. Prominent among these were the National Metal Trades Association (NMTA), the National Founders' Association, the American Anti-Boycott Association (AABA), and the Citizens' Industrial Association (CIA), founded in 1903 and led by prominent NAM officials, including David Parry, James Van Cleave, and C. W. Post.[10] At first, the members of these associations were primarily smaller and medium-sized concerns from the Midwest, while the largest corporations joined the NCF in the hopes that arbitration and conciliation would settle labor strife to their advantage. By 1903, however, when Parry founded the CIA, even large corporations like International Harvester, US Steel, and National Cash Register had embraced an open-shop stance and withdrawn from the NCF's collective bargaining committee (although they remained interested in the NCF's welfare programs).[11]

Employers who joined the open-shop movement saw unions as trusts that fettered the ambitions of the most efficient and skillful workers and thus

8. Greene, *Pure and Simple Politics*, 88.

9. Richard Gable, "Birth of an Employers' Association," *Business History Review* 33 (Winter 1959): 535–45, 539.

10. Greene, *Pure and Simple Politics*, 88–89; Taft, *The AFL in the Time of Gompers*, chap. 16; Chad Pearson, *Organizing America's Anti-Union Movement* (Philadelphia: University of Pennsylvania Press, 2016), especially chap. 1. For a contemporary account, see John Keith, "The New Unions of Employers," *Harper's Weekly*, January 23, 1904, pp. 130–33.

11. David Montgomery, *The Fall of the House of Labor: The Workplace, the State, and American Labor Activism* (New York: Cambridge University Press, 1991), 272–74.

impeded the progress that individual effort was supposed to bring.[12] Unions had rules setting productivity rates, which prevented employers from offering incentive pay. They refused to accept labor-saving devices. Because of jurisdictional agreements, they often required that three or four different skilled workers work on a specific job when one person could do it.[13] Trade unions could drag an entire enterprise into jurisdictional battles among different trades, as unions themselves were trying to establish a foothold in new industries. One dispute between masons and electricians over whose union was responsible for making the wall holes for electrical wiring, for instance, lasted ten years.[14] Often, a "walking delegate" would take an employer to task for using the wrong union for a particular type of job. One employer hired iron union men to install a low iron railing in an office front, only to be told that the job belonged to the carpenters' union, because it involved hammering nails into a wooden floor.[15] The AFL tried to resolve such conflicts between, for instance, furniture workers and carpenters, or lathe operators and machinists, but had little authority over autonomous unions, and thus the disputes often became problems for employers, who risked hiring the "wrong" union and sparking a strike. Similarly, individual unions could deploy boycotts in ways that even the AFL found frivolous. Boycotts of a company's product were an effective bargaining chip for unions, but often they hurt other unions at the company in question. The AFL tried to dictate the terms under which a boycott would be acceptable, but the unions on good terms with a company might still protest the decision, causing disunity in the AFL.[16]

Union violence was another impetus for the growth of employers' associations. Most famously, the militant leaders of the International Bridge and Structural Iron Workers—in defiance of AFL policy—sabotaged the property of employers who refused to use union labor. The leaders of this union, Frank Ryan and John McNamara, secretly led the dynamiting of eighty-seven structures built by non-union labor between 1906 and 1911, including the Llewellyn Iron Works in Los Angeles. This team was also responsible for

---

12. See especially Pearson, *Organizing America's Anti-Union Movement*, 3–19; see also chapter 1.

13. These standard complaints are discussed in Mark Hendrickson, *American Labor and Economic Citizenship* (New York: Cambridge University Press, 2013), 44–45.

14. Keith, "The New Unions of Employers," 131; Taft, *The AFL in the Time of Gompers*, chap. 12. For examples of union competition causing trouble for employers, see Ray Stannard Baker, "Organized Capital Challenges Organized Labor," *McClure's* 23, no. 3 (July 1904): 281.

15. Keith, "The New Unions of Employers," 130.

16. Taft, *The AFL in the Time of Gompers*, 264–65.

bombing the *Los Angeles Times* building in 1910, which killed twenty news-paper workers. The *Times* was targeted because of its editor, the anti-union Harrison Gray Otis. The culprits and their accomplices eventually pled guilty to these deeds, but not before Gompers and the AFL vigorously denied their guilt and raised money for their defense. In all, thirty-eight members of the union were found guilty of charges related to the dynamiting. Although these actions were the doings of a small group of men in one union, they were large in scale and easily confirmed employers' charges that unions used unlawful and violent means to achieve their dubious goals.[17]

Savvy employers could perhaps have exploited the many divisions among and between unions and workers. Those employers who joined open-shop organizations, however, not only were tired of getting dragged into trivial and unpredictable disputes, but also felt that the goal post kept moving in negotiations with unions: the more the employer conceded, the larger and more frequent their demands. They became convinced that the collectiv-ism represented by unions would impede progress and bring nothing but chaos, compulsion, and, finally, state servitude.[18] Thus, instead of negoti-ating, they chose to organize and fight. In doing so, they gave life to the radical idea that there was class warfare in the United States, a claim they simultaneously denied.

Similar to cartels and unions, local employers' associations forced their members to comply with the association's decisions in labor disputes so as to present a unified front. They did this by imposing literal bonds that member employers paid to the organization, which would be forfeited if they failed to go along with the association's decision. Such forfeiture was worded in contracts as "damages," rather than "fines," and therefore was apparently not technically illegal.[19] The employers' associations were thus able to enforce blacklists and lockouts among their members. Employers who chose not to join their local citizens' alliance or employers' association and contin-ued to deal with unions eventually could be forced out of business. This sounds like collusion—exactly what employers found objectionable about unions—but they insisted it was the only way to fight the unions. Employ-ers' associations also held "open-shop drives" to enlist new members and support, recruited workingmen into their organizations and trained them

17. On this episode, see ibid., chap. 17, and "The Dynamiters," *American Industries* (August 1911): 22–26.

18. A paraphrase of a statement by open-shop leader George B. Hugo, quoted in Pearson, *Organizing America's Anti-Union Movement*, 3.

19. Keith, "The New Unions of Employers," 131.

as machinists and tradesmen to replace striking workers, and used injunctions, spies, and company unions to prevent (or provoke) strikes and subvert independent unions.[20]

They also brought suits against unions for "conspiracy to restrict trade" under the Sherman Antitrust Act. Their most successful case was the Danbury hatters case, which led to *Loewe v. Lawlor*, a 1908 Supreme Court decision affirming that unions could be prosecuted as trusts under the Sherman Act. After hatmaker D. E. Loewe & Company refused to sign on to a collective bargaining agreement in 1902, the United Hatmakers of North America, backed by the AFL, struck and boycotted the company. The American Anti-Boycott Association took up Loewe's case, investing $20,000 in prosecuting it and arguing that the union conspired to restrict interstate trade. After the decision in 1908, the case dragged on for nine more years, costing the hatters' union and the AFL over $422,000 in fines and fees.[21]

These methods were effective, and most labor historians agree that they severely restricted union growth after 1904. Given that the AFL's entire strategy hinged on the union shop, there was no room for "win-win" solutions for these two groups.[22] Each group's success depended on the other's failure. In the land of individualism, at a time of cooperation, each claimed that its organization was necessary to confront and defeat the organization of the other.

NAM's "Open-Shop" Turn

The attendees at NAM's 1902 convention in Indianapolis elected open-shop activist David Parry as the organization's new president. Other contenders included a Brooklyn leather-belting manufacturer who was an outspoken exporter and former Brooklyn mayor. Although favored to win, the Brooklyn exporter lost to Parry, whose election may have benefited from the convention being held on Parry's home turf but also reflected the rising interest among NAM members in the open-shop movement.[23] Parry, who

20. Greene, *Pure and Simple Politics*, 90; Gable, "Birth of an Employers' Association," 538–40; Montgomery, *Fall of the House of Labor*, 270–75; Taft, *The AFL in the Time of Gompers*, chap. 26.
21. Robertson, *Capital, Labor, and State*, 112.
22. See "Address of Samuel Gompers . . . before the Arbitration Conference, held at Chicago, Ill., December 17, 1900, under the Auspices of the National Civic Federation," available at https://archive.org/details/addressofsamuelg00gomp; David Parry, presidential address, *NAM Proceedings*, 1903.
23. See the description of the 1903 convention in *Iron Age* 69 (April 17, 1902): 27–29; *New York Times*, April 15, 1902, p. 7.

was simultaneously organizing the CIA, quickly changed NAM's focus. In October 1902, NAM sent out a circular declaring its intention to fight two bills sponsored by the AFL and pending in Congress, one for an eight-hour day for government employees, the other prohibiting the use of injunctions against striking workers.[24] In December, Parry sent out another set of circulars, attacking the AFL as socialist and calling for employers to unite against it. These themes were well rehearsed by the time Parry took the stage at the 1903 NAM convention in New Orleans to announce a "new direction" for the organization.

In a barrage of hyperbolic rhetoric, Parry spelled out the dangers that organized labor (the AFL) posed to manufacturers and American democracy:

> Organized labor knows but one law, and that is the law of physical force—the law of the Huns and Vandals, the law of the savage. All its purposes are accomplished either by actual force or by the threat of force. It does not place its reliance in reason and justice, but in strikes, boycotts, and coercion. . . . It is, in fact, a despotism springing into being in the midst of a liberty-loving people.[25]

The AFL, he continued, had "grown into an army, presumably 2,000,000 strong," and was now bringing bills before Congress that would engraft upon the nation "its sprigs of socialism."[26] Parry decried the impending eight-hour bill's likely adverse effect on industry and its denial of individual rights to those workers who wanted to work longer than eight hours. The anti-injunction bill, which would have limited employers' use of court-ordered injunctions against striking workers, would "legalize strikes and boycotts," according to Parry, and take away employers' only defense against organized coercion and violence.[27] Parry assured his audience that he was not attacking unions per se, but rather their "theories and methods." This caveat tells us that Parry's brand of anti-unionism was not necessarily a popular position at this time, even among industrialists.

Parry rejected "conciliation" and arbitration, favored stances of the NCF and "enlightened" businessmen. For Parry, conciliation with unions

---

24. "Big War Begins on Union Labor," *Chicago Daily Tribune*, October 25, 1902; "Oppose the 8-Hour Bill," *New York Times*, October 8, 1902, p. 1.

25. *NAM Proceedings*, 1903, p. 16, quoted in Gable, "Birth of an Employers' Association," 541–42.

26. As reported in "Manufacturers Hear an Attack on Unions," *New York Times*, April 15, 1903, p. 3.

27. Ibid.

demanded an acknowledgment of their legitimacy as economic organizations, which would compromise one's fundamental convictions: "The principles of organized labor are untenable to those believing in the individualistic social order."[28] Like Gompers, Parry also rejected compulsory arbitration, wherein labor problems were decided by an allegedly neutral third party; neither believed that the third party would be neutral. Gompers, however, did favor conciliation, otherwise known as "collective bargaining," which was, as Parry understood, a recognition of labor's power.

Most historians have emphasized Parry's alarmist rhetoric, but what also stands out in his 1903 convention speech is his focus on *organization*. If unions threatened the "individualistic social order," what about collectivities like corporations and trade associations? Parry grappled with this conundrum. At first he seemed to suggest that unions were the reason businessmen had to forsake individualism and organize: "The day of individual isolation is dead. The time has gone when individual employers can stand alone." Employers needed to fight organization with organization. But then Parry stated that organization was a good in itself: "Organization is the modern machine for accomplishing results beneficial to all." In fact, he continued, the day might come when organizations would have to be given the rights enjoyed by individuals: "The law of individual freedom seems to be correctly applicable to individuals in their associative capacities."[29] Later, in a different context, he objected to state-level antitrust laws, stating that the consolidation of widely scattered activities under one management was advancing the cause of civilization.

The speakers who followed Parry at this historic convention likewise spoke about the changing times begetting the need for organization in ways that seemed to contradict Parry's concern about "our individualistic social order." Farm equipment manufacturer A. B. Farquhar celebrated the efficiency of large organizations and, like Parry, decried the inefficiency of state-level antitrust legislation. Going further, however, Farquhar said that the problem was not centralized administration, which advanced civilization, but rather *special privileges*, which benefited some trusts over others.[30] He was referring to the tariff (which caused a bit of a stir), but it is hard to read his words and not hear echoes of Gompers. Then, in taking a position distinctly contrary to Parry's, US Commissioner of Labor Carroll D. Wright

28. *NAM Proceedings*, 1903, p. 60.
29. Ibid., 57–59.
30. Ibid., 257–65.

asserted an equivalence between organized capital (the corporation) and organized labor (unions), suggesting that they could work together to allay their mutual suspicion of each other.[31] These other speakers indicate not only a diversity of opinion within NAM about the labor problem but also a shared recognition and indeed celebration of "the age of organization." NAM was not interested in the preservation of nineteenth-century proprietary capitalism or its "limited state" corollary. It was firmly in the camp of Theodore Roosevelt with regard to the need for trusts, organization, and federal coordination—except in the realm of labor relations.

Following the speechifying, NAM adopted ten "labor principles," which amounted to ten different ways of saying that NAM respected the individual rights of all workers but reserved employers' right to be "unmolested and unhampered in the management of their business." They rejected the union-shop principle on the basis that every man ought to be free to work regardless of whether or not he joined a union—that is, unions were fine if they didn't insist on a closed shop.[32]

NAM's stand against the union shop was seen by many as a declaration of war. Newspaper headlines blared, "Manufacturers Hear an Attack on Unions," and "Big War Begins on Labor." The business community was critical of the turn. The *Wall Street Journal* disapproved in an editorial titled "Nothing Is to Be Gained by Violence." Republican Mark Hanna—the businessman's businessman—said that Parry's views "did not reflect the modern tendency in thought" and that the manufacturers in NAM were "splendid, broadminded men" who did not share the pessimistic and inflammatory views of their president. Hanna singled out Parry's criticism of conciliation and arbitration as particularly wrongheaded.[33] When Parry condemned the AFL in a speech before the Furniture Association of America, a furniture-maker from New Rochelle, New York, stood up and asked members to protest the speech they had just heard; if they did not, "we shall go down as opposed to union labor, while I do not think that to be the case." He continued: "If ever I heard anarchy, I heard it tonight from that platform."[34] Even NAM members were not all on board. Upon receiving NAM's circular about its fight against the eight-hour bill, the head of the Gold Medal Camp Furniture Manufacturing Company in Racine, Wisconsin, replied: "The time

31. Recounted in Steigerwalt, *The National Association of Manufacturers*, 113–14.
32. For the list of ten labor principles, see Gable, "Birth of an Employers' Association," 543.
33. "Hanna Replies to Parry," *New York Times*, April 19, 1903, p. 1.
34. "D. M. Parry Condemns Organized Labor," *New York Times*, July 28, 1903, p. 7.

is coming when the eight hour system will be generally observed and the writer feels the sooner the better."[35]

For Parry and company, such negative responses were evidence of the need for "propaganda," or education, about "the individualistic social order." The AFL's unlikely success had persuaded NAM leaders that "public opinion is the guiding force in the nation today," a belief that it would hold all through the twentieth century.[36] Like the AFL, NAM issued hundreds of pamphlets designed to win over opinion leaders, workingmen, and ultimately the broader public. Titles included "Class Legislation," "The Doom of the Boycott," and "Americanism: The True Solution of the Labor Problem." In publications, articles, pamphlets, advertisements, and speeches, NAM representatives and propagandists blasted union collectivism and recorded the absurdities of a topsy-turvy world in which unions controlled the factory floor instead of employers. They argued that unions were essentially "trusts" that were seeking control of the labor market and colluding to impede trade. These efforts would eventually evolve into a full-blown, permanent public relations campaign for the "individualistic social order," also known as the "American free enterprise system."[37] Countering (and combating) the narratives put forward by organized labor, newspapers (the "mainstream media" of the day) and, later, the New Deal wing of the Democratic Party would become NAM's main priority for the rest of the twentieth century. It would take its educational campaign to local communities, rotary clubs, churches, high schools and colleges, trade conventions, and political campaigns, adapting the newest media and networking innovations to counter labor and liberals' portrayals of US capitalism and employers.

Parry even wrote a successful science fiction novel, *The Scarlet Empire*, published in 1906 by Bobbs-Merrill. Surprisingly well plotted, the dystopian novel tells the story of a young idealist who, failing to make it in the free enterprise system, throws himself off a bridge in Coney Island. Instead of drowning, he is rescued and taken to an undersea socialist community and sees for himself how socialism undermines human dignity. The story was standard antisocialist fare, yet told with a wit and grace that one would not expect from a carriage manufacturer. The book

---

35. Gold Letter Camp Furniture Manufacturing Company to David Parry, July 1, 1902, reprinted in US Senate Judiciary Committee, *Maintenance of a Lobby*, vol. 1, p. 18.

36. Quoted in Bonnett, *Employers' Associations in the United States*, 336.

37. Ibid., 87–89.

was serialized in *American Industries* and stayed in print for most of the twentieth century.[38]

NAM also fought the AFL in the courts. NAM president James Van Cleave, owner of Buck's Range and Stove Company, directly confronted Gompers on the use of the boycott in what culminated in the Supreme Court case *Gompers vs. Buck's Stove and Range Company* (1911). It was perhaps the most direct conflict between the two organizations and was followed closely by the press over seven years. Both Gompers and Van Cleave saw it as a test case to determine once and for all the validity of the secondary boycott; both also hoped to use the struggle to gain support for their own organization.[39] Like the Danbury hatters case, this case involved a manufacturer—Van Cleave—who refused to sign a collective bargaining agreement. In 1906, the Metal Polishers, Buffers, Platers' Union at Van Cleave's company struck, and the AFL added the company's name to its "do not patronize" list, knowing that it was directly challenging NAM itself. Van Cleave requested an injunction to prevent the boycott, and Gompers removed the company's name from the boycott list, but continued to write and speak about the metal polishers' complaints against Buck's Stove and Range Company. Gompers knew he was violating the injunction, but he saw it as a matter of free speech: "So long as I retain my health and my sanity, I am going to speak on any subject on God's green earth," Gompers told an Indianapolis crowd after the injunction was instated. "I have not yet surrendered and I am not likely to surrender, the fight of freedom of speech and freedom of the press. . . . I shall discuss the merits of the Buck Stove and Range Company injunction. . . . I can't help it. I must discuss it. I will explode if I don't."[40]

In 1908, Van Cleave's lawyer, the AABA's Daniel Davenport, urged the federal district court in Washington, DC, to find the AFL guilty of contempt for violating the injunction in Gompers's speeches and by continuing to write about it in the AFL's journal, *American Federationist*. The court found Gompers and several other AFL officials guilty of contempt and sentenced them to varying prison terms, which they never served. Unlike Gompers, the courts did not see it as a freedom of speech case, but rather as a conspiracy

38. David Parry, *The Scarlet Empire*, edited by Jerome Clubb and Howard Allen (Carbondale: Southern Illinois University Press, 2001), introduction.

39. Ken I. Kersch, "The *Gompers v. Buck's Stove* Saga: A Constitutional Case Study in Dialogue, Resistance, and the Freedom of Speech," *Journal of Supreme Court History* 31, no. 28 (2006): 28–57; see also Robertson, *Capital, Labor, and State*, 112–13; Greene, *Pure and Simple Politics*, 153–54.

40. Quoted in Kersch, "The *Gompers v. Buck's Stove* Saga," 37.

to restrain trade; the issues that animated the many appeals and retrials (which continued through 1914!) were mainly procedural, as if the courts were avoiding the free speech elements of the case. Van Cleave died in 1910, and his company chose to settle with the union and pull out of the ongoing litigation. The company also left NAM.[41] But the case continued without Buck's Stove and Range Company. The Supreme Court in 1911 dismissed the case, in part because of Van Cleave's death but also on the procedural grounds that Gompers and two other AFL officials should have been tried for civil (not criminal) contempt. The same judge who had found AFL officials in contempt in 1908 retried them in a second—civil—contempt case, which was likewise dismissed by the Supreme Court in 1914 because of a new statute of limitations.[42]

The Buck's Stove and Range case illustrates not just the kind of tactics NAM was deploying and not just its vendetta-like targeting of the AFL, but also the changing political landscape that was in fact what the real contest was about. At various points in the case's history, both sides claimed victory, but at the end of the day it was Gompers who had most expertly used the free speech issue to get voters, the press, and politicians to take a side. Previously, the two major political parties had tried to finesse the workingman's vote, which was divided and nowhere near a unified bloc vote. But in the electoral contests of 1908 and 1912, both parties were forced to take a position on this case, with the Democrats supporting Gompers's interpretation and the Republicans supporting NAM. What you see here is the beginning of a politically meaningful working-class vote for the party that was willing to cultivate it.[43]

NAM also confronted the AFL in Congress and state legislatures, where it coordinated lobbying against AFL-supported bills at the federal, state, and local levels. To help with these efforts, NAM created the National Council for Industrial Defense (NCID), which by 1909 consisted of 227 local, state, and national employers' associations and trade organizations. These associations did not meet NAM's membership qualifications (not being individual companies), nor were they able to contribute in any sustained way for its services.[44] But, President Van Cleave insisted, the members of these

41. Ibid., 47, citing "Gompers Is Jubilant," *New York Times*, July 27, 1910, p. 6.
42. For details on the rest of the case, see Kersch, "The *Gompers v. Buck's Stove* Saga," 47–52.
43. Ibid., 37–39.
44. NCID members made contributions "as needed," rather than in the form of regular dues. This was a source of confusion for congressional investigators in 1913. See US House Select Committee on Lobby Investigation, *Charges against House Members and Lobby Activities of the National*

associations were essential to NAM's lobbying efforts. They had connections to state legislators and other officials. They could write, telegram, and otherwise contact legislators on their own dime and send representatives to Washington at their own expense. Since NAM lacked these connections, said Van Cleave in a letter to his closest associates, "even if we should never secure any financial contributions from the Council organizations we need them to show the right strength in Washington." Indeed, the purpose of Van Cleave's letter was to persuade his colleagues to use NAM funds to finance the NCID.[45] For all practical purposes, the NCID was basically NAM. As President Van Cleave explained, NAM's Legislative Committee and the NCID were like Siamese twins: "You cannot and need not be able to tell where the one ends and the other begins. The Council was organized and exists under the leadership of the National Association of Manufacturers, and this leadership is exercised through the Legislative Committee."[46]

This was a period of great legislative activity. As Van Cleave noted, over forty thousand bills were introduced in Congress in 1907–1909, and over forty-five thousand bills in state legislatures during that same period. In 1909, thirteen thousand laws were enacted at the federal and state levels. NAM was on the lookout for those statutes that affected "natural and artificial persons" (the latter being corporations) by seeking to "increase their liabilities, restrict their liberty, change their mode of operations, subtract from or add to their legal remedies, and affect the control and disposition of their property."[47] Mainly, however, NAM in this period focused its lobbying on combating the AFL's eight-hour bill for government contractors, the AFL's anti-injunction bills, and the AFL's attempt to exempt labor unions from the Sherman Antitrust Act.

The AFL had made some progress in attaining congressional support for its proposals in the 1890s, but that changed with NAM's legislative offensive in 1903 and the election of Illinois Republican Joseph G. Cannon as House speaker in the same year. A onetime ally of Abraham Lincoln's, Speaker Cannon began his political career during the Civil War. By the time he became House speaker, he was an "old guard" Republican, wary of the increasing influence of labor and progressives. Cannon worked closely with NAM to

Association of Manufacturers and Others, vol. 4, September 9–13, 1913, esp. 2919–21; Steigerwalt, *The National Association of Manufacturers*, 125.

45. Van Cleave to Parry, October 16, 1908, in US Senate Judiciary Committee, *Maintenance of a Lobby*, vol. 2, appendix, pp. 2223–24.

46. "Report of the Legislative Committee," *American Industries* 10, no. 11 (June 1909): 22.

47. Ibid.

make sure that there was "balance" on House committees that they believed favored labor and reformers. In control of committee appointments and the Rules Committee, he became a singularly powerful and obstructionist House speaker.[48] From 1903 to 1910, Cannon, NAM, and other "standpatters," such as Congressman Charles Littlefield of Maine and James Tawney of Minnesota, successfully kept the AFL's eight-hour bill for government employees and its anti-injunction bills from coming to the House floor.[49]

A common tactic was to tie up bills in hearings, as described by NAM/NCID secretary Marshall Cushing to NAM members: "A week ago we demanded hearings and got them and now the game is to string them out indefinitely."[50] At the hearings, a tightly coordinated group of manufacturers who were active in NAM and other open-shop organizations gave predictable testimony about the damage to their enterprise that would be wreaked if a certain bill passed.[51] Or, as Cushing's telegram to a NAM member in a position to influence Georgia congressman William G. Brantley put it, "Kindly telegraph Brantley today asking him to make certain that new Jenkins anti-injunction bill has no show tomorrow, next day, or at any time."[52] Hundreds of such telegrams were sent out asking members to pressure their congressmen one way or the other. Although it is impossible to know how many NAM members followed through with such requests (some opposed these efforts), most historians agree with Julie Greene's conclusion: "As a result of the NAM's political campaign, the AFL abruptly ceased to enjoy any political success even as its leaders intensified their efforts."[53]

---

48. See Greene, *Pure and Simple Politics*, 255; Robert Remini, *The House: A History of the House of Representatives* (New York: HarperCollins, 2006), 269–75; Janice A. Petterchak, "Conflict of Ideals: Samuel Gompers v. 'Uncle Joe' Cannon," *Journal of the Illinois State Historical Society* 74 (Spring 1981): 31–40.

49. Robertson, *Capital, Labor, and State*, 161–62; Greene, *Pure and Simple Politics*, 94–97.

50. Quoted in Greene, *Pure and Simple Politics*, 96, citing US Senate Judiciary Committee, *Maintenance of a Lobby*.

51. See, for example, the testimony of Mr. W. B. Bowles of the Long Arm Systems Company of Cleveland, Ohio, also representing NAM and the NMTA, in "Eight Hours of Laborers on Government Work," hearings before the US House Committee on Labor, 1906.

52. Cushing to F. B. Gordon, January 24, 1905, in series 1, box 43, "Corporate Records, 1903–1905" file, NAMR; see also US Senate Judiciary Committee, *Maintenance of a Lobby*, vol. 1, appendix, 38–47, for examples.

53. Greene, *Pure and Simple Politics*, 96. From 1909 to 1913, the NCID spent $167,163 to stop this legislation. US House Select Committee on Lobby Investigation, *Charges against House Members and Lobby Activities of the National Association of Manufacturers and Others*, vol. 4, September 9–13, 1913, p. 2919.

Much of what we know about NAM's political influence in these years comes from congressional investigations instigated by what became known as "the Mulhall scandal." In 1913, "Colonel" Michael Martin Mulhall, a former employee of NAM and NCID, sold his story to the *Chicago Tribune* and the *New York World*, accusing his former employers of bribery, secret deals, and interference with elections. Echoing the words of recently elected President Wilson, the headlines told of "an invisible government" corrupting the democratic process for private profit. Upon the revelation of Mulhall's charges in the papers, both houses of Congress subpoenaed NAM's records and began investigations into political lobbying that focused almost solely on NAM. The result was a media frenzy, four volumes of testimony, and four remarkable volumes of NAM leaders' private correspondence.[54]

Like a latter-day WikiLeaks, the newspapers reported each new piece of testimony with zeal, quoting copiously from Mulhall's letters and testimony. "Great Slush Fund Given by the Lobby to Grease Wheels," said the *Atlanta Constitution*, reporting that manufacturers raised between $500 and $700 every year to oppose legislation.[55] Another headline charged, "He Gave Money to Congressman," reporting on Mulhall's payments to labor-friendly Illinois congressman J. T. McDermott and his secretary, Mr. McMichaels, to report information on Gompers's activities and advance information on upcoming bills.[56] Each new document confirmed the worst tales of Progressive Era muckrakers.

The congressmen of course denied all charges. They'd never met the man, they said. He was a shady character with a proven record of lying, they charged. James Emery, NAM's general counsel, informed the papers (and the committees) that NAM had fired Mulhall in 1911 because of his "unreliability" and his questionable personal life.[57] Republican operative Arthur Vorys said that it was hardly news that NAM supported Republican

54. The Senate Judiciary Committee's hearings were published as *Maintenance of a Lobby*, and those of the House special investigating committee as *Charges against House Members and Lobby Activities of the National Association of Manufacturers and Others*; both filled four volumes, and both were published in 1913.

55. "Great Slush Fund Given by the Lobby to Grease Wheels," *Atlanta Constitution*, July 17, 1913, p. 1.

56. "He Gave Money to Congressman," *Atlanta Constitution*, July 25, 1913, p. 10; US House Select Committee on Lobby Investigation, *Charges against House Members and Lobby Activities of the National Association of Manufacturers and Others*, vol. 4, appendix A, pp. 2809–14. In total, between $1,500 and $2,000 was paid to McDermott and McMichael for their assistance.

57. "Emery Flays Col. Mulhall," *Chicago Tribune*, June 30, 1913; "Mulhall Fired for Unreliability," *San Francisco Chronicle*, June 30, 1913, p. 2. Mulhall had deserted his wife and five children, and an apparent second "wife" had been accompanying him on business.

candidates.[58] Yes, the NAM was "guilty" of lobbying, said former NAM president John Kirby, but seeking to influence Congress was not illegal; it was the basis of the democratic process. NAM had openly declared its intentions to influence the passage of legislation it favored and to stop that which it did not. That was the purpose of the organization. That was what its members paid it to do. There was no secret about this, he asserted.[59]

Historian Albert Steigerwalt concluded that the Mulhall charges were overblown and disproven over the course of the hearings. No charges were ever brought against anyone in NAM. Nor did any legislative proposals emerge from the hearings, suggesting, according to Steigerwalt, that the whole case was inflated by the antitrust, anti–big business rhetoric of the Wilson administration. There may be some truth to that. Speaker Cannon did not, after all, need NAM's involvement to keep labor bills from the floor; he would have done so regardless. And while NAM did send letters to congressmen asking if it could count on their support for a specific piece of legislation, a surprising number of congressmen responded either no they could not, or, more indignantly, they would do what was best for their constituents.[60] Moreover, there is evidence that Emery and NAM officials sought to avoid questionable activity. With regard to the failed Indiana gubernatorial campaign of Republican James Watson, for instance, the correspondence shows that Van Cleave had not followed Mulhall's recommendations for fear of exposure and legal charges.[61] NAM's lobbying transgressions—its $15 payments to congressional pages and Democratic congressmen, for instance—appear mild compared to the billions of dollars spent by lobbyists today.

Nonetheless, the documents do reveal some shady behavior. NAM hand-chose James Watson to run for the Republican nomination. David Parry spelled out the job before them: "Watson really is a man of really no means at all, and it is going to be hard sledding to nominate him, and we are going to have the fight of our lives to elect him; both of which will take some money."[62] The documents also show NAM's direct involvement in

58. "NAM Sought to Influence Tariff," *Chicago Tribune*, July 19, 1913, p. 2.

59. "Mulhall Fired for Unreliability," *Chicago Tribune*, June 30, 1913; Steigerwalt, *The National Association of Manufacturers*, 140.

60. See, for instance, Parry circular dated October 6, 1902, and responses, in US Senate Judiciary Committee, *Maintenance of Lobby*, vol. 1, appendix, 25–46.

61. "NAM Sought to Influence Tariff," *Chicago Tribune*, July 19, 1913, p. 2.

62. David Parry to James Van Cleave, December 30, 1907, in US Senate Judiciary Committee, *Maintenance of a Lobby*, vol. 2, appendix, 1242.

strikebreaking. "Mulhall Sent to End Strikes in Many Cities," announced a *Chicago Tribune* page one headline in early July 1913. Companies called up Emery seeking help with their labor troubles. Emery in turn would dispatch Mulhall, who would travel to the city in question and hire agitators to break up strike meetings and pay striking workers to inform on the unions' plans and strategies.[63] Sometimes he'd find a way to convince (or pay) someone to call off a strike. His cash came from NAM/NCID, which kept strict records of the payments made, ranging from $25 to $50 for informants to between $100 and $200 for replacement workers. Mulhall broke up strikes by fifty thousand printers in Philadelphia in 1906, twenty-three thousand shoe workers in St. Louis in 1907, and machinists at the Long Arm Systems Company in Cleveland, also in 1907. In 1908 it was anthracite miners in Pennsylvania, and in 1909 shoe workers in Portsmouth, Ohio, and hatters in Danbury, Connecticut. In Danbury, some of the hat manufacturers apparently were willing to settle with the union and "did not welcome the assistance of the N.A.M." But Mulhall swept in anyway and reunited the manufacturers against the unions.[64] He also enlisted the help of a local church leader through, in part, a generous $300 donation to the church.[65]

Mulhall and his associates were scoundrels. They sometimes involved NAM in bizarre deals, such as, for instance, a scheme in 1908 to bribe Gompers to give up his labor activism and enlist him in the antilabor cause. When NAM president Van Cleave was finally approached about it, he refused to have anything to do with it.[66] Van Cleave may well have been genuine in his disdain for Mulhall's below-board machinations, but the fact was that he had hired Mulhall and his ilk to do this kind of dirty work and for the most part was happy with the results. Marshall Cushing, NAM's general secretary and

---

63. "Mulhall Sent to End Strikes in Many Cities," *Chicago Daily Tribune*, July 2, 1913, p. 1; see also US Senate Judiciary Committee, *Maintenance of a Lobby*, vols. 1 and 2 appendices.

64. Mulhall describes his activities in Danbury in numerous letters to the NCID, but see especially Mulhall to Ferdinand [Schwedtman], June 16, 1909, in US Senate Judiciary Committee, *Maintenance of a Lobby*, vol. 3, appendix, 2930.

65. Ibid. This was about a year after the Supreme Court case, *Loewe vs. Lawlor*, which also concerned the Danbury hatters. The Supreme Court made the use of the boycott illegal, but did nothing to mitigate the dispute, which continued. Reports in papers indicate that the strikers won the use of the union label, although the manufacturers won an open shop. Both sides submitted to arbitration. See "Danbury Strike Off," *New York Herald*, June 9, 1909, p. 5.

66. This is recounted in newspaper accounts of the Mulhall controversy in 1913 and the Buck's Stove and Range case in 1908, which are examined earlier in the chapter. See "Gompers Bribe Story Amplified by Ex-Editor," *New York Tribune*, July 1, 1913, p. 5; "Seek to Intimidate," *Washington Post*, July 19, 1913, p. 2; "Denies Bribe Story," *Washington Post*, September 25, 1908, p. 1.

the man who had organized much of this activity, left NAM in 1907 to start his own strikebreaking detective firm.[67] NAM in this period was thus not simply a "clearinghouse" for employers seeking to maintain an open shop, but an organization with a hands-on policy of actual strikebreaking that tied it to the world of small-time thuggery and con-men.

The Mulhall scandal was a huge embarrassment to NAM and all of US industry at a sensitive time. The *New York World* called NAM's actions "terrorism" on behalf of "gluttonous industry," comparing the organization to the union leaders convicted of bombing the *Los Angeles Times* building: "Under their [NAM's] shelter, men and interests have been dynamited as truly as any of the victims of the structural iron workers plot."[68] While more sympathetic to the business community, the *Journal of Commerce and Commercial Bulletin* scolded NAM for subjecting "themselves to attack and discredit" when they should have been acting as "bulwarks against over-radical movements," concluding: "Their usefulness is thus largely destroyed."[69] The scandal and hearings brought an end to NAM's direct political and strikebreaking activities. NAM would continue to lobby for and against specific legislation, of course, but it removed itself from the world of congressional intrigue, strikebreaking, and thuggery.

Although labor historians see NAM's efforts as successful in thwarting the AFL, that success was short-lived. Democrats won control of Congress in 1910 and passed the eight-hour bill for federal contractors, which President Taft signed in June 1912. Progressive Woodrow Wilson was elected in 1912, and in 1914 the Clayton Antitrust Act exempted union activity from the Sherman Antitrust Act. Injunctions could no longer be issued because a union was impeding trade. This was what the AFL had been seeking—and what NAM had been blocking—since 1903. True, the unions in some key industries, such as steel, were in steep decline, but this had more to do with technological innovations and unions' stubborn adherence to a skilled-trade model than it did with NAM lobbying. Moreover, union membership was increasing in other trades, such as construction, which led to higher wage standards in general.[70] During World War I, the AFL doubled its membership, from two

67. See an unnamed operative (probably Mulhall), letter to Van Cleave, June 8, 1907, in US Senate Judiciary Committee, *Maintenance of a Lobby*, vol. 1, appendix, 968–70; Edward Levinson, *I Break Strikes!* (New York: Robert McBride, 1935), 27.

68. Editorial in *New York World*, reprinted in "Press Opinions on the Revelations Made by the Mulhall Documents," *Chicago Tribune*, July 2, 1913, p. 6.

69. Quoted in Steigerwalt, *The National Association of Manufacturers*, 148.

70. See Swenson, *Capitalists against Markets*, 175–81.

million to four million.[71] In the end NAM may have only succeeded in consolidating a burgeoning workingmen's vote in the Democratic Party.

Finally, it is not clear that NAM's militant anti-unionism improved its
membership, as some have argued. Although membership did increase
during those years, it continued to increase at the same rate after NAM
adopted a less militant antilabor stance in 1913. Membership typically rose
with economic growth. Historians' arguments that anti-unionism increased
membership are based on comments by Emery and Van Cleave concerning
the importance of "the labor issue" to unity and membership.[72] But Emery
and Van Cleave were militant open-shop partisans trying to persuade others
of the institutional importance of the labor issue. Historians largely ignore
those NAM officials who were repulsed by the fixation on anti-unionism
and had to be persuaded that this was a good use of NAM resources. Cotton
manufacturer and prominent NAM member D. A. Tompkins, for instance,
wrote to Van Cleave in 1907 expressing concern about the appointment of
Emery as NAM's legal counsel, since Emery was still connected to the Citizens Industrial Association: "This Citizen's Union [*sic*] has been for several
years trying to take possession of the Treasury of the National Association
of Manufacturers under the plea that the National Association is in a better position to collect money. . . . I have steadily and vigorously opposed
any such arrangement, but if Mr. Emery is still representing the Industrial
Union [*sic*], they have finally succeeded in landing their plan."[73] Ten months
later, Van Cleave was asking permission for NAM to financially support
the NCID (headed by Emery) by making the case that it would bring in
members.[74] Thus, while certain NAM officials may have believed that militant anti-unionism brought in members, there is no real evidence that it did.

After the Mulhall controversy and the complete failure of its militant approach, NAM began moderating its open-shop activities. Its new

71. Albion Guilford Taylor, *Labor Policies of the National Association of Manufacturers* (1928:
New York: Arno Press, 1973), 19; Cyrus Ching, *Review and Reflection: A Half Century of Labor
Relations* (New York: B. C. Forbes and Son, 1953), 27.

72. See especially Greene, *Pure and Simple Politics*, 92.

73. See D. A. Tompkins to Van Cleave, December 12, 1907, and an operative (probably Mull-
hall), letter to Van Cleave, June 8, 1907, both in US Senate Judiciary Committee, *Maintenance of
Lobby*, vol. 2, appendix, 1208, 968–70.

74. Van Cleave letter to Parry that also went to Tompkins, Miles, Kirby, and Emery, Octo-
ber 16, 1908, in ibid., 2223–24; see also Van Cleave to members of the Executive Committee,
October 17, 1908, in ibid., 2232–33. Tompkins assented, but fiscal concerns led F. H. Stillman, a
Bridgeport, Connecticut, metal man and NAM treasurer, to vote "no" on the proposition. See
Stillman to Van Cleave, October 19, 1908, in ibid., 2236.

president, a bicycle manufacturer from Connecticut named George Pope, suggested in his first presidential address in 1914 that perhaps workers were attracted to unions because management had failed to take their concerns seriously: "The employer has offered so little and whatever relief has been obtained has been under such pressure, the workman concludes it has been his individual victory to secure concessions of any nature."[75] NAM had long been interested in industrial improvement, but in 1913 it adopted a new program of "industrial betterment" that focused on working conditions, safety and training, and employee morale. The association would continue its battle for the open shop, but it would shift its labor policy from sabotaging unions to professionalizing management. This position would be more consistent with its cooperative, progressive trade association work, although the organization would never quite live down (or give up) its anti-union belligerence.

75. Quoted in Steigerwalt, *The National Association of Manufacturers*, 170.

4

Managing Labor

The 1920s were prosperous years for US business, which enjoyed the return to "normalcy" in the form of three business-oriented Republican presidents and the abeyance of Progressive Era zeal, at least in the political arena. But reform did not disappear in industry. The AFL's Progressive Era victories, immigration restriction, and the public relations fallout of tragedies such as the Triangle Shirtwaist fire (1911) and the Ludlow massacre (1914) led industrial leaders of all stripes to reappraise their labor practices.

Many turned to the new field of industrial relations, which applied the insights of scientific management to labor relations, promising to engineer more harmonious and hence more productive relations between and among workers, foremen, supervisors, and employers. In part an antidote to unionism, its larger and more significant aim was to allay inefficiencies caused by labor disputes, high turnover, and unemployment.[1] It sought to replace the coercive and inefficient "drive system" with a managerial strategy

---

1. The field of industrial relations included different schools of thought and was also known as "human relations," "employee relations," or "personnel relations." See Sanford Jacoby, *Modern Manors: Welfare Capitalism since the New Deal* (Princeton, NJ: Princeton University Press, 1997); Sanford Jacoby, *Employing Bureaucracy: Managers, Unions, and the Transformation of Work in American Industry, 1900–45* (New York: Columbia University Press, 1985); Richard Gillespie, *Manufacturing Knowledge: A History of the Hawthorne Experiments* (New York: Cambridge University Press, 1991); Guy Alchon, *The Invisible Hand of Planning* (Princeton, NJ: Princeton University Press, 1985); Burleigh Gardner and David Moore, *Human Relations in Industry*, rev. ed. (1945; Chicago: Richard D. Irwin, 1950).

that emphasized proper training, worker well-being, long-term planning, and teamwork. Eventually staffed by college and business school graduates (as opposed to factory men who had risen "in the line"), industrial relations departments fostered a cooperative, professional, liberal sensibility toward employees that was compatible with NAM's modernizing trade association work.

The industrial relations formula, in emphasizing reason over "emotion" in dealing with labor, implicitly rejected the hotheaded emotionalism embodied by past NAM leaders like Parry, Van Cleave, and Kirby.[2] Industrial relations experts viewed labor relations as a cooperative endeavor that involved the input of outside experts, community members, and other professionals, which is to say, "the public." Employers needed to understand industrial problems from multiple perspectives, said the experts, including that of organized labor. By participating in the larger discussion, the employer would not become labor's target.

Confronted with the failure of previous approaches, and facing a postwar strike wave and immigration restrictions, NAM leaders adopted this more moderate, professional industrial relations approach to labor management in the 1920s. Still committed to a union-free workplace, NAM reconceived the open shop as good industrial relations. This paved the way for the employment of "nontraditional" workers, such as women, the disabled, and, later, people of color. While unions remained focused on skilled workers, this more modern approach to management was necessarily inclusive of all employees. Indeed, one of its hallmark features was attention to the social demographics of workforces in order to understand how employees might work better together.

The National Industrial Conference Board

NAM's commitment to understanding labor relations in a larger social context can be seen in its participation in the creation in 1915 of the National Industrial Conference Board. A proto–think tank, the NICB would collect and analyze data on employee relations, labor supply, safety, production, and other areas of concern to provide the basis for effective lobbying and

---

2. See especially John Broderick, *Pulling Together: The Story of Human Relations in Industry* (Schenectady, NY: Robson and Adee, 1922); Clarence Hicks, *My Life in Industrial Relations* (New York: Harper & Brothers, 1941), 64–122; Ching, *Review and Reflection*, chap. 2. Ching was an active NAM member and the head of US Rubber Company (later Uniroyal).

the promulgation of what would later be called "best practices."[3] Among its founders were NAM president George Pope, as well as three militant open-shop NAM leaders whose names you may recall from the previous chapter: James Emery, F. C. Schwedtman, and John Kirby. These men joined a group of business leaders who were looking for a more scientific approach to labor relations. Staunchly anti-union, they nonetheless understood that the confrontational method had failed and feared that its continued use threatened to bring in more government regulation.

The NICB took a solution-oriented, scientific approach to labor relations, trying to get out in front of potential problems before they became labor disputes and public relations disasters. General Electric's Magnus Alexander came up with the idea, arguing that industry should have anticipated the inevitability of workmen's compensation and come up with a coordinated effort to enact and institute the reform (instead of what had been a haphazard and jumbled response).[4] Implicit in this attitude was the idea that workers might have legitimate claims in the workplace that needed to be taken into account in industrial planning. Industry needed to come up with scientific standards for establishing fair policies around hiring, firing, grievances, workload, hours, and pay.[5] If employers were fair and forthright in their labor policies, the thinking went, perhaps workers would be less likely to turn to "outside" organizations (like the AFL or the state) and more likely to work with employers to find integrated win-win solutions to common disputes.[6]

Also implicit in Alexander's reasoning was the need for uniform standards across industries. NICB founders believed "a few bad eggs" were responsible for the business community's damaged reputation. One of their aims was to educate "backwards" employers about efficient scientific labor relations.[7] The "bad eggs" did not just mar the business community's reputation, but also made the labor market more volatile by making themselves

3. See H. M. Gitelman, "Management's Crisis of Confidence and the Origin of the National Industrial Conference Board, 1914–1916," *Business History Review* 58, no. 2 (Summer 1984): 153–77; David Eakins, "Policy Planning for the Establishment," in *A New History of Leviathan: Essays on the Rise of the Corporate State*, edited by Ronald Radosh and Murray Rothbard (New York: Dutton, 1972), 191–98.

4. Noble, *America by Design*, 236–37.

5. Norman J. Wood, "Industrial Relations Policies of American Management, 1900–1933," *Harvard Business Review* 34, no. 4 (Winter 1960): 403–42, 408–12.

6. Gitelman, "Management's Crisis of Confidence," 165–66; Bonnett, *Employers' Associations in the United States*, chap. 13.

7. Gitelman, "Management's Crisis of Confidence," 165–66.

more competitive in the short run vis-à-vis those businesses committing resources to scientific and progressive labor policies. Uniformity in labor practices was desirable because it evened the playing field, removing whatever competitive advantage the old drive system may have held. As the head of the National Metal Trades Association said in praise of the NICB: "It is bringing about uniformity of thought and action among employers, woefully lacking in the past. We are thinking together."[8]

The NICB was founded and funded by anti-union militants and large corporations like General Electric, General Motors, and John Deere, leading many historians to regard it as merely a tool of the open-shop movement.[9] In some ways perhaps it was. But that misses the neutralizing, professionalizing influence of scientific management on labor relations: it bettered the lives of all workers, the unskilled included, even if it also thwarted the unionization of skilled male workers. Independent of union pressure, efficiency-seeking employers would have embraced standards and techniques that increased employees' investment in their work and loyalty to the company, especially in a tight labor market.[10] It just made good economic sense, as proponents of what became known as "corporate social responsibility" would later put it. Although unionists, intellectuals, and labor historians would remain suspicious of any kind of "cooperation" between management and its workers that did not recognize independent unions, the NICB's acknowledgment of workers' interests and needs was a huge step forward in labor relations. It was the hallmark of the "enlightened businessman."

The NICB was just one of many organizations funded by the heads of the largest corporations to study labor relations and help employers reform and standardize their practices. Others included the Special Conference Committee, the National Association of Corporation Schools (later the American Management Association), Industrial Relations Counselors, Inc. (a Rockefeller-funded consulting firm that worked with companies to reform their practices), and NAM itself.[11] At first glance, it seems as though there was a tremendous amount of redundancy in these organizations, especially

8. Quoted in Brady, *Business as a System of Power*, 204.

9. See for instance, ibid., 204; Howell John Harris, *The Right to Manage: Industrial Relations Policies of American Business in the 1940s* (Madison: University of Wisconsin Press, 1982), 17–19.

10. This is the argument of Wood, "Industrial Relations Policies."

11. Brady, *Business as a System of Power*, 214; Hicks, *My Life in Industrial Relations*, 41–63; Robert Ozanne, *A Century of Labor-Management Relations at McCormick and International Harvester* (Madison: University of Wisconsin Press, 1967), 163–64; Roland Marchand, *Creating the Corporate Soul* (Berkeley: University of California Press, 1998), 22–25.

in terms of leaders and sponsors. Why the need for the NICB when NAM was developing its research departments and had as part of its mission the coordination and standardization of industrial policies? One way to see it is that the proliferation of these kinds of organizations indicated the unsettled, but nonetheless networked, way in which labor relations reforms took hold. As each organization developed and debated the parameters of workers' rights and needs, it created different variations of the new management style, depending on the context of its own constituency or niche. For instance, the NICB became less "political" than initially envisioned and was eventually a well-respected research body, while NAM continued to juggle differences among its members as both a lobbyist and a research group. But both organizations propagated the principles of modern industrial relations.

Labor-Employer Relations during War

The First World War aided businessmen and professionals who sought to coordinate and standardize labor relations. Under the exigency of war, all sectors of society were forced to embrace the credo of the trade associations: cooperation. Nowhere was this more evident than in labor relations. Immigration came to a stop just at the moment when employers were losing employees to the armed services and being asked to increase production. Among the many government bureaus and commissions created to coordinate production and enforce cooperation were the National Defense Council and the National War Labor Board, both charged with engendering "cooperation" between organized labor and capitalists. Although genuine cooperation would not be achieved, the experimental endeavor accelerated employers' embrace of modern industrial relations techniques.

In consultation with the newly created NICB and AFL leader Samuel Gompers, the National Defense Council arranged a policy of sorts wherein labor and industry agreed that neither would take advantage of the wartime emergency to push for advantages that they could not achieve in normal times: "Neither employers nor employes shall endeavor to take advantage of the country's necessities to change existing standards."[12] The idea was to preserve the status quo from before the war. NAM heartily endorsed this agreement. Employers would not push to open a closed shop, nor would employees strike to "close" an open shop. The labor shortages, however,

---

12. Quoted in "Changing Existing Standards," *American Industries* 18, no. 4 (November 1917): 33–35; see also Taft, *The AFL in the Time of Gompers*, 346–47.

put labor in a position to change the status quo. By proffering cooperation, Gompers expertly entered a conversation that previously would have
included only employers and the government. He was able to win from
the government prevailing union wages and hours as the standard even in
non-union plants.[13] Unfortunately, he was not able to prevent workers from
striking. In just one month (September 1917), according to the Department
of Labor, there were 171 strikes in the war industries.[14]

The National War Labor Board was created in 1918 to deal with the many
strikes and industrial disputes occurring despite Gompers's efforts. Consisting of five representatives from labor and five from industry, and headed
by former president William Howard Taft, the War Labor Board tried to
finesse the open-shop question. It determined that workers had the right to
organize, to choose their own representatives, and to bargain collectively,
and that employers could not interfere with that right. But it also said that
workers could not coerce non-union workers to become union members,
and that employers in mixed union–non-union plants could continue the
practice of bargaining only with those workers in their employ—that is, not
with outside union agents.[15] Officially, the government stood with employers for an open shop, but in practice the policy contributed to the expansion of union power, especially in those areas where unions already had a
foothold. In Seattle, for instance, where the government had embarked on
a massive shipbuilding effort, the labor movement was strong enough to
instate what amounted to a closed shop.[16] Union membership increased
nationally from three million in 1917 to five million by 1919.[17]

NAM endorsed the War Labor Board and urged its members to comply
with it (much as Gompers urged his unions to comply).[18] NAM attorney
James Emery extolled the government agency as a "remarkable social experiment" and explained to readers that it was not the product of state pressure (as in Britain), but rather the result of adopting "reciprocal voluntary
restraints"; thus, it was not in violation of America's liberal tradition.[19] An
article in *American Industries* extolled the new era of "business socialism"

13. Taft, *The AFL in the Time of Gompers*, 347–57.
14. As reported in James Emery, "The Functions of the War Labor Board," *American Industries* (May 1918): 15.
15. Taft, *The AFL in the Time of Gompers*, 356.
16. See William Breen, "Administrative Politics and Labor Policy in the First World War,"
Business History Review 61, no. 4 (Winter 1987): 582–605.
17. Wood, "Industrial Relations Policies," 412.
18. "Resolutions Adopted by the Convention," *American Industries* (June 1918): 15.
19. Emery, "The Functions of the War Labor Board," 15.

that was accompanying the war, whereby a robust social cooperation anticipated "the establishment of a complete harmony and cooperation among
all the classes in the various channels of industry."[20] NAM president George
Pope instituted the "National Industrial Conservation" movement, which
produced prowar materials advocating for state-directed "cooperation."[21]
Employers in general, however, balked at the new strictures, even if patriotism and production quotas prevented them from actively resisting them.
Just as Gompers had trouble keeping unions in line, so too was NAM unable
to persuade all employers. Despite the rhetoric of "cooperation," then,
neither labor nor industry fully committed to that principle. In the mean-
time, industry was also experimenting with new techniques of personnel
management.

This experimentation can be seen in the hiring and training of nontraditional workers, such as women. The employment of women was an attempt
to deal with the labor shortage, and its novelty required a more intentional
approach to training and management. One challenge was the actual training of women, but another, more significant, challenge was convincing male
workers and male management that women could do the work, that they
should be paid equal to men, and that they would not stick around after the
war. That is, employers were learning to understand that the *social context*
of the workplace was more important in determining worker productivity
than individual merit, which was the main insight of a variation on industrial
relations called "human relations."[22]

As usual, NAM stood ready to help its members adjust to such changes. In
September 1918, *American Industries* ran an article on incorporating women
into "men's jobs." The good news was that "women are able to do anything
men are doing in our factories except where brute strength is required." The
other good news was that they were willing to work for the war effort but
would happily return home after the war.[23] The article detailed what was
necessary to integrate women (a "shop mother," low-heeled shoes, rest-
rooms), but emphasized that such accommodations were minimal: "Forget
sex. Training is training, for a man or a woman." The article exhibited some
unexamined stereotypes—cautioning against using women in excessively

20. Felix Orman, "The New Order of Business, *American Industries* 18, no. 3 (October 1917): 11.

21. "Winning the Third Party in Industry," *American Industries* (November 1917): 14–15.

22. The "Human Relations in Industry" movement was built on Elton Mayo's Hawthorne
experiments of the 1920s; see Gillespie, *Manufacturing Knowledge*.

23. H. E. Miles, "Women in Industry," *American Industries* 19, no. 2 (September 1918); 20–21;
see also *NAM Proceedings*, 1918, pp. 54–56.

dirty work, noting that their hands were more subtle—but ended on a progressive note: "One thing is certain: for the first time woman is put where she belongs in terms of her individual aptitude, not limited by the mere conventions and traditions of sex."[24] And for this reason, women should be paid the same as men—or even more: "Sex is no element in machine production. We have been slow to learn this. We must pay for results regardless of who runs the machine, man or woman."[25] The context for NAM's position on "equal pay" was, as usual, its contentious experience with white, male workers, who often, according to employers, worked slowly so as to set a slower standard for a day's work. Whether it was patriotism or a need to prove themselves, women worked almost twice as hard as men, and employers were delighted to pay them almost twice as much.[26]

NAM's president also made a point of promoting the rehabilitation of injured soldiers for work after the war. *American Industries* published several stories about hiring workers with disabilities that likewise emphasized the context into which such workers would be integrated.[27] NAM's emphasis on rehabilitating the disabled soldier may have begun as a patriotic (or public relations) gesture, but the research and attention devoted to the topic raised the possibility of developing and training groups of other "nontraditional" workers (such as, perhaps, people of color) to address the labor supply calculus. Although manufacturers hired Southern black workers during the war and similarly used professional industrial relations consultants to help in that endeavor, neither *American Industries* nor NAM seemed interested in that potential labor pool at this time.[28]

NAM remained committed to helping employers hire women and the disabled throughout the twentieth century, long before the Civil Rights Act

24. Miles, "Women in Industry," 21.

25. Ibid., 21; "Would You Give Men's Wages to Women?" *American Industries* (May 1918): 10; the article's answer was yes.

26. Doing less than one could was called "goldbricking," or "soldiering," and it was a rational response about output in the conflict between employer and employee. It was this tendency that scientific management was designed in part to curb. See Frederick Winslow Taylor, *The Principles of Scientific Management* (New York: Harper & Brothers, 1911).

27. See "Re-education of Disabled Soldiers," *American Industries* (November 1917): 23–25; "Rebuilding the Crippled Soldier," *American Industries* (April 1918): 26–27; *NAM Proceedings*, 1918, pp. 81–82. With regard to the non-English-speaking immigrant, see "Industry's Part in Americanization Work," *American Industries* (July 1919): 17.

28. Nevertheless, NAM member companies, such as International Harvester and Lukens Steel, were hiring blacks at this time; see Jennifer Delton, *Racial Integration in Corporate America* (New York: Cambridge University Press, 2009), 1–2, 19–20; see also Hendrickson, *American Labor and Economic Citizenship*, chap. 6.

(1964) or the Americans with Disabilities Act (1990). NAM's attention to the recruitment and training of nontraditional workers affirmed the idea that what mattered most for productivity was not the individual worker but rather his or her context—what one textbook called "the web of social relations"—in which work was accomplished. Women could do the work; the trick was to get other workers to accept them. In addressing this challenge, NAM was reinforcing the modern ideas of "interdependence," cooperation, and coordination from social science; these ideas were embraced by the trade association movement in general, but they also challenged the traditional rugged individualism that NAM businessmen liked to champion. On the other hand, those making the case for the worthiness of women and the disabled as workers emphasized their individual capabilities in a way that championed the individualism—and hence rights—of all people, regardless of gender, nationality, or disability. That is, NAM's non-union labor management strategies were *progressive* in their embrace of social interdependence and *liberal* in championing individual rights. It was precisely these marginal nontraditional populations that the labor movement had been slow to include.

Another experimental policy that gained traction during the war was the employee representation plan (ERP), or "shop committee," which would later become known disparagingly as "company union." While the AFL reflexively opposed ERPs and employers would later, in the 1920 and 1930s, use company unions to avoid unionization, during the war and its immediate aftermath ERPs were seen as a bold experiment in industrial democracy. Originally, the War Labor Board had recommended employee representation plans as a way for employers to collectively bargain with employees in plants that, like most, were unorganized. Employers were not thrilled by the suggestion, which many considered "revolutionary," but eventually they came to see the benefits of interacting with their employees and being informed as to their grievances and concerns.[29] Progressive Era reformers such as Herbert Croly and Walter Weyl saw the plans as an alternative to the conflict-oriented bargaining of the union movement, which inevitably led employers to dig in their heels. Reformers believed that union representatives were, understandably, always negotiating to better the position of their union and were not concerned about the success of the company;

---

29. Wood, "Industrial Relations Policies," 410–11, 413–44; see also David Brody, "The Wagner Act and the Question of Workplace Representation," Cornell University, ILR School, January 1994, https://digitalcommons.ilr.cornell.edu/cgi/viewcontent.cgi?article=1458&context=key_workplace.

thus, just as understandably, employers were resistant to negotiating with them. But what if the employees of a company could negotiate an agreement that depended on and contributed to the success of the company? Wouldn't they then share a common interest with the employer? As reformer and professor Henry Seager put it in 1919: "The psychology of collective bargaining through shop committees is predominately cooperative; that of collective bargaining through trade or labor union officials is predominately contentious."[30] With its emphasis on cooperation, the shop committee idea was consonant with the idea of industrial relations and trade associations. It also represented a progressive alternative to employer autocracy.

The war created a context in which manufacturers could see labor relations, not as a struggle against unions, but rather as an essential part of macroeconomic planning and managerial strategy. While not specifically endorsing any particular reforms, NAM's journal *American Industries* apprised its readers of the changing scope of labor relations in the United States and Europe, reviewing books on the topic and emphasizing the growing importance of cooperation and coordination.[31] Although anxious for the government to withdraw from labor relations after the war, NAM leaders were interested in promoting patriotic unity and cooperation with the war agencies, much as Gompers wanted to do with labor organizations. Both organizations struggled to keep their members in line, but the experience introduced both industry and unions to what would later, with the New Deal and World War II, become the norm of state-mediated labor relations.

Postwar Labor-Employer Relations

After the war, there was a scramble to define labor relations. As noted, union membership had doubled during the war, especially in shipbuilding, railroads, textiles, and the construction trades. As employers started on the path back to "normalcy," organized workers tried to maintain and expand their gains. Over four million workers struck in 1919, which was double the number of strikers during any other year between 1880 and 1937.[32] Most

30. Quoted in Gary Dean Best, "President Wilson's Second Industrial Conference, 1919–1920," *Labor History* (Fall 1975): 505–20, 512.

31. See, for instance, "Industrial Reconstruction in Britain," *American Industries* 18, no. 9 (April 1918): 43; "Second Wartime Convention," *American Industries* 18, no. 9 (April 1918): 7; see also Miles, "Women in Industry"; "Would You Give Men's Wages to Women?"; "Re-education of Disabled Soldiers"; and "Rebuilding the Crippled Soldier."

32. Terry Boswell et al., *Racial Competition and Class Solidarity* (Albany: State University of New York Press, 2006), 86.

notably, some 350,000 steelworkers walked off the job in October 1919 in a coordinated attempt to organize that industry. At the same time, government officials launched a frenzied campaign against labor radicals, socialists, communists, and immigrants suspected of radical aims. Sparked in part by the Russian Revolution and the creation of an international Communist Party, the postwar "red scare" contributed significantly to political unrest, which lessened the public's sympathy for the labor movement.

The Wilson administration attempted to deal with the unrest by reviving the government-mediated "cooperation" of the war years. Wilson called the First Industrial Conference in October 1919 in hopes of staving off the steelworkers' strike, but the AFL was unable to avert the strike and the conference, consisting of representatives from labor, industry, and "the public," was utterly unable to offer any settlement. Although the conference was not meant to be about the strike, the AFL insisted that it be addressed, while the steel companies refused to recognize the striking unions and the government found itself no longer in a position to uphold workers' right to organize. The AFL walked out.[33] Flush with wartime profits and strikebreakers, the steel companies were able to break the strike and retain an open shop. US Steel reinstated the twelve-hour day. A second Industrial Conference was held in December, with Herbert Hoover at the helm. This conference made some headway in discussing strategies for labor dispute settlements, industrial democracy, and employee representation plans, but the labor contingent had lost the power it commanded during the war. Congress did not act on any of the conference recommendations, and employers, buoyed by the victory against the steelworkers' strike, revived a new, more professionalized open-shop movement.[34]

NAM created an Open Shop Department in 1920. Its new head, Noel Sargent, was an amalgam of the old open-shop militant and the new educated professional. An economist with a master's degree from the University of Minnesota, Sargent was also an avid proponent of the "American Plan," which was basically the open shop backed by the cooperative ethos of fair and scientific personnel policies. He generated numerous tracts and studies that emphasized the economic inefficiency of the closed shop (as opposed to its viciousness or immorality). Sargent seemed aware of the missteps of his predecessors and adopted a calm, measured style, backing

33. Best, "President Wilson's Second Industrial Conference," 507; see also Hendrickson, *American Labor and Economic Citizenship*, 39–42.

34. Best, "President Wilson's Second Industrial Conference," 519–20.

up his claims with statistics and facts from government and university institutes. He avoided exaggeration and limited his claims.[35] He recast the closed shop not as a threat to employers' prerogative or as the path to socialism (as Parry had argued), but as contributing to unemployment, a social problem that most directly affected workers. As he noted, open-shop proponents embraced economic and industrial progress (which could include technological innovations that led to deskilling), while the proponents of the closed shop wanted only to maintain the position of "the minority of workers who are members of labor organizations."[36] These were not unreasonable views; indeed, they were part of what historian Mark Hendrickson has called the "New Era" capitalism of the 1920s, and variations of them were adopted by Herbert Hoover, researchers, and government officials.[37] Sargent would stay with NAM for almost forty years, becoming one of its most prodigious researchers and spokesmen and also expanding and supporting the organization's commitment to industrial relations.[38]

In 1925, the NAM Open Shop Department became the Industrial Relations Department, with divisions dedicated to employee relations, education, and women.[39] Not everyone in NAM was happy with the new emphasis. Old-style industrialists, many of whom were on the executive committee, continued to see labor relations as the sole prerogative of the boss/owner and there continued to be disagreement on this issue within the organization.[40] President John E. Edgerton, however, seemed to be interested in negotiating these tensions and appeasing the curmudgeons, while also creating a space for reformist impulses. So while NAM revived its open-shop campaign and continued its battle with the AFL, the campaign was tempered and sharpened by the professionalism of the new industrial relations staff, which was as concerned about unemployment, workplace conditions,

35. See, for instance, his contribution to "American Trade Unionism—Discussion," *American Economic Review* 12, no. 1 (March 1922): 80–96.

36. Ibid., 94.

37. Hendrickson, *American Labor and Economic Citizenship*, 1–34. Hendrickson has an updated spin on the concept, but it is basically what Ellis Hawley called "voluntarist corporatism."

38. For information on Sargent, see "Of Those Who Served, 1954," series 1, box 101, NAMR.

39. See Allen Wakstein, "The National Association of Manufacturers and Labor Relations in the 1920s," *Labor History* 10 (1969): 163–76. The National Council of Industrial Defense was similarly renamed the National Industrial Council; see *NAM Proceedings*, 1926, 64.

40. See Wakstein, 169–71, for the details of these divisions.

and affordable transport as it was in trading punches with the AFL.[41] This was not Martin Mulhall's NAM.

It was during this period that NAM led a campaign against a proposed constitutional amendment banning child labor. Aware of how the amendment's proponents would label opponents as being "for" child labor, NAM insisted that it was against "constitutional encroachment" that undermined local responsibility and self-government, and that its own members complied with state laws against child labor.[42] Indeed, it supported state child labor laws as a way to avoid federal overreach, a strategy that would lead it to support many a progressive law at the state level. NAM formed the National Committee for the Rejection of the Twentieth Amendment, bringing together farmers, who were most dependent on child labor, and various civic organizations. In 1925, the amendment had already been rejected by thirty-four states and ratified by only four. As with so many of these campaigns, it is difficult to ascertain what influence NAM's activities played in the amendment's defeat. At a time when fewer than 40 percent of "children" were enrolled in high school and family farms and stores depended on their teenagers' contribution, the eighteen-year limit alone was enough to sink this amendment.[43]

By 1926, President Edgerton was celebrating NAM's developmental work in industrial relations and downplaying its anti-union activities. NAM was not organized to combat organized labor, Edgerton said at the thirty-first annual convention, but rather to organize and improve industry; it was a progressive organization, not a reactionary one.[44] Edgerton praised NAM's role in founding the Chamber of Commerce and National Industrial Conference Board, organizations that fostered cooperation and a scientific approach to the problems of industry and labor. He endorsed a cooperative attitude toward employees and labor relations that recognized their mutual interdependence. As evidence of the effectiveness of this approach, he cited the dwindling number of labor disputes between 1918 (when there were

41. Bonnett writes: "In the matter of industrial betterment the committees of the NAM have generally been too progressive to receive the whole hearted endorsement of a majority of the other members of the Association"; see Bonnett, *Employers' Associations in the United States*, 359.

42. *NAM Proceedings*, 1925, pp. 47–48. On the campaign, see Jan Dolittle Wilson, *The Women's Joint Congressional Committee and the Politics of Maternalism, 1920–30* (Champaign: University of Illinois Press, 2007), chap. 5.

43. This argument is explained in Wilson, *Women's Joint Congressional Committee*, chap. 5. On high school enrollment, see US Department of the Interior, "Statistics of Public High Schools, 1927–28" (Washington, DC: US Government Printing Office, 1929).

44. *NAM Proceedings*, 1926, pp. 61–62.

3,353) and 1925 (when there were 1,301). Summoning Frederick W. Taylor and Commerce secretary Herbert Hoover, he noted that prosperity rested on a vital relationship between high wages, reasonable hours, and healthful conditions, on the one hand, and decreased waste, better executive organization, and technological innovation, on the other.[45]

Despite Edgerton's sunny rhetoric, NAM was still committed to union-free workplaces; its new labor philosophy was in some ways old wine in new bottles. Although it was more moderate, its position was not quite as evolved as that of other business-oriented groups—such as the Republican Party of the 1920s. Unlike NAM, the pro-business Republican Party did not formally endorse the open-shop movement of the 1920s. Its rising star, Herbert Hoover, who was secretary of commerce during both the Harding and Coolidge administrations, recognized unions (and trade associations) as a vital part of American democracy. Hoover frankly endorsed the AFL's beneficent influence "in stabilizing industry, and in maintaining an American standard of citizenship"—although by the late 1920s Hoover thought that unions were becoming obsolete, owing to corporations' adoption of more scientific labor relations and reforms.[46] Hoover, moreover, supported a constitutional amendment prohibiting child labor, a universal eight-hour day, and collective bargaining, all positions opposed by NAM. Despite these differences, the Republican Party was home to the majority of NAM's membership and its best hope for legislative influence. NAM's softer approach to labor relations reflected its conformity to the business and political climate of a generally prosperous era.

NAM and Immigration

One of the most culturally and politically contentious issues of the early twentieth century was immigration, which the Republican Party and the AFL sought to restrict and NAM (and industry in general) sought to maintain. Industrialists and employers had opposed immigration restriction for as long as the AFL had fought for it. It was a stark class issue: the capitalist class wanted a steady supply of labor, and the working class sought to limit the labor supply in an effort to raise wages and gain leverage. In 1911,

---

45. *NAM Proceedings*, 1926, p. 67.

46. From a 1925 speech by Herbert Hoover quoted in *The Memoirs of Herbert Hoover*, 102. On the Republican Party's stance on the open shop, see Robert Zieger, *Republicans and Labor, 1919–1929* (Lexington: University of Kentucky Press, 1969), 70. On Hoover's changed position on unions, see Hendrickson, *American Labor and Economic Citizenship*, 11.

NAM member and foundry man William Barr told the *New York Times* that immigrants were a blessing to the country, which needed their labor; they adjusted themselves to American standards, he argued, and because they returned to their home countries when work was slack, there was no need to worry about unemployment among Americans.[47] Barr was clearly addressing growing public concerns about unregulated immigration.

After the war, there was more support for immigration restriction, not just from nativists and labor but also from a public dismayed at the surfeit of unassimilated newcomers and the influx of possible radicals (of the sort that had just staged a revolution in Russia). In 1917, Congress passed a literacy test requirement with the aim of limiting immigration, and in 1921 it passed an emergency quota act that limited immigration from any (European) country to 3 percent of its population in the United States at the time of the 1910 census. The emergency act was temporary, but there was tremendous support for a permanent law based on the same principle.[48] Giving in to public pressure, NAM supported the regulation of immigration, such that certain, narrowly defined "undesirables" would be prohibited, but opposed restriction in general. Arguing against a restrictive bill in 1919, NAM's new president, Stephen Mason, said that it would "extinguish the light in the hand of the Goddess of Liberty at the entrance to New York harbor."[49] Although Mason was frank about manufacturing's need for workers, like many progressives then and now, he saw immigration as the heart of American democracy and its restriction as a betrayal of democratic promises.

Confronted once again with unfavorable public opinion, the business class sought to put a more positive social spin on immigration. Uniting with the representatives of a variety of racial and ethnic groups, business leaders, including many in NAM, formed the Inter-Racial Council (IRC) in 1919. The purpose of this group was to help immigrants adjust to their new life, foster better relationships between natives and the foreign-born, "stabilize industrial conditions," and stem the tide of emigration (immigrants returning to their native countries).[50] The organization was committed

47. "Freer Immigration Asked by Employers," *New York Times*, May 16, 1911, p. 9.

48. Alan Dawley, *Struggles for Justice* (Cambridge, MA: Harvard University Press, 1991), 277–82.

49. Stephen Mason, "The Proposal to Suspend Immigration," *American Industries* 19, no. 7 (February 1919), 7.

50. From an IRC pamphlet presented at US House Committee on Immigration and Naturalization, "Proposed Restriction on Immigration" (hearings), 66th Cong., April 22, 1920, pp. 108–9. See also William Barr, "Sound Business and Sound Statesmanship," *The Rotarian* (September 1920): 117–19. The "races" included Armenian, Assyrian, Belgian, Canadian, Chinese, Czecho-Slovakian,

to Americanization, in that it sought to help immigrants adjust to life in the United States, but it also sought to eliminate "racial denunciation" and discrimination. It offered tips for employers on how to create what we would now call "an inclusive climate" for the foreign-born. "Train your foreman to respect the foreign-born" was the topic of one newsletter sent to employers.[51] The object was retention of labor, but by means of cultural and ethnic tolerance.

Headed by Pierre and Coleman du Pont and William Barr (who was also head of the open-shop National Founders' Association), the Inter-racial Council also sought to stave off immigration restrictions. The congressional hearings leading to restrictions convey the political difficulty that business executives faced. The chair of the House Committee on Immigration and Naturalization was Congressman Albert Johnson, a Republican from Washington. A eugenicist, Johnson grilled the IRC representatives, accusing them of wanting "free immigration" and being unconcerned about bringing in socialists and radicals. The IRC's secretary did his best to explain how their program in fact promoted Americanization and fought against socialism, even if it also sought to end the literacy test for immigrants (which it did). When Chairman Johnson said: "Let me see if I have it correctly: you have the Interracial Council, which has one big idea . . . and that is the need for 5,000,000 laborers in this country," he was suggesting that the IRC was acting in the selfish interests of "Big Business" rather than to safeguard the nation.[52] Thus, businessmen always claimed to support *some* restrictions, such as those that would keep out the mentally and physically indigent, while still hoping to convince Americans of the vital importance of a flexible labor supply.

Some historians argue that businessmen and industrial leaders supported the immigration restriction legislation of the 1920s.[53] The argument is that the recession of 1920–1921, combined with the electrification of plants,

---

Danish, Estonian, Finnish, Greek, Italian, Lettish, Lithuanian, Magyar, Norwegian, Polish, Russian, Swedish, and Syrian; not included were African Americans.

51. IRC newsletter, June 16, 1919, box 1993, "Inter-Racial Council, 1919–1921" file, Lukens Steel Company papers, Hagley Museum and Archives; see also US House Committee on Immigration and Naturalization, "Proposed Restriction on Immigration," 127.

52. US House Committee on Immigration and Naturalization, "Proposed Restriction on Immigration," 106–7. The IRC rep denied this charge: "On the contrary the principle [*sic*] object is to create a better understanding between the foreign born and native born residents of America."

53. See, for instance, Peter Swenson, *Capitalists against Markets*; Stanley Vittoz, "World War I and the Political Accommodation of Transitional Market Forces: The Case of Immigration Restriction," *Politics and Society* 8, no. 1 (1978): 67–73; Dawley, *Struggles for Justice*.

which increased productivity per worker, obviated the need for cheap immigrant labor. Surplus labor at a time of recession led to unrest; in addition, the war had made the United States a creditor nation, thus lowering the price of capital relative to the price of labor. This led even the most conservative industrialists to invest in electrification and other plant efficiencies.[54] The non-agricultural workforce grew in the 1920s, but not in the area of manufacturing, but rather in construction, service, and trade. The proportion of the workforce engaged in manufacturing actually declined by 7 percent.[55] These conditions enabled business to support restriction.[56] This argument is very persuasive, but it misses the role that immigration played in thwarting unionization. It was not just a labor supply that industry needed, but strikebreakers or some other kind of surplus labor supply to turn to after firing union agitators.

The argument about the changing political economy is persuasive, however, and there is some evidence that NAM was concerned about immigration as a social problem, especially during the recession of 1920–1921. In December 1920, for instance, *American Industries* published an article about "The Immigration Menace," which raised the specter of immigrant hordes and unemployment. The editors published the article, but commented that the solution was not to prevent immigration entirely, but rather to make sure that immigrants were guided into American ways.[57] Those who maintain that NAM supported restriction do not, however, cite that article but rather a 1923 *American Industries* symposium, which, they argue, suggests NAM support for restriction.

The 1923 symposium compiled the views of leading businessmen and NAM members on immigration and specifically what would eventually become the Johnson-Reed Bill of 1923.[58] Almost all of the forty-eight published responses said that *some* restriction was necessary, to keep out "undesirables," but after that acknowledgment, most of them (three-quarters) expressed disappointment and dismay with the then-current restrictions (quotas set at 3 percent), which they found too restrictive, too arbitrary, or

54. Vittoz, "World War I and the Political Accommodation of Transitional Market Forces," 64–65.

55. Ibid., 65. This would explain NAM's declining membership in the 1920s. See especially laments in *NAM Proceedings*, 1925, p. 55.

56. Citing NAM, Swenson, a sociologist, argues that business support for immigration legislation indicated a nascent cross-class alliance between some parts of industry and labor that helps explain the coming of the welfare state; see Swenson, *Capitalists against Markets*, 187–88.

57. "The Menace of Immigration," *American Industries* (December 1920).

58. "The Problems of Our Immigration," *American Industries* 23, no. 7 (February 1923): 5.

too inflexible. Many wanted a "selective" policy to ensure that productive sorts of immigrants would come in, but their understanding of who was productive was not a question of nationality or race, but rather an individual's character. Some suggested an immigration board that could set immigration rates according to need, rather than arbitrary exclusion. A few supported a registry to track the whereabouts and employment of new immigrants. There were also some, however, who wanted "free immigration" and decried all artificial barriers to trade. There were no wholly nativist responses. Out of forty-eight responses, only three saw the need for more restrictions, and of those, only one saw immigration as a racial issue. More common was the concern that, because Americans were not welcoming enough to immigrants, some were leaving. To keep them, the nation "should extend and make more human its method of receiving immigrants."[59] They believed that a good Americanization plan was a better way to deal with radicalism than exclusion.

Throughout this symposium, there is little evidence that manufacturers opposed immigration or wanted to see more stringent restrictions. In hindsight bolstered by data, there may not have been a labor shortage at this time, but manufacturers themselves listed labor shortages as the main reason they opposed continued restrictions. In 1924, NAM's Immigration Committee reported on the pending legislation. After a strong statement condemning unrestricted immigration, they made a case for the economic necessity of a flexible immigration policy that responded to the needs of the market, suggesting that the country's economic health was as essential to its future as "good citizens" (the stated goal of restrictive legislation).[60] The committee's complaint about the proposed legislation was that it was permanent; their alternative proposal was an immigration board that, like their proposed tariff board, could study the labor situation and set rates according to verified need rather than prejudice. The Immigration Committee endorsed a registry that would be used to enforce the new legislation and collect data, as long as it was kept to a minimum. Thus, NAM's stated position was not exactly opposition to the new legislation, yet neither was it support.

---

59. That was how Edgerton summed up his opinion; see ibid.

60. "Recommendation of Immigration Committee of the National Association of Manufacturers," *American Industries* (April 1924): 31–32. See also a similar recommendation in James Emery's statement to the National Republican Club, January 27, 1923, *NAM Washington Service Bulletin*, no. 116 (February 1, 1923): 1.

The Immigration Committee's report seems crafted to show that the manufacturers were socially responsible and concerned, not just acting on their own interests. They had tried, for instance, to make the most efficient use of labor they already had: "We believe it every employer's duty to endeavor constantly to make more efficient use of the existing labor saving devices, improved training methods, stabilizing production and employment, [and] resisting organized efforts to impose burdens upon manufacturing or transportation"—in other words, the new industrial relations techniques.[61] Despite these efforts, they might still need more labor; hence their need for flexible immigration policies. At one time a NAM committee might have blamed the AFL or used it to inflame opposition, but that is not in evidence here. The only mention of organized labor is in the statement just quoted, and it is pretty oblique. The committee's findings drew from the "reports and recommendations" of government departments and the NICB, which, as the report itself notes, had indicated that "the only test of our conclusions is their conformity to the public interest."[62]

As a final gesture of its social responsibility, the report ends with what will eventually become a social good—good race relations: "We urge our fellow members to afford within their resources every reasonable facility and in their communities to join in practical efforts to aid the alien in obtaining a working knowledge of our language, customs, traditions, and law. Let us meet the stranger with sympathetic understanding and just treatment as we would hope to be met were we strangers in a strange land."[63] "Americanization" has gotten a bad historical reputation, but this call to help newcomers adjust is a subtle way of criticizing those who called immigrants "un-American" and yet offered no help in making them the "good citizens" they complained they could not be. Manufacturers were interested in stemming the outflow of immigrants, of course, but their practical methods for labor retention fit perfectly with the burgeoning movement for racial and cultural tolerance.

Historians have since shown that immigration restriction, which was in place from 1921 to 1965, helped the labor movement develop solidarity and consolidate its power among workers. According to Liz Cohen, immigration restriction and the consequent assimilation lessened the influence

61. "Recommendation of Immigration Committee of the National Association of Manufacturers," 32.

62. Ibid., 31.

63. Ibid., 32.

of ethnicity in workers' lives and allowed a labor culture of solidarity to take root in workplaces and communities.[64] More recently, Jefferson Cowie affirmed that argument, adding that the homogeneity of American culture during these years contributed not only to a strong labor movement but also to the support for government activism in the form of New Deal liberalism.[65] Although African Americans and other people of color were citizens and certainly part of the population, they were a minority; their existence was marginalized and their rights limited. As the United States became more diverse after the Civil Rights Act of 1964 and the Immigration and Naturalization Act of 1965, the New Deal coalition and the labor movement gradually fell apart. Not that NAM leaders could have predicted any of this in 1924, but they were rightfully, from their perspective, worried about the effects of immigration restriction on unions and consistently opposed it.

Women in the Workplace

Women first became a concern for NAM in its battles against protective legislation. One of the successes of Progressive Era labor activists and feminists was state-level legislation limiting women's work hours. NAM saw such restrictive legislation—whether at the state or federal level—as a violation of the freedom to contract, an overstepping of government's power, and a blow to employers' rights. In *Muller v. Oregon* (1908), the Supreme Court ruled otherwise, arguing that the state had a compelling interest, more a responsibility, in protecting the health of women, who were the "weaker sex," and thus maximum-hour laws for women workers were constitutional. Thwarted legally, NAM began a two-pronged campaign: it deemed such laws discriminatory against women workers, who were rights-bearing adults, and it urged corporations to voluntarily pay attention to the health and welfare of all workers regardless of gender, a position not unlike that of the head of the Women's Bureau.[66]

---

64. Lizabeth Cohen, *Making a New Deal: Industrial Workers in Chicago, 1919–1939* (Cambridge: Cambridge University Press, 1990).

65. Cowie, *The Great Exception.*

66. The discrimination inherent in protective legislation was a point of contention within the women's movement as well, and many feminists likewise opposed such laws as discriminatory; see Nancy Woloch, *A Class of Her Own: Protective Laws for Women Workers* (Princeton, NJ: Princeton University Press, 2015); Dawley, *Struggles for Justice*, 282. On the Women's Bureau, see Hendrickson, *American Labor and Economic Citizenship*, chap. 5, which argues that the Bureau used gender as a way to fight for the rights of all laborers.

As we have seen, the war brought women into the workplace. The assumption during the war—stated in part to help men accept women in industrial work—was that women would leave industry once the men came back. But that did not happen, or at least not to the degree it would happen after World War II. Indeed, in creating a Women's Bureau, the Department of Labor was essentially saying—as its new director, Mary Anderson, said—that women were in industry to stay. In 1920, *American Industries* published a three-page article by Anderson, who conveyed that message with statistics and census reports. Having mastered "chemical analysis, acetelyne [*sic*] welding, core making, and operation of cranes," women had enlarged their horizons and were not about to go backwards: "Their mastery makes that enlargement permanent."[67] Nor were they prepared to work for less: "They are acting in concert and are concerned about hours, wages, conditions, equal pay for equal work, and equal opportunities in all occupations." Changes in family structure, said the author, had compelled more women to work, making the idea of a "family wage" for men obsolete. Anderson was an activist on behalf of women, but she also thought that attending to women's needs in industry would be a way to improve labor conditions for all.[68] As she wrote in the article, "she will carry man with her to improved conditions."[69]

The rise of personnel officers and industrial relations departments after the war brought a whole new type of woman worker into industry: the career woman, or professional woman, as distinguished from "women workers," which referred to working-class women. The professional woman was the product of women's advances in education and politics in the early twentieth century. Women had secured the vote in 1920 and were graduating from college in ever-greater numbers. Many of these female graduates were able to enter the new professional field of industrial relations, also known as employee relations, personnel, labor relations, and human relations. The very newness of the field had prevented it from becoming monopolized by males.[70] A good example of one of these women is Sara Southall, who worked her way up to an executive position in International Harvester's

67. Mary Anderson, "Woman's Future Position in Industry," *American Industries* (December 1920): 27–29, 28.
68. Hendrickson, *American Labor and Economic Citizenship*, 181.
69. Anderson, "Woman's Future Position in Industry," 29.
70. See Jacoby, *Employing Bureaucracy*; Rakesh Khurana, *From Higher Aims to Hired Hands: The Social Transformation of American Business Schools and the Unfulfilled Promise of Management as a Profession* (Princeton, NJ: Princeton University Press, 2007); Rosabeth Moss Kanter, *Men and Women of the Corporation* (1977; New York: Basic Books, 1984).

Industrial Relations Department over the course of the 1930s and 1940s and became a nationally recognized expert on women workers and race relations in the workplace.[71] NAM would eventually hire women to staff its research, foreign trade, and industrial relations divisions, some of whom would rise to leadership positions within the organization.

NAM's awareness of professional and activist women as a particularly active component of "the public" is indicated by its efforts to cultivate them as a possible constituency. In May 1923, *American Industries* published the views of eleven "representative" prominent women on the issue of the open shop. They included suffrage leaders, the heads of women's clubs, one company head, one woman in public relations, and one woman in the "Mutual Service" department of a manufacturer. Of the eleven, only two defended the rights of organized labor, and that in itself is somewhat of a surprise, given that the point of the exercise was to show that even women supported the open shop. But at least eight of them felt compelled to add that the closed shop was unnecessary if employers were practicing modern labor relations. As public relations specialist Edna Dunlop put it, "It has always seemed to me that the first union must have been organized at a time when the employer had the idea that his employes were far below him and to be considered merely cogs in a machine. This is not the modern idea."[72] The one woman who was an employer, Vira Whitehouse, head of Whitehouse Leather Products Company, Inc., said that from the perspective of the union, the open shop represented an "intolerable injustice." She thought that it had to be galling for union members whose hard work and sacrifice had brought about wage increases and improvements to see those who had stood by and might even have opposed their efforts now sharing in these gains. "From their point of view," she wrote, "the closed shop is but a necessary protection and a matter of justice." Whitehouse said that at her plant she has both closed and open shops and had harmonious relations with both.[73]

In 1926, NAM created a Woman's Bureau, dedicated to the idea that women were a permanent and useful part of industry, not a problem to be studied but an opportunity to expand upon. Its director was Mrs. Marguerite Benson from the Illinois Manufacturers Association. She was introduced at

71. See Delton, *Racial Integration in Corporate America*, 134–35; Sara Southall, *Industry's Unfinished Business* (New York: Harper & Brothers, 1950).

72. Edna J. Dunlop, "Finds the Open Shop Brings Contentment," *American Industries* 23 (May 1923): 23–24.

73. Vira B. Whitehouse, "Sees the Open Shop as Fair and liberal," *American Industries* 23 (May 1923): 22. The headline does not reflect the gist of what Whitehouse actually said.

the annual convention in a panel that inaugurated the Bureau and featured US Steel's Elbert Gary, as well as six women speaking not just on "women in industry" but also on women in business and professional associations and women in management and supervisory positions.[74] Also speaking at the convention was Jane Norman Smith, the chairwoman of the National Woman's Party, whose fiery speech on behalf of the Equal Rights Amendment condemned the male monopoly that structured the labor market and opposed the protective legislation that reinforced it. This was the speech of a feminist. It demanded women's full equality with men in every realm and an end to the notion of women as "dependent." It was countered by a male lawyer who warned of the dangers that such a radical amendment posed to the American family and way of life, but this speech sounded quaint compared to Smith's ringing call for individual rights, a favorite cause of NAM's.[75]

With the formation of its own Woman's Bureau, NAM not only embraced the enlightened philosophy of industrial relations, a hallmark of the corporate liberal future, but also opened up career opportunities for women in NAM. Women found jobs as researchers, writers, and department heads in NAM's rapidly growing research departments dedicated to bringing modern, progressive business and management trends to America's capitalists.

———

NAM's embrace of the new modern techniques for managing labor was indeed part of its open-shop campaign, but it was also beneficial and even progressive from the standpoint of what today we would call an inclusive workplace. NAM leaders were of course creatures of their time and held prejudices and assumptions about race and gender that are now outmoded. At the same time, however, they had remarkably open attitudes about welcoming immigrants into the country and women into the workplace. That these attitudes were mostly a response to labor supply issues does not make them any less noteworthy, historically speaking. Indeed, as employers concerned about labor supply, they moved beyond merely having open attitudes and toward putting in place economic structures, such as personnel departments and job training programs, that actively integrated immigrants, women, the unskilled, the handicapped, and eventually racial minorities into the workplace.

74. *NAM Proceedings*, 1926, pp. 55–57, 294–313.
75. Ibid., 190–203.

Although the 1920s were economically prosperous, NAM's membership declined significantly in this decade, presaging the Great Depression. This decline could be attributed to two recessions, in 1923–1924 and again in 1926–1927, and it could also have been the result of mergers—the most common cause of membership decline, as we will see. NAM reorganized its membership strategy in 1923, hoping to stem the effects. In 1925, the Membership Department was unable to report an increase in membership, which hovered around 3,000, down from its high of 5,350 in 1922. In 1926, the department reported a 6 percent decrease.[76] Nonetheless, NAM leaders were optimistic. In October 1929, they reported that business had never looked better.[77]

76. Ibid., 76; *NAM Proceedings*, 1925, p. 55; Taylor, *Labor Policies of the National Association of Manufacturers*, 17.

77. "Survey Shows Business Good," *Los Angeles Times*, October 15, 1929, p. 10.

5

New Deal Blues and Global Boons

The Great Depression was a crisis for the United States and the world. Industry ground to a halt. So too did international trade. Capitalism itself was called into question. Democracy likewise seemed shaky, as events in Spain and Germany showed. NAM, meanwhile, lost fully three-quarters of its membership.[1] The election of a Democratic president was bad enough for the Republican-dominated NAM, but Franklin Roosevelt was also, it seemed, a Democrat with distinctly socialistic leanings, surrounded by people sympathetic to organized labor. In the face of this disaster, NAM reorganized and slowly emerged as the first line of resistance to the new New Deal state—thus conforming perfectly to New Dealers' view of capitalists as class-bound reactionaries.

Much has been written about the reactionary anti–New Deal NAM, and I will review that history here because it is significant in terms of the organization's identity, the struggle for workplace control, and US history in general. But some New Deal policies—such as the National Industrial Recovery Act of 1933, the Reciprocal Trade Agreements Act of 1934, and the establishment of the Export-Import Bank in 1934—furthered NAM's agendas in industrial rationalization and trade expansion, highlighting the tension between the conservative principles of its leaders and the progressive prerogatives of global capitalism.

1. In 1931, NAM had only 1,000 members, down from 3,090 in 1927, and compared to a high in 1922 of 5,350. It was forced to end publication of *American Industries* in 1930. See Tedlow, "The National Association of Manufacturers and Public Relations during the New Deal," 25.

Confronting the New Deal

President Edgerton had led NAM for eleven prosperous years when he resigned in 1931 at the low point of NAM membership and a high point of economic panic. A Southern textile mill owner, Edgerton had helped professionalize the open-shop movement and worked with the Republican government in Washington to streamline trade and industry. The men who stepped in to reorganize NAM were hard-edged conservative industrialists from large multi-plant corporations, who believed that the crisis created an opportunity for organized labor that threatened not only their own control of the workplace but also American democracy. Even before Roosevelt's election in 1932, they sought to revive NAM as a first line of defense against the labor movement. These "Brass Hats," as they were dubbed, included Robert Lund of Lambert Pharmaceuticals (maker of Listerine) and NAM president in 1932–1933; Lammot du Pont, president of DuPont and board chair of General Motors; J. Howard Pew of Sun Oil Company (later Sunoco); Tom Girdler, president of Republic Steel; and Ernest Weir, head of National Steel. These men had ties to and in some cases helped found anti–New Deal organizations such as the American Liberty League and Crusaders for Economic Liberty.[2]

The Brass Hats' big plan was a public relations offensive to get business's "story" to the public. By 1937, NAM was spending 55 percent of its budget on "public information," up from just 7 percent in 1934.[3] To run the campaign, they created a new executive vice president position and hired Walter Weisenberger, a former newspaperman and Chamber of Commerce exec from St. Louis, to fill it. Weisenberger surveyed six thousand factory employees around the nation about business, government, and labor and then crafted a campaign in accordance with that data, being careful not to alienate the "regular" worker in this battle against organized labor for the hearts and minds of the public. Initially, he used every media channel available to get the message out: paid advertising in national and local newspapers, magazines, billboards, radio, school programming, speakers' bureaus, motion pictures, filmstrips, pamphlets, and community exhibits.[4]

2. Tedlow, "The National Association of Manufacturers and Public Relations during the New Deal," 29–30; Philip H. Burch Jr., "The NAM as an Interest Group," *Politics and Society* 4, no. 1 (1973): 97–130; Lichtman, *White Protestant Nation*, 62–75; Phillips-Fein, *Invisible Hands*, 13–15.

3. Tedlow, "The National Association of Manufacturers and Public Relations during the New Deal," 33.

4. Ibid., 32–33.

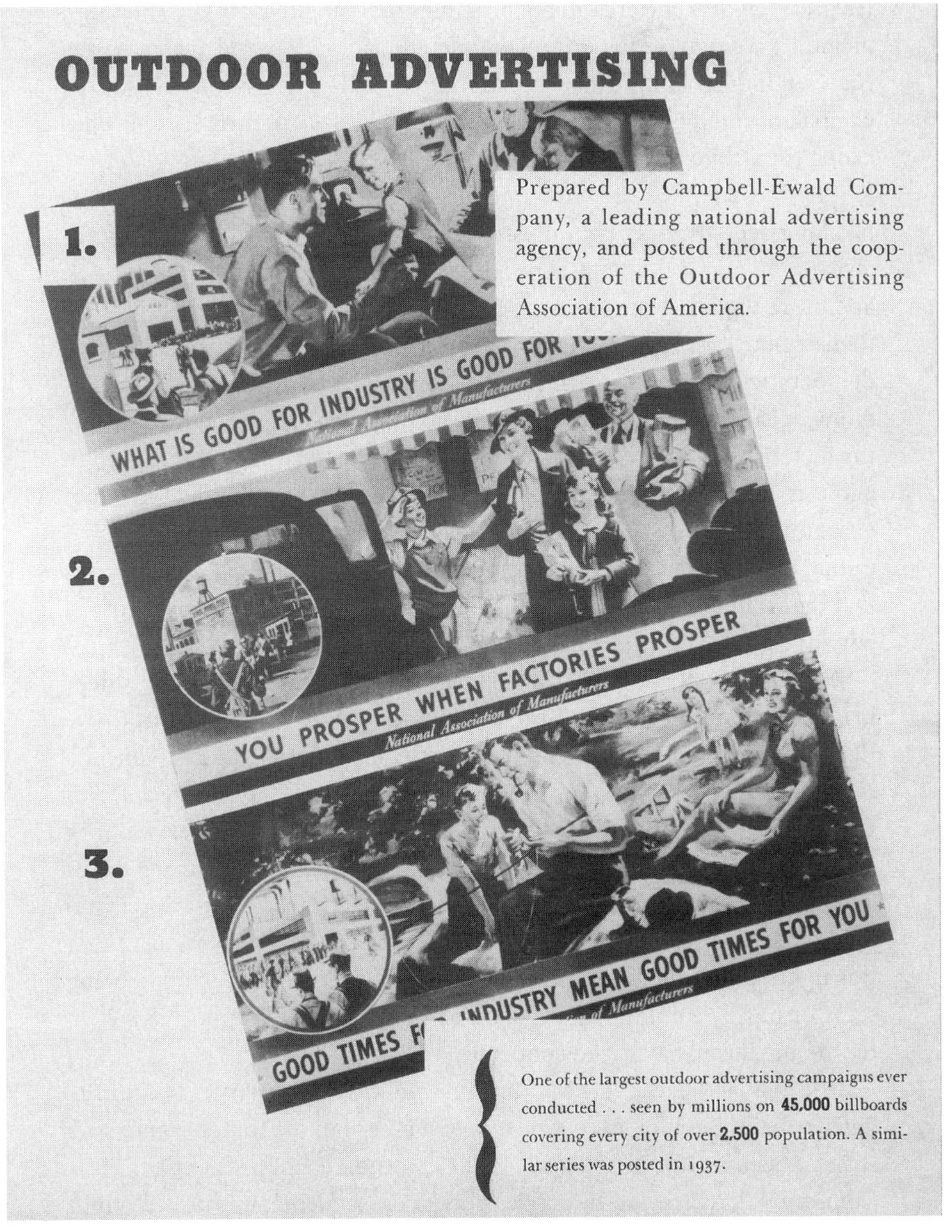

FIGURE 5.1. NAM "Free Enterprise" campaign, 1938. From the NAM-sponsored National Industrial Information Committee (NIIC), reporting to members on how it was taking industry's case to the public. Copyright © National Association of Manufacturers; courtesy of Hagley Library and Museum.

He presided over the creation of programs that targeted key communities, including women, farms, churches, and education. NAM also created the National Industrial Information Committee (NIIC) to raise money for the campaign, and the National Industrial Council (NIC) to further aid in educating the public at the state level.

The message was the same one that NAM and other business groups had long been trumpeting: industry means prosperity, high wages, affordable goods, and technological progress, all of which make life easier, safer, and more dignified. Alone among nations, America had figured out how to distribute more goods and more opportunities to more people by tying democratic ideals to free market principles. In America, an essential harmony existed between the worker, the consumer, and the industrialist—the fortunes of each rested on the prosperity created by economic growth and the capitalist system. The key to this success was individual freedom ensconced in the US Constitution, which was necessary for innovation and initiative and threatened only by an overreaching state or organizations that demanded mandatory membership in order for a man to be gainfully employed.

Neither the strategy nor the message was new. Every NAM president in a time of crisis felt that business's "message" was not getting out there. Else why would there be a crisis? With each new crisis, NAM had launched another public education campaign, which back in 1903 President David Parry had approvingly called "propaganda" (see chapter 3). What was new about this moment was new labor legislation that spurred organizing drives and strikes and was accompanied by a massive and apparently successful public relations campaign by New Dealers and labor organizations. NAM was fighting to hold on to its piece of social hegemony, which was being transformed by a politically popular counternarrative in support of collectivism, organized labor, and cooperation.

The new labor laws were NAM's worst nightmare come true. The Norris-LaGuardia Act, which narrowed employers' use of the injunction to stop strikes, became law in 1932. In April 1933, the Senate passed the Black-Connery Bill, which cut the official workweek to thirty hours in an attempt to put people back to work. NAM and other business groups rallied to stop it in the House.[5] But then, in June, the National Industrial Recovery Act

5. Bernard Bellush, in *The Failure of the NRA* (New York: W. W. Norton, 1975), argues that FDR never supported the Black-Connery Bill, which he considered impractical. Benjamin Kline Hunnicutt, in *Free Time: The Forgotten American Dream* (Philadelphia: Temple University Press, 2013), says that FDR caved in to NAM pressure and dropped his support for the bill.

(NIRA)—section 7(a) of which protected workers' right to bargain collectively in independent unions—was passed. NAM leaders supported the NIRA in general, but were dismayed by how labor leaders and some NRA officials were, in their eyes, misinterpreting section 7(a)'s position on company unions. NAM believed that company unions (employee representation plans) were an acceptable vehicle for collective bargaining, whereas labor officials did not. Thus, NAM advised members to ignore the new National Labor Relations Board (NLRB) rulings until a court decided on the matter.[6] The NIRA was declared unconstitutional in 1935. But Senate prolabor forces had already begun to replace section 7(a) with what became the Wagner Act, which codified labor's collective rights to organize independent unions and take collective action, including strikes, while discouraging company unions and prohibiting employers from interfering in union elections. The Wagner Act took employers' traditional argument about "freedom of contract," which employers had used in opposing federal labor legislation, and applied it to workers' relationship with unions, arguing that employers could not interfere with workers' rights to freely associate and contract with independent unions to represent their interests.[7]

Apprehensive employers looked to NAM to avert the pending legislation. It was the Wagner Act, more than NAM's expensive PR campaigns, that brought employers back to the organization. They objected to the long and ill-defined list of employers' liabilities and what they saw as the coercion of workingmen into the "ranks of a country-wide labor unit."[8] Steel man Ernest Weir saw the pending Wagner Act as an AFL plot to eliminate "its chief competitor," the employee representation plan, which many large companies had adopted to represent their employees in the wake of NIRA's section 7(a).[9] Weir called the Wagner Act "one of the most vicious pieces of legislation ever proposed," adding that it would "write into law a principle of eternal warfare between employer and employee."[10] NAM vigorously opposed the Wagner

6. See *NAM Annual Report*, 1934, p. 10, series 12, box 192, NAMR. The reference in this report is to the "old" NLRB, which was set up to enforce section 7(a) of the NIRA and was distinct from the NLRB formed by the Wagner Act in 1935.

7. Brody, "The Wagner Act and the Question of Workplace Representation"; Jerold Auerbach, *Labor and Liberty: The La Follette Committee and the New Deal* (Indianapolis: Bobbs-Merrill, 1966), 51–53.

8. Graton and Knight to "The President," April 5, 1934; see also other letters, series 12, box 194, "Wagner Act" file, NAMR.

9. Ernest T. Weir, "Present Relations of Business to Government," *Vital Speeches* (April 22, 1935): 476–80.

10. Ibid., 477–78.

Act, questioning its constitutionality, suggesting amendments, testifying before Congress, and writing editorials. But to no avail. The law passed. Roosevelt signed it in July 1935.

NAM's Legal Department issued a statement to members that unfair labor practices were not related to interstate commerce, that is, not within the reach of federal law, and that the act did not then apply to all manufacturers.[11] NAM hoped that the Wagner Act would be amended or struck down by the Supreme Court, as the NIRA had been. Instead, the Supreme Court upheld it in April 1937. But that did not quell the criticism. Opinion-makers such as Walter Lippmann, Dorothy Thompson, and Arthur Krock all commented on the Wagner Act's bias toward organized labor.[12] While the act delineated what organized labor could do and, more vaguely, what employers could not do, it offered no corresponding clarity about what labor could not do and what actions were legal for employers. By 1938, 52 percent of Americans believed that the Wagner Act should be amended.[13]

Far from resolving the "labor problem," the Wagner Act unleashed a wave of strikes and retributions as unions struggled to make it real and employers, including prominent NAM members, actively resisted it. Beginning in May 1936, James H. Rand Jr., NAM director and president of the Remington-Rand Corporation, fought for over two years against the AFL's attempt to bargain for its workers in his upstate New York office machine plants. Rand hired security forces and enlisted local police to protect the company's property, deployed labor spies to incite violence and spread misinformation, began to close plants, and formed citizens' committees to turn locals against the strikers. Rand packaged up all of these acts, which the Wagner Act had prohibited, as the "Mohawk Valley Formula" in a speech directed at other beleaguered employers and published approvingly in NAM's *Labor Relations Bulletin* in June 1936.[14] Even after the strike was over, Rand continued

---

11. Auerbach, *Labor and Liberty*, 53, citing US House, "Hearings before the Special Committee to Investigate the National Labor Relations Board," XIII, 2578–80. The Liberty League issued a similar statement. Progressive Republican senator William Borah also held this position, as quoted in *Fact and Fancy in the TNEC Monographs*, compiled by John Scoville and Noel Sargent (New York: NAM, 1942), 397.

12. Quoted in *Fact and Fancy in the TNEC Monographs*, 398, in discussion of reasonable disagreement on the Wagner Act.

13. "Fight on Measure Due in Next Congress," *Washington Post*, November 13, 1938, p. B3.

14. See Ahmed White, *The Last Great Strike: Little Steel, the CIO, and the Struggle for Labor Rights in New Deal America* (Berkeley: University of California Press, 2016), 56–57. The NLRB investigated this strike.

to resist the settlement and fired the workers involved (also illegal under the Wagner Act).

A month later, nearly seventy thousand workers represented by the Steelworkers Organizing Committee (SWOC, later to become the United Steelworkers of America-CIO) walked off their jobs at four steel companies that were collectively known as "Little Steel." US Steel Corporation had recognized SWOC in 1936, but leaders of the Little Steel companies, led by Tom Girdler of Republic Steel, took a page from Rand's Mohawk Valley Formula and prepared to fight, stocking up on barbed wire and tear gas, arming company agents, and enlisting local law enforcement to protect their property and break the strike. For two months in 1937, the companies battled strikers at thirty mills across Illinois, Ohio, Pennsylvania, Michigan, and New York. In Chicago, a group of men, women, and children attempted to picket the Republic Steel mill and were met by Chicago police armed with revolvers, nightsticks, and gas weapons. In what became known as the Memorial Day Massacre, the police killed ten strikers and seriously wounded thirty others with gunfire.[15] At its height in June 1937, the strike involved over eighty thousand workers. By the end, six others lost their lives and hundreds more were injured. The companies declared victory and gradually fired many of the striking workers. Girdler and Weir blamed strikers for the violence and continued to publicly resist the Wagner Act.[16]

The Little Steel violence and employers' continued intransigence led to investigations not only by the new National Labor Relations Board, set up to enforce the Wagner Act, but also by the Senate Committee on Education and Labor, which formed a subcommittee to investigate violations of free speech and labor rights. The La Follette Committee, as it was known, investigated the anti-union activities of US companies, but also targeted employers' associations.[17] So it was that NAM, along with the National Metal Trades Association and Associated Industries of Cleveland, found itself, again, the target of a congressional investigation.

In operation from 1936 to 1941, the La Follette Committee helped turn public opinion in favor of unions and the Wagner Act. Headed by progressive Republican senator Robert La Follette Jr. of Wisconsin, the power center of the committee was a labor journalist and NLRB staffer named Heber

15. For a moving description of the massacre, see ibid., 1–3.
16. See ibid., chap. 12.
17. Auerbach, *Labor and Liberty*, 144.

Blankenhorn, who created a persuasive public relations campaign that, as one historian put it, "crucially aided the CIO in gaining a foothold in the mass production industries."[18] That was the main purpose of the subcommittee, according to Blankenhorn. Every time the NLRB encountered trouble, Blankenhorn recalled, the La Follette Committee took "the heat off it." A White House memo noted that the subcommittee was doing as much to legitimate the Wagner Act as the NLRB and the Supreme Court.[19] That was certainly how it seemed to business community supporters, as well as to progressive journals like *The New Republic*.[20]

NAM cooperated with the committee. It handed over its financial information, membership lists, correspondence, minutes, and publications. NAM's lawyers indicated that there was certain material that NAM was not legally bound to deliver, even under subpoena, but the board made the decision to supply it anyway: "Conscious of the fact that this association has never violated the rights which are the subject matter of inquiry and having nothing to conceal, we waive such privilege to the extent herein indicated."[21] NAM had nothing to hide. Indeed, in preparation for the hearings, Walter Weisenberger wrote to Senator La Follette that, in view of the committee's interest in NAM's educational programs, he should provide enough time for the committee to view *all* of its films and presentations. The full flavor could not be conveyed by one or two random pieces but had to be appreciated in full.[22]

What did the committee uncover? It found "a community of interests" among the Little Steel companies involved in labor violence and the memberships of NAM and the American Iron and Steel Institute. It found that from 1933 to 1937 the six Little Steel companies contributed $140,000 in dues to NAM; that Girdler, Weir, and Charles Hook, president of ARMCO, another Little Steel company (but, significantly, not involved in the strike), had all served on NAM's board or executive committee; that NAM had promoted ERPs, or company unions (which the Wagner Act had deemed illegal); that NAM had raised and spent large amounts of money on a "propaganda" campaign designed to thwart support for labor unions and "promote

18. Gilbert Gall, "Heber Blankenhorn, the La Follette Committee, and the Irony of Industrial Repression," *Labor History* 23 (1982): 246–53.

19. Ibid., 248, citing Blankenhorn manuscript about the La Follette Committee.

20. See collected newspaper clippings and an untitled document dated March 25, 1938, series XII, box 195, NAMR; and "The Pinkertons Testify," *The New Republic*, March 31, 1937, pp. 227–30.

21. Board of directors meeting minutes, November 23, 1937, series 12, box 194, NAMR.

22. Weisenberger to La Follette, February 14, 1938, series 12, box 194, NAMR.

organized disregard" for the Wagner Act; and that NAM had sought to retard unionization and "to render public opinion intolerant of the aims of social progress through legislative effort."[23] None of this was a secret. NAM itself had announced to the press in December 1935 that it intended to "rid the nation of the New Deal."[24] NAM officials nonetheless distanced themselves in their testimony from the inflammatory actions of Rand, Girdler, and Weir. In a move no doubt urged by Weisenberger, they pointed to their employee relations programs, their desire for harmony, and their interest in reducing unemployment.

As with the Mulhall hearings of 1913, no legal wrongdoing was found. The biggest offense seemed to be a well-financed public relations campaign on behalf of capitalism. But as conservatives around the country pointed out, NAM's $750,000 campaign paled next to the US government's million-dollar campaign to educate the public on New Deal programs, which could more aptly be called "propaganda," as it sought to justify state policies.[25] The La Follette Committee identified booklets instructing employers how to form ERPs as evidence of malfeasance, whereas NAM saw them as part of its professionalizing, developmental work.[26] The committee found NAM's lobbying scandalous, whereas NAM saw it as free speech, and a service to its members. In all these activities NAM was negotiating, testing, trying to shape the new labor regime of the Wagner Act in ways more favorable to industry. Its activities were conservative, certainly, but not a violation of labor rights, which were and always have been contested. Even the CIO thought that the battle would be won on the shop floor, not in the halls of Congress.[27]

Still, the La Follette Committee hit a nerve. By 1938, NAM had softened its anti–New Deal animus. Its 1939 platform seemed to call for cooperation with labor and government. It identified the main problem facing America, not as "socialistic government," but rather as the question of how to apply the principles of democracy and private enterprise to "the conditions and

23. White, *The Last Great Strike*, 66–72; quotes from Auerbach, *Labor and Liberty*, 146, 147.

24. Louis Stark, "Business Fights New Deal," *New York Times*, December 15, 1935, p. E7.

25. "Public Propaganda," *Baltimore Sun*, March 5, 1938, and others in clippings document, series XII, box 195, NAMR.

26. On the context in which ERPs were "illegal" under the Wagner Act, see Brody, "The Wagner Act and the Question of Workplace Representation."

27. On the CIO's unwillingness to rely on the NLRB and its strategy of "building strength by more direct means," see White, *The Last Great Strike*, 273–74. NAM's critique of the La Follette Committee can be found in *Fact and Fancy in the TNEC Monographs*, 387–407.

requirements of present-day society."[28] It admitted that industry had made its "share of mistakes" and that it had a responsibility to both the nation and its workers to maintain uniform employment. It recognized that "mutually satisfactory labor relationships [were] essential to industrial efficiency." Noticeably absent from the platform was any mention of the open shop or the Wagner Act. It criticized specific government programs, but the overall tone was one of conciliation. The opening address at the convention that year was given by Gerald Swope, the progressive president of General Electric, a supporter of labor legislation, and a corporate liberal par excellence. Newspapers seemed genuinely surprised, proclaiming in headlines, "Manufacturers Endorse Cooperation with Labor" and "Industrialists Vote to Give Government Cooperation."[29]

The platform vote was presented as "unanimous," but it had been leaked that it was actually the result of a "bitter fight in the resolutions committee."[30] As one columnist noted, the platform resembled that of a political party that is "torn within itself but feels bound to present a united front."[31] This indicates that by 1938 the Brass Hats were no longer in control (although they remained active in the organization). The president that year was Charles Hook, head of ARMCO (a Little Steel company) and a critic of NAM's confrontational style. A longtime advocate for cooperation and fair play in labor relations, Hook was appointed by President Roosevelt to serve on the Business Advisory Council (BAC), which worked closely with government agencies to implement New Deal policies.[32] Hook had his allies in NAM who likewise opposed the Brass Hats' "get tough" posturing, but it is uncertain whether they would have prevailed had the La Follette Committee not garnered such bad publicity for NAM—a point underscored by the *Washington Post*, which saw in the platform "a smarter sense of public relations than the NAM exhibited in the early days of the New Deal."[33]

28. Quoted in "A Middle Ground," *New York Times*, December 10, 1938, p. 16.

29. "Manufacturers Endorse Cooperation with Labor," *Christian Science Monitor*, December 9, 1938, p. 1; "Industrialists Vote to Give Government Cooperation," *Washington Post*, December 9, 1938, p. 1; see also "Industry Urges Accord with US and Labor," *Chicago Daily Tribune*, December 9, 1938, p. 35.

30. "Industrialists Vote to Give Government Cooperation," *Washington Post*, December 9, 1938, p. 1.

31. Ernest Lindley, "A Tempered Tone," *Washington Post*, December 12, 1938, p. 9.

32. On Hook, see John William Tebbet, *The Human Touch in Business* (Dayton, OH: Otterbein Press, 1963). On the BAC, see Kim McQuaid, *Uneasy Partners: Big Business in American Politics, 1945–1990* (Baltimore: Johns Hopkins University Press, 1994).

33. Lindley, "A Tempered Tone."

A more conciliatory approach might help with public relations, but the Brass Hats had been right about one thing: the New Deal philosophy, which even the most conciliatory NAM leaders regarded as a socialistic threat to free enterprise, seemed to be catching on. Baffled by the widespread acceptance of New Deal ideas, NAM officials struggled to understand how their "time-tested" ideas about individualism, competition, and limited government could have fallen so out of favor. They never considered the ways in which their own organization had contributed to this development—but that it did so is the only way to explain why so much of the New Deal was actually in line with NAM's agenda.

Industrial Cooperation and the National Recovery Administration

The "new" economic ideas that undergirded much of the New Deal were familiar to NAM. New Deal policies to "kick-start" the economy and stabilize employment embraced a systems-oriented approach to the economy similar to the one NAM had been cultivating since 1895. Founded at a moment of economic crisis, NAM was part of a trade association movement that sought to reduce industrial costs and competition, allocate resources efficiently, and iron out fluctuations in employment, output, and demand.[34] Long before the New Deal, trade associations and NAM had looked to the government to stabilize currency, coordinate markets, and put in place structures to encourage trade. They had used the language of cooperation and interdependence to standardize and coordinate industry, and the management philosophies they developed had acknowledged workers' experiences, needs, and rights.

Herbert Hoover had embraced the trade association ethic of cooperation and coordination in his tenure as commerce secretary and as president. A stout defender of individualism and limited government, Hoover nonetheless understood that Adam Smith's model of independent competition not only was unable to meet modern economic problems, like unemployment and depression, but also contributed to them. Hoover viewed the economy as a system with various parts that could and should be regulated, if not by the state then by responsible trade associations or farm cooperatives. Like NAM, he believed that there was a role for government in developing

---

34. See chapter 1; see also Ellis Hawley, "Herbert Hoover and Economic Stabilization, 1921–22," in *Herbert Hoover as Secretary of Commerce*, edited by Ellis Hawley (Iowa City: University of Iowa Press, 1981), 44–47.

industries that would make business more efficient, such as aviation, ship-ping, and radio.[35] The federal government could also cultivate international trade, possibly with loans. NAM did not blink an eye at any of these progres-sive departures from "time-tested" ideas of free market competition and individualism. In fact, it worked closely with Hoover to promote this agenda.

The Roosevelt administration continued the general direction of Hoover's economic policies—but on steroids and with a noxious prolabor union bent.[36] The New Deal's economic centerpiece was the National Indus-trial Recovery Act (NIRA), which had the stated purpose of promoting "the organization of industry for the purpose of cooperative action among trade groups."[37] Once organized, these organizations would devise codes of fair competition, which would set standard wages, hours, and a method to ensure the compliance of the entire industry so that nonconformists did not profit from undercutting the standard. This was essentially the codification of Hoover's voluntary program of systematizing and regulating industries.

The NIRA wasn't simply about propping up trade associations, however. In the eyes of many, it was a license to monopoly. Many of these trade asso-ciations had spent the 1920s trying to evade antitrust laws and to stabilize prices by agreeing to restrict output.[38] Although NAM itself was not the kind of industry-specific trade association that would benefit from ending anti-trust laws, many of its members expected NAM to take a strong anti-antitrust position, which it did. The Depression confirmed to many the dangers of

35. See especially Evan B. Metcalf, "Secretary Hoover and the Emergence of Macroeconomic Management," *Business History Review* 49, no. 1 (Spring 1975): 60–80; Ellis Hawley, "Herbert Hoover, the Commerce Secretariat, and the Vision of an Associative State, 1921–1928," *Journal of American History* 61 (June 1974): 116–40; Himmelberg, *The Origins of the National Recovery Administration*.

36. What the New Deal was about, of course, has been contested historically and politically. My understanding of it as a continuation of Progressive Era attempts to contain capitalism is a condensation of arguments found in these works: Alan Brinkley, *The End of Reform: New Deal Liberalism in Recession and War* (New York: Alfred A. Knopf, 1995); Cowie, *The Great Exception*; Jason Scott Smith, *Building New Deal Liberalism: The Political Economy of Public Works, 1933–1956* (New York: Cambridge University Press, 2006); Jordan K. Schwartz, *The New Dealers: Power Politics in the Age of Roosevelt* (New York: Alfred A. Knopf, 1993); David Plotke, *Building a Demo-cratic Political Order* (New York: Cambridge University Press, 1996); Gerstle and Fraser, *The Rise and Fall of the New Deal Order*.

37. Quoted in Sargent and Galt, "The National Industrial Recovery Act," 1.

38. The similarity between Hoover and Roosevelt was a focus of the Revisionist historians of the 1960s, most notably, Murray Rothbard, "Hoover and Myth of Laissez-Faire," in *A New History of Leviathan: Essays on the Rise of the Corporate State*, edited by Ronald Radosh and Mur-ray Rothbard (New York: Dutton, 1972); James J. Martin, "Business and the New Deal," *Reason* (December 1975). http://reason.com/archives/1975/12/01/business-and-the-new-deal.

overproduction and hence the need for planning, which in practice would mean output restriction. Indeed, the aim of the NRA and its partner, the Agricultural Adjustment Administration (AAA), was to restrict production to raise prices, which would allow companies to start hiring again.[39]

NAM leaders supported the endeavor and actively shaped the legislation.[40] After sinking the Black-Connery Bill, which had sought to limit hours and raise wages, NAM counsel James Emery proposed a business-centered approach to industrial recovery and reemployment, whereby antitrust laws would be temporarily suspended, eliminating "cutthroat competition" and allowing businesses to agree on minimum wages and maximum hours. It would be, he wrote, "an experiment of self-government within industry."[41] Together with Chamber of Commerce head Henry Harriman, Emery convinced the drafting committee to consider this proposal, promising that the suspension of antitrust laws would allow business to develop a reemployment plan. NAM sent a delegation to discuss the bill with the drafting committee, which was surprisingly open to industry's approach. It also formed a business steering committee, headed by James Rand of Remington-Rand, to lobby lawmakers. Even before the bill passed, NAM began to prepare its members. In a publication dated May 23, 1933, NAM staff members Noel Sargent and John Galt explained the rationale behind the legislation, how it would work, and how companies could form trade associations. It highlighted section 7(a), which instructed companies that codes must provide that "employees should have the right to organize and bargain collectively through representatives of their own choosing," and that no employee or anyone seeking employment "shall be required as a condition of employment to join any company union or to refrain from joining a labor organization of his own choosing," and that employers must comply with maximum hours and minimum wages, as approved by the president.[42] NAM here was basically agreeing to mandated collective bargaining, minimum wages, and maximum hours. At this point, section 7(a) still allowed company unions, but banned employers from forcing workers into them. This was distasteful, but acceptable given the opportunity to achieve liberation from antitrust laws and the long-standing goal of self-regulation.

Despite the boon to trade associations embodied in the NIRA, there was much for NAM to object to, including its licensing provisions, its lack

39. Bellush, *The Failure of the NRA*, 2–5.
40. Himmelberg, *The Origins of the National Recovery Administration*, 204–6.
41. Quoted in ibid., 204.
42. Sargent and Galt, "The National Industrial Recovery Act," 5.

of import controls, and section 7(a), which was contested from the start. The licensing provisions gave the president unprecedented power over business, but most business leaders seemed not to care and the president never used it. Imports became a problem because the NIRA was designed to raise prices and wages among American producers, but this left them vulnerable to importers. In October 1933, President Roosevelt issued an executive order to control imports that endangered the NIRA codes, and in June 1934, the Reciprocal Trade Agreements Act further expanded executive import control power, in part to alleviate this problem.[43] Section 7(a) caused the most trouble. The NAM group was able to rewrite it by accepting collective bargaining but leaving a statement that protected the open shop. Congress changed the language to prohibit employers from interfering with organizing efforts in a way that left open the possibility of a closed shop. NAM leaders tried to rally businessmen to oppose the bill, but most businessmen were not interested in stopping the legislation on that point. In November, NAM issued a strong statement against parts of the NIRA, claiming that it had the support of twenty-six industry groups, but the groups it listed denied that they supported the statement.[44] Nonetheless, despite its hostility to key parts of the NIRA, NAM renewed its endorsement of it in December 1933.[45]

Even before the Supreme Court declared it unconstitutional in May 1935, the NIRA was a failure in the eyes of labor, consumers, progressives, and economists. It had raised prices without a corresponding increase in employment. The much-vaunted standardization of prices and wages had done nothing to increase purchasing power and indeed had left consumers and workers worse off than before.[46] Plus, the approval of the codes was a slow and cumbersome process, their enforcement completely neglected. The program was in shambles, provoking a whole new round of antibusiness, antimonopoly rhetoric. Historians blame its head, "General" Hugh Johnson, and other administrators for ceding control of the process to industry reps, who, as it turns out, were completely unable to govern themselves.[47] Although NAM had been overtly hostile to parts of the defunct program, it praised its original

43. "Heeds Import Menace," *New York Times*, October 25, 1933, p. 1; this will be discussed later in the chapter.

44. Himmelberg, *The Origins of the National Recovery Administration*, 207; "NRA Threat Seen in Industry Move," *New York Times*, November 2, 1933, p. 15.

45. "Roosevelt Backed by Trade Leaders on Money and NRA," *New York Times*, December 9, 1933, p. 1; "NAM Looks Ahead for the NRA," *Business Week*, November 24, 1934, pp. 7–8.

46. Bellush, *The Failure of the NRA*, chap. 3.

47. This is the thesis of both Bellush and Himmelberg.

mission and urged all trade associations "to take immediate steps within its sphere to stabilize wages, hours, working conditions and competitive practices on a voluntary basis."[48]

Trade Expansion

NAM began life as an advocate for reciprocity: bilateral agreements that would allow certain countries and goods into the highly protected US market in return for US access to their markets. To facilitate such agreements, it promoted an independent commission that would remove tariff agreements from congressional control and logrolling. As we have seen, this was a delicate operation, since the party with which it had the most influence—the Republican Party—was a staunch defender of tariff "protection," as were many NAM members. NAM always insisted that high protective tariffs in some areas were perfectly compatible with reciprocity, but manufacturers in protected industries saw any change in the tariff regime as a "slippery slope" to free trade.

In 1934, Franklin Roosevelt signed into law what NAM trade expansionists had been seeking since 1895. The Reciprocal Trade Agreements Act (RTAA) of 1934 transferred tariff-making authority from Congress to the executive branch, which would, in consultation with an independent tariff commission, be in charge of making reciprocal trade deals with individual countries. Although not a complete victory for "free trade," it did set the country on the path to lowering US import duties over the course of the twentieth century, from a high of 52.8 percent in 1930 to 9.9 percent in 1967 to just 5.2 percent in 1982.[49] A watershed moment in the history of US trade, it represented a transfer of institutional power from Congress to the executive branch.[50] Speaking for its mostly Republican constituency, NAM seemed to oppose the RTAA, which was the brainchild of the internationalist, free-trade Democrat Cordell Hull. But on closer inspection, NAM's "opposition" was an opposition to Hull's original version of the law, not to the law that was passed and signed. NAM successfully lobbied for key restrictions that made the RTAA the weird combo-platter of reciprocity and protection that NAM had always imagined could exist.

48. "The Manufacturers' Stand," *New York Times*, May 29, 1935, p. 11.

49. Nitsan Chorev, *Remaking US Trade Policy: From Protectionism to Globalization* (Ithaca, NY: Cornell University Press, 2007), 2.

50. According to trade analysts, it is the "single most important change in the institutional history of US trade policy"; quoted in Tim Woods, "Capitalist Class Relations, the State, and New Deal Foreign Trade Policy," *Critical Sociology* 29, no. 3 (2003).

THE PREHISTORY: SMOOT-HAWLEY

Widely regarded as one of the worst economic policy choices of the twentieth century, the Smoot-Hawley Tariff raised US duties to their highest level in over a century. Signed into law by President Hoover at the onset of the Great Depression, it was condemned by Democrats and economists for exacerbating the Depression and stifling trade. Its passage through Congress was a circus of battling interest groups, each lobbying for higher rates for their product, be it wool, skins, dyes, or shoes, a process captured by political scientist E. E. Schattschneider's famous study of interest groups in politics.[51] Ironically, Hoover shared an antipathy to this political logrolling and had pursued the new tariff legislation in an attempt to shift tariff-making authority over to an independent commission.[52]

NAM stood on the sidelines in the Smoot-Hawley debate. It made no endorsement either for or against the measure. In 1927, NAM had issued a resolution endorsing the protective tariff but proposing its removal from the vagaries of congressional control. In 1929, as Congress was preparing to revise the tariff, NAM restated that position, but more emphatically endorsed "the validity and economic necessity of Executive Rate Adjustment with the aid of a qualified Commission"—meaning that it favored giving the president more power to set tariff rates.[53] Hoover sought to incorporate into Smoot-Hawley a flexible tariff provision that would have put tariff revisions in the hands of a bipartisan commission. Senate Republicans opposed this, but eventually accepted a weaker version of it. Hoover signed the bill, mostly to avoid further divisions at a time of crisis.[54] After the bill passed, NAM issued a statement of support, but one focused not on the most obvious feature of the bill (higher duties), but on the flexible tariff provision: "The new law, for the first time in the history of the country, should result in taking the tariff out of logrolling and political maneuvering and relieve business from the disastrous effects of general revisions

51. E. E. Schattschneider, *Politics, Pressure, and the Tariff* (Englewood-Cliffs, NJ: Prentice-Hall, 1935).

52. Hoover had spent most of his career in Washington (as commerce secretary and then as president) fighting for more liberal trade policies; see *The Memoirs of Herbert Hoover*, chap. 11.

53. "Chronological Documentation of NAM Positions on the Tariff and Reciprocity Agreements since 1895," series 1, box 105, NAMR.

54. Edward Kaplan, *American Trade Policy, 1923–1995* (Westport, CT: Greenwood Press, 1996), 37.

for years to come."[55] This is not how the Smoot-Hawley Tariff is usually characterized. It was the best possible spin NAM could put on a bill that divided its membership.

THE RECIPROCAL TRADE AGREEMENTS ACT

The person most responsible for the Reciprocal Trade Agreements Act was Cordell Hull, a Wilsonian Democrat and free-trade advocate from Tennessee who had been appointed secretary of state by Roosevelt. A zealous internationalist, Hull had helped write President Wilson's tariff-slashing Revenue Act of 1913 (known as the Underwood Tariff).[56] While workers (and manufacturers) believed that tariffs protected jobs and raised wages, Hull believed that they created industrial monopolies, raised prices for consumers, and eliminated opportunities to export American goods, thereby stifling job growth. They protected American manufacturers from competition, yes, but that made American companies slow to adopt innovations that would make them more efficient and productive—that is, competitive. Problems like European debt repayment could be solved if the United States lowered its tariffs so that Europeans could sell their goods in the US market. Hull believed that trade barriers were a source of international competition that led to trade wars, and then to real wars.[57] He saw closed borders as akin to closed minds; condemning economic nationalism as "provincialism, a narrowing of ideas," he warned that, "without the knowledge and customs and manners and learning of the rest of the world, which is one of the benefits of extensive international commerce, nations inevitably tend to decline and decay."[58]

Hull's ideas were very much in line with an ascendant internationalist group of bankers and multinational corporations, who, like Hull, sought to topple trade barriers. The First World War had removed European powers from the field of international investment, and the United States had emerged as the major supplier of capital in the world. Major multinational corporations like General Electric, Great Northern Railway, Westinghouse, Armour, AT&T, and W. R. Grace backed a new venture to coordinate and direct investment into overseas enterprises and into shipping and financing

55. Quoted in "Manufacturers Approve Tariff as Business Aid," *New York Herald Tribune*, June 17, 1930, p. 6.

56. Butler, *Cautious Visionary*, 3.

57. Ibid., 7–11; Kaplan, *American Trade Policy*, 43–44.

58. Quoted in Kaplan, *American Trade Policy*, 51.

infrastructure.[59] The largest American corporations were increasing their foreign direct investment (FDI), mainly by building new factories abroad, which allowed them to circumvent foreign trade barriers. Typically, these corporations offered some kind of patented, specialized good, such as automobiles, electrical appliances, communication devices, and office equipment, although industries like mining and petroleum also had almost 18 percent of their fixed capital investment in FDI. By the end of the 1920s, all of the major car companies had gone multinational.[60] In terms of trade policy, these internationalist-oriented bankers and manufacturers wanted to make sure that the foreigners to whom they loaned or sold goods had the money to do business with them. The best way to do this was to lower US tariffs on imports so that they could sell goods in American markets and thereby secure dollars to repay or pay US bankers and multinational corporations.

The vast majority of American manufacturers, however, did not have foreign investments, nor did they produce for the export market. As H. L. Derby, head of NAM's Tariff Committee, was fond of noting, "ninety-five percent of the markets for American goods are in America."[61] One reason this remained true was high tariffs—why would American manufacturers compete in an international market when their home market was guaranteed? This group of manufacturers, often called "nationalists" (as opposed to "internationalists"), still held sway in the Republican Party, as indicated by the passage of the Smoot-Hawley Tariff, but there was also sympathy for the tariff among Democrats in the Al Smith, Northeastern wing of the party, which represented workers.

There was then a clash of interests between protectionist, nationalist capitalists, mostly in the Republican Party, and free-trade, multinationalist capitalists who were increasingly drawn to the anti-tariff policies of Secretary Hull and the Democratic Party. NAM's members and leaders inhabited both camps—or perhaps it is more accurate to say that its leaders included (1) protectionists, especially in the steel, chemical, and textile industries; (2) representatives from large multinational corporations with FDI; and (3) aspirational exporters who supported a reciprocal trade policy that

59. Woods, "Capitalist Class Relations, the State, and New Deal Foreign Trade Policy," 399; Mira Wilkins, *The Maturing of Multinational Enterprise: American Business Abroad from 1914 to 1970* (Cambridge, MA: Harvard University Press, 1975), 20–22.

60. Woods, "Capitalist Class Relations, the State, and New Deal Foreign Trade Policy," 399; Wilkins, *The Maturing of Multinational Enterprise*, 68–77.

61. "Higher Tariff Plea Is Made in Debate," *New York Times*, April 11, 1932, p. 17.

removed tariff-setting responsibility from Congress. Despite the presence of large multinational corporations in its leadership, NAM never argued for lower tariffs to encourage imports. But neither did it take a purely nationalist view. Its position was for reciprocal trade deals with certain countries to create export markets. Although NAM's rhetoric was often protectionist, the organization's goal was a more efficient process for making reciprocal trade deals. In the end, that is exactly what it got.

Although the Roosevelt administration was wary of entering the politically charged field of tariff reform, it did take some steps that prepared affected populations for the possible fallout of lowered tariffs. First, Roosevelt took the United States off the gold standard, which had the effect of devaluing the dollar internationally and making American exports more competitive vis-à-vis imports. Between February and December 1933, American exports nearly doubled.[62] This enabled the United States to reduce tariffs without facing destructive competition from imports. Second, Roosevelt's domestic programs contained provisions that protected industry, farmers, and workers from the possible fallout of lower tariffs. The point of both the AAA and the NRA was to raise prices. Because that could conceivably create a space for cheaper imports, both programs contained mechanisms for executive adjustment on a product-by-product basis. With the Wagner Act and the social security legislation of 1935, Roosevelt released American workers from their dependence on the tariff. Having unions to secure high wages and federal insurance for unemployment made workers less susceptible to protectionists' arguments about the tariff as a guarantor of jobs.[63]

As originally pitched by a State Department–chaired committee on commercial policy, the RTAA was intended to expand American export markets through the negotiation of bilateral trade agreements on an unconditional most favored nation (MFN) basis. Unconditional MFN meant that all nations so designated would be privy to concessions negotiated by another trading partner. For instance, if the United States and England made an agreement that allowed England to import woolen jackets into the United States at lowered tariffs, all nations with MFN status could sell their woolen jackets

62. Stephen Haggard, "The Institutional Foundations of Hegemony: Explaining the Reciprocal Trade Agreements Act of 1934," *International Organization* 42, no. 1 (Winter 1988): 91–119, 110.

63. On New Deal programs as prep for tariff reduction, see ibid., 108–10; Andrew Wender Cohen, "Unions, Modernity, and the Decline of American Economic Nationalism," in *The Right and Labor in America*, edited by Nelson Lichtenstein and Elizabeth Tandy Shermer (Philadelphia: University of Pennsylvania Press, 2012).

in the United States under the same agreement.[64] Unconditional MFN was controversial because it seemed to use the bilateralism of reciprocal trade to lower tariffs multilaterally. The main controversy in 1934, however, was not over MFN, but rather the shift of tariff-making authority to the president. The Constitution explicitly gave that authority to Congress. As with other New Deal programs, Roosevelt was asking for a constitutional revision, or "reinterpretation," that empowered the executive branch at the expense of Congress. Republicans balked. Roosevelt couched his request for tariff-making authority in the language of national emergency, assuring Congress that the purpose was to benefit industry and agriculture. He explained that domestic recovery depended in part on international trade. He noted that other countries' leaders had this authority and were busy making trade deals. The United States risked being left out or discriminated against in the absence of an authoritative and reliable negotiating mechanism in the executive branch.[65]

Unlike most Republicans, NAM leadership had no problem departing from constitutional precepts on this issue. The proposed RTAA was consistent with NAM's longtime support for reciprocity agreements as a way to expand trade. In 1929, NAM had adopted a resolution in support of removing tariff rate adjustment from Congress: "We are convinced of the validity and economic necessity of Executive Rate adjustment with the aid of a qualified commission . . . [and urge] the retention of administrative as distinguished from legislative rate adjustment of the tariff."[66] However, because the executive at the time was Roosevelt, NAM did attempt to limit that presidential authority. In his appearance before Congress, NAM counsel James Emery expressed support for the idea of reciprocal trade agreements negotiated by the president, but requested (1) congressional ratification of treaties, (2) mechanisms by which industries could make their case during negotiations, and (3) a limited term for the act.[67] Congress amended the bill to

64. Haggard, "The Institutional Foundations of Hegemony," 110–11. For a nice primer on MFN status, see Justin D. Doenecke and Michael R. Adamson, "Most-Favored-Nation Principle," at *American Foreign Relations*, n.d., http://www.americanforeignrelations.com/E-N/Most-Favored-Nation-Principle.html. The unconditional MFN was very controversial and would later become a point of contention within NAM, but initially it was not.

65. Franklin Roosevelt, "Message to Congress Requesting Authority Regarding Foreign Trade," March 2, 1934, http://www.presidency.ucsb.edu/ws/index.php?pid=14817&st=commercial+agreement&st1=.

66. "Chronological Documentation of NAM Positions on the Tariff and Reciprocity Agreements since 1895," p. 8, series 1, box 105, NAMR.

67. Woods, "Capitalist Class Relations, the State, and New Deal Foreign Trade Policy," 411–12; see also "Industry Backs Tariff Plan, but Points Out Peril," *Chicago Daily Tribune*, March 14, 1924, p. 5.

meet the spirit of these requests. It made the RTAA renewable every three years, provided a commission to hear industrialists' concerns, and required congressional approval for rate reductions of more than 50 percent.[68] With these amendments, Congress got the approval as well of the US Chamber of Commerce and other industry groups, and it passed the RTAA on June 12, 1934.

As noted, NAM's leadership at this time was dominated by the "Brass Hats," executives from large and, in many cases, multinational corporations. NAM presidents in the 1930s came from pharmaceuticals, food processing, publishing, steel, and machine tools. The directors, executive committee, and committee heads exhibited the same variety; no one industry seems to have dominated leadership structures, but it is worth noting the presence on the board of directors of multinational companies like IBM, Colgate-Palmolive, Eastman-Kodak, General Foods, and General Mills.[69] The loudest, most conservative voices in NAM, however, came from the steel and chemical industries, two of the most nationalist, protectionist industries. Although never president, Lammot du Pont (DuPont) and Edgar Queeny (Monsanto) were regulars on the executive committee throughout the 1930s. The Tariff Committee chair, H. L. Derby, was the head of two large chemical companies, American Cyanamid Company and Kalbfleisch Corporation. The Tariff Committee over which Derby presided included representatives from smaller, nationalist companies in the textile, machine tool, and paper industries, but also large multinationals like Armstrong Cork, Union Carbide, Allis-Chalmers, and Pillsbury. When it came to representing NAM in Congress, NAM preferred to send its longtime counsel, staff member James Emery, who reconciled the protectionist interests of the Tariff Committee with the organization's commitment to trade expansion. Just as the Roosevelt administration worked to reconcile the interests of the internationalist and nationalist industries in the RTAA, so too did NAM leadership perform the same task within NAM, thereby preserving the veneer of unity that allowed the organization to "represent industry" in the halls of Congress.

Twenty-nine RTAA treaties were made between 1934 and 1945, reducing the US tariff by nearly three-quarters. By 1939, US exports had risen by more than $1 billion.[70] Some see the RTAA as the beginning of the globalization of American trade policy, and thus as a victory for "free trade,"

68. Woods, "Capitalist Class Relations, the State, and New Deal Foreign Trade Policy," 413.

69. NAM annual reports, which list the directors, are available in the Hagley Library and Research Center.

70. LaFeber, *The American Age*, 375.

despite the qualifications.[71] Others, however, suggest that its impact was minimal, pointing out that most of the reciprocal trade agreements that the United States made were with small countries and that while tariff rates dropped from 53.6 percent in 1933 to 25.5 percent in 1945, this was still about what they had been before Smoot-Hawley. Stephen Haggard says that the RTAA ushered in, not "free trade," but rather a compromise with it.[72] Both perspectives are evident in NAM's support for a heavily circumscribed RTAA.

The story does not, however, end there. The RTAA came up every three years for renewal, which gave the Tariff Committee plenty of opportunities to criticize it. While the MFN clause provoked little ire in the first round, it became the focus of NAM discontent in 1937, when the Tariff Committee adopted a resolution stating that unconditional MFN was "inconsistent with the theory of reciprocal tariffs."[73] Here was the slippery slope. Unconditional MFN extended the benefits of bilateral trade deals to other nations without getting anything in return. Rather than calling for the removal of unconditional MFN, however, the resolution demanded only that the commission consult with affected groups in industry, labor, and agriculture. This did not stop John Hooper of the American Machine and Foundry Company of Brooklyn, and a member of the NAM Tariff Committee, from requesting its exclusion when he testified before the Senate Ways and Means Committee about the RTAA's extension.[74] A 1938 Tariff Committee study of the effects of the new agreements with Britain, Canada, and a slew of Latin American countries found that the unconditional MFN clause "cannot be generally adopted to advantage."[75] Full of facts and figures, the study contained no clear policy directives, which was typical of NAM publications on the tariff. Newspaper reports necessarily reflected NAM's ambivalence on the issue. Reporters recognized NAM criticism of the RTAA but were unclear about what it meant, since the organization continued to support the RTAA. It was hard to find the punch line in NAM statements, which were deliberately

71. See Chorev, *Remaking US Trade Policy*; LaFeber, *The American Age*; Butler, *Cautious Visionary*.

72. Haggard, "The Institutional Foundations of Hegemony," 92, 101; Claude Schwob, "Did the Reciprocal Trade Agreements Act of 1934 Initiate a Revolution in American Trade Policy?" *Historical Social Research (Historische Sozialforschung)* 34, no. 4 (2009): 377–89.

73. NAM, of NAM Positions on the Tariff and Reciprocity Agreements since 1895," p. 9, series 1, box 105, NAMR.

74. "Urge Senate Pass on Treaty Agreement," *New York Times*, January 26, 1937, p. 6.

75. "Tariff Committee Report," December 1938, series 1, box 105, NAMR.

vague.[76] Despite the Tariff Committee's dissatisfaction with the RTAA, there was no criticism of it in NAM's 1938 platform. The issue continued to be contentious within the organization well into the postwar era, but the forces favoring international trade expansion generally prevailed.

THE EXPORT-IMPORT BANK

Another way to deal with the trade problem was for the US government to supply credit to foreign companies so that they could purchase American exports. This was the purpose of the Export-Import Bank, established by executive order in February 1934.[77] Roosevelt argued that the bank was necessary to implement the provisions of the National Industrial Recovery Act, the Reconstruction Finance Corporation Act, and the Bank Conservation Act, all of which had been passed by Congress. Although the new bank facilitated these particular New Deal programs, it also met the demands of exporting capitalists, who had long argued that because other governments made credit available to foreign companies to buy their exports, US companies were at a comparative disadvantage in the international marketplace.[78] NAM itself had made this argument in the past, although the main lobbyist for the bank was the National Foreign Trade Council (NFTC).

NAM was not publicly involved in the creation of the bank. It did, however, recommend the original plan for such a bank to the State Department. By the 1930s, NAM had abandoned most of its earlier "hands-on" exporting work, such as translation, letters of introduction, and shipping, in part because the US Commerce Department was finally addressing these needs. But it remained active in networking with foreign trade organizations, such as the American-Russian Chamber of Commerce and the Soviet trade agency AMTORG (see chapter 2).[79] Roosevelt's recognition of the Soviet Union in 1933 was good news for those seeking to do business with the Soviets, but obstacles remained: the question of trading with a noncapitalist nation, the repayment of a pre-Revolution American loan, and the Soviet

76. See, for instance, "Producers Favor Bi-Lateral Pacts," *New York Times*, October 23, 1938, p. 65.

77. Franklin D. Roosevelt, "Executive Order 6581 Creating the Export-Import Bank of Washington," February 2, 1934, *The American Presidency Project*, https://www.presidency.ucsb.edu/node/208209.

78. Richard Feinberg, *Subsidizing Success: The Export-Import Bank in the US Economy* (New York: Cambridge University Press, 1982), 2–16.

79. Siegel, *Loans and Legitimacy*, 81–101.

Union's lack of dollars. The idea of the Export-Import Bank was originally developed to help with these issues and establish trade with the Soviets.[80]

Robert F. Kelley, the chief of the State Department's Division of Eastern European Affairs, was charged with instituting the new bank. In February 1934, NAM general secretary Noel Sargent sent Kelley recommendations, developed jointly by NAM and the American-Russian Chamber of Commerce, for "dealing with American exports to Russia and imports from that country."[81] Several "plans" were presented, the variations of which concerned how best to get US government loans to "Russia," where, they stressed, there was "one customer exclusively, viz. The Russian Government"—by which they meant Joseph Stalin. Among the plans considered were a special committee, a government-owned and -operated bank, or a network of privately owned banks. Although the unique situation of "Russia," with its lack of private companies, was the alleged reason for endorsing a government-owned bank, the report said that its recommendations could be used "in the operation of all export and import business," signaling its approval of government loans to foreign companies.[82]

This is an extraordinary document. It suggests that NAM staff had no principled objection to doing business with a communist dictator, nor indeed to government-owned and -operated banks. True, Sargent could not bring himself to call the Soviet Union by its real name, but he clearly had no problem with finding a mechanism that would allow the United States to compete with other Europeans for Soviet business. I point this out not to reveal NAM's hypocrisy, but rather to suggest, again, its bifurcated nature. NAM directors and members were industrialists who believed fervently in free enterprise and individualism. The staff seemed to have a more practical, savvy, and capitalistic business sense, especially when it came to globalization, which belied NAM's message of parochial free enterprise. This did not escape the notice of the Executive Committee or the Tariff Committee, which periodically criticized the International Department for its "service agency" work. In September 1939, the Executive Committee stated: "While the NAM is interested in public policies which affect the conduct of foreign trade, it is not its proper function to act as a service agency for its members

80. Michael Cassella-Blackburn, *The Donkey, the Carrot, and the Club: William C. Bullitt and Soviet-American Relations, 1917–1948* (Westport, CT: Praeger, 2004), 120–26. A second bank was established for Cuba, and Congress combined the two banks in 1936.

81. Noel Sargent to Robert Kelley, February 8, 1934, folder 7, box 3, Robert F. Kelley Papers, Georgetown University, Washington, DC.

82. "Russian Business—Recommendations," attached to ibid.

directly interested in either export or import trade with foreign countries."[83] This was probably a good policy in terms of conflict-of-interest concerns— and it made no specific reference to the Russian business or the International Department. But this complaint, which is about internationalists' activism, would come up again in the Cold War era, pitting those interested in using the government's power and money to forge trade connections against traditional conservatives who saw this as an expansion of government control (see chapter 7).

———

The most conservative NAM leaders loathed the New Deal and all that it signified. It mattered little to them that New Deal policies furthered NAM's ongoing aims in rationalizing industry, long-term economic planning, and international trade. The empowerment of an independent labor movement was enough to negate whatever benefits manufacturing would see from the new regime. But others in the organization were more ambivalent; particularly among the international and industrial relations staff, which had gradually grown over the decade, who saw real opportunities in some of the New Deal policies. Unfortunately, historians have heard only the loudest voices and have continued to view NAM as the voice of the reactionary right—a perspective that has obscured NAM's success in shaping the global future.

83. Executive Committee meeting minutes, September 28, 1939, series 13, box 250, NAMR.

PART II

Dominance, 1940–1980

The Second World War ended the Depression and showed what feats could be accomplished when industry, government, and labor cooperated. After the war, a brief struggle between these three entities over what the postwar world would look like led to a series of compromises, one of which was the Taft-Hartley Act concerning labor relations. Crafted by more moderate elements of NAM, the Taft-Hartley Act was seen as a defeat for labor and liberals, which it was. But it provided the legal framework for a consensus of sorts, in which industry agreed to accept the legal existence of unions, per the Wagner Act, and unions agreed to keep their demands within the rules laid out in Taft-Hartley. Both sides still mobilized against the other, but they did so politically and under agreed-upon rules, and each grew strong under this arrangement. The memberships of both NAM (in absolute numbers) and labor (as a percentage of the private sector workforce) peaked in the 1950s.

Industry also became government's partner in mapping out a more integrated international economy through the United Nations, the Bretton Woods Agreement, which created the International Monetary Fund and World Bank, and a steady lowering of US tariffs. The Cold War impeded full international cooperation, but spurred US efforts to share (or impose) the benefits of capitalism with the so-called developing world.

Both developments contributed to the "liberal consensus," which marked an era when both political parties laid to rest "rugged individualism" and endorsed a highly progressive tax system, public spending, social security, government-backed mortgages, civil rights, international involvement, and collective bargaining as normal features of modern industrial democracy.

Symbolic of this consensus was the large, multidivisional, professionally managed manufacturing corporation, governed by a socially responsible stakeholder ethos that attempted to reconcile and respect the interests of its various stakeholders—employees, customers, and communities as well as shareholders. NAM conservatives resisted this consensus in the 1950s, but were ousted in 1961, a transformation that paved the way for a "new" NAM to deal with the social upheavals of the 1960s, including civil rights.

6

The Road to Taft-Hartley

Like most Americans, NAM opposed US involvement in the European war between 1939 and 1941, issuing a clear statement of "industry's hatred of war."[1] Its leaders wanted to refute charges that manufacturers were war-profiteering "merchants of death," and like many Republicans, they were wary of giving President Roosevelt war powers. When war came, however, NAM got on board, pledging to Roosevelt: "Industry will build two battleships for every one that sinks, it will match every enemy bomb with a dozen. It will blacken the skies with planes to replace the ones shot down."[2]

The Second World War was just about the best thing that could have happened to American industry, which retrieved its golden crown with amped-up patriotism and miraculous feats of production. But would NAM capitalize on industry's redemption? Would it work with government for a prosperous postwar economy? Or would it return to being the negative, defensive organization it had been in the wake of the New Deal? Could it trim labor's sails without triggering memories of its reactionary past? Could it make peace with collective bargaining? Could it play well with others? Those were the questions that occupied many a NAM memo at this time and guided its most stunning achievement, the Taft-Hartley Act of 1947. Condemned by labor, liberals, and most historians, the Taft-Hartley Act curbed union gains and allegedly marked a turn to the right. But it also represented

---

1. *NAM Annual Report*, 1939, p. 6.
2. Quoted in "The Purposes and Operations of the National Association of Manufacturers . . . ," statement by Noel Sargent, May 6, 1944, series 1, box 42, NAMR.

NAM's acceptance of collective bargaining with industrywide unions. It was a peace of sorts, a settlement, in NAM's long-running war against big unions.

It was NAM "moderates" who advocated for what became the Taft-Hartley Act, not the conservative hardliners. Taft-Hartley required business to accept the legitimacy of unions and collective bargaining. In exchange, the act put limitations on unions' right to strike, while expanding management's right to manage.[3] Hard-line conservatives rejected this compromise, while NAM's more moderate and pragmatic conservatives were able to unite all of the major business groups around it, a rare moment of real leadership for NAM at a time when the direction of the US economy was up for grabs.

The Moderating Impact of Public Relations

NAM had already begun to moderate its official attitude toward the end of the 1930s in response to the fallout from the La Follette Committee, which had investigated NAM's anti-union activity. It was still conservative, of course, but in a less shrill and confrontational way. Ironically, it was the public relations professionals whom conservatives brought in to fight the New Deal who became the foremost voices of moderation. Public relations exec Walter Weisenberger had been hired to "get business's story out" to the public. But as executive vice president, he also sought to make NAM a more effective organization, which meant curbing its ideological excesses. Weisenberger believed that in order to effectively represent manufacturers' interests NAM had to accept the New Deal and the union shop as political realities and work within the new system to win gains for management, which would be couched in an appeal to the general public interest, not ideological principle. Polls indicated that Americans were not interested in abstractions like "free enterprise" and "individual competition," but rather wanted good jobs and consumer goods. NAM needed to emphasize how industry improved peoples' lives, not how it preserved freedom.[4]

---

3. For a full, but manageable, discussion of the Taft-Hartley Act, see Harris, *The Right to Manage*, 118–27. See also Christopher Tomlins, *The State and the Unions: Labor Relations, Law, and the Organized Labor Movement in America* (New York: Cambridge University Press, 1985), chap. 8; R. Alton Lee, *Truman and Taft-Hartley: A Question of Mandate* (Lexington: University of Kentucky, 1966); Elizabeth Fones-Wolf, *Selling Free Enterprise: The Business Assault on Labor and Liberalism, 1945–1960* (Urbana: University of Illinois Press, 1994), 42–48.

4. Andrew Workman, "Manufacturing Power: The Organizational Revival of the National Association of Manufacturers, 1941–45," *Business History Review* 72, no. 2 (Summer 1998): 279–317, 292.

Accordingly, Weisenberger tried to re-spin NAM's public image: instead of being only *against* things (such as government control, or the closed shop), NAM would take positive positions *for* things (such as lower prices, or employment stabilization). As part of this reform, Weisenberger hoped to refocus public relations efforts solely on NAM's reputation as a public-oriented business group and curtail what he saw as the diffuse defense of American capitalism.[5] He beefed up NAM's professional staff, which carried out its many programs and conducted research for committees that came up with official policies. Between 1933 and 1945, an increase in staff from under 30 to 450 brought in a slew of educated administrative types, who were typically less ideologically conservative than the hard-line industrialists who sat on the board.[6]

These changes created tension in the organization, especially between the staff and more conservative members of the board of directors. The executive staff, led by Weisenberger and Noel Sargent, often represented NAM's views before Congress or in press statements. Keenly aware of tone and nuance, they sometimes aggravated more conservative NAM leaders, who thought that they were watering down the official NAM position. Weisenberger and his colleagues would have called it "spin." They were conveying the position, but in a way that was more appealing to the general public. But hard-line conservatives were suspicious. The NAM Executive Committee passed a resolution in 1941 declaring that "officers of the Association have no power to later modify" statements adopted by the board of directors: "When Association officers appear before legislative committees or other public bodies their prepared statements naturally include and will be based upon positions that have been approved by the Association, and cannot in the nature of things be subject to review and alteration by either the Public Relations Department [staff members] or the Public Relations Committee [other NAM members]."[7] These resolutions indicate that the majority of the Executive Committee believed that officers were watering down NAM positions—and that the PR advocates were abetting them. Similarly, in 1943, the board of directors specifically requested that the staff "exercise care" when representing NAM's position on reciprocal trade agreements to "fully

---

5. Ibid., 292.

6. Ibid., 290, 288. The 450 figure comes from NAM general secretary Noel Sargent, in response to an inquiry about the NAM staff. See Sargent to H. Whycliffe Rose, January 17, 1945, series I, box 42, "Correspondence 1945" file, NAMR.

7. Executive Committee meeting minutes, April 21, 1941, p. 3, series 13, box 250, NAMR.

conform to the position taken by the Board."[8] Part of the board's concern was the correct articulation of NAM's evasive positions on the tariff, but it was also true that staff researchers were more committed to international trade and tariff reduction than many board members. Years later, hard-line conservative William Grede specifically attacked "public relations" for subverting the conservative agenda.[9] But at this time, in the 1940s, both NAM moderates and conservatives had such a deep reverence for "public relations" as a panacea that could solve all their problems that they gave Weisenberger a wide berth.

In 1941, NAM conservatives inadvertently bolstered Weisenberger's mission when they derailed any chance that NAM would influence the structure of government-industry cooperation during the war by refusing to participate on any industry-labor panel that did not guarantee an open shop. President Roosevelt called their bluff, creating the National War Labor Board (NWLB) with more cooperative industrial representatives, leaving NAM leaders stewing when it codified a "maintenance of membership" policy that essentially upheld the union shop in wartime plants. NAM tried to fight it, but came off as unpatriotic and uncooperative. Realizing they had been beat, many conservatives, such as NAM president and Thompson Industries head Frederick Crawford, began to cooperate with the NWLB and were increasingly open to Weisenberger's efforts to lessen the influence of ultraconservatives on NAM policy.[10]

Another factor pushing NAM leaders to be more savvy in their public relations were *corporate liberals*, those self-styled moderate industrialists from large, capital-intensive corporations who embraced certain aspects of the New Deal order and whose increasing numbers and stature on the Committee for Economic Development (CED) and Business Advisory Council (BAC) threatened to outmaneuver the more conservative, labor-intensive NAM industries in representing business interests to the public.[11] In 1942,

8. Noel Sargent to Walter Weisenberger, February 6, 1947, series 1, box 105, "Reciprocal Trade Positions" file, NAMR.

9. See William Grede to Clark C. Thompson, September 24, 1953, box 25, folder 6, William J. Grede Papers (hereafter WJGP), 1909–1979, MSS 341, Wisconsin State Historical Society, Madison, WI, as well as other correspondence found in box 24, folder 1, that also indicates disgust at staff departments.

10. Workman, "Manufacturing Power," 289. NAM conservatives acknowledged bitterly the reality of government control for the duration. See, for example, Bruno Neumann to Walter Weisenberger, January 31, 1942, series 1, box 42, NAMR.

11. Workman, "Manufacturing Power," 283. On the rivalry between corporate liberals and business conservatives, see McQuaid, *Uneasy Partners*, 19–35.

one of their ilk, Seattle businessman Eric Johnston, became president of the US Chamber of Commerce. Despite their rivalry, the Chamber and NAM had been allies in opposing the New Deal. Now, here was the new head of the Chamber of Commerce mending fences with the White House and getting a lot of good press in the process.[12] Although such isolation caused ultraconservatives to dig in more deeply (in a "go down fighting" kind of vein), other NAM conservatives worried about NAM's further marginalization, which made them more amenable to Weisenberger's style of pragmatic moderation.

In 1945, Johnston began planning a postwar labor-management conference. At first it seemed as though NAM would again be left in the dust. Johnston had gone ahead and forged an agreement with the AFL's William Green and the CIO's Phillip Murray, leaving NAM's new president, Ira Mosher, with the awkward choice of acquiescing to corporate liberals or cranky nonparticipation. Determined not to replay the disastrous 1941 conference (which had resulted in the NWLB), Mosher bided his time.[13] Luckily (and predictably), the AFL and CIO disagreed with each other and pulled out of Johnston's agreement.[14] The path was thus cleared for NAM to propose a new program for industry-labor cooperation that emphasized the "positive" themes of economic security, steady wages, and labor peace, but in line with NAM values.[15]

By the time President Truman got around to proposing an official labor-management conference in August 1945, NAM had a well-researched labor policy program all ready to go. Working with the Industrial Relations Committee, Mosher took a leadership role in determining the conference's planning and agenda, reaching out to the Chamber of Commerce before the conference to form a united business front in the face of government officials and labor representatives. Under Mosher's leadership, industry reps agreed upon "a constructive program for the public welfare," backed up by

12. Jack Alexander, "Young Man in a Snakeskin Belt," *Saturday Evening Post*, August 28, 1945, 10–11; "A New C of C," *Business Week*, August 8, 1942, 19–20; Workman, "Manufacturing Power," 294.

13. See "Report on the President's 1945 Labor-Management Conference," January 1946, series VII, box 143, NAMR. The NAM board voted not to sign Johnston's charter, but were willing to have Mosher discuss a different labor-management plan with Johnston and the unions. See Memorandum to Mr. Mosher, et al., May 24, 1945, "Board of Directors Meetings," series 13, box 236, NAMR.

14. Workman, "Manufacturing Power," 293–99; see also Harris, *The Right to Manage*, 106–17.

15. See Committee on Labor Management Relations meeting minutes, June 13, 1945, series 13, box 236, NAMR.

opinion polls and best practices, covering "every item listed on the agenda of the meeting."[16] During the conference, NAM staff provided business reps with regularly updated position papers, press releases, and agreed-upon talking points backed up by data, not NAM's past ideological cant. Mosher avoided any kind of specific policy arrangements and instead focused on general areas of consensus for a future voluntary agreement between labor and management.

Others—the press, liberals, Democrats—saw the conference as a bit of a bust because no agreement was reached. But an actual labor-management agreement was never the point for Mosher. The aim was avoiding such an agreement without appearing to obstruct, and Mosher accomplished that perfectly by being prepared, avoiding ideological outbursts, and seeking cooperation with business rivals. This was an important victory for those in NAM who sought to adopt a more pragmatic public relations approach to attaining conservative ends.

The American Individual Enterprise System

In 1940, the NAM board appointed members to an Economic Principles Commission to study the "free enterprise system." Made up of business executives and academic economists (including Ludwig von Mises), the commission sought to objectively analyze "the philosophy, operations, and achievements of the American economic system."[17] Published in 1946 as a two-volume book, *The American Individual Enterprise System* was intended to lend legitimacy to NAM's conservative economic ideas and stave off whatever economic alternatives might emerge from wartime turmoil. It also laid the groundwork for NAM's internal acceptance of an amended Wagner Act, as opposed to the outright repeal advocated by NAM ultraconservatives.

Reviewers of the book were tepid in their responses, wryly noting its ringing defense of "free enterprise," its reliance on pre-1929 studies, and its incoherent organizational scheme. Keynesian James Tobin called the book "an apologia for the status quo ante 1933, in the course of which extreme opinions on controversial issues masquerade as economic principles." Its relentless anti-statism, noted Tobin, was "most evident in their attack on the use of fiscal policy as an anti-cyclical device. Judging from the energy

16. "Report on the President's 1945 Labor-Management Conference," p. 5, January 1946, series VII, box 143, NAMR.

17. NAM Economic Principles Commission, *The American Individual Enterprise System: Its Nature, Evolution, and Future* (New York: McGraw-Hill, 1946), ix.

the authors devote to this campaign, Keynes and Hansen, rather than Marx and Hitler, are the real enemies of free enterprise."[18] The reviewers were mostly right. The commission's book was a clunky defense of American "free enterprise" and lacked the sharp nuances of Schumpeter's *Capitalism, Socialism, and Democracy* (1942) or Hayek's *Road to Serfdom* (1944), both of which also defended capitalism in the face of rising socialism.

Despite its conservative agenda, however, parts of *The American Individual Enterprise System* sound like concessions to modern liberalism and can be seen as an attempt to persuade NAM members that *some* government regulation was necessary, even in America. That is, there were many ways in which it departed from, or softened, the traditional ideological laissez-faire conservatism held by many of the older, more conservative NAM members. There was, for instance, the ridiculous title, which never really caught on as a descriptor for what was more commonly known in these circles as the American free enterprise system. In explaining why they had not used such standard terms as "free enterprise" or "private enterprise," the book's authors argued that those phrases failed to convey the way modern industry had changed American capitalism. American enterprise was not completely "free." Some rules and regulations, the authors argued, were necessary to the smooth running of industrial capitalism.[19] Nor was the American economy entirely private. There was public spending, such as on roads, dams, and education, that benefited both society and the economy. Although capitalism was rooted in competition, there were many noncompetitive aspects to the modern economy.[20] But behind those rules and regulations, behind public spending, behind the noncompetitive agreements, there were private individuals who formulated those rules and policies "through cooperation in trade associations" and "through their freely selected governmental representatives."[21] Despite the emphasis on *individualism*, this sounds a lot like what would become known as *liberal pluralism*—the idea that a neutral administrative state reconciled the interests of competing groups and organized voters.[22]

18. James Tobin, review of *The American Individual Enterprise System*, *Review of Economics and Statistics* 30, no. 1 (February 1948): 77–79.

19. NAM Economic Principles Commission, *The American Individual Enterprise System* (hereafter *AIES*), 2–3, 11.

20. Ibid., 3.

21. Ibid., 2–3.

22. Expressions of liberal pluralism include David B. Truman, *The Governmental Process: Political Interests and Public Opinion* (New York: Alfred A. Knopf, 1963); V. O. Key Jr. *Politics, Parties, and Pressure Groups* (New York: Thomas Crowell Co., 1964), Robert Dahl, *Who Governs?*

While the authors of this effort rejected New Dealers' interest in national planning or a hybrid "third way" between socialism and democracy, they seemed to accept public spending and federal regulations as necessary to the modern industrial enterprise—and not antithetical to individualism. Noting that "laissez-faire" never meant "anarchy," the authors admitted that government legislation had always shaped the economy: what was the tariff but an "artificial stimulus" to US industry?[23] Reviewing such legislation as the Sherman Antitrust Act (1890) and the Food and Drug Act (1906), the authors insisted—not unlike New Dealers—that the goal of government regulations historically was not curtailment of individual freedom: "This has been shown by the fact that when the public has found that there was needless regulation it has reversed the action and repealed the statute. In other words, the public has not regarded regulation as establishing a principle of government management of private enterprise." Similarly, public spending on roads, schools, and even utilities had been "in the hope that such centralized direction and control would confer greater benefits than were being obtained under private ownership." These projects had been attempts to "increase the nonmonetary income of the American public, not attempts to undermine the driving motivation that comes from the system of individual enterprise."[24] This disquisition hearkened back to the NAM of the Progressive Era, when it was a champion of government regulation that expanded trade and rationalized industry.

This book also laid out the blueprint for what would become the Taft-Hartley Act. The authors acknowledged a need for something like the Wagner Act to protect employees' right to organize. They explained that the Wagner Act attempted to do that by prohibiting employers from interfering with that right and by creating procedures for determining who represented employees in collective bargaining. The authors seemed okay with all of this (in a way that NAM leaders like Tom Girdler and William Grede were definitely not). Their quibble was that, in practice, with procedures put in place by the National Labor Relations Board, the process became grossly unfair to employers. Employers, for instance, were not allowed to prevent employees from joining unions, but unions were allowed to coerce workers to join unions (the union, or closed, shop). The NLRB was not an objective

Democracy and Power in an American City (New Haven, CT: Yale University Press, 1961); Harold D. Lasswell, *Politics: Who Gets What, When, How* (New York: McGraw-Hill, 1936).

23. *AIES*, 28–29.

24. All quoted material from ibid., 11.

interlocutor of labor relations, according to the authors, but rather labor's ally, serving as investigator, prosecutor, jury, and judge against employers. The Wagner Act constrained the activities of employers, but not those of unions.[25]

To remedy this situation and to restore economic efficiency to the process, the book's authors put forth ten amendments to the Wagner Act, including a free speech provision for both employers and employees, a prohibition of employee coercion from any source, a separation of the various functions of the NLRB, and a clear definition of unions' legal responsibilities.[26] The implicit acceptance of the Wagner Act by a NAM-sponsored group of businessmen and economists signaled to NAM members the future direction of NAM policy: it was firmly in the camp of amending the Wagner Act, not repealing it.

Reconversion: Curbing the New Deal at Home

While pragmatic conservatives were pushing more moderate positions within NAM, outside the organization they were in full attack against the expansion of the New Deal. Wartime unity had quickly given way to an all-out power struggle as various groups—including business, labor, liberals, and farmers—tried to claim their piece of the postwar pie. The year 1946 saw a massive strike wave, congressional contests over price controls and full employment, a new lobby act, and a resurgent conservatism as Republicans won control of both houses of Congress in midterm elections, an apparent repudiation of New Deal liberalism.

STRIKE WAVE

As it did after the last war, labor moved to maintain its wartime gains. Under NWLB guidance, membership in organized labor (now consisting of the AFL, the CIO, and the Railroad Brotherhoods) had grown from less than nine million before the war to almost fifteen million by its end.[27] The NWLB had rationalized union procedures and policies, making unions stronger, more centralized, and more professional.[28] Anticipating a postwar

25. Ibid., 216–17.
26. Ibid., 217.
27. Lee, *Truman and Taft-Hartley*, 4; Harris, *The Right to Manage*, 43.
28. See Harris, *The Right to Manage*, 47–58, for discussion of the ways in which the NWLB shaped union organization.

contraction of jobs and wages, major unions launched a tremendous strike wave in 1945–1946 to press for job security and higher wages while they remained at peak power. Still under government price controls, corporations were unwilling to raise wages until the government ended the controls.[29] At its peak in January and February 1946, over a million workers were involved. While striking workers represented only 14.5 percent of the total labor force (as compared to 20.8 percent in 1919), their actions affected key industries such as coal, steel, railroads, and meat and thus didn't go over well with the president or the public at this time of uncertainty.

Newspapers highlighted union in-fighting and the showy antics of labor "bosses" like John L. Lewis; their sensationalist strike coverage emphasized the deleterious effects on prices and everyday necessities.[30] Conservative groups and the business community likewise blamed the strikes for food shortages and the general economic turmoil of reconversion. NAM geared up its PR machinery to educate the public about the social costs of strikes. In the multimillion-dollar campaign, advertisements appeared in local newspapers around the nation and materials were tailored and distributed to farming communities, women's groups, and religious organizations. NAM's aim was to gain public and thus political support for its attempt to reform the Wagner Act.[31] By June 1946, upwards of 90 percent of the public, according to a Gallup poll, thought that there should be some restrictions on union activities.[32]

Even liberal Democrat Harry Truman was frustrated by labor's tactics. People expected the president to make sure that goods and services like meat, oil, coal, and transportation were available and accessible. But as president, Truman also felt compelled to control inflation, which was why he insisted on continuing price controls, making it difficult, in turn, for employers to raise wages. Labor itself seemed willing to forgo price controls if it meant higher wages.[33] In February 1946, Truman relaxed selected price controls in some industries. This helped resolve strikes in steel, but labor leaders in the railroad and coal industries remained recalcitrant. Frustrated, Truman seized control of the railroads in May 1946, declaring to union heads

---

29. Barton J. Bernstein, "The Truman Administration and the Steel Strike of 1946," *Journal of American History* 52, no. 4 (March 1966): 791–803.

30. Lee, *Truman and Taft-Hartley*, 9–21. For fuller discussions, see Fones-Wolf, *Selling Free Enterprise*, chaps. 1–2; Harris, *The Right to Manage*, chap. 4.

31. Fones-Wolf, *Selling Free Enterprise*, 39–44; Lee, *Truman and Taft-Hartley*, 10–11.

32. Lee, *Truman and Taft-Hartley*, 18.

33. Tomlins, *The State and the Unions*, 255.

that he was not going to let them "tie up the country" and threatening to conscript striking workers into the US Army—a move that even Republican senator Robert Taft opposed.[34] This threat finally brought the unions around, but Truman had not only undermined his relationship to labor but also contributed to undermining labor's cause in the public eye.[35]

All of which is to say, labor was not making any friends in 1946. Congress passed the Case Bill in May 1946, which restricted labor's ability to strike. Truman vetoed it, but it was a sign of things to come.

PRICE CONTROLS AND FULL EMPLOYMENT

Truman's administration consisted of New Deal Keynesians, many of whom sought to build on their wartime achievement of a managed economy. They urged Truman to maintain price controls to allay inflation. They also sought legislation that required the federal government to guarantee full employment.[36] In both cases, their larger goal was economic stabilization. Although neither of these policies was very radical (compared to what Europeans were doing), NAM and most conservatives equated them with rising socialism and "government control." Even corporate liberals, who had gone along with wartime price controls, were keen to end them sooner rather than later.

There was a great deal of confusion within the Truman administration over how quickly wartime controls could be disbanded without shocking the economy into runaway inflation. But Chester Bowles, who headed the Office of Price Administration (OPA), wanted to keep them (and his office) as a matter of postwar policy. While liberals were trying to figure out how much and what kind of Keynesianism the postwar era would require, conservatives acted. Once again, NAM stood ready to lead, uniting the business community and sponsoring yet another public relations campaign, this time against the extension of the OPA and price controls, which required congressional reauthorization in the spring of 1946.[37] Even before the war's end,

34. Quoted in Lee, *Truman and Taft-Hartley*, 35; see also ibid., 37–38. On price controls (discussed later), see Bernstein, "The Truman Administration and the Steel Strike of 1946," 791–92; Andrew H. Bartels, "The Office of Price Administration and the Legacy of the New Deal, 1939–1946," *The Public Historian* 5, no. 3 (Summer 1983): 5–29, 25–26.

35. Lee, *Truman and Taft-Hartley*, 38.

36. See, for instance, Bartels, "The Office of Price Administration and the Legacy of the New Deal," 5–29; Stephen Bailey, *Congress Makes a Law: The Story behind the Employment Act of 1946* (New York: Columbia University Press, 1950), chap. 1.

37. See Barton J. Bernstein, "The Removal of War Production Board Controls on Business," *Business History Review* (Summer 1965); Barton J. Bernstein, "Clash of Interests: The Postwar

Congress had criticized price controls for preventing manufacturers from obtaining reasonable profits and inhibiting the production of some lines of goods.[38] After Truman lifted the lid on wages and prices in the steel industry (in February), small businesses and farmers demanded similar relief and public support for the OPA began to sour. In June, conservative Republicans and Southern Democrats passed a law that renewed but severely weakened the OPA. After Truman vetoed it, price controls lapsed, causing prices to shoot up. Congress passed another bill in late July that Truman was forced to sign, but the weakened OPA was ineffective and eventually disbanded.[39] The battles over price controls that summer gave NAM a platform for its warnings against government intervention.

The full employment bill was a bit trickier because NAM leaders had been expressing support for employment stabilization—in other words, full employment. The precise shape of "full employment," however, was still up for grabs. Liberal Keynesians imagined that full employment required the federal government to guarantee employment *as a right* for all citizens and that this goal could be met, if necessary and after careful study, through government spending and investment. The Committee for Economic Development, the Brookings Institution, and various national planning organizations largely agreed with this assessment, arguing that such a policy would ensure the purchasing power and demand necessary to economic growth.[40] NAM and the Chamber of Commerce agreed that regular employment was a positive goal that encouraged productivity and growth, but predictably, they thought that this should be an industrial goal not a something forced or engineered by the federal government.[41]

The original Full Employment Act of 1945 was introduced in the Senate in January 1945. Careful to avoid offending free enterprisers, the bill declared that it was US policy "to foster free competitive enterprise and the investment of private capital in trade and commerce." But then it also stated that all Americans who were able to and seeking work "had a right to useful, remunerative, regular, and full-time employment," and that it was the responsibility of the federal government to provide "such volume of Federal investment

---

Battle between the Office of Price Administration and the Department of Agriculture," *Agricultural History* 41, no. 1 (January 1967): 45–58; Fones-Wolf, *Selling Free Enterprise*, 34–35.

38. Tomlins, *The State and the Unions*, 255.

39. Bartels, "The Office of Price Administration and the Legacy of the New Deal," 26–27.

40. On the politics of growth, see Lizabeth Cohen, *A Consumers' Republic: The Politics of Mass Consumption in Postwar America* (New York: Vintage, 2008).

41. Bailey, *Congress Makes a Law*, 3–36.

and expenditure as may be needed to assure continuing full employment," if private investment proved inadequate to the task.[42] As the bill made its way through Congress in the latter half of 1945, it faced opposition not only from NAM, the Chamber, and other trade associations but also from the American Farm Bureau Federation and conservative groups like the Committee for Constitutional Government. Although the efforts of these organizations were not coordinated, there was agreement among them that the bill gave unprecedented power to the federal government, undermined private initiative and business confidence, and threatened individual freedom. They were skeptical of the government's ability to forecast economic conditions, let alone its capacity to devise a feasible national employment plan.

NAM's campaign against the original full employment bill reflected both its new cooperative pragmatism and its familiar conservative ideology. Testifying before the Senate in August 1945, NAM president Ira Mosher recited a statement, prepared by NAM's research staff, that endorsed the goal of full employment, praised the bill's sponsors for their openness to alternative points of view, raised some concerns about the current bill, and offered NAM's own plan for achieving full employment, called "A Program for Permanent Prosperity." NAM's plan included tax reform to free up private money for investment, a government committee to study money and credit, stricter enforcement of antitrust laws, curbs against labor, and a progressive but gradual reduction in tariffs.[43] Under questioning, Mosher stated his personal opposition to what he regarded as a government spending bill that would sap the confidence of business.[44] As per usual, NAM sponsored a well-orchestrated public education campaign against the bill that reflected the views of conservatives, farm groups, and indeed many in Congress. The campaign didn't attack the concept of full employment, but rather the specific "big government" aspects of the bill, and crucially, it offered an alternative solution. This was not the surly, hunkered-down, tone-deaf NAM of the 1930s, but rather a NAM on board with modern realities, a NAM willing to work with liberals and labor to find solutions.[45] Its new attitude was on display at its annual meeting in December 1945, which

42. Quoted in ibid., 243–44.

43. Recounted in ibid., 133–34. For details on NAM's plan, see "Full Employment Backed by Mosher," *New York Times*, December 6, 1945, p. 1.

44. Bailey, *Congress Makes a Law*, 134.

45. At least when it stayed on message. NAM was still producing a variety of conservative tracts, as described in ibid., 134–35, but there was a more careful and conciliatory tone coming from NAM president Mosher and his successors, Robert Wason (1946) and Earl Bunting (1947).

featured commerce secretary and New Dealer Henry Wallace as the opening speaker. The meeting also featured an official from the US Steel Workers of America (CIO), as well as President Truman's message of thanks to American manufacturers.[46] A PR stunt? No doubt, but one that demanded key concessions to the liberal state.

The full employment bill was recrafted in conference committee in January 1946. The reworked bill removed any statement of employment as an individual right, as well as specifications for when the government would be required to "prime the pump" to alleviate projected recession. A product of compromise, the reworked bill passed both houses and was signed by Truman in February as the Employment Act of 1946. Liberals at the time and historians since have seen the resulting bill as "toothless" and so weakened as to be irrelevant.[47] But the Employment Bill of 1946 did endorse the idea that the federal government had a responsibility to maintain "maximum employment, production, and purchasing power." Plus it created—per the original bill—a Council of Economic Advisers to the President, which would advise the president on how the government might best fulfill that responsibility, as well as a requirement that the president transmit to Congress crucial economic information and recommendations based on his consultations with the council. In the decades to come, the Council of Economic Advisers would play an important role in formulating US economic policy with an eye to avoiding recession and stabilizing employment. The council was key, for instance, in formulating the Federal Aid Highway Act of 1956 as something akin to a jobs program under President Eisenhower.[48] During the 1960s and 1970s, it was led by Keynesians. So the Employment Act of 1946 was not a total policy defeat for liberals, although it was a political defeat at the time.

It is difficult to measure the impact, if any, of NAM campaigns against strikes, price controls, and full employment legislation on public opinion,

46. See "Full Employment Backed by Mosher," *New York Times*, December 6, 1945, p. 1.

47. Bailey's excellent book, *Congress Makes a Law*, set the tone. A political scientist and liberal who admittedly favored the bill in its original Keynesian form, Bailey is fair in his presentation of events but puts forth what has become the dominant interpretation—that the Employment Act was a severely weakened bill with "no teeth" and served as a lesson in how uninformed pressure groups and an antiquated process shaped economic policy in the mid-twentieth century. Bailey would later testify before Congress on NAM's possibly illegal lobbying tactics. See Karl Schriftgiesser, *The Lobbyists: The Art and Business of Influencing Lawmakers* (Boston: Little, Brown, 1951), 166–67.

48. See Stephen E. Ambrose, *Eisenhower*, vol. 2 (New York: Simon & Schuster, 1984), 76, 159; Saul Engelbourg, "The Council of Economic Advisers and the Recession of 1953–1954," *Business History Review* 54 (1980): 192–214.

or for that matter on lawmakers. NAM's apparent success in these campaigns, compared to its failures with regard to the New Deal, might have been a reflection of the public mood rather than a manipulation of it.[49] Still, many saw NAM's hand behind the liberal defeats. In a front-page editorial addressed to NAM, the *Philadelphia Record* wrote: "Gentleman, you win. Your campaign to kill the OPA has succeeded. Your association is more responsible than any other organization for ending price control."[50] Contemporary liberal accounts of these events, from *The New Republic* to books such as Stephen Bailey's *Congress Makes a Law* and Karl Schriftgiesser's *The Lobbyists*, likewise credited, or charged, NAM with orchestrating public opinion, emphasizing not just the tremendous resources the organization applied to the task but also the overlapping membership networks of NAM leaders, large corporations, and ultraconservative groups.[51] Concern about the influence of "big business" and money on politics led to the Lobby Act of 1946.

The Lobby Act

Senator Robert La Follette would not let up on NAM. In May 1946, La Follette sponsored an act to regulate the role of lobbyists in politics. It was directed at all the "peddlers of influence" opposing Truman's Fair Deal—the American Medical Association (AMA), the real estate lobby, "the power lobby," and big business. But as in previous attempts to stem lobbying (see chapter 3), NAM's well-financed and highly publicized campaigns seemed to make it a specific target.

In 1945, Congress had formed a committee to investigate the possible reorganization of Congress. It chose as its chair Senator Robert La Follette Jr., a progressive Republican fresh off his investigation of labor rights violations (see chapter 5). Lobbying per se had not been an original focus of the La Follette–Monroney Committee.[52] But the postwar struggle between different groups trying to protect or expand their interests—and the amounts of money involved in these efforts—shocked lawmakers and citizens alike. Much of the testimony the committee heard focused on the heavy-handed

---

49. This is suggested with regard to labor by "Renovation in NAM," *Fortune*, July 1948, p. 167.

50. "Praise and Attack for Veto in Press," *New York Times*, July 1, 1946, p. 19.

51. Bailey, *Congress Makes a Law*, 132–45; Schriftgiesser, *The Lobbyists*, 79.

52. This account is from Schriftgiesser, *The Lobbyists*, chap. 6; and Belle Zeller, "American Government and Politics: The Federal Regulation of Lobbying Act," *American Political Science Review* 42, no. 2 (April 1948): 239–71.

tactics used by "organized pressure groups." In March 1946, a Democratic congressman from Illinois called for an investigation of "any and all groups which have or are engaged in present propaganda campaigns or lobby to defeat legislative measures," such as price control, veterans' housing, and the like. Republican congresswoman Margaret Chase Smith had likewise called for some kind of regulation.[53]

Lobbying could not be prohibited, of course. Citizens have a constitutionally protected right to petition the government and try to influence its policies. But there was something about the fancy new public relations campaigns, the mass forms of communication, the manipulation of public opinion, and the concentrated power of organized groups—be they on the left or the right—that seemed to blur the line between a congressperson's constituency and something called "public opinion," which could be twisted and spun and even manufactured. As one reporter covering the OPA debate put it, "Congress as a whole does not know just where spontaneity in plea and edict from the public ends and where cold organized lobby takes over."[54] Political scientists and democratic theorists likewise struggled to reconcile modern interest groups with traditional democratic precepts (not unlike their struggle to reconcile the New Deal state with traditional ideas of limited government).[55]

The solution was transparency. The proposed law would in no way restrict groups' ability to contact members of Congress or print materials, but it would require all persons and organizations involved in lobbying Congress to register and disclose their membership and finances. Included was anybody or any organization that directly or indirectly received money or payment, the principal purpose of which was to influence the passage or defeat of congressional legislation.[56] Exempted were people who appeared before Congress in support of or opposition to legislation who were not paid, expert witnesses giving testimony, and, crucially, "organizations formed for other purposes whose efforts to influence legislation are merely incidental to the purposes for which formed."[57] There was a substantial fine for those found in violation of the act.

53. Schriftgiesser, *The Lobbyists*, 79.

54. "Citizens Groups Pound Congress on OPA Issue," *New York Times*, May 5, 1946, p. E7.

55. The answer in both cases was pluralism. See Dahl, *Who Governs?*; and V. O. Key Jr., *Politics, Parties, and Pressure Groups* (New York: Crowell, 1958).

56. For exact language, see Zeller, "American Government and Politics," 243–44.

57. Quoted in ibid., 254.

The Lobby Act was Title III of the larger Legislative Reorganization Act of 1946, which was signed into law by President Truman in August 1946. There was relatively little congressional opposition to it, perhaps because the larger bill contained higher congressional salaries and benefits.[58] NAM was concerned about Title III, which seemed after all very much directed at its activities, but made little effort to oppose it.

At first the big lobbies seemed to comply. In November, papers reported those individuals who filed as business lobbyists, including two Chamber of Commerce reps and NAM's Walter Chamblin.[59] By 1948, there were 818 registered lobbyists. Of these, 128 represented various unions, eighteen utility companies, twelve the sugar industry, nine oil, six wool, six livestock, and three the New York Stock Exchange. Also noteworthy were the thirty-six reps for the Townsend Plan (an old-age pension), fifteen for veterans' associations, and three for the National Council for the Prevention of War. These figures are from Ruth Finney's reporting in *American Mercury*, which also noted wryly the "lone representative of the once-powerful Anti-Saloon League."[60]

Finney's roll call highlighted the ineffectiveness of the law. The information given—mainly individual salaries—gave no indication of how much money was actually being spent. Moreover, no one from the real estate lobby had registered, and only a few individuals from the Chamber or NAM, universally seen as the "big lobbies," had registered. Even the CIO and AFL were balking, claiming, like NAM and the Chamber, that they were exempt from the law because their "principal purpose or activity"—the law's words—was not lobbying, but rather service to their members, and that a relatively small portion of their income went to influencing Congress.[61] But when the Justice Department clamped down, they all grudgingly registered. NAM filed under protest, claiming that the $146,186 it had spent on legislative activities

58. "Stream-lined Set-up Asked for Congress," *New York Herald Tribune*, March 5, 1946, p. 1.

59. "Files as Business Lobbyists," *New York Times*, November 21, 1946. Chamblin was the head of the Government Relations Committee. Three other NAM members registered as well; see Schriftgiesser, *The Lobbyists*, 93.

60. Ruth Finney, "Washington Lobbies," *American Mercury* (February 1948): 286–93, 287–88 (figures).

61. Schriftgiesser, *The Lobbyists*, 100–101; "Trade, Labor Groups Yield, File as Lobbies," *New York Herald Tribune*, April 19, 1948, p. 2; "Senators Hear Lobbying Act Is Widely Violated," *New York Herald Tribune*, February 18, 1948, p. 4; "Lobby Act Form Filed by NAM under Protest," *New York Herald Tribune*, May 1, 1948, p. 2.

was less than 3 percent of its $5 million income for 1947.[62] As journalists quickly noted, however, that $146,186 didn't include the money spent on NAM's far vaster public relations work in 1947. NAM eventually brought a federal suit against the law, which it won in 1952 when a three-judge federal court declared key sections of the Lobby Act unconstitutional (because of the law's imprecision in describing the offense) and gave NAM a permanent injunction against prosecution under them.[63]

NAM's Liberal Platform

In its annual meeting in December 1946, NAM adopted its most liberal platform ever, when it conceded finally that workers had a right to organize unions and even endorsed collective bargaining as a positive good. It was rewarded with salutary, if astounded, write-ups in the press.[64] The "liberal platform," as it was dubbed, was both the fruition of Weisenberger's reforms and a strategic parry in shaping what would become the Taft-Hartley Act. But it didn't come about without a fight.

Given the Republican victories in the 1946 midterm elections, it seemed increasingly likely that there would be a legislative attempt to curb or repeal the Wagner Act. To make the most of this opportunity, NAM had to have a comprehensive labor relations program that could unify the business community at large. This task fell to the staff of NAM's Industrial Relations Department and the members of its Industrial Relations Committee, guided by Inland Steel's Clarence Randall. An active NAM leader, Randall would become the chairman of Eisenhower's Commission on Foreign Economic Policy in 1953. He fancied himself a progressive of sorts; his memoir is sprinkled with references to his bohemian friends, Gandhi, and the flack he took for supporting progressive education in Chicago.[65] It makes sense that he would be in charge of this effort to moderate NAM's labor policy. Representatives from this group met with other (non-NAM) trade association leaders

---

62. "Lobby Act Form Filed by NAM under Protest," *New York Herald Tribune*, May 1, 1948. CEOs would also defy the Buchanan Committee, which was tasked with investigating lobbies. See "Inland Steel Head Defies Buchanan," *New York Times*, June 14, 1950, 23.

63. "US Court Rules Key Sections of Lobby Law Unconstitutional," *New York Herald Tribune*, March 19, 1952, p. 1; National Association of Manufacturers et al. v. McGrath, US District Court, District of Columbia, March 17, 1952.

64. "Liberal Program on Labor, Economy Announced by NAM," *New York Times*, December 5, 1946, p. 1; "Head of NAM Pledges to Carry Out New Liberalized Labor Program," *New York Times*, December 7, 1946, p. 5.

65. Clarence Randall, *Over My Shoulder: A Reminiscence* (Boston: Little, Brown, 1956).

and corporate heads, seeking their input on basic principles for collective bargaining and labor relations.[66] The aim was to develop a policy that the entire business community—not just NAM—could get behind.

Randall and industrial relations aficionados promoted an ethos that emphasized cooperation over conflict. This was not a gambit to avoid unionization—although some corporate heads surely saw it as such—but rather part of a professional belief that harmonious employer-employee relations, in which employees were heard and safe and paid well, would lead to higher productivity.[67] For industrial relations types, collective bargaining was, as one NAM memo put it, "a useful tool for the maintenance of good employee relations."[68] Because this group charged with devising a labor relations program not only accepted collective bargaining but saw it as a positive good for employee relations, it was not interested in repealing and replacing the Wagner Act, but rather worked to get better terms for management.

Randall presented the Industrial Relations Committee's plan to the NAM board of directors in November 1946. The plan opened with a statement of principles that encouraged member companies to adopt policies that supported employment stabilization, high wages based on productivity and incentives, transparency and cooperation between employees and management, and safeguards for the health, dignity, and self-respect of all employees. If followed, these principles would promote cooperation and harmony, minimize industrial conflicts, and ensure that more goods at lower prices would be available to the consumer.[69] The plan stated clearly that "the right of employees to organize in union is, and should continue to be protected by law," indicating its support of the Wagner Act, but then it laid out amendments to that act that would curb its alleged excesses and restore the legal balance between management and labor. Among these amendments was an emphatic and familiar statement that workers had a right *not*

---

66. Harris, *The Right to Manage*, 120.

67. See chapter 4. NAM made a number of new hires in the Industrial Relations Department, including two women, Sybyl S. Patterson as assistant director and Phyllis Moehrle as a researcher, as well as a new director for the department, Carroll E. French, who had come from the relatively progressive, Rockefeller-funded Industrial Relations Counselors, Inc., after he was assured that NAM had changed its reactionary ways. On French, see Harris, *The Right to Manage*, 120. Patterson and Moehrle both graduated from Hunter College and had careers in industrial relations before coming to NAM in 1945. See NAM staff booklet, 1954, series 1, box 101, NAMR.

68. Quoted in Harris, *The Right to Manage*, 120.

69. Ibid., 120. The original report can be found as an appendix in the board of directors meeting minutes, December 3, 1946, series 13, box 237, NAMR.

to join a union; that jurisdictional strikes, sympathy strikes, or any strikes not involving legitimate differences of wages, hours, or working conditions should be banned; and that employers' right to "free speech" (that is, anti-union messaging) needed to be secured.[70]

NAM conservatives filed their own report, which was presented to the board by Chrysler's B. E. Hutchinson. Entitled "Dissenting Viewpoint on Report of the Committee on Industrial Relations Program," it called for the repeal of not only the Wagner Act but also the Norris-LaGuardia Act of 1932 (preventing injunctions) and the Fair Labor Standards Act of 1938 (establishing wage and hour laws). The dissenters blamed the increase in strikes and work stoppages on these federal intrusions into the realm of industry and demanded that the government stop using legislation to prop up labor unions. The recent election results indicated that the country was "fed up" with organized labor. Now was the time for industry to act.[71] The state and local groups represented on NAM's National Industrial Council supported the dissenting view, but thought that the two reports could be reconciled.[72]

The board meeting minutes obscured whatever debate ensued. It was moved and seconded that the dissenting view replace the Industrial Relations Committee Report, but that was voted down. Hutchinson wanted the record to show that the Chair refused his (Hutchinson's) request for a record vote, which means it is difficult to tell how much support the dissenting group actually had. This issue clearly divided the organization, but unlike with the tariff, the leadership at this time forced the issue and NAM came out squarely for a more moderate, liberal, approach to labor relations.

There were more disputes at the actual three-day meeting, but the "moderates" prevailed. In addition to the new labor program, NAM also passed resolutions supporting international economic cooperation, world peace, support for congressional investigation of communists, employment stabilization, higher wages for teachers, and preferences and training for returning veterans, including those now handicapped.[73] These resolutions represented a return to positions that NAM had held earlier, before the New Deal changed the political and economic atmosphere so completely. The opening speaker, Secretary of Commerce Averill Harriman, called for

70. Ibid.

71. "Dissenting Viewpoint on Report of the Committee on Industrial Relations Program," November 25, 1946, appendix in board of directors meeting minutes, December 3, 1946, series 13, box 237, NAMR. Most accounts state that the dissenters were centered in the automobile and steel industries, but given Randall's prominent role in the steel industry, that seems unhelpful.

72. Board of directors meeting minutes, December 3, 1946, series 13, box 237, NAMR.

73. "Liberal Program Outlined by NAM," *New York Times*, December 7, 1946, p. 5.

both labor and management to be more responsible, while the new president, Earl Bunting, head of O'Sullivan Rubber (rubber heels and plastics), told newspapermen that the new NAM was "aimed right down the middle of the road," with a constructive program that would benefit the public at large.[74] But it was Walter Weisenberger, NAM's executive director, who clearly acknowledged that NAM's blind opposition to the New Deal had left it—and the country—in a worse position: "How much better if business had met these problems head on . . . instead of simply protesting."[75] If America was to buck the global trend of collectivization, it would need NAM to be statesmanlike and concerned about long-term public interest, not short-term profit. Most surprisingly, perhaps, and in clear refutation of NAM conservatives, Weisenberger said that the recent election did not mean that American voters wanted "reaction," but rather that they were looking for a program of "constructive liberalism"—of the sort NAM was proposing at this meeting.[76]

The meeting was a tour de force performance for Weisenberger, who expertly got the message out to the press: A new NAM. A NAM that leads. Of course, the platform was not really liberal, as liberal commentators were quick to point out. It did, after all, lay the groundwork for Taft-Hartley, as well as call for a 20 percent tax cut. But it was a break with NAM's recent past, and it put NAM at the forefront of the business community, a position that finally justified its members' dues. In July 1948, *Fortune* would report that a renovated NAM "now says yes as well as no."[77]

The Taft-Hartley Act

In 1947, Republicans in the 80th Congress moved forward with the goal of curbing the perceived excesses of labor and the New Deal. New Jersey Republican congressman Fred Hartley presided over the House Committee on Education and Labor, which conducted hearings in February and March 1947 on ways to revise the Wagner Act.[78] NAM president Ira Mosher presented NAM's plan before the House Committee, while general counsel

74. "Smuts Brands Communism as Sly Aggression," *New York Herald Tribune*, December 7, p. 1.

75. "Liberal Program on Labor, Economy Announced by NAM," *New York Times*, December 5, 1946, p. 1.

76. Ibid. See also "Split over 'Liberal' Labor Policy Seen in NAM," *Christian Science Monitor*, December 24, 1946, p. 15.

77. "Renovation in NAM," *Fortune*, July 1948, pp. 72–75ff.

78. Lee, *Truman and Taft-Hartley*, 56. Also serving on the committee were newly elected congressmen John F. Kennedy and Richard Nixon.

Raymond Smethurst presented it to the Senate Labor and Public Welfare Committee, chaired by Republican senator Robert Taft.[79] Hundreds of other groups and individuals presented their hopes and fears as well, preserved in over four volumes of testimony and evidence.[80] Mirroring NAM, labor would conduct a $1 million PR campaign against the "slave-labor" bill.[81]

The House passed its bill on April 17 by 308 to 107. A majority of 93 Democrats, mostly from the South, joined Republicans. The bill contained much of what NAM had been advocating—the prohibition of jurisdictional strikes, secondary boycotts, and wildcat strikes; a mandatory "cooling off" period before a strike; a guarantee of employers' free speech rights; and the prohibition of the closed shop. House Democrats—the liberal ones anyway—argued that the bill had been "written by NAM" or the Chamber or both, and that it served the interests of "Big Business."[82] Congressman John Blatnik introduced a point-by-point comparison of the bill to NAM's 1946 legislative proposals, copies of which had been sent to all legislators.[83] The Senate debate was more substantive, according to historian Alton Lee, with the majority arguing that the Wagner Act had been an experiment and experience over the past decade showed that there were areas where it could be improved. The minority argued that it was working and that the draconian measures proposed would lead to an increase in labor strife.[84] In May, the Senate passed Taft's version of the bill, 68 to 24, with the help of 21 Democrats, mostly from the South.

What would become the Taft-Hartley Act (officially, the Labor Management Relations Act of 1947) was crafted in committee with the aim of overcoming Truman's expected veto. This meant that conservative House Republicans made a great show of demanding harsher terms and then "conceding" them in the interests of compromise. The final bill outlawed the secondary boycott, the closed shop, refusal of bargaining, jurisdictional strikes, union contributions to elections, strikes by federal employees, welfare funds administered only by unions, exorbitant initiation fees, and interference in employers' free speech. It featured an increase in NLRB membership, a "cooling off" requirement before a national emergency strike,

79. Business report, February 28–March 26, 1947, series 13, box 237, NAMR.

80. Lee, *Truman and Taft-Hartley*, 56.

81. Ibid., 81.

82. Ibid., 62–68.

83. Ibid., 63; Harry Millis and Emily Clark Brown, *From the Wagner Act to the Taft-Hartley: A Study of National Labor Policy and Labor Relations* (Chicago: University of Chicago, 1950), 370–71.

84. Lee, *Truman and Taft-Hartley*, 70.

a requirement that union officials sign a non-communist affidavit, and a provision protecting state "right to work" laws that prohibited compulsory union membership.[85]

The reconciled bill passed both houses by more than a two-thirds majority and was sent to Truman for consideration. Truman faced an avalanche of telegrams and postcards begging him to veto the bill, which he eventually did. Congress voted to overrule the veto on June 23, 1947, and the bill became law.[86]

It would be hard to overstate the anger and outrage that liberals and labor felt toward this bill, which represented not just a political loss but also, and more important, a genuine frustration with conservatives' inability to rationally govern in a modern industrial society. It seemed, as the NLRB head put it, that the shield that the Wagner Act had given the workingman had been transformed into a sword to be used by the state against unions.[87] What Republicans and NAM had seen as legislation that "balanced" the playing field, labor saw as a punitive and repressive "slave-labor" bill. It would lead to more, not less, industrial strife. Truman's veto of the act was in many ways the opening salvo of his upcoming presidential campaign, in which he would scold the Republican Congress for the practical inefficiencies and hypocrisies of the bill and its limited ability to accomplish the high-sounding claims Republicans made on its behalf. At a time when liberals and labor were hopelessly divided, the Taft-Hartley Act more than anything would reunite them in returning Democrats to power in both the House and the Senate in 1948, as well as reelecting Harry Truman.

Conservatives, for their part, were likewise disappointed. Publisher Frank Gannett brushed aside the freedom-of-speech provisions as "picayune," given that the essence of the Wagner Act had been preserved. According to conservative columnist Henry Hazlitt, the Taft-Hartley Act, in retaining all of the Wagner Act's legal compulsions against employers—which, in a bid for "balance," had now been *expanded* to include unions—left untouched "what was centrally unsound in the original law."[88] This is exactly what Samuel Gompers had once feared and why he had opposed relying on the state, rather than the strength of the union, to secure union rights.

85. Ibid., 77.

86. Ibid., 99–101.

87. Ibid., 92.

88. Tomlins, *The State and the Unions*, 280; Henry Hazlitt, "To Improve the Taft-Hartley Law," *Newsweek*, April 12, 1948, p. 74.

NAM's success was a double-edged sword. On the one hand, it showed NAM's influence and power, which affirmed its claims to be the "voice of industry" and justified its existence to its supporters. Its officials had very strategically planned out and worked for this outcome. On the other hand, however, it resurrected the specter of NAM as a corrupt and powerful lobby. Charges that NAM had written the bill lingered, prompting a NAM denial in a January 1948 statement, "Who Wrote the Taft-Hartley Bill?," which, if anything, seemed to confirm NAM's "guilt."[89] But the truth, as most historians eventually concluded, was that the provisions that ended up in the House bill had been kicked around for many years; they had appeared in a 1940 attempt to amend the Wagner Act, as well as in the Case Bill of 1946. Some of them had even been proposed by President Truman. Moreover, NAM did not control the legislative process—Republicans did.[90] At the end of the day, the bill was not as bad as labor and liberals feared. It affirmed "labor" as a serious actor in post–World War II politics, a check on business, and a voice for the middle class. As historian James Patterson has written:

> By the 1950s most observers agreed that Taft-Hartley was no more disastrous for workers than the Wagner Act had been for employers. What ordinarily mattered most in labor relations was not government laws such as Taft-Hartley, but the relative power of unions and management in the economic marketplace. Where unions were strong they usually managed all right; when they were weak, new laws did them little additional harm.[91]

As with trade, passage of the Taft-Hartley Act was an instance of NAM contributing to the stability of the New Deal order, otherwise known as the liberal consensus, a brief time in US history when progressive ideals and policies dominated politics, even if they were sometimes trimmed around the edges by the political process.

---

89. See Richard Gable, "NAM: Influential Lobby or Kiss of Death?" *Journal of Politics* (May 1953): 254–73, 254; and Millis and Brown, *From the Wagner Act*, 370.

90. Lee, *Truman and Taft-Hartley*, 66; Harris, *The Right to Manage*, 123–24; Millis and Brown, *From the Wagner Act*, 361. In 1949, the lawyer who had written the House bill described, in testimony for an unsuccessful bill to repeal Taft-Hartley, how he had cobbled together the bill from earlier bills he had worked on in consultation with two other labor law attorneys. See Lee, *Truman and Taft-Hartley*, 64–65.

91. James T. Patterson, *Grand Expectations: The United States, 1945–1974* (New York: Oxford University Press, 1996), 52.

7

Trade, Tariffs, and the Postwar Economic Order

In 1944, Assistant Secretary of State Dean Acheson spoke at NAM's annual meeting, extolling the importance of trade to postwar recovery. International markets could add $10 billion to the American economy, he said; they could create at least three million jobs in industry as well as outlets for the agricultural products of another one million Americans.[1] The United States needed to create the "circumstances favorable to increased trade" throughout the world, such as stable exchange rates and currencies, the elimination of trade barriers, and the reduction of tariffs. Hear, hear, said the manufacturers.

The Second World War and its aftermath gave Americans an opportunity to create an international order based on economic growth and the US dollar. Anchored by the Bretton Woods Agreement, the new economic regime sought to stabilize international currencies and minimize barriers to the movement of goods, services, and technology.[2] Executed by a Democratic

---

1. "Acheson Stresses Big Foreign Trade," *New York Times*, December 9, 1944, p. 12. On Acheson's testimony, see Doug Irwin, *Clashing over Commerce: A History of US Trade Policy* (Chicago: University of Chicago Press, 2017), chap. 10.

2. Irwin, *Clashing over Commerce*, chap. 10; Patrick Hearden, *Architects of Globalism: Building a New World Order during World War II* (Fayetteville: University of Arkansas Press, 2002); Benn Steil, *The Battle for Bretton Woods* (Princeton, NJ: Princeton University Press, 2013); Charles Maier, "The Politics of Productivity: Foundations of American Economic Policy after World War II," *International Organization* 31, no. 4 (Autumn 1977): 607–33.

administration, the bipartisan plan went hand in hand with a domestic program that emphasized job security, consumer spending, and labor rights.
Although NAM was skeptical of the domestic part of this agenda, it supported a foreign policy leading to a more integrated global economy; it had,
after all, been founded on that very principle. Accordingly, NAM departed
from conservative principle and championed the United Nations (UN),
alongside such progressives as Eleanor Roosevelt and labor leader Walter
Reuther. It urged the creation of an international trade organization and
supported the Marshall Plan. It sponsored international trade conferences
and worked closely with the UN's Economic and Social Council (ECOSOC),
the International Labor Organization (ILO), the International Chamber of
Commerce (ICC), and a variety of other international organizations.

The Cold War impeded full global economic integration, but it also provided an opportunity for free enterprise to show its superiority to state-
directed economic systems. The US Department of State depended on trade
associations like NAM and the US Chamber of Commerce to perform and
coordinate the "private enterprise" aspect of American capitalism. The
State Department certainly could not control or regulate American economic expansion: that would have been statist (in other words, socialistic),
exactly what the American free enterprise system eschewed. And yet there
needed to be a high degree of coordination, standard-setting, and information exchange in order to globalize capitalism. Much of this work was done
by NAM and the many international organizations to which it belonged and
which it financially supported. But that work fostered tensions, especially
with regard to tariffs.

Tariff reduction was key to the postwar trade agenda. Here, NAM was,
as usual, divided. But times were changing. The Cold War fight against
communism required a commitment to international capitalism and freer
trade. State-instigated tariffs were antithetical to postwar free-market conservatives, a movement influenced by Austrian émigrés and enthusiastically embraced by NAM leaders. Even parts of the Republican Party were
embracing economic internationalism.[3] As a result, protectionists had
fewer allies. NAM still had to treat the issue gingerly; once again, it refused
to take an official position on the tariff, angering both internationalist and

---

3. On Hayek's and Mises's attitudes toward trade, see especially Quinn Slobodian, *Globalists:
The End of Empire and the Birth of Neoliberalism* (Cambridge, MA: Harvard University Press, 2018).
On Republicans, see Arthur Larson, *A Republican Looks at His Party* (New York: Harper Bros.,
1956); Republican Party platform of 1948, June 21, 1948, *The American Presidency Project*, http://
www.presidency.ucsb.edu/ws/index.php?pid=25836; Irwin, *Clashing over Commerce*, chap. 10.

protectionist members. In the end, however, internationalists prevailed and put the organization on the side of economic globalization.

Working toward the Democratic Liberal Internationalist Economic Order

The idea of establishing international institutions and agreements to create a more connected, cooperative, and integrated global economy was bipartisan and national, even international, representing more than anything else the desire to avoid future wars and depressions. That was the spirit in which Washington policymakers pushed forward their international vision.[4] But an integrated world economy had also been a longtime goal of the Democratic Party. Republicans were increasingly on board with the Democratic trade agenda, especially after Dwight Eisenhower, an internationalist, became president in 1953. But the party's protectionist conservative wing openly opposed not just freer trade but also the international treaties and agencies that global economic integration required.[5] So, once again, NAM's trade agenda was being led by liberal Democrats, not by the party to which its members belonged. This might be one reason the public seemed so unaware of NAM's support for progressive trade policies.

To be sure, NAM globalists were not in complete agreement with the Democrats' internationalist vision. NAM wanted freer trade, but it was wary of government spending and bureaucratic controls, and its internal divisions often limited or qualified its support. Nonetheless, a significant number of individual NAM leaders spoke often and eloquently on behalf of freer trade and foreign economic development in a way that contributed to the postwar bipartisan consensus on US international economic involvement.

NAM was active in the International Chamber of Commerce, which had likewise embraced a version of the internationalist ideal. Founded in Paris in 1920, the ICC gathered international economic statistics, propagated the idea of a single world economy, and called for the removal of barriers to trade and the free movement of capital. Described by historian Quinn Slobodian as "the global public sphere of capitalists," the ICC consisted of national contingents of businessmen and experts.[6] NAM contributed funds and representatives to its American branch from the beginning. This is probably

4. Mazower, *Governing the World*, chap. 7.

5. See Thomas Zeiler, "Managing Protectionism: American Trade Policy in the Early Cold War," *Diplomatic History* 22, no. 3 (Summer 1998): 337–60.

6. Slobodian, *Globalists*, chap. 1.

where NAM's Noel Sargent met Ludwig Von Mises, who was a member of both the ICC and the Vienna Chamber of Commerce, the latter of which was a dominant influence on the ICC.[7] Like liberal internationalists, the ICC believed that the growing economic interdependence of all nations made economic nationalism dangerous; in this it affirmed the views of Democrats in the United States and the US State Department.

In 1944, NAM president Robert Gaylord (of Ingersoll Milling Machine Company of Rockford, Illinois) and general secretary Noel Sargent were part of a group of fifty-four business and industry leaders who hoped to offer the impending UN direction in creating "a world of expanding trade and equal trading opportunities for all."[8] Organized in cooperation with the Carnegie Endowment for International Peace and headed by Chase National Bank chairman Nelson Aldrich, the group warned that unless multilateral trade was set up between private traders, government monopolies and trading blocs would reinstitute the kind of economic nationalism and hoarding of raw materials that had led to depression and the current war. What these businessmen feared most was government intervention if private enterprise failed to step up to the plate. The group included corporate liberals like Thomas Watson (IBM), the Chamber of Commerce's Eric Johnston, Paul Hoffman from the Committee for Economic Development, and Marion Folsom (Eastman-Kodak), as well as economists, experts, and other NAM members. They used the internationalist language of world peace, full employment, and freer trade to make their case for an integrated world economy. They appealed to the UN structure as a way to secure their international agenda and, notably, hoped the new international economic charter would include "countries whose foreign trade is either completely or partially conducted by state enterprise," a reference to the Soviet Union, a US ally at the time.[9]

In November 1944, NAM sponsored an international business conference in Rye, New York, attended by industry representatives from fifty-two countries, including the Soviet Union. Sponsored jointly by NAM, the US Chamber of Commerce, the National Foreign Trade Council, and the ICC,

7. Through the Vienna Chamber of Commerce, neoliberals were able to make the ICC "an important institutional partner"; see ibid. Von Mises was a regular consultant to NAM, and he contributed to *The American Individual Enterprise System: Its Nature, Evolution, and Future* by NAM's Economic Principles Committee (New York: McGraw-Hill, 1946), discussed in chapter 6.

8. Quoted in "New Group Offers World Trade Plan," *New York Times*, July 5, 1944, p. 25.

9. Ibid. This position is notable because it suggests that liberal internationalism was not just a version of Cold War anticommunism—that is, a geopolitical strategy—but had an earlier incarnation as a vision of a truly integrated world economy.

the conference was the brainchild of NAM secretary Noel Sargent, who along with NAM's 1943 president, Frederick Crawford (Thompson Industries, later TRW, a supplier of auto parts), and Inland Steel president Wilfred Sykes approached Secretary of State Cordell Hull about the advisability of such a conference in a time of war.[10] Hull thought it was a terrific idea and gave the go-ahead. Sargent and assistant secretary Vada Horsch spearheaded the nineteen-month organizing effort. The conference was "nonpolitical," meaning it would consist of nonstate actors from industry. No binding decisions would be made; instead, the conference would provide an opportunity for businesspeople from around the world to air concerns and issues. Discussion would focus on cartels, the commercial policies of other nations, the protection of foreign investment, economic development, foodstuffs and raw materials, and international monetary relations.[11] The invitations took a page from Cordell Hull's playbook, proclaiming:

> In a world in which the problems and the welfare of every country will be linked more closely than ever with those of every other country, understanding and cooperation among such leaders and between the business interests and the nations they represent are essential steps to national and international progress and to the development and maintenance of an enduring international peace.[12]

The theme of peace and international understanding permeated the conference. Chamber of Commerce head Eric Johnston delivered a typically "one-world" speech about the importance of cultural understanding.[13] Given the sponsors, it was no surprise that the conference identified the need for some kind of "international economic organization to organize, supervise, and manage the policies and mechanisms agreed upon by the various nations in carrying out a rational program of international trade and distribution."[14] This set the stage for work to begin on the (never realized)

10. This description comes from a NAM pamphlet, "The Story of the International Business Conference" (1944), and a memo titled "Record of the Proceedings," prepared for Mr. Chen, head of the Chinese delegation, by NAM assistant secretary Vada Horsch, according to a letter dated December 20, 1944; both documents in series 12, box 192, "International Business Conference" file, NAMR.

11. The international monetary relations section was headed by Polish-American neoliberal economist Michael Heilperin; see Slobodian, *Globalists*, chap. 4.

12. Quoted in NAM, "The Story of the International Business Conference," p. 4, series 12, box 192, "International Business Conference" file, NAMR.

13. In "Record of the Proceedings," series 12, box 192, "International Business Conference" file, NAMR.

14. Ibid.

International Trade Organization (ITO), the forerunner of the World Trade Organization (WTO), which was eventually created in 1994.

Secretary of State Edward Stettinius Jr. (previously of US Steel and General Motors) invited NAM president Gaylord to participate in the United Nations Charter Conference in San Francisco in the spring of 1945, along with representatives from forty-one other US organizations. Gaylord came armed with NAM's positions on double taxation (no), currency convertibility (yes), cartels and state-run enterprises (no), and protection of investment and property from nationalization (yes).[15] Cartels had long been an obstacle to trade from the US perspective. Common in Europe and Japan, cartels were cooperative agreements among firms to regulate markets, often with state backing; some cartels were state-enforced, others were private and voluntary, but either kind made it difficult for individual US firms to compete against a large conglomerate with state protection, especially if they had to follow US antitrust laws. NAM saw cartels as an unfair barrier to trade and, under the banner of "free competition," sought to prohibit them in international trade.[16] Similarly, European currencies were not freely convertible to dollars but instead were subject to official exchange controls that hindered the flow of American imports into European markets and were regarded as a trade barrier.[17] The State Department, however, would continue to tolerate European cartels and currency restrictions to avert economic bickering and preserve the Cold War alliance.[18]

In speaking to the press about the conference, Gaylord endorsed the work of the IMF, the UN, and other agencies, suggesting as well that business would have a large role to play in "protecting world peace against aggression," which it would do through an international trade organization. He endorsed a UN declaration on human rights, saying, "You can't have economic rights

15. "Memorandum for Consideration by Mr. Gaylord," undated, series 1, box 42, NAMR; summary of Steering Committee meeting minutes, World Trade Policy Committee, April 17, 1945, series 13, box 236, NAMR. These positions match the neoliberal positions discussed by Slobodian, *Globalists*, chap. 3, and they might well have been influenced by the ICC, although they are very much in line with NAM's historical positions on these issues.

16. Ironically, cartels were just another form of industrial cooperation, not unlike unions or trade associations themselves, which was one reason neoliberals rejected them, as discussed in Slobodian, *Globalists*, chap. 3. On resemblances between trade associations and cartels, see chapter 2; Jeffrey Fear, "Cartels and Competition: Neither Markets nor Hierarchies," working paper, 2006, https://www.hbs.edu/faculty/Publication%20Files/07-011.pdf.

17. Irwin, *Clashing over Commerce*, chap. 10.

18. On the State Department's prioritization of politics over economics, see Alfred Eckes Jr., *Opening America's Market: US Foreign Trade Policy since 1776* (Chapel Hill: University of North Carolina Press, 1995), chaps. 5–6.

without human rights," before segueing into a lesson on the evils of cartels.[19] Even organized labor—also represented at the conference—was in agreement. In 1945, and particularly at the UN conference, there was a great deal of unity—of which NAM was part.[20] So successful and unified was business after the UN conference that they met again in London to continue the discussion—corporate liberals, free-traders, bankers, and NAM, all now in favor of working within the Bretton Woods framework.[21] The same group met again in Paris under the auspices of the ICC, seeking official status with the newly formed UN Economic and Social Council.[22] NAM was given consultative status with that body in 1947, along with the ICC and the Carnegie Endowment for International Peace.[23]

By the end of 1946, the press was reporting that NAM had "tacitly accepted a large part of both the New Deal and the Good Neighbor policy"— that is, the Democrats' program, including tariff reductions.[24] There were key differences, of course. NAM wanted the government to push back harder against cartels and currency restrictions, it wanted economic organization to remain under private control, and it opposed government spending. But with respect to the vision of multilateral international trade and even foreign aid, NAM was very much on the same page as the government.

THE MARSHALL PLAN / FOREIGN AID

The Marshall Plan—or the European Recovery Program (ERP)—was in many ways the lynchpin of liberal Democratic international policy, with its hallmark combination of humanitarianism and economic interest.[25] The

19. "World Group Seat Asked by Business," *New York Times*, May 11, 1945, p. 13.

20. "Unity Is Revealed on Economic Plan," *New York Times*, May 18, 1945, p. 13. The *Times* article emphasized the commonalities between the AFL, CIO, and NAM.

21. Robert Mullen, "US Businessmen to Meet in London on World Trade," *Christian Science Monitor*, July 6, 1945, p. 1. Some NAM leaders, probably influenced by neoliberals, disapproved of Bretton Woods for leaving in place exchange controls and allowing for full employment plans, but by and large Bretton Woods was seen as a step in the right direction.

22. "Winthrop Aldrich Departs for Paris," *New York Herald Tribune*, June 11, 1946, p. 9B.

23. "NAM and International Relations" (memo), August 17, 1948, p. 9, series 1, box 76, NAMR. This memo was part of an investigation into the scope of NAM international activities that was conducted by the organization in 1948 (to be discussed later). See "Social Council Backs NAM Consulting Role," *New York Times*, August 8, 1947, p. 25.

24. Russell Parter, "NAM Advocates Reforming Economic Foreign Policy," *New York Times*, December 15, 1946, p. F1.

25. See Benn Steil, *The Marshal Plan: Dawn of the Cold War* (New York: Simon & Schuster, 2018); Greg Behrman, *The Most Noble Adventure: The Marshall Plan and How America Helped*

United States tied the more than $13 billion it provided for the rebuilding of Europe to the adoption by Europeans of more liberal trade policies. This aid was a first step in addressing the "dollar gap"—the shortage of hard-currency dollars in Europe that prevented Europeans from paying for US exports. The aim was to provide aid so that Europeans could build up their productive capacity to produce goods it could sell to the United States for dollars and thus become real paying trading partners.[26] Liberal Democrats saw this as a humanitarian alternative to the militarism of Truman's nascent Cold War policies—a way to fight communism through aid and trade rather than bombs and guns. Conservative Republicans, however, strongly opposed the Marshall Plan, which they believed used taxpayers' money to bolster socialist European governments. Republican senator Robert Taft supported the idea of helping to rebuild Europe, but like many conservatives, he thought Truman's request of $17 billion over four years was too much of a tax burden, inflationary, and a disincentive to European private-sector investment.[27] Taft eventually came round, but many conservatives—including NAM members J. Howard Pew and Ernest Weir—opposed it.

NAM leadership supported the Marshall Plan. It sent Herbert Schell, president of Sidney Blumenthal & Co., Inc. (textiles) and a member of its International Relations Committee, to represent NAM's perspective at the House hearings held in January 1948. Schell testified that NAM had considerable experience and expertise in the area of international trade and was "enthusiastically in favor of the purpose and objective of the European recovery plan," which was that the United States would give material and financial aid in order to help war-torn European countries regain a state of economic independence via production and sound fiscal policies.[28] It would be to the advantage of the United States for Europe to be economically healthy and capable of resisting the spread of communism through free enterprise and economic security. NAM did recommend, however, certain safeguards to ensure the program's success. While professing no desire to

---

Rebuild Europe (New York: Free Press, 2007); Michael Hogan, *The Marshall Plan: America, Britain, and the Reconstruction of Western Europe* (New York: Cambridge University Press, 1987).

26. See Hogan, *The Marshall Plan*, chap. 6. Hogan describes the Marshall Plan as a "New Deal synthesis" that sought a neocapitalist order based on productivity, growth, and labor-management cooperation. See also Maier, "The Politics of Productivity."

27. Steil, *The Marshal Plan*, 215–16; Behrman, *The Most Noble Adventure*, 135, 148–49.

28. Herbert Schell, "United States Foreign Policy for a Post-War Recovery Program," statement before the House Committee on Foreign Affairs hearing, January 28, 1948, part 1 (Washington, DC: US Government Printing Office, 1948), 659–987.

"dominate or interfere in the political life of any other government," NAM nonetheless wanted countries receiving aid to be required to adopt currency reforms, stabilize their exchange rates, balance their budgets, concentrate on production, and be prohibited from undertaking further economic nationalization. "Europe should produce more and experiment less," said Schell, referring to the postwar rise of European social welfare states.[29]

Domestically, NAM wanted the government to pay for the program by cutting existing domestic programs. Nodding to Taft's concerns, Schell hoped that Congress would also balance the budget, reduce taxes, and arrest the inflationary spiral of monetary expansion. Finally, the program should not be administered by an existing government agency, NAM recommended, but rather by a corporation created for this purpose, controlled by a board appointed by the president with the advice and consent of the Senate. Board members would be recognized men of industry, commerce, and agriculture approved by major trade organizations. The secretary of state, the president of the Export-Import Bank, and the commerce secretary might also be part of this board.[30]

NAM internationalists were aware of the ERP's perceived "liberalism," and the savviest talked about it in a folksy, pragmatic, "the world is changing" tone rather than the voice of a liberal "one-worlder." Inland Steel's Clarence B. Randall was a NAM board member who went to work for the Economic Cooperation Administration (ECA), which was set up in 1948 to administer the Marshall Plan in Europe. Speaking before a group of Chicago industrialists, Randall began by scoffing at one-worlders to show he wasn't one of them. He also admitted that there was some truth to the reservations of some American businessmen about the Marshall Plan. Britain and Germany did seem interested in nationalizing the steel industry, he noted, but what could the United States do about it? It was up to the Germans and British to decide how to organize their own economies. He talked about how things were different in Europe and how it took some getting used to. For instance, the head of the steel committee for the new Organization for European Economic Cooperation was—of all things—a woman! A Miss Betty Ackroyd, "an attractive young woman" about the age of his daughter. As it happened, however, "it made sense" that the "key figure in the reconstruction of the steel industry in Europe" was a woman. Miss Ackroyd had

29. Ibid., 664.
30. Ibid., 665–66.

graduated from Oxford when war broke out; after all the men went to fight, she came up through British industry on merit. She was intelligent, honest-minded, and "chairs a meeting like nobody's business," but, he concluded, her presence at the head of the steel committee showed why it was difficult to rush off to do a job in Europe: it was so different there.[31]

Randall's speech is evidence of the liberalizing effect of international trade on American businessmen. Rhetorically and probably personally, Randall identified with the conservative men in the room, most of whom were bewildered by nationalization and women in industry, but also completely on board with the US foreign economic policy.[32] A member of NAM's International Relations Committee and the future head of President Eisenhower's Commission on Foreign Economic Policy, Randall saw the Marshall Plan as a temporary emergency program to get European trade back on track so that Europeans could produce and sell without US aid or loans and thereby eventually purchase American exports.[33] In this case, the key to preserving traditional principles such as private initiative, competition, and the free market was a little government spending in the form of foreign aid (and eventually a reduction in US tariffs).

NAM supported Truman's renewal of the ERP in 1949, despite the program's socialistic tendencies. Acknowledging the "complexities" inherent in the program, the official NAM position was that progress had been made and that the ECA's director, Paul Hoffman (of Studebaker Corporation and the CED), could be trusted to limit its excesses.[34] A major part of the ERP was offering "technical assistance" to help European factories become more efficient, that is, more Americanized. This was the kind of developmental work that NAM specialized in, and it was excited to export its expertise to Europe.[35] At one point, there was even talk of opening a NAM European office, one purpose of which would be to counter the excessive power of socialistic trade unions, as well as the CIO, which had established an

31. Clarence Randall, "The ECA as I See It," September 23, 1948 series I, box 76, "ERP" file, NAMR.

32. NAM also filed a memo on behalf of gender equity and pay equality with the UN's ECOSOC in 1948, series I, box 187, NAMR.

33. Clarence B. Randall, *A Foreign Economic Policy for the United States* (Chicago: Chicago University Press, 1954), 12.

34. "Statement on the European Recovery Program," February 17, 1949, and other statements, series I, box 76, "ERP" file, NAMR.

35. The technical assistance program is discussed in Hogan, *The Marshall Plan*, chap. 4. On "development," see Mazower, *Governing the World*, chap. 10.

outreach effort in Europe.[36] Although NAM never opened a European office, it maintained its presence there as a member of the ICC and as part of the US Foreign Operations Administration, a temporary government office that coordinated technical assistance and cooperative economic endeavors.[37]

Surprisingly, NAM also supported Truman's "Point Four" program aimed at developing so-called undeveloped areas and getting US capital out into the world.[38] Conservatives in NAM opposed Point Four, which they saw as another foreign aid boondoggle using American taxes to do what those countries should be doing for themselves.[39] NAM internationalists, on the other hand, argued that their participation was necessary to stem further aid or loans, but they were also interested in the profits that could be made from private capital investment in underdeveloped areas. Thus, this faction wanted the government to "encourage a larger flow of capital and technology abroad" by "creating necessary conditions to enable private initiative to function effectively," including "convertible currencies, free foreign exchange, balanced budgets, non-discriminatory laws, fair and efficient administration, and reliable courts."[40] It wanted the government to do this through the negotiation of bilateral treaties with the target nations, which would ostensibly protect investment against currency inconvertibility, nationalization, and war.[41]

In NAM's initial proposal in support of Point Four, it was unclear how those guarantees would be kept. Would the US government underwrite the risk and reimburse those corporations that lost profits? Would the nation in

36. See specifically A. M. Lederer to Earl Bunting, September 10, 1951, and Robert Yoakum, "Victor Reuther Asserts NAM Is Aiding Red Line in Europe," *Paris Herald Tribune*, April 7, 1951 (clipping), series 1, box 43, "European Office" folder, NAMR.

37. Under the auspices of this office, the NAM held, for instance, a management study group for Norwegians and a meeting for French women industrialists. See documents in series 1, box 76, "International Relations—Foreign Operations Administration" files, NAMR. On the Foreign Operations Administration, see President Dwight D. Eisenhower, "Letter to Secretary of State Dulles Regarding Transfer of the Affair of the Foreign Operations Administration to the Department of State," April 17, 1955, *The American Presidency Project*, http://www.presidency.ucsb.edu/ws/index.php?pid=10454.

38. See Mazower, *Governing the World*, 273–81.

39. See Henry Hazlitt, "Illusions of Point Four" (Irvington, NY: Foundation for Economic Education [FEE], 1950). Some NAM leaders were active in FEE, so there was a diversity of opinion within the organization on this topic. As discussed in the following chapter, a large contingent of NAM conservatives were also isolationists, in the tradition of Robert Taft, and opposed foreign aid.

40. "The Bold New Plan: A Program for Undeveloped Areas with Statement of Principles Prerequisite to the Free Flow of Foreign Investment Capital," NAM Economic Policy Division Series 11, May 1949, p. 4, series 1, box 76, "Point Four" file, NAMR.

41. This matches European neoliberal thinking to a tee; see Slobodian, *Globalists*, chaps. 3–4.

question be able to do this? Could some kind of insurance pool be set up? These were controversial points that the drafting committee deliberately avoided.[42] By 1950, however, after a bill proposed that the US government underwrite these risks, NAM adopted an official policy of opposition to US government guarantees for foreign investment abroad.[43] But there was still a debate within NAM about whether government guarantees might be necessary in order for private capital to step up.[44] The conservatives won this particular point, but the very fact that NAM supported diplomatic initiatives for foreign investment (as it had in its earliest years) and that a sizable contingent wanted the government to underwrite the risk (à la government-backed mortgages at home) indicated that NAM saw a positive, even necessary, role for government in trade.[45]

THE INTERNATIONAL TRADE ORGANIZATION AND THE GENERAL AGREEMENT ON TARIFFS AND TRADE

In the spring of 1947 in Geneva, the State Department participated in the first-ever round of trade negotiations known as the General Agreement on Tariffs and Trade (GATT), which was the forum by which select nations would establish the "rules of the game" and policies for international trade. As with the Marshall Plan, the US government's aim was to address the dollar gap, in this case by reducing US tariffs to encourage imports so that countries could earn dollars. Truman had signed off on a list of items on which the United States could make concessions. Conservative Republicans objected to US participation, but Truman orchestrated a compromise and the Geneva conference proceeded. When it concluded in October 1947, twenty-three nations had agreed to lower trade barriers and preferences.[46] The Geneva conference also drafted a charter for an international trade organization.

---

42. "Dear Sirs," J. C. Stark letter to James McGraw and John Suman, April 8, 1949, series 1, box 76, "Point Four" file, NAMR.

43. "For Release in Morning Papers of Thursday June 15, 1950," series 1, box 76, "Point Four" file, NAMR.

44. For opposing and affirmative views of the question, see "United States Government Guarantee of American Private Investment Abroad," series 1, box 76, "Point Four" file, NAMR.

45. NAM conservatives continued to dissent, but their presence on the Foreign Aid and Technical Assistance Subcommittee just indicates NAM's continuing interest in foreign aid and technical assistance. See business report, June–September 1959, p. 13, series 13, box 242, NAMR.

46. See Irwin, *Clashing over Commerce*, chap. 10. For details on the Geneva conference, see Susan Ariel Aaronson, *Trade and the American Dream: A Social History of Postwar Trade Policy* (Lexington: University Press of Kentucky, 1996), 79–83.

Although the draft was far from perfect, the State Department nonetheless convened a UN conference in Havana to refine the charter and officially establish the International Trade Organization (ITO).

NAM was an early advocate of some kind of international trade organization that would provide rules and standards for international trade. It promoted this idea in its 1944 International Business Conference in Rye, New York, at various UNECOSOC meetings, and in communications to the State Department. On the eve of the much-anticipated Havana conference, NAM issued a statement in support of the ITO, but it was critical of the various drafts for failing to address its concerns about cartels and the protection of foreign investment. Spelling out its expectations in a constructive manner, the document enthusiastically affirmed NAM support for the endeavor, stating: "We believe that the United States and the world as a whole need such an organization to help remove chaos in international trade, to promote mutual benefits in international trade, and consequently to assist in promoting world understanding and world prosperity."[47]

This first attempt to create a world trade organization was rocky to say the least. Despite the air of goodwill and cooperation, each nation was understandably trying to get its interests and concerns met. The British emphasized lowering trade barriers rather than forgoing their imperial preferences, and they wanted exceptions for maintaining full employment at home. Not represented at Geneva, the smaller, so-called developing nations were not happy with the dominance of British and US influence (the countries with the largest share of world trade), and particularly resented the US demands for protections of foreign investment, which they regarded as economic imperialism.[48] The final agreement contained over 106 articles, including provisions that allowed nation-states to retain control of their economies (that is, to restrict trade) for purposes of full employment and economic development. Nonetheless, fifty-three countries, including the United States, signed the agreement in March 1948.

Unlike a trade *agreement*, such as GATT, US membership in an international organization needed approval by Congress. Understanding its weaknesses, Truman delayed submitting the ITO to Congress until after the 1948 election. But even with Democratic congressional victories that fall, the ITO

47. "NAM Position on the Geneva Draft of the Charter for an International Trade Organization," October 29, 1947, in board of directors meeting minutes, 1947, p. 3, series 13, box 237, NAMR.

48. For details, see Irwin, *Clashing over Commerce*, chap. 10, Chorev, *Remaking US Trade Policy*, 50–56; Aaronson, *Trade and the American Dream*, chaps. 5–7; Slobodian, *Globalists*, chap. 4.

was doomed because none of the major business organizations that typically supported international trade expansion supported it. Along with NAM, the US Chamber of Commerce, the National Foreign Trade Council, and the US contingent of the ICC all opposed the ITO, which, they felt, condoned restrictive and discriminatory policies, accommodated centralized government planning, required excessive government regulations and controls, and committed signatories to state planning for full employment.[49] Nor was the State Department all that enthusiastic about it by 1949, when Truman finally submitted it to Congress for a vote. Acheson feared that a congressional fight over the ITO might jeopardize the renewal of the Reciprocal Trade Agreements Act (RTAA), which allowed the United States to participate in GATT negotiations. So the administration dropped the ITO, which collapsed without US participation.

The Tariff Question

In a telling moment in NAM's congressional testimony about the Marshall Plan, Republican congressman Jacob Javits of New York asked NAM rep Herbert Schell if he saw any threat to the American businessman if the program were to restore European production to 150 percent of where it was in 1939. Would that produce "undue competition" for American manufacturers? Schell said no, the world was progressing, Americans were not afraid of competition. Javits pushed back slightly, asking if the United States no longer needed tariff protection. Here Schell clarified his response: "I did not say we did not need protection. That suggests a rather complicated tariff discussion which purely as a time-saver we should avoid I believe."[50] Yes, avoiding the question was purely a "time-saver"—and nothing at all to do with the many manufacturers represented by NAM who did fear European competition.

Hanging over all of NAM's talk of international cooperation and free enterprise were the substantial number of its dues-paying members who expected NAM to uphold the tariff. Membership rates were prorated, so it was not as if NAM needed the dues of small and midsized manufacturers. What it did need, however, were membership numbers so that it could claim that it represented "over 20,000 manufacturers." Membership numbers

---

49. Chorev, *Remaking US Trade Policy*, 52; Irwin, *Clashing over Commerce*, chap. 10. NAM member Philip Cortney led the opposition from the neoliberal, free-market side in his book *The Economic Munich* (New York: Philosophical Library, 1949), discussed in Slobodian, *Globalists*, chap. 4.

50. Schell, "United States Foreign Policy for a Post-War Recovery Program," 671.

bolstered NAM's legitimacy and credibility in Washington and the business world. Plus, some of NAM's largest members, such as Monsanto Chemical Company, supported high tariffs. Thus, protectionists' concerns could not be completely ignored. Some have since seen these fears as misplaced. The United States had substantially reduced its tariffs by the 1950s to no ill effect; imports remained low because European production was still recovering from the war and thus did not threaten US manufacturers.[51] Nonetheless, in the midst of great uncertainty, these fears were very real and, as it turned out, prescient.

Tensions were especially acute whenever the RTAA came up for renewal. Mandated to be renewed every three years, RTAA gave the executive branch the power to reduce tariff rates in reciprocal trade treaty negotiations. NAM took an officially supportive, if convoluted, position on each RTAA renewal from 1934 to 1945, endorsing both the need for protection and the need to "adjust" tariffs to encourage trade, as well as proposing various amendments, which were generally ignored.[52]

In 1945, in preparation for postwar reconstruction, the State Department asked to be able to reduce tariff levels by 50 percent of 1945 levels—not of 1934 levels, as had previously been done. President Roosevelt, just weeks before his death, urged Congress to accept the State Department's request. Even so, the 1945 renewal encountered rough waters, arousing the ire of small to midsized producers and their Republican representatives.[53] Sensing the tension, NAM officially opposed the additional tariff reduction request and, like many Republicans, supported a one-year renewal only.[54] But NAM president Ira Mosher gave speeches arguing on behalf of ongoing tariff reduction: "If a high level of employment is to lead to expanding exports of American goods and services, then we must prepare to take goods and services in return."[55] The bill passed as written, and the State Department increased its tariff-reducing powers for another three years.

---

51. Irwin, *Clashing over Commerce*, chap. 10. For very different views, see Eckes, *Opening America's Market*, chap. 6; and Judith Stein, *Pivotal Decade: How the United States Traded Factories for Finance in the Seventies* (New Haven, CT: Yale University Press, 2010), chap. 1. Both Eckes and Stein argue that the United States consistently put foreign policy before economic interests, to the detriment of American industry and workers.

52. See "Chronological Documentation of the NAM Positions on the Tariff and Reciprocity Agreement since 1895," pp. 9–13, series 1, box 105, NAMR.

53. Irwin, *Clashing over Commerce*, chap. 10.

54. "Chronological Documentation of the NAM Positions on the Tariff and Reciprocity Agreement since 1895," p. 13, series 1, box 105, NAMR.

55. Ira Mosher, address before the Economic Club, March 1945, in ibid.

Republicans in the House voted no, but almost half of Senate Republicans broke ranks to vote yes.

In the wake of the 1945 RTAA renewal, the Marshall Plan, and NAM's increased activity on behalf of freer trade, NAM protectionists were becoming restless. In 1947, Noel Sargent wondered if it would be possible for NAM to even take a position on the 1948 RTAA renewal. A committee formed to study the tariff had made little progress and was unlikely to reach an agreement that would be approved by the board.[56] Sargent suggested that since other organizations would support the RTAA, perhaps NAM didn't need to take a position. He also implied that renewal would likely go through with or without NAM support, noting that Republican politicians talked protection to placate their constituencies but were in fact more and more likely to endorse RTAA renewal out of hand.[57]

In the end, NAM took no position on RTAA renewal in 1948. The executive committee decided against a study of the tariff or the effects of RTAA, "in view of the sharp divergences of viewpoints among industrialists."[58] A Republican Congress weighed renewal down with "peril point" provisions and limited it to one year.[59] A new Democratic Congress redid the whole thing the following year, removing the provisions and strengthening the president's authority.

The next renewal came up in 1953, during the Eisenhower administration, which had brought with it a Republican congressional majority. Although Republicans were increasingly supportive of RTAA, an active contingent of protectionists were able to siphon off once-solid Southern Democrats who now represented a growing number of transplanted (and import-threatened) textile factories.[60] Eisenhower opted to go for a one-year renewal of the RTAA and formed a commission on foreign economic trade to provide fair and balanced recommendations for RTAA policy in the future. He appointed as its head Inland Steel's Clarence Randall, who was

56. Noel Sargent to Walter Weisenberger, February 6, 1947, series 1, box 105, NAMR.

57. Irwin, *Clashing over Commerce*, chap. 10.

58. Executive Committee meeting minutes, April 24, 1947, series 13, box 250, NAMR; see also Bauer, de Sola Pool, and Dexter, *American Business and Public Policy*, 334–36.

59. The "peril point" is the lowest tariff rate on a commodity before the tariff has an adverse effect on local producers. The provision provided a limit below which the president could not cut tariffs on specific products. See Irwin, *Clashing over Commerce*, chap. 10.

60. Southern Democrats, who had once protested "the tariff of abominations," were increasingly interested in protection, owing to both the transplanted textile industry and the decreasing importance of cotton exports since the application of New Deal cotton subsidies. See Irwin, *Clashing over Commerce*, chap. 11, for this fascinating discussion.

also a loudly internationalist presence on NAM's International Relations Committee. It was at this time that all hell broke loose at NAM.

It is hard to pinpoint where exactly the trouble started, but the International Relations Committee's recommendation that NAM adopt more internationalist positions regarding the tariff and other trade restrictions was certainly a provocation. Based on a 400-page study put together by the staff of NAM's International Economic Affairs Department, the International Relations Committee developed and adopted (by fifty-eight votes to two) a detailed policy position in favor of gradually lowering tariff rates and other restrictions.[61] The reasoning was familiar: Europeans and others needed to be able to sell their goods in US markets in order to accrue the dollars they needed to buy US exports.[62] At the same time, NAM president Charles Sligh Jr. (Sligh Furniture Companies in Michigan) was traveling the country calling for lower tariffs.[63] Sligh's proselytizing, along with the International Relations Committee's recommendations, prompted Monsanto Chemical Company, then the sixth-largest US chemical producer, to very publicly resign from NAM, an event widely covered in the press.[64] A Monsanto vice president explained that the company "cannot honestly align itself with an organization whose beliefs are contrary to our own." NAM responded that free-trade statements were matters of opinion, not official NAM policy, and as if to back that up, the board of directors promptly rejected the International Relations Committee's well-researched position, reviving the NAM policy of taking no position on the tariff.[65] This action did not mollify Monsanto, which wanted NAM to stand up for the protection of certain industries. Nor did it please internationalists, such as Philip Cortney, president of Coty, Inc. (a beauty products company) and a member of NAM's International Relations Committee, who resigned from the NAM board of directors over the matter.

61. Bauer, de Sola Pool, and Dexter, *American Business and Public Policy*, 334–35. The vote is recorded in Philip Cortney to Directors of the NAM, December 22, 1953, box 4, folder 6, WJGP.

62. "Preamble and Policy Statement on the Tariff and Related Issues Adopted by the NAM International Relations Committee," considered but not approved by the NAM board of directors, October 29, 1953, appendix B, series 13, box 240, volume 47, NAMR.

63. "NAM Head Calls for Cuts in Tariffs," *New York Times*, October 9, 1953, p. 37; "Asks Gradual Cut in World Trade Curbs," *Chicago Daily Tribune*, June 25, 1953, p. D6.

64. "NAM Too Liberal on Trade?" *Business Week*, November 21, 1953, p. 170; Edward Ryan, "NAM Directors Vote "No" on Tariffs," *Washington Post*, November 20, 1953, p. 27; see also "100-0 1953" file, series 1, box 284, NAMR.

65. "NAM Too Liberal on Trade?" *Business Week*, November 21, 1953, p. 170; Edward Ryan, "NAM Directors Vote "No" on Tariffs," *Washington Post*, November 20, 1953, p. 27.

It is worth examining Cortney's criticism because it illuminates the tensions inherent in the entire NAM project of a united front of manufacturers in the mid-twentieth century. In a flurry of letters copied to top leaders of NAM's board, Cortney politely expressed outrage at NAM's backwardness, cowardice, and lack of principled leadership: "It still seems incredible to me that the Board of Directors should have adopted the resolution that the governing body of American industry has no opinion regarding one of the most vital national issues."[66] By not taking any position on the issue at this time, wrote Cortney, NAM was essentially supporting high tariffs. It might as well be the American Tariff League. NAM spent millions educating the American public on economic principles, yet it could not educate its own members "as to the proper attitude they should adopt towards these problems if we are not to be discredited in the eyes of the American people."[67] And it was not just this issue but others also, such as the gold standard and the minimum wage, on which NAM likewise refused to provide leadership. Cortney understood that the NAM leadership took neutral positions in order not to lose members, but all that meant to him was that NAM shirked its leadership responsibility for a "certain amount of dollars," choosing to represent narrow interests rather than provide national guidance.[68] Convinced that the majority of members supported his position, Cortney suggested holding a referendum on important issues rather than ducking them.[69]

The chairman of the NAM board, William Grede (Grede Foundries, Inc., Milwaukee), responded respectfully to Cortney's protest. Part of NAM's conservative wing, Grede himself had likewise been disappointed by NAM's inability to take strong positions on issues like the minimum wage. But Grede nonetheless defended the organization's attempt to keep the peace by being neutral. Grede and Cortney were in ideological agreement about unions, free enterprise, and monetary policy; both were fans of Hayek and involved in the Mont Pelerin Society.[70] Thus, at one level, the disagreement in the NAM leadership was not just—or even mainly—about "free trade" versus "protection," but rather about the nature of organizational integrity: should

66. Cortney, "to My Fellow Directors," November 12, 1953, and Cortney to H. W. Prentis Jr., November 6, 1953, both in box 4, folder 6, WJGP. A Milwaukee foundryman, William J. Grede was NAM president in 1952 and chairman of the board of directors in 1953.

67. Cortney to H. W. Prentis Jr., November 6, 1953, box 4, folder 6, WJGP.

68. Cortney to William J. Grede, November 30, 1953, box 4, folder 6, WJGP.

69. Ibid.; Bauer, de Sola Pool, and Dexter, *American Business and Public Policy*, 334–35.

70. Cortney is heavily featured in Slobodian, *Globalists*, chap. 4, for opposing the ITO and tying economic rights (such as the right to transfer capital across borders) to human rights.

an organization prioritize institutional cohesion or principled positions? The NAM leadership, represented by Grede, chose institutional cohesion, although that decision provided anything but.

The Randall Report came out in January 1954, in time for Congress to consider the RTAA renewal in June. The report called for a gradual reduction of tariffs, renewal of the RTAA, and other policies designed to lessen international trade restrictions and promote trade. In forming the commission, Congress had attempted to "balance" the representation, including protectionists in the mix of ten congressmen and seven presidential appointees. But Eisenhower's choice of a known internationalist to head the commission raised the ire of many. Journalist Walter Lippmann suggested that the whole rushed gambit was meant to persuade the three ultra-protectionists on the commission to change their minds, reflecting Ike's misplaced pursuit of "consensus" rather than real debate.[71] In an effort at "fairness," the report was weighted down with qualifications and concessions, and thus it was a disappointment to internationalists, who were looking for a forthright, fact-based case for the economic value of lower tariffs. Moreover, a minority group filed a separate report anyway, undermining the whole purported purpose.[72] US allies and free-traders were disappointed in the report, but so too were protectionists. However, as a *Christian Science Monitor* reporter noted, it was actually historically significant that a Republican administration endorsed a call—however mild and qualified—for lower tariffs.[73] And despite the Randall Report's weakness, Eisenhower himself made a strong statement on behalf of open markets when he asked Congress to renew the RTAA in March.[74]

Meanwhile, NAM's executive committee voted six-to-five against having Randall, a prominent NAM director, speak on President Eisenhower's foreign economic policy at the annual meeting.[75] So here we have a prominent

71. Walter Lippman, "The Randall Commission Theory," in his syndicated column "Today and Tomorrow . . . ," *Washington Post*, January 25, 1954, p. 15. For an argument that Eisenhower attempted to coordinate assent from the three major business associations, see Bauer, de Sola Pool, and Dexter, *American Business and Public Policy*, 334.

72. US Commission on Foreign Economic Policy, "Report to the President and the Congress," and "Minority Report," January 1954 (Washington, DC: US Government Printing Office, 1954).

73. Joseph Harsch, "State of the Nations: The Randall Commission Report," *Christian Science Monitor*, January 29, 1954, p. 1.

74. "The President's Trade Policy," *New York Herald Tribune*, March 31, 1954, p. 18; Irwin, *Clashing over Commerce*, chap. 11.

75. Entry from November 1, 1954, box 4, volume V, "Washington 1954," *Journals of Clarence B. Randall on Foreign Economic Policy*, Clarence B. Randall Papers, MC109, Public Policy Papers, Department of Rare Books and Special Collections, Princeton University Library, Princeton, NJ. I

NAM leader who, two years earlier, had been voted NAM's "Man of the Year" and who was chosen by President Eisenhower to formulate economic policy being shunned by the organization in order to maintain peace. Randall ended his relationship with NAM, noting that the organization had "demonstrated conclusively that [its] resolutions on behalf of liberty, and freedom of speech, and the enterprise system were a fraud" and that it was "merely the embodiment of self-interest, and not dedicated to general welfare."[76] Nonetheless, Randall did end up speaking at NAM's annual meeting, exhorting NAM members to apply "the same principles of rigorous competition" it embraced at home to the international economy.[77] Those in attendance cheered. Others, such as Dow Chemical, resigned from NAM.[78]

Other Tensions with Internationalists

Even aside from the tariff issue, NAM's international activities caused consternation among many of its members. Partly this reflected divisions within the Republican Party of the 1950s. The internationalist Eisenhower wing was supportive of international institutions and treaties that would foster cooperation and goodwill, especially in the shadow of potential nuclear holocaust. Meanwhile, the conservative wing feared that organizations like the UN or even GATT threatened US sovereignty. In the mid-1950s, Ohio congressman John Bricker proposed a series of constitutional amendments aimed at checking Eisenhower and preventing international treaties and executive orders from subverting US laws or Congress. Groups like the US Chamber of Commerce, the Daughters of the American Revolution, and the American Legion backed the Bricker amendment, leading Eisenhower to quip that it was an attempt to "save the United States from Eleanor Roosevelt."[79] NAM stood with Eisenhower, but conservative Republicans in both its leadership and membership did not make it easy.

---

thank Janick Marina Schaufelbuehl for the reference. See also discussion in Executive Committee meeting minutes, October 26, 1954, series 13, box 251, NAMR.

76. Entry from November 1, 1954, box 4, volume V, "Washington 1954," *Journals of Clarence B. Randall on Foreign Economic Policy*, Clarence B. Randall Papers, MC109, Public Policy Papers, Department of Rare Books and Special Collections, Princeton University Library.

77. Max Forester, "NAM Hears Randall Appeal for Freer Trade," *New York Herald Tribune*, December 4, 1954, p. 16.

78. Entry from November 1, 1954, box 4, volume V, "Washington 1954," *Journals of Clarence B. Randall on Foreign Economic Policy*, Clarence B. Randall Papers, MC109, Public Policy Papers, Department of Rare Books and Special Collections, Princeton University Library.

79. Quoted in Stephen E. Ambrose, *Eisenhower*, vol. 2 (New York: Simon & Schuster, 1984).

It is difficult to make generalizations about which NAM members stood where with regard to this split. It is safe to assume that, in *general*, large multinational corporations were in the Eisenhower wing, while smaller and midsized enterprises that relied on the tariff were more conservative. But NAM conservatives like J. Howard Pew of Sunoco and Lammot du Pont supported the Bricker amendment even though they headed large multinational corporations, while leaders of smaller companies could be internationalist. Internationalist Philip Cortney was head of a relatively small company (Coty, Inc.) that employed just 1,300, but its business was international and relied on imports.[80] Harold McClellan, NAM director and head of the privately held Old Colony Paint Company in Los Angeles, was likewise an internationalist; in 1959, he organized the United States Exhibition in Moscow, the site of the famous Nixon-Khrushchev "Kitchen Debate."[81]

Within NAM, internationalists were under close scrutiny. As early as 1945, Executive Vice President Walter Weisenberger had scolded Noel Sargent for NAM's overreach in international work. NAM's general secretary since the 1920s, Sargent attended myriad international conferences, representing NAM in the many international organizations to which it belonged. Weisenberger felt that this activity kept Sargent from his regular duties, but also that it might infringe on other organizations doing similar work.[82] In 1948 a special committee was formed to investigate the question. It found NAM's international activities to be beneficial to the organization.[83] Again in 1955, the Executive Committee, ostensibly instigated by budgetary concerns, appointed another subcommittee to investigate the scope of NAM's international activities.[84]

Such scrutiny was not just a reflection of Republican Party divisions. NAM members had genuine concerns. Some objected to sharing technical and market information with foreign manufacturing groups—which

80. On Pew, see correspondence in "Bricker Amendment" folder, box 13, J. Howard Pew Personal Papers, accession 1634, Hagley Library and Museum, Wilmington, DE; information on Coty, Inc., from *Moody's Industrial Manual* (New York, 1960), 2055–56.

81. "Harold McClellan, Paint Concern Head," *New York Times*, August 4, 1979; Walter Unna, "Exchanging Fair Exhibits," *Washington Post and Times Herald*, November 21, 1958, p. A9.

82. Weisenberger to Sargent, March 9, 1945, series 1, box 76, "International Affairs" file, NAMR.

83. See Patrick McMahon to Kenneth Miller, October 24, 1945, and "Report of the Special Committee on International Relations, Approved by the Board," September 17–18, 1948, both in series 1, box 76, "International Affairs" file, NAMR.

84. This investigation likewise found no ill effect, but recommended cost limitations on an upcoming international conference; Executive Committee meeting minutes, February 2, 1955, and October 27, 1955, series 13, box 251, NAMR.

was what international conferences were about. Sharing information was central to the development and rationalization of a global capitalist economy, just as it had been in the early twentieth century at the national level. Indeed, one of the main functions of trade associations had been this kind of information-sharing (see chapter 1). But for some it meant sharing trade "secrets" with foreign competitors, and many NAM members balked at that possibility.[85]

Then there was the issue of Soviet trade. As a Cold War measure, the United States had adopted export controls that limited trade with the Soviet Union and Eastern Europe in the name of national security.[86] NAM globalists thought that the controls were too broad. Although they agreed that the United States and its allies should not give away military secrets, they wanted restrictions lifted in other "nonstrategic" areas. They usually kept their preferences on the down low, given the rampant anticommunism of the day, especially among NAM members. But in 1953, the Eisenhower administration considered loosening restrictions for Western Europe.[87] Emboldened by Eisenhower's move and concerned about missing the boat on Soviet trade opportunities, the International Relations Committee adopted a heavily qualified statement in support of lifting restrictions on the Soviet bloc in order to spur growth in Europe and lessen its dependence on America. It was also hoped that the West would receive valuable goods in "exchange for goods it ships to the east."[88] The NAM board vetoed the International Relations Committee resolution on Soviet trade, affirming NAM's belief in "security above profits."[89] Other business leaders had also offered tentative support for a "thaw" in Soviet-American relations. All of which led to a full-on attack by fierce Cold Warriors like editorialists Joseph and Stewart Alsop and AFL-CIO head George Meany. Meany in particular took great pleasure

85. See Executive Committee meeting minutes, October 26, 1954, p. 4, series 13, box 251, NAMR; "Report of Mr. Henning W. Prentis, Jr.," appendix D in board of directors meeting minutes, September 16, 1954, series 13, box 240, NAMR.

86. As one historian put it, "In export control policy, the United States has acted in defiance of globalization"; Michael Mastanduno, "The United States Defiant: Export Controls in the Postwar Era," *Daedalus* 120, no. 4 (Fall 1991): 91–112, 92.

87. See Robert Mark Spaulding Jr., "'A Gradual and Moderate Relaxation': Eisenhower and the Revision of American Export Control Policy, 1953–1955," *Diplomatic History* 17, no. 2 (Spring 1993): 223–49.

88. See Clayton Kirkpatrick, "NAM Board Vetoes Trade with Russia," *Chicago Daily Tribune*, June 30, 1954, p. C7; see also "100-0 1954: Statement on East West Trade" file, submitted on April 30, 1954, series 1, box 284, NAMR.

89. Kirkpatrick, "NAM Board Vetoes Trade with Russia."

in castigating the business community for not being "sufficiently alert to the danger of world communism."[90]

Snafus like this raised the ire of the NAM conservatives in control of the Executive Committee, who were increasingly suspicious of the staff's developmental and international work.[91] Consisting of about fifteen former presidents and directors, the Executive Committee controlled NAM's purse strings. In September 1957, it recommended that the International Relations Committee be eliminated.[92] The board of directors rejected this idea, and indeed, despite internal antipathy, NAM's international activities continued apace.

Internationalism thrived at NAM not just because large multinational corporations wanted it to, but also because of the moderating influence of the NAM staff. In their study of trade associations and tariff legislation, political scientists Raymond Bauer and Ithiel de Sola Pool noted that the NAM staff was "almost to a man in favor of a liberal trade policy."[93] Exemplifying this observation was not a man, but a woman named Vada Horsch, who organized and chronicled NAM's activities in the international field. A graduate of the University of Wisconsin, Horsch came to NAM in 1932 and served on the Industrial Relations Committee and the International Relations Committee before being promoted to NAM assistant secretary in 1947. As assistant secretary, she worked closely with the Executive Committee and the board of directors until her retirement in 1966.[94]

As manager of NAM's International Economic Affairs Department, Horsch worked with her counterparts in Europe and Latin America to develop trade and encourage intercultural understanding. She held a leadership role in the US Inter-American Council, a Uruguay-based group committed to opening markets in Latin America. She cofounded and led the Lafayette Fellowship Foundation, which provided scholarships to French

90. "Meany Warns US on Soviet Trade," *New York Times*, January 20, 1956, p. 6; Joseph and Stewart Alsop, "Only Soviets Lose Nothing if Truce Fails," *Boston Daily Globe*, August 8, 1951, p. 1.

91. See the Executive Committee meeting minutes from 1954 to 1960, in which the committee refuses to fund studies for water conservation and nuclear energy. This issue is discussed in chapter 8.

92. See "Recommendations on NAM Activities in the International Field . . . ," September 9, 1957, in board of directors meeting minutes, series 13, box 241, NAMR; and Executive Committee meeting minutes, September 18, 1957, series 13, box 251, NAMR. The board of directors was considerably larger and more representative than the Executive Committee and voted on all public positions, as well as on committee decisions.

93. Bauer, de Sola Pool, and Dexter, *American Business and Public Policy*, 335.

94. See "Of Those Who Served," 1954 (which contains biographies of NAM staff), series 1, box 101, NAMR.

students for study in the United States.[95] Whether organizing visits to Chicago meatpacking plants or arranging tea parties for Argentinian diplomats' wives, Horsch was a favorite with foreign dignitaries, who wrote letter after letter singing her praises. The governments of France, Italy, and Ecuador all awarded Horsch citations for her work.[96] Horsch pushed NAM directors to connect with other organizations and groups, urging cooperation with the National Foreign Trade Council and the inclusion of Latin America in international trade conferences (when some pushed for exclusion of Latin American countries). At a time when ultraconservatives were isolating NAM, Horsch—and the staff in general—was a consistent voice for connection and inclusion.[97]

The flip side of liberal internationalism's connection and inclusion was what many see as economic imperialism. NAM's work on the Inter-American Council and the like facilitated US penetration of Latin American markets. The NAM member companies opening plants in Latin America included Allis-Chalmers in Mexico, Harnischfeger, International, and Chrysler in Brazil, W. R. Grace in Puerto Rico, and IT&T in Chile.[98] Corporations built factories in these countries to jump tariffs and gain access to markets— that is, to make a buck and establish US hegemony. But they also produced goods to help Latin American nations develop their own industries. In 1955, 94 percent of US corporations' output in Latin America was sold in Latin American markets.[99] At this time, the United States supported "import substitution industrialization," a policy embraced by developing nations that allowed them a heavy hand in protecting their industries to develop self-sustaining economies.[100] Some market cheerleaders in NAM even applied Marshall Plan reasoning to Latin America, arguing that US trade in the region would bring the dollars to these countries that they needed to buy

95. "Woman Executive Sights French Industrial Surge," *Christian Science Monitor*, May 17, 1957, p. 13; "Activities and Policy Positions Related to International Economic Matters," prepared by Vada Horsch, April 13, 1960, series 12, box 194, NAMR.

96. "Activities and Policy Positions Related to International Economic Matters," prepared by Vada Horsch, April 13, 1960, series 12, box 194, NAMR.

97. See, for instance, Horsch to Kenneth Miller, November 17, 1955; Horsch to Lightner, March 25, 1958; "Activities and Policy Positions Related to International Economic Matters," all in series 12, box 194–95, NAMR. The ultra-conservatives are discussed in chapter 8.

98. See Senator Alexander Wiley's remarks in praise of the Inter-American Council's work in *Congressional Record*, March 10, 1958, p. A2177, as found in Wiley to H. W. Balgooyen, March 11, 1958 series 12, box 194, NAMR.

99. Panitch and Gindin, *The Making of Global Capitalism*, 104.

100. Ibid., 104–5. Apparently, this was one of many more moderate policies later replaced by WTO policies, which are less accepting of participating countries' trade barriers.

FIGURE 7.1. Vada Horsch receiving the French Legion Medal of Honor, 1958. The man on the left is NAM board member and internationalist Philip Cortney of Coty, Inc. Copyright © National Association of Manufacturers; courtesy of Hagley Library and Museum.

from US companies.[101] The bottom line, however, was that there was money to be made in helping developing nations build an industrial infrastructure of their own.

THE INTERNATIONAL LABOR ORGANIZATION

NAM members were rabidly anticommunist. Promoting global capitalism sometimes meant working with the Soviet Union, however, and that was a constant source of tension. The International Labor Organization (ILO)

101. See the pro-RTAA editorial, Vision Incorporated, "Keep the Open Door Open," March 14, 1958, in series 12, box 194, "International Relation" file, NAMR. For a more thorough discussion of US economic imperialism, see Walter LaFeber, *Inevitable Revolutions: The United States in Central America* (New York: W. W. Norton, 1993); Greg Grandin, *Empire's Workshop: Latin America, the United States, and the Rise of the New Imperialism* (New York: Holt, 2007); and, of course, Williams, *The Tragedy of American Diplomacy.*

was a case in point. Founded in 1919 as part of the League of Nations, the ILO aimed to establish international labor standards, protections for workers, and social justice for all peoples. It became part of the UN in 1946, at the urging in part of the US State Department, which hoped to keep any international labor organizations in the capitalist network.[102] The US government provided 25 percent of its annual budget, roughly $1.5 million. By 1960, the ILO had eighty member countries sending two governmental reps, one employer rep, and one labor rep each.[103] The State Department asked NAM and the US Chamber of Commerce to nominate the employers' rep for the United States, which gave them a voice, albeit a tiny one, in setting international labor standards and norms.

The ILO's organizational structure assumed and validated the idea that government, employers, and labor had separate and distinct interests, thus upholding and naturalizing the structure of "free enterprise." This idea was strained when the Soviet Union barged in on the project in 1954, accompanied by three of its communist satellites.[104] Because there was no such distinction among employers, the state, and workers under communist rule, the communist nations presented a unified front and thus skewed the already left-leaning ILO further leftward. This alarmed the American business reps, who accused communists of using the ILO as a propaganda platform.

Both the Chamber and NAM lodged objections with the US government. Although they threatened to leave, they were also wary of who the government might replace them with if the United States chose to remain in the ILO. In response to the request from NAM and the Chamber, the Departments of State, Labor, and Commerce conducted an investigation into the matter. The conclusion was that the United States did indeed have an interest in participating in the ILO, and that, if it withdrew, it would miss

102. Hearden, *Architects of Globalism*, 76–77; see also Walter Galenson, *The International Labor Organization: An American View* (Madison: University of Wisconsin Press, 1981), 4–9.

103. Galenson, *The International Labor Organization*, 11; "International Labor Organization Committee Findings," n.d., c. 1957, series 12, box 195, NAMR. These were the findings of a special committee formed by the US Departments of Commerce, Labor, and State, appointed in May 1956.

104. Galenson, *The International Labor Organization*, 23–47. The Soviet Union had withdrawn from the organization in 1937, but returned in 1954, during the Cold War. See Yves Beigbeter, "The United States' Withdrawal from the International Labour Organization," *Relations Industrielles/Industrial Relations* 34, no. 2 (1979): 223–40.

an opportunity to proselytize on behalf of capitalism and basically hand over to the Soviet Union control of an international labor organization. In fact, the departments requested that Congress increase the US contribution to the ILO to $3 million![105]

The United States remained in the ILO, but the controversy continued. In 1960, a committee proposed that NAM support legislation demanding the withdrawal of the United States. The board voted no. In 1961, a committee proposed that NAM withdraw its participation. Under pressure, the board decided to suspend NAM's participation in the ILO for one year, but not to withdraw completely.[106] The struggle was between the ultraconservative, McCarthyite anticommunists, most of whom were also economic nationalists, and the free-trade anticommunists, represented by Philip Cortney, NAM board chair Stanley Hope, and the US State Department, who hoped to establish US economic hegemony internationally.[107] Stanley Hope was the former head of Esso Standard, later Exxon Mobil, the second-largest corporation in the United States in the 1950s, and part of a multinational industry interested in seeing the United States remain in the ILO. Indeed, in 1962 a representative of the American Petroleum Institute urged NAM to maintain its membership.[108] Hope would be among those sidelining the ultraconservatives in 1961 (see chapter 8) and bringing in a more multinational-friendly governing structure. By 1962, NAM had resumed its regular role in the ILO.[109] Thus, despite their members' complaints and various resolutions

105. The Senate did not approve the request. After failing to get the United States to withdraw from the ILO, Ohio Republican senator John Bricker was successful in capping the US contribution to $1.75 million. See "Senate Vote Freezes ILO Fund," *Christian Science Monitor*, April 20, 1956, p. 1; see also Galenson, *The International Labor Organization*, 31–33; "International Labor Organization Committee Findings," c. 1957, series 12, box 195, NAMR.

106. The suspension was the result of the board vote of forty-six in favor and thirty-two against not meeting the required two-thirds majority; Charles Sligh, memorandum to NAM staff, February 28, 1961, series 12, box 192, NAMR.

107. In fact, Cortney and ILO rep Cola Parker, who was also a cofounder of the John Birch Society, exchanged words for which apologies were proffered; see chapter 8 and also "Statement to the National Association of Manufacturers Board of Directors," December 5, 1961, series 13, box 242, NAMR 8.

108. Executive Committee meeting minutes, June 13, 1962, series 13, box 251, NAMR. On Hope, see "Stanley Hope Dead; Had Served as Head of Esso Standard Co.," *New York Times*, June 23, 1982, p. B11.

109. For the Executive Committee vote against further study of ILO, see Executive Committee meeting minutes, December 3, 1962, series 13, box 251, NAMR.

against the ILO, both NAM and the Chamber continued to participate in the ILO.[110]

These instances and others suggest that internationalists had a troubled relationship with conservatives. But the two groups were not mutually exclusive either. The next chapter examines NAM's post–World War II conservatives in greater depth.

110. NAM would not be as active in the ILO as the Chamber of Commerce. NAM, for instance, did not send a representative to ILO hearings in 1963. These events are described in "International Labor Organization Committee Findings," n.d., c. 1957, and in "Brief Chronology of Developments Regarding the Communist Issue in ILO," January 1957, both in series 12, box 195, "ILO" folder, NAMR. None of this controversy made it into Vada Horsch's reporting on NAM's service to the ILO. When the United States finally left the ILO, it would be at the instigation of the AFL-CIO in the 1970s.

8

Conservatives vs. Managers

The 1950s were good years for US manufacturing, which faced little competition from a world still recovering from the Second World War. Manufacturing as a percentage of the GDP peaked in 1953, at 28.3 percent, and remained above 25 percent until the mid-1960s. NAM likewise seemed to share in this bounty, its membership hovering between 19,000 and 21,000 during the years 1954 to 1960 and peaking in 1957 at 21,801. Its staff had grown to 400, and in addition to its New York City headquarters and Washington, DC, office, it had twelve regional and five divisional offices. Yet, despite all of this good news, trumpeted in press releases and publications, NAM remained divided about its mission, worried about its membership, and beset by negative press.

Businessmen and journalists alike regarded NAM's ideological "backwardness" as a hindrance to business's interests and unrepresentative of the business community. Malcolm Forbes called NAM's endorsement "the kiss of death." Inland Steel's Joseph Block said of the 1950s-era NAM: "It has stereotyped positions that are inflexible; it has a reputation for being reactionary and rigid." Another executive characterized NAM leaders as "stewing in their own juice and issuing feudal and futile pronouncements."[1] Partly, this was about corporate liberals criticizing NAM to highlight their own

---

1. Osborn Elliot, *Men at the Top* (New York: Harper and Bros., 1959), 206. See also Malcolm Forbes, "The NAM Would Do Better Dead," *Forbes*, August 15, 1951, p. 10; Richard Gable, "NAM: Influential Lobby or Kiss of Death?"; and less adamantly, Alfred Cleveland, "NAM: Spokesman for Industry?" *Harvard Business Review* (May 1948): 353–71.

enlightened and reasonable moderation. But mostly this criticism was fairly earned by a group of "ultraconservatives," whose control of the purse strings and ties to far-right groups like the John Birch Society (JBS) were increasingly at odds with NAM's internationalism, professional goals, and membership quandaries, areas overseen by the NAM staff. It would be wrong to call the NAM staff "liberal," but its outlook was more pragmatic, more influenced by business and management schools, and less committed to "rugged individualism" than that of NAM's conservative leaders.

The tensions created by ultraconservatives would lead to a restructuring of NAM that sidelined the "old guard" and gave NAM its first full-time paid president and a more pragmatic, issues-based approach to its work. Much has been written about NAM's conservatives, especially with regard to the rise of the right in US politics, but my account highlights the fissures among and between corporate capitalists and conservatives in the mid-twentieth century.

The Return of "Classical Liberalism"

Pragmatic NAM leaders were able to take NAM in a more flexible direction after the war, but ultraconservatives always found a home in the organization. Indeed, the postwar strike wave, the rise of moderates in the Republican Party, and the contests over postwar reconversion all contributed to a "digging in" on the part of NAM conservatives, who were heartened by and involved in a number of new conservative organizations dedicated to combating statism and New Dealism.[2]

After the war, there was a renewed interest in classical liberalism of the old John Locke, Adam Smith sort, which was given new life by Austrian economists Ludwig Von Mises and Friedrich Hayek. Von Mises was already a familiar presence at NAM; an active participant in the International Chamber of Commerce (ICC), he had long been a consultant for NAM projects and a speaker at its meetings.[3] Hayek was the author of a surprise anticollectivist blockbuster, *The Road to Serfdom* (1944), and founder of the Mont Pelerin Society in 1947. Conceived as a kind of study group, MPS consisted of a distinguished group of mainly European economists and intellectuals, including Von Mises and Milton Friedman, who were bent on curtailing collectivism, statism, and the cradle-to-grave welfare systems

---

2. See Phillips-Fein, *Invisible Hands*; Burch, "The NAM as an Interest Group."
3. On Von Mises and Hayek, see Slobodian, *Globalists*, chaps. 1–2.

adopted by postwar Europe.[4] NAM's Jasper Crane, retired from DuPont, convinced a number of his NAM colleagues to contribute to MPS, including J. Howard Pew (Sun Oil Company, later Sunoco), William Grede (Grede Foundries, Inc.), and B. E. Hutchinson (retired from Chrysler). In September 1958, Crane helped organize the first MPS meeting in the United States in Princeton, New Jersey, where Grede and other NAM members gave talks on their pet subjects, liberty and individualism.[5] Hayek had a vexed relationship to businessmen, whom he regarded as intellectually unsophisticated, and they in turn were skeptical of many of his positions. He wanted their funding, however, and they supported his efforts on behalf of free-market individualism.

Philip Cortney, the Romanian-born president of Coty, Inc., was an avid Hayek follower, especially with regard to removing barriers to international trade. The author of *The Economic Munich*, a critique of the proposed International Trade Organization, Cortney was one of the few NAM conservatives who seemed to understand (and embrace) the implications of Hayek's arguments for global markets. As chair of NAM's International Relations Committee, Cortney constantly tried to explain the Hayekian perspective on the gold standard and free trade, often with the aid of economist Michael Heilperin, but to no avail.[6] His lack of success suggests that NAM businessmen had little patience for the highly abstract and internationalist ideas coming from the Mont Pelerin group.

NAM conservatives were more comfortable giving money to homegrown organizations dedicated to getting the message out to regular Americans, who they believed had been duped by New Dealism and the labor movement. They supported Leonard Read's Foundation for Economic Education (FEE), founded in 1946, which published and distributed pamphlets on the wisdom of individualism and capitalism that were very much in line with Hayek's ideas.[7] The American Enterprise Association, founded in 1938 to provide "unbiased" information to Congress, was another favorite. Funded by large corporations, it floundered after a congressional investigation (of the

---

4. On Hayek and NAM businessmen, see Phillips-Fein, *Invisible Hands*, 34–51.

5. Ibid., 50–51.

6. See chapter 7. NAM economist Ralph Robey wrote a long letter to William Grede about Cortney's obnoxious and condescending behavior in one committee meeting; see Ralph Robey to William Grede, August 22, 1952, box 4, folder 6, WJGP.

7. On FEE, see Phillips-Fein, *Invisible Hands*, 41–56; and Brian Doherty, *Radicals for Capitalism: A Freewheeling History of the Modern American Libertarian Movement* (New York: PublicAffairs, 2007), chap. 4.

sort NAM was all too familiar with). In 1954, a General Electric executive revived the organization and hired William J. Baroody, whose fund-raising and recruitment created a network of like-minded businessmen and a think tank now known as the American Enterprise Institute (AEI).

More traditionally conservative (and most popular among NAM members) was *The Manion Forum*, a weekly radio broadcast and media outlet founded in 1954 by Notre Dame law professor Clarence Manion. Whereas FEE and AEI promoted classical liberal ideas, including free trade, *The Manion Forum* was heavy on anticommunism and isolationism.[8] It played to the conservative Republicans who felt abandoned by the moderate internationalists in their own party and who supported Ohio senator John Bricker's many amendments to end US international involvement.[9] Much of the NAM base was made up of conservative Midwestern Republican isolationists whose anger was directed not just at the United Nations and Eisenhower's internationalism but also at NAM's complicity in it. These conservatives found a home and a cause in *The Manion Forum*, which would be crucial to Barry Goldwater's bid for the Republican presidential nomination in 1964.

Perhaps the oddest of the new organizations to beguile NAM businessmen was Robert LeFevre's Freedom School, founded in 1956 in Larkspur, Colorado. A former member of something called the "I AM" cult, LeFevre was a charismatic autodidact and anticommunist who caught the libertarian bug and opened a school in the Rocky Mountains on land cleared by him, his wife, and former female acolytes from his old cult days.[10] An anarchist, a pacifist, and a bit of a bohemian, LeFevre was not every libertarian's cup of tea, and he eventually made enemies of onetime allies at the FEE.[11] Nonetheless, he was able to attract serious libertarians to teach at his school, including Ludwig Von Mises, F. A. Harper, Frank Chodorov, Rose Wilder Lane, and Milton Friedman. But LeFevre himself was the main attraction. One of the school's graduates described him as "a convincing cross of a professor, a father figure, and a religious—not quite charlatan, but a

8. Phillips-Fein, *Invisible Hands*, 81–85.

9. On the Bricker amendment, see Dwight D. Eisenhower, *Mandate for Change, 1953–1956* (New York: Doubleday, 1963), 278–85; on the isolationists, see Justin Doenecke, *Not to the Swift: The Old Isolationists in the Cold War Era* (Lewisburg, PA: Bucknell University Press, 1979).

10. For an excellent overview of LeFevre's career and philosophy, see Doherty, *Radicals for Capitalism*, 312–37.

11. The FEE's Leonard Read taught one session there, but he was put off by LeFevre's extremism, which he thought was anarchistic. For LeFevre's nixing of Grede's recommendation of Read as a Freedom School trustee, See LeFevre to Grede, April 22, 1960, box 7, folder6, "Freedom School" file, WJGP. See also Doherty, *Radicals for Capitalism*, 320.

spellbinder."[12] His donors included textile magnate Roger Milliken, the young Charles Koch, and NAM directors Robert Gaylord and William Grede. As president of Grede Foundries, Inc., in Milwaukee, Grede convinced members of the Milwaukee Employers Association to not only attend and fund the school but also to fund a scholarship for Milwaukee youth. Gaylord of Ingersoll Milling Machine Company did the same through the Rockford (Illinois) Chamber of Commerce.[13]

Responses to the school were generally positive, at least according to LeFevre's supporters. But six students wrote with alarm to the Rockford Chamber of Commerce about their Freedom School experience. They were concerned that the Chamber might have been misled about the school and its teachings. For one thing, it did not seem to have many students and there was little evidence of local support. More distressing, however, was LeFevre's message that there should be no government, no police department, no fire department, and no public schools, not to mention his message that "all religion is a myth" and his opposition to voting, which Lefevre taught them was a capitulation to government. The school displayed no American flag on its grounds. The students said that they could not believe the Chamber would endorse what amounted to anarchy. Although grateful for the opportunity, they thought the Chamber should know what was going on; it was their opinion that LeFevre was a huckster.[14] Even positive letters, such as one from a businessman who had just returned from a session, indicated some warning signs. James Vollmar said that he spent the first few days "in bitter opposition" to LeFevre, and then "suddenly, as if someone had pushed a button, I saw everything so clearly." Still, the man regretted that he could not defend his new faith as expertly as LeFevre.[15]

The folks at the Milwaukee Employers Association saw the Rockford students' criticism of the Freedom School as evidence of socialism's influence on "today's youth." For their part, they had received no negative responses: "Certainly we have not had one hundred percent conversions to strict libertarians . . . but without exception among those I have talked to so far they have returned with a much deeper concept of the nature of the trend toward Socialism and the root causes of it."[16] And that after all was the main point.

12. Quoted in Doherty, *Radicals for Capitalism*, 319.

13. Ibid., 316–17, 320. On Charles Koch's involvement with the school, see also Mayer, *Dark Money*, 43–45.

14. Letter to Chamber of Commerce, Rockford, IL, September 1, 1959, box 7, folder 6, WJGP.

15. James Vollmar to C. W. Anderson, September 2, 1959, box 7, folder 6, WJGP.

16. [?] to Francis Spence, September 24, 1959, box 7, folder 6, WJGP.

Despite LeFevre's unconventionality, NAM conservatives loved him, and their continued support for him was a measure of how beleaguered they felt.[17]

Beleaguered in NAM

Even though NAM was regarded as one of the most conservative organizations in America, conservatives like Grede and Gaylord were not happy with it. They saw themselves as fighting a lonely, losing battle against not only New Deal collectivism but also organizational pragmatism and NAM's professional, college-educated staff. Despite their leadership positions, they felt like they had little influence over NAM, which depended on funding from larger, less conservative corporations. The committee system worked against any kind of ideological coherence on specific issues. Conservatives were constantly objecting to committee endorsements of, for instance, the minimum wage, unemployment compensation, or, as we have seen, reduced tariffs.[18] They worried that do-gooders were gaining influence in NAM. Here is Robert Gaylord complaining about the NAM report endorsing unemployment compensation in 1956:

> If the real purpose of the report is to embrace compulsory unemployment compensation as a "social responsibility" so the self-labeled "liberals" will not consider the NAM a reactionary, hidebound organization refusing to recognize the realities of present day life, it is "too little, too late," nor will a public profession of something we do not actually believe in effectively serve even that purpose.[19]

In point of fact, the Employment Health and Benefits Committee was only endorsing common practice, which recognized that a dynamic free enterprise system created involuntary unemployment and that the best way to deal with this was through "sound public unemployment programs," a position to which NAM members had long ascribed.[20] Ignoring this con-

17. Grede and LeFevre would have a falling-out over the John Birch Society: LeFevre saw political activism like that of the JBS as validating the system, while Grede saw it as a responsibility in a democratic society. See Craig Miner, *Grede of Milwaukee* (Wichita, KS: Watermark Press, 1989), 240–43.

18. See Elliot, *Men at the Top*, 208–9; see also correspondence in box 24, folder 1, WJGP.

19. Gaylord to Grede, September 10, 1956, box 24, folder 1, WJGP.

20. Report of W. G. Caples, chairman of the Employment Health and Benefits Committee, September 12, 1956, series 12, box 192, NAMR.

text, Gaylord dismissed the policy as a ploy on the part of reformer-types who wanted to make NAM "relevant." Grede concurred. He too saw NAM efforts to hide their real principles as an ill-advised public relations gambit, generated by public relations departments not on the basis of sound economics "but rather on the basis of what is popular with the public." Large corporations were particularly guilty of this practice, he noted, suggesting that their broad ownership or industrial dominance had led them to "develop a sense that they are a public corporation and therefore, must be responsive to the popular public opinion."[21] Indeed, William Caples, the head of the offending committee, was a vice president at Inland Steel, one of the largest steel concerns in the nation.

Historians have likewise tended to see larger corporations as more "socially responsible" and concerned with their public images, and they have characterized NAM conservatives as the owners and operators of small and midsized companies. NAM was proud that 83 percent of its member companies were small plants employing fewer than five hundred people (the standard cutoff separating small and midsized plants from large ones), and most of the owners of these smaller plants were no doubt conservative—but they were not NAM leaders. The most conservative NAM leaders, rather, were from large, labor-intensive, mostly privately held plants that employed upwards of two thousand workers. Grede was the owner and operator of Grede Foundries, Inc. a large, multi-plant, privately held company, but he had also been president (for five years) of J. I. Case, a publicly listed, multinational corporation with ten thousand employees.[22] His allies included Ernest Swigert of the Hyster Corporation, which was not listed in *Moody's* until 1960 but had over two thousand employees, as well as factories in Scotland, the Netherlands, and Brazil. Robert Stoddard was president of the Wyman-Gordon Company, a private, family-owned and -operated, Massachusetts-based producer of titanium-forged aircraft engine and missile components and a major government contractor, with four thousand employees. Robert Gaylord headed the privately held Ingersoll Milling Machine Company in Rockford, Illinois, with over two thousand employees. Fred Koch's Wood

21. Grede to Clark C. Thompson, September 14, 1953, box 25, folder 6, WJPP. Thompson was from that National Industrial Conference Board and was surveying employers about their views on public relations.

22. Case employment figures are from *Moody's Industrial Manual* (New York, 1960); Moody's listed only publicly traded companies. During the war, Grede Foundries, Inc., consisted of four plants, employed 1,200 people, delivered 100,000 tons of casings, received $24 million in revenue, and paid $3.5 million in taxes. See Miner, *Grede of Milwaukee*, 77.

River and Refining Company, described by one journalist as "a motley collection of oil pipeline assets," had revenues of $250 million, or $2 billion in today's dollars. JBS cofounder Cola Parker headed the Kimberly-Clark Company, a Wisconsin-based company with factories all over the world; the maker of Kleenex, Kotex, and other paper products, it was publicly listed and had over thirteen thousand employees.[23] Although not connected to the JBS, Lammot du Pont (of I. E. Du Pont de Nemours and Company) and Howard Pew (of Sun Oil) were prominent NAM conservatives from large multinational corporations who contributed more than $30,000 in annual dues to NAM. JBS founder and head Robert Welch was one of the few who fit the stereotype: he was an official at his brother's Cambridge, Massachusetts, candy company (producer of Junior Mints), which was bought out by Nabisco in 1963. So while some ultra-conservative NAM leaders came from smaller, privately held corporations, most came from large companies, and some were from large, publicly traded conglomerates. If anything seemed to unite those who became involved in the JBS, it was being from Wisconsin or being in a heavy equipment or heavy machinery industry—which is to say, being in Grede's orbit.

Bill Grede had become popular among conservatives for his successful evasion of unionization. He had acquired his first foundry in 1920 (at the age of twenty-three) and had adopted welfare capitalism techniques (eight-hour day, paid vacation, weekends off) to stave off unions.[24] New Deal legislation and the war made avoiding unions more difficult, but Grede managed to do so through delaying tactics with the United Steelworkers of America (USWA) reps who were trying to unionize Grede Foundries, Inc., which produced ductile iron and steel and employed 1,200 people in the late 1940s.[25] The end of the war forced a confrontation, and two of Grede's plants struck in 1946, the year of the big strike wave. Grede deployed the same tactics, arguing every point of the contract, grilling employees about whether they wanted everything

23. On Hyster, see *Moody's Industrial Manual* (New York, 1960); Mildred McClary Tymeson, *The Wyman-Gordon Way* (Worcester, MA: Wyman-Gordon Co., 1959), 131; "Bay State Company Plays Role of Blacksmith to Space Age," *Boston Globe*, July 17, 1960, p. 44. Several sources call Hyster the largest producer of its product in the world; see Jon Van, "Flexibility, Change Way of Life at Ingersoll," *Chicago Tribune*, November 5, 1991. On Koch, see Leslie Wayne, "Pulling the Wraps Off Koch Industries," *New York Times*, November 20, 1994; on Kimberly-Clark, see *Moody's Industrial Manual* (New York, 1956).

24. Even more critical assessments of him acknowledge his employee-friendly policies, which were, after all, a deterrent to unionization. See, for instance, Tula Connell, *Conservative Counterrevolution: Challenging Liberalism in 1950s Milwaukee* (Urbana: University of Illinois Press, 2016), 128–37.

25. Glenn Fowler, "William J. Grede Is Dead at 92," *New York Times*, June 7, 1989, p. A24. See also Miner, *Grede of Milwaukee*, 40–41, 77.

in the contract, working to divide employees from the national union reps, raising wages for nonstriking workers, and promising to welcome back all striking workers at any time. He even extended their health insurance through the strike.[26] This went on for over a year, by which time the Taft-Hartley Act had passed and the union's case was thrown out because it had not signed the new anticommunist affidavit. The key to Grede's success was his willingness to talk, listen, and argue; he saw the strike as an opportunity to proselytize and defend his philosophy of radical individualism against New Deal collectivism.[27] In 1956, J. I. Case Company, a large manufacturer of farm equipment and tractors, brought in Grede to help with its own labor troubles.

Some NAM leaders and staff members felt that Grede's extremism was damaging to the organization. But these views just contributed to Grede's rising stock in a generally conservative organization. Unlike some other conservatives, Grede apparently had a light touch and was a skilled speaker. In 1952, he was elected NAM president. Presidents served a one-year term and then became board chairs, after which they often served on the Executive Committee; thus, Grede was able to wield influence throughout the 1950s, as were several of his closest JBS allies, including Cola Parker and Ernest Swigert, who served as NAM presidents in 1956 and 1957, respectively. The three would be regular fixtures on NAM's Executive Committee, as well as the far larger board, which approved committee recommendations and determined NAM's public pronouncements.

Not surprisingly, NAM conservatives were rabid anticommunists and supporters of Joseph McCarthy (also from Wisconsin). Keen to "get the message out," they gravitated toward committees on public relations, communications, or education. Robert Welch, for instance, was a fixture on the Education Committee in the 1950s. At one time dedicated to promoting education for careers in manufacturing, the Education Committee became increasingly obsessed with making sure teachers understood the dangers of communism. This caused tension in the NAM Education Department, which had cultivated connections with professional educators.[28]

26. Recounted in elaborate detail in Miner, *Grede of Milwaukee*, 89–98. For a more critical perspective, see Connell, *Conservative Counterrevolution*, 127–39.

27. This tactic of trying to win over employees was deployed as well by General Electric's Lemuel Boulware; see Herbert Northrup, *Boulwarism: The Labor Relations of the General Electric Company* (Ann Arbor: University of Michigan, Bureau of Industrial Relations, 1965); Phillips-Fein, *Invisible Hands*, 97–104.

28. See, for instance, Executive Committee meeting minutes, September 18, 1957, and February 6, 1960, series 13, box 251, NAMR, as well as materials in series 12, box 192, "Education" file, NAMR.

In 1958, Welch founded the John Birch Society, dedicated to raising awareness of and eradicating communist influence in America. By "communist," Welch didn't mean actual Communists or even the Soviet Union. He meant whatever it was that was making Americans forsake their liberal (individualist) tradition of limited government. He meant whatever it was that was making President Eisenhower endorse the United Nations or send troops to Little Rock, Arkansas, to protect black children and overrule Arkansas law. Communism was a convenient explanation for the inexplicable and horrific political direction the country was taking. Even the head of NAM's Public Relations Department understood this: "As I see it the fight is not against a symbol, which is Communism, but against very specific measures such as the progressive income tax, government controls, government ownership of power resources, etc."[29] Communism was indeed an effective symbol, and by fighting it, the JBS hoped to return the country to a time before income tax, social security, reciprocal trade treaties, and NATO—all of which NAM had in fact made peace with, if not directly supported. Like Manion, and unlike Hayek, Welch was an economic nationalist, theoretically opposed to the kind of internationalist policies pursued by NAM.

As a NAM member, Welch was well positioned to build up the JBS. NAM contained a ready-made network of well-connected men seething about the New Deal, unions, free trade, and now civil rights. Grede threw his prestige behind the project. As his biographer notes, "there is no doubt that Bill Grede's organizational and fundraising skill . . . were a major factor in the initial rapid growth of the John Birch Society."[30] Membership lists were closely guarded, but in 1960 Welch reported to the JBS Council that there were three hundred members from over forty states in the home chapter and eighty-two working chapters. The Anti-Defamation League estimated that in 1962 there were over five hundred chapters.[31]

The mainstream press and regular Republicans were quick to dismiss the JBS as a fringe group of haters and extremists, especially after someone leaked a passage from Welch's writing that accused President Eisenhower of being a communist agent.[32] *Fortune* called the group "bizarre" and undemo-

29. Quoted in Miner, *Grede of Milwaukee*, 117.
30. Ibid., 215.
31. Figures from ibid., 222.
32. This bit of information was published in the *Milwaukee Journal* in 1960, but not picked up by the major news outlets until March 1961. See ibid., 216; and "Group Calls Eisenhower a Red," *New York Times*, March 9, 1961.

cratic.[33] Eventually, even William F. Buckley, editor of the *National Review* and spokesman for the nascent conservative movement, would declare the JBS beyond the pale.[34] Grede defended the organization. Welch's views were his own, he said, not those of the JBS, which was a fine, patriotic, anticommunist organization.[35]

The NAM board of directors was not so sure. At the September 1960 board meeting in Hot Springs, Arkansas, the board discussed the quandary raised by Welch's belief (never renounced) that Eisenhower was a communist agent and the fact that three former NAM presidents (Grede, Swigert, and Parker) were founding members of the JBS. The major news outlets had not yet gotten the story, but members of the NAM board were concerned that NAM would be tainted by association and wanted to get out ahead of it.[36] Those implicated doubted that the story would have any impact on NAM and thought it would probably blow over. The board disagreed and adopted a statement declaring NAM's belief in the loyalty and integrity of President Eisenhower and disassociating itself from any individual or group that believed otherwise.[37] That any organization at this time would have to make such a statement was remarkable, but especially an organization that was basically Republican. The statement was regarded by all as a censure, and when the story finally did break the following spring, NAM was able to present it as such—even though NAM reps hedged, saying that it was not repudiating the JBS per se, but only clarifying that Welch's statement was not a view shared by the organization. As one NAM director put it (to the likely horror of other NAM directors), "you can't find much fault with an outfit that's dedicated to fighting Communism."[38]

That December, the NAM board approved the employment of a management consulting firm to survey NAM and make recommendations for improvement.[39] Robert Heller & Associates of Cleveland, Ohio, a firm used by many of NAM's directors, was chosen for the job. The resulting report,

33. "The NAM and the JBS," *Fortune*, May 1961, p. 74.

34. "The John Birch Society and the Conservative Movement," *National Review*, October 19, 1965, pp. 914–16.

35. Miner, *Grede of Milwaukee*, 219–35.

36. See executive session of board of directors meeting minutes, September 13, 14, 15, 1960, in series 13, box 242, NAMR.

37. Ibid. Also described in Miner, *Grede of Milwaukee*, 217–24. This censure was not made public until April of the following year; see John D. Morris, "Birch Unit Pushes Drive on Warren," *New York Times*, April 1, 1961, p. 1.

38. Quoted in "The NAM and the JBS," *Fortune*, May 1961.

39. Minutes of the Board of Directors Meeting, Dec. 6, 1960 in NAMR, Series 13, box 242.

issued in 1961, called for a total restructuring of NAM's administration and governance. Old-timers and conservatives were baffled. Things were tough, sure, but it wasn't NAM's governance that was the problem, they said to each other. An examination of the NAM staff and its challenges offers us some clues as to the necessity for the shake-up.

The Staff

The bad publicity incurred by NAM conservatives frustrated the NAM staff, who tracked and rebutted critical articles as part of their jobs. Assistant Secretary Vada Horsch, who served as secretary to both the International Economic Affairs Department and the Industrial Relations Committee, was dismayed that profiles on NAM tended to caricature its most conservative political aspects while ignoring the organization's more progressive nonpolitical achievements.[40] The positive achievements included not only support for employment stabilization, the United Nations, and reducing trade barriers but also the numerous management workshops, technical publications, and safety institutes, which shared the latest innovations and efficiencies with member companies. In her rebuttals, Horsch emphasized and defended the kind of developmental work she and her peers did as staff.

After a *Harvard Business Review* article came out in 1948, Vada Horsch used the opportunity to gently suggest that they all step back and think about why it was written.[41] Despite its errors and obvious biases, she wrote, publication of the article "may stimulate soul-searching and constructive thinking as how and why such an article could be written" and what means could be adopted to correct the situation.[42] She suggested that conservatives were being allowed to define NAM's image, rather than the good work NAM actually did. That was certainly how the many positive responses to Horsch's review interpreted it. Harry Stinnett of Curtis Publishing Company complimented Horsch's moderate tone, noting: "It's too bad that you can't speak more often for the Association."[43] Edgar Smith of General Motors

---

40. Vada Horsch to Mr. Sargent, March 16, 1948, series 1, box 43, NAMR.

41. Alfred Cleveland, "NAM: Spokesman for Industry?" *Harvard Business Review* (May 1948): 353–71. Horsch's response is "Comments on Article by Alfred S. Cleveland," May 20, 1948, series 12, box 192, NAMR.

42. "Comments on Article by Alfred S. Cleveland," May 20, 1948, series 12, box 192, NAMR. Horsch's name is not on the document, but the responses it elicits are all addressed to her. In addition, the memo goes over themes Horsch consistently emphasized.

43. Harry Stinnett to Miss Vada Horsch, June 28, 1948, series 12, box 192, NAMR.

Overseas Operations praised Horsch's review, adding that big companies did *not* dominate NAM, as Cleveland argued, and that it would be a good thing if they actually did because "the bigger companies are on the whole more liberal" than the smaller companies.[44] Taking her own advice, Horsch gained authority to collect material for an official NAM history, focused on its progressive achievements.[45]

The developmental work that Horsch pointed to as NAM's primary business was philosophically at odds with the vision of NAM conservatives. As we have seen in previous chapters, staff work involved sharing information, standardizing industry, and taking a more collective, socially responsible approach to managing workplaces—sometimes working with the government to do so. Historically, this kind of developmental work—performed by organizations like NAM, the US Chamber of Commerce, the National Industrial Conference Board, and the American Management Association—helped bring about a more rationalized, organized, and effective capitalism that displaced and superseded traditional, "individualist" American capitalism, which so many NAM conservatives were obsessed with bringing back—at least philosophically.

NAM's 1954 budget indicated an almost even split between the conservatives' capitalist propaganda (called "public relations") and, well, everything else, including lobbying, recruitment, and the developmental work of the staff. Forty-seven percent of NAM's $5.5 million budget in 1954 went to public relations for capitalism, which was a sharp increase over the 24 percent that public relations got in 1950—and an indication of the increasing influence of conservatives by the mid-1950s. Nonetheless, NAM operations managed to hold on to 52 percent.[46]

What kind of work was the staff doing with that budget in the 1950s? In addition to expanding international trade (described in chapter 7), NAM was instructing its member companies in how to act more like large, publicly owned corporations, especially in terms of management and organization. NAM's Industrial Relations Department sponsored management institutes, produced pamphlets, reprinted speeches about the importance

44. Edgar Smith to Miss Vada Horsch, May 26, 1948, series 12, box 192, NAMR.

45. For a variety of reasons, this project never came to fruition, but some of its results can be seen in Vada Horsch, "NAM Past and Present," September 4, 1951, updated June 10, 1963, series 1, box 43, NAMR; see also series 12, "Vada Horsch" files, NAMR.

46. Membership Advisory Development Committee meeting, February 1955, review of 1954 notes: 19,788 dues-paying members with total annual billing of $5,467,000; series 8, box 148, NAMR.

of good employee-management relations, and disseminated related policies on how to define job positions and criteria, set salaries, and handle other basics of personnel administration. The Industrial Relations Department also advocated for "human relations" in management, which was a management trend almost universally adopted by large corporations, whether unionized or not.

Developed in the 1920s by social psychologist Elton Mayo (see chapter 4), the human relations school had been refined by a new generation of industrial sociologists by the 1950s. Employed by major universities and funded in some cases by large corporations, these social scientists based their work on the idea that human beings were group-oriented and worked best when integrated into a team that was integrated in turn into the larger organization.[47] The job of a manager was not to bribe workers with incentives, but to orchestrate an environment that led to job satisfaction and high performance by fulfilling the human need to belong and to be appreciated. Human relations experts urged managers to see the factory as a social system in which everyone had a place; the manager's role was to coordinate the relations between the various parts, teams, and departments to create a smooth-running operation. In this conception, unions were just another group that had to be folded into the whole. Although not every CEO embraced the human relations approach, the heads of their industrial relations departments usually did (since it was taught in management schools), and its ideas and jargon dominated the workplace, even at organizations, like NAM, that were ostensibly committed to individualism and competition.

In his 1950 book *The New Society*, management expert (and another Austrian émigré) Peter Drucker argued that large corporations were fundamentally changing American society and its individualist values.[48] His main point was that in a modern industrial society the individual was obsolete. Individuals no longer produced anything, said Drucker, deliberately

47. The best description of the group-based ideas of midcentury social science is in Daniel T. Rodgers, *Age of Fracture* (Cambridge, MA: Harvard University Press, 2011), 4–5. On human relations as a management technique, see Stuart Chase, *The Proper Study of Mankind: An Inquiry into the Science of Human Relations*, rev. ed. (1948; New York: Harper & Row, 1956); William Foote Whyte, "Human Relations Theory—A Progress Report," *Harvard Business Review* 34, no. 5 (September/October 1956): 125–32; William Foote Whyte, *Participant Observer: An Autobiography* (Ithaca, NY: ILR Press, 1994), 141–49. For a more critical perspective, see Sanford Jacoby, *Modern Manors: Welfare Capitalism since the New Deal* (Princeton, NJ: Princeton University Press, 1997); Daniel Bell, "Adjusting Men to Machines," *Commentary* 3 (January 1947): 79–88; and Harris, *The Right to Manage*.

48. Drucker, *The New Society*.

targeting the American myth of rugged individualism and self-sufficiency. The producer, wrote Drucker, "is actually the organization of large groups of men standing in definite relationship to each other. . . . By himself, the human being, whether worker or manager, is incapable of producing."[49] *Fortune* editor William H. Whyte Jr. agreed with Drucker that corporations had all but erased the individual, but Whyte's classic *Organization Man* (1956) was a scathing critique of this development.[50]

The idea that management was fundamentally about coordinating different groups of people made sense for large corporations, which were indeed massive systems of production. But the practices adopted by large corporations, NAM felt, were just as suited for smaller companies, which NAM urged to rationalize their labor practices by, for instance, setting up proper employment offices and clear procedures.[51] Larger corporations were setting the tone even within NAM, that bastion of American individualism. This contradiction did not go unnoticed. In *The Organization Man*, William Whyte skewered businessmen's constant talk of individualism while their own corporations emphasized the group over the individual.[52] NAM officials also noted the contradiction in their speeches, and at least one attempt was made to reconcile it. In opening NAM's 1953 Institute on Industrial Relations with an address titled "New Focus on the Human Equation in Industry," Senior Vice President Kenneth Miller (staff) pondered the tension between individualism and the new human relations philosophy, which emphasized groups and belonging.[53] Miller held to the idea that treating individuals with respect and dignity and offering them incentives to improve their standing would bring forth their best work. But, he admitted, this idea was at odds with the "newer sociological thinking," which held that "the individual is happiest when he is a member of a satisfied group."[54] Miller quoted an expert from New York State's School of Industrial Relations, who said, "An employee doesn't come to his full stature as a man except in group associations. He is more than ready to surrender a portion of his

49. Ibid., 44.

50. William H. Whyte Jr., *The Organization Man* (Garden City, NY: Doubleday/Anchor, 1957).

51. See, for instance, Carl Schneider, "Personnel Relations in Small Companies and Unorganized Companies," speech delivered at the NAM Institute of Industrial Relations, March 1953, series 7, box 136, NAMR.

52. Whyte, *The Organization Man*.

53. Kenneth Miller, "New Focus on the Human Equation in Industry," speech delivered November 2, 1953, reprinted by NAM Employee Relations Division, series 7, box 136, NAMR.

54. Ibid., 2.

individualism," argued the expert, for the direct satisfaction of belonging.[55] Having identified the tension, Miller then brushed it away, arguing that one's satisfaction as an individual is fulfilled by being in a group, and that a group in turn benefits from the cooperation of individuals who want to make a contribution. Having dispensed of the contradiction, Miller focused on the importance of transparency and equal opportunity before speaking of the danger of union monopolies.

At a practical level, anti-unionism was compatible with a human relations approach designed to counter the comradery and community of the union. Indeed, NAM members probably used human relations to inoculate against unionism, and NAM continued its lobbying and PR campaigns against the newly merged AFL-CIO. But the philosophy behind human relations was very much at odds with the individualistic philosophy of NAM conservatives like William Grede.

NAM embraced the human relations approach in its own management. Its procedures for the "induction and orientation" of new employees stressed the role of training in developing a loyal and efficient workforce. The orientation leader was instructed to be warm, genuine, and enthusiastic and to let the new employee be shown around by an old-timer: "Induction takes on the warmth of personal friendship when one of the old time employees sponsors the new employee on the first day." Even though it was difficult to determine "just when an employee feels he belongs and is part of the team," it was the responsibility of the supervisor to keep an eye on him to ensure that he did become part of the team.[56] Other procedures instructed on how to listen, how to encourage employees to talk about problems, and how to, essentially, be kind and welcoming yet still enforce the many rules and regulations undergirding a productive, efficient workplace.

As per its instructions to members, NAM hired a firm in 1954 to conduct a survey of its staff, a definitive component of the human relations approach of measuring what we would today call "climate."[57] What it found was that NAM employee satisfaction was only average compared to some of its member companies. As was true at other companies, the supervisory and professional staff were more favorably disposed toward their workplace

55. Ibid.

56. NAM, "Induction and Orientation Procedure," n.d., series 1, box 101, "NAM Personnel" file, NAMR.

57. The survey included questions about whether staff understood with and agreed with the NAM mission to defend free enterprise, so here again we see some of the tension between NAM conservatives and the staff's more liberal management approach.

than those in lower positions, but staff were generally satisfied with their own jobs and their colleagues, and most felt that NAM was an okay place to work. There were complaints, however, about poor salary, poor communications, constant bickering, and deteriorating teamwork. Several echoed the sentiment of this comment:

> NAM has an employee relations division that tells members how to attain good relations with employees, but the Association itself takes none of its own advice. Very poor personnel policies (if any) and poor personnel administration.[58]

Others were critical of NAM's pretense of being "nonpolitical," when it was clearly Republican and antilabor.[59]

The survey confirmed that the staff was not as supportive of NAM's policies and positions as its members were; for instance, "84% of NAM members, as compared to only 63% of the Staff, say they usually agree with the NAM's positions on national affairs."[60] And the New York office's non-supervisory staff—the workers, if you will—were the least favorably disposed toward NAM. Indeed, one gets the feeling that what is being measured in the last section of the survey are the staff's ideological positions—did they share NAM's mission? Certainly NAM's leader-members saw the staff as more liberal, as did outside researchers. Although the survey seemed to provide empirical confirmation of this impression, what the data mainly showed was that the staff was as confused and divided about NAM's mission as its members.

To remedy that confusion and address some of the complaints, NAM inaugurated an in-house staff publication called *The Gear* in November 1954, a month after receiving the survey analysis. Experts recommended these types of publications to inculcate employees with that crucial sense of belonging and purpose. As the new editor noted, "The far-flung operations of the NAM prevent the personal acquaintanceships that are essential to understanding and 'family' spirit." The publication was "truly an employee publication, by and for the employees of NAM," and created, marveled the editor, "at management's own insistence."[61] Of course it was.

---

58. "Staff Members Talk about the NAM," by the Opinion Research Corporation, Princeton, NJ, September 14, 1954, p. 24, in NAMR, Series 7, Box 148.

59. Ibid., 25.

60. Ibid., 60.

61. Jane Almert, "First Gear Hits Staff," *The Gear* 1, no. 1 (November 1954): 1. *The Gear* is available at the Hagley Library and Museum.

MEMBERSHIP WOES

NAM staff also recruited and managed members. Indeed, this was the essential, moneymaking part of the business, overseen by the Membership Department. The vast majority (83 percent) of NAM members were small companies, whose net worth was less than $500,000. For these members, rates were prorated. Those worth between $400,000 and $499,000, for instance. would pay $300 a year in dues, while a company worth less than $100,000 would pay $100.[62] Larger companies would pay a base of $300 and an additional $10 per $100,000 of net worth, but many contributed much larger amounts.[63]

Even though the 1950s were the peak of manufacturing in the United States, as well as the peak of NAM membership, the Membership Department had discerned that NAM was shedding members as fast as it was signing them up. A memo from 1955 noted that "it has been the Association's boast that we speak for more than 20,000 members," and yet during 1954 NAM had sustained a net loss of 574 members, leaving them with only 19,778 members, below their boast.[64] Indeed, in 1954 NAM had seen 3,246 resignations, or 15.9 percent of its membership. The memo-writer proposed a new plan that would focus on retention as much as recruitment. For the next three years, they managed to stem the rate of resignations and boost membership to its high in 1957 of 21,801. But they were still losing between 12 and 13 percent of their members per year via resignations. Then, in 1958, a record 3,628 members resigned, or 16.6 percent, the largest resignation rate in the post–World War II years and the beginning of a steady decline of membership that would leave NAM with only 12,231 members by 1972.[65]

There is little evidence that companies quit NAM because of its conservatism. Indeed, a majority of those leaving were small concerns, which tended to be more conservative and resentful of government regulations, and a survey indicated that former members thought NAM accurately reflected their views on national affairs.[66] But the same survey also indicated a "high degree of dissatisfaction" among NAM's larger members, "particularly

---

62. As explained in *The Gear*, January 1955.

63. In 1968, the largest corporations, such as General Electric, General Motors, US Steel, and DuPont, paid as much as $65,000 a year; see series 7, box 148, NAMR.

64. "NAM 1955 Development Plan," p. 1, series 7, box 148, NAMR.

65. Membership data, 1949–1968, June 28, 1968, series 7, box 148, NAMR.

66. "Survey of Former Members' Views on the NAM," condensed from Opinion Research Corporation Survey, 1954, p. 2, series 1, box 46, NAMR.

among the second-line executives"—in other words, the younger ones.[67] Larger companies were the key to addressing budgetary concerns, and in this regard NAM's extremism could be a factor, as it was when George Romney, president of American Motor Corporation (AMC), pulled his company (along with its $6,700 per year dues) out of NAM. Romney cited the need to economize as the reason for the withdrawal, but when pressed by reporters, he admitted that "the most important factor" had been "a sense of fundamental disagreement with certain policies and attitudes of the association."[68] These disagreements concerned unemployment compensation and attitudes toward union negotiations.

NAM's Executive Committee attributed membership loss to the 1958 recession, which saw a 47 percent decline in Detroit automobile production and deep cuts in textiles, lumber, and mining.[69] In the next four years, NAM lost 2,800 members, a decrease that led to a shortfall in its budget. A subcommittee was set up to investigate ways in which NAM could economize in light of the declining membership. On the chopping block was one of its major propaganda efforts, its award-winning TV show *Industry on Parade*.[70] Strenuously defended by Lammot du Pont, the show was only reinstated in response to the AFL-CIO's counter-effort, *America at Work*.[71] NAM also reduced the number of $50 memberships, the service costs of which exceeded their value. This move saved money, but also contributed to declining membership.[72]

As it turned out, the most important factor in membership loss was mergers and buyouts—the inevitable consequence of the type of capitalism NAM promoted. Successful companies acquired other companies. That was how companies grew. Entries in *Moody's Industrial Manual*, an annual listing of publicly traded companies for prospective investors, vividly illustrate that

67. "Committee Report and Recommendations on Opinion Research Survey," November 1954, series 1, box 46, NAMR.

68. "American Motors Quits NAM," *New York Times*, February 2, 1957, p. 9.

69. On recession, see William M. McClenahan and William H. Becker, *Eisenhower and the Cold War Economy* (Baltimore: Johns Hopkins University Press, 2011), chap. 3 and epilogue. On NAM's response, see NAM Special Subcommittee of the Executive Committee meeting minutes, September 15, 1958, series 13, box 251, NAMR.

70. This NAM-produced TV show ran from 1950 to 1960 on NBC, highlighted industrial processes and capitalism in general, and was made available to community groups; see Samuel Dodd, " 'Industry on Parade': Developments in Invention and Research," *Atlantic*, August 4, 2011, https://www.theatlantic.com/technology/archive/2011/08/industry-on-parade-developments -in-invention-and-research/242422/.

71. NAM Executive Committee meeting minutes, June 24, 1959, series 13, box 251, NAMR.

72. H. L. Derby to William Grede, November 27, 1961, box 24, folder 3, WJGP.

the history of individual companies—as well as the history of capitalism—has been the history of mergers and acquisitions. Even before deindustrialization became a recognizable phenomenon in the 1970s, mergers and acquisitions had already begun to reduce the number of manufacturing concerns in the 1950s.[73] The continuing focus of the Membership Department on retention to stem the decline, however, made discussions about NAM's "product," as well as its public image, very salient. And the ultra-conservatives were not helping NAM's image.

The Shake-up

The consulting firm hired to assess NAM's organizational efficacy completed its work in 1961 and issued the Heller Report, which recommended, among other things, a more geographically diverse Executive Committee and a full-time paid president from outside the organization who would occupy the position for at least five years. Previously, the president had been a representative of a member company and served only one year. The Heller Report also recommended that the president be responsible for NAM management and administration, a task previously held by the executive vice president, a staff position. Essentially the consulting firm proposed reorganizing NAM by having a full-time *staff* member at the helm.

In July 1961, the Executive Committee and the board approved the first stage of the Heller recommendations and rewrote the NAM constitution and bylaws. There is no official record of the restructuring discussions, which took place in closed committees, but the Executive Committee was going forward with the report's recommendations. While conservatives still sat on the Executive Committee, they had been damaged by the JBS scandal. Now newer members like Donald Hardenbrook of American Creosoting Corporation, Milton Lightner of Singer Manufacturing Company, Stanley Hope of Esso Standard Oil Company (later Exxon-Mobil), and John McGovern of US Rubber Company seemed to be pushing forward the Heller Report's recommendations. These men were from large, multinational conglomerates; Singer Manufacturing still employed over 49,000 workers, while US Rubber

---

73. Bluestone and Harrison identify a merger wave from 1949 to 1955; see Barry Bluestone and Bennett Harrison, *The Deindustrialization of America: Plant Closings, Community Abandonment, and the Dismantling of Basic Industry* (New York: Basic Books, 1982). Deindustrialization had a regional impact, hitting some areas, such as Detroit in the 1950s, more than others; see Thomas Sugrue, *The Origins of the Urban Crisis: Race and Inequality in Postwar Detroit* (Princeton, NJ: Princeton University Press, 1997).

had over 61,000; in 1955, Esso Standard was the second-largest corporation in the United States after General Motors.[74]

Conservatives and the retired oldsters who corresponded with them (and were still somehow kept in the loop) stewed about the impending changes. They could not understand the need for such a drastic restructuring. Membership decline was the result of mergers and liquidations, not poor management, wrote Harry L. Derby, formerly of American Cyanamid Company. Derby recalled that NAM in 1932 had fewer than 1,600 members and an income of $200,000, but under the current management structure its membership had grown to over 18,000, with an income of $6 million. Why mess with success?[75] A convalescing Grede complained privately to Ernie Swigert about being sidelined by the likes of Hardenbrook, whom he had seen on TV: "If what he said on that TV show represents NAM thinking and the present philosophy of the Executive Committee, I ought to resign."[76]

Some of the tension around the Heller Report seems to have been entangled with conservative criticism of the International Economic Affairs Committee, particularly with regard to its support for the new Organization for Economic Cooperation and Development (OECD), the International Labor Organization (ILO), and the World Court—three pieces of a new globalist infrastructure. JBS member Cola Parker tried unsuccessfully to reduce funding for NAM's work with the OECD and then questioned the timing of the International Economic Affairs Committee's new recommendations with regard to the Heller Report discussions.[77] The minutes are rather oblique as to what the new recommendations were, but a letter from the committee's chairman, Meade Brunet (of RCA), to JBS conservative Robert Love offers some clarity. Brunet tried to persuade Love to reconsider supporting US participation in the World Court. At issue was a resolution clause change

74. *Moody's Industrial Manual* (New York, 1959). Esso Standard began as Standard Oil of New Jersey after Standard Oil was broken up, but it quickly acquired other Standards and became Eastern States Standard Oil, or Esso. After acquiring Humble Oil, it became Exxon, and then Exxon-Mobil. Esso was at the forefront of international investment; see Daniel Yergin, *The Prize: The Epic Quest for Oil, Money, and Power* (New York: Free Press, 2008). Per corporate policy, Hope had retired from Esso at age sixty-five, in 1958; he subsequently became president of the Soundscriber Corporation. Hope served as NAM president in 1959. See "Stanley Hope Dead; Had Served as Head of Esso Standard Co.," *New York Times*, June 23, 1982, p. B11.

75. H. L. Derby to William Grede, November 27, 1961, box 24, folder 3, WJGP.

76. Grede to Swigert, July 26, 1962, box 24, folder 3, WJGP.

77. See Executive Committee meeting minutes, February 14, 1960, December 4, 1961, and June 13, 1962, for mentions of these items. In the June 13, 1962, meeting, a letter was presented by the president of the American Petroleum Institute urging NAM to remain in the ILO; for more on this controversy, see chapter 7.

(supported by the International Economic Affairs Committee) that conservatives felt undermined US sovereignty; Brunet argued that it did not.[78]

In December 1961, President John F. Kennedy delivered a speech before NAM that focused on foreign policy and America's role in international economic development. If anything said that liberal internationalists were in charge of NAM, it was this invitation, extended by Hardenbrook, McGovern, and crew. Joking about the oddity of his coming before the organization, Kennedy acknowledged that most of the people in the room had probably voted for his Republican opponent, "except for a very few who were under the impression that I was my father's son."[79] This quip was a reference to his father's isolationism before World War II. But if Kennedy was suggesting that this kind of isolationist conservatism was clearly a thing of the past, he did so before an audience that no doubt included just such isolationists.

Thus, the regime change was not only a response to the bad press the JBS conservatives brought to NAM at a time of declining membership but also, and more directly, a move by NAM internationalists to sideline NAM isolationists. Historians of US postwar conservatism have underemphasized the split within the post–World War II conservative revival between Hayekian free-trade libertarians and traditionally Republican, Manion Forum, JBS conservatives, who were isolationists and economic nationalists—and understandably so, given that major conservative figures like Grede and Cola Parker were supporters of both Hayek *and* the JBS. But they were exceptions. The divide within NAM between internationalists (including the staff) and isolationists matches and reinforces the divide in the country between more moderate conservatives and the ultraconservatives who joined the JBS. Historian Jonathan Soffer has argued that NAM's restructuring, which sidelined smaller, independent firms, was a response to the increased influence of large government defense contractors among its members.[80] That argument is useful, but it should be kept in mind that large government contractors were also multinational corporations seeking an international economic infrastructure to make investment in the developing world safe and profitable.

In September 1962, the Selection Committee introduced Werner P. "Gully" Gullander, the new full-time, paid NAM president.[81] Gullander had

78. Meade Brunet to Robert Love, February 9, 1962, box 24, folder 3, WJGP.

79. "Text of President Kennedy's Speech before the NAM," *New York Times*, December 7, 1961.

80. Jonathan Soffer, "The National Association of Manufacturers and the Militarization of American Conservatism," *Business History Review* 75 (Winter 2001): 775–805.

81. Executive Committee meeting minutes, September 6, 1962, series 13, box 251, NAMR. The NAM board (in executive session) unanimously elected Gullander president for a five-year

been an executive vice president at General Dynamics Corporation, a major government contractor and developer and manufacturer of submarines, space vehicles, and missiles, employing over 84,000 people, with net sales in 1962 of $1.8 billion.[82] Donald Hardenbrook, chairman of the American Creosoting Corporation and a vice president at its parent company, Union Bag–Camp Corporation, was made chairman of the board of directors, the highest nonpaid official position at the NAM, which would be filled on a yearly basis.[83] Stanley Hope (retired from Esso Oil because of mandatory age limits) was made chair of the Executive Committee and Milton Lightner became Finance Committee chair.[84] By 1964, the Executive Committee would be purged of all of the old guard conservatives, replaced by executives from multinational corporations like General Electric, US Steel, US Rubber, and Crown Zellerbach. Large corporations had long supported NAM financially, but their executives had never been this dominant on the Executive Committee.[85]

Keenly aware of NAM's image problem, Gullander admitted that "we have been talking to ourselves for too many years."[86] NAM needed to talk to the public. Gullander told the Executive Committee that NAM was a bipartisan organization and that it was "important to work with the Administration in power"—which was the liberal internationalist, Democratic Kennedy administration.[87] Gullander also raised staff salaries and initiated the kind of liaison-building developmental programs that Vada Horsch, for one, saw as NAM's primary contribution.[88] With the help of the social changes of the 1960s, this new guard would finally revamp NAM, transforming what the press saw as backwards-looking, nationalistic grumps into forward-looking, market-oriented internationalists.

---

term, beginning November 1, 1962. See board of directors meeting minutes, September 19–21, 1962, series 13, box 242, NAMR.

82. *Moody's Industrial Manual* (New York, 1964).

83. "NAM Elects Permanent Head under Plan for Reorganization," *New York Times*, September 20, 1962, p. 45.

84. Executive Committee meeting minutes, September 6, 1962, series 13, box 251, NAMR.

85. See Executive Committee meeting minutes, September 14, 1964, series 13, box 251, NAMR.

86. Quoted in "Industry Lobbyist Says Public's Boss," *Minneapolis Star*, 1970, clipping found in series 1, box 45, NAMR.

87. Executive Committee meeting minutes, September 14, 1964, series 13, box 251, NAMR.

88. See, for instance, Executive Committee meeting minutes, March 25, 1964, series 13, box 251, NAMR.

9

A Changing Workforce

Assuming the NAM presidency at the dawn of the 1960s, Werner Gullander sought to restore capitalism's reputation as a progressive force and refashion NAM into an organization that embraced change. Gullander purged the John Birchers, deleted support for states' rights from NAM's "Industry Believes" statement, and stood ready to work with the government on economic policy issues. "A Changing World" was the theme of NAM's annual meeting in 1962, and "NAM Meets the Challenge of Change" was the title of its 1964 annual report. Treasury Secretary Henry Fowler, a New Dealer who had begun his career in the Tennessee Valley Authority (TVA), opened NAM's 1965 meeting, which also featured a pollution control advocate and a representative from Students for a Democratic Society (SDS).[1] By 1968, NAM was encouraging members to attend environmental teach-ins and holding conferences on inner-city unemployment, water pollution, drug abuse, and mental illness.

As we have seen, NAM had a history of periodically casting off its conservative husk and refashioning itself as a progressive contributor to American society. But this time it actually had some substantive impact, particularly in the area of civil rights and equal opportunity for African American workers. Although NAM was officially neutral about the Civil Rights Act of 1964, it

---

1. Frank Prial, "A New NAM?" *Wall Street Journal*, May 31, 1966, p. 1; Murray Kempton, "Laughter at the NAM," *The New Republic*, December 18, 1965, 19–20; "NAM Meets the Challenge of Change," in *NAM Annual Report*, 1964; "Deletion of Policy on State-Local Initiative vs. Federal Control," September 1965, series 1, box 105, NAMR.

did sponsor seminars and workshops to help member companies integrate their plants and comply with the law. It also worked with the government to develop affirmative action guidelines for contractors and training programs for minority youth in inner cities.[2] In other words, it translated to industry the civil rights movement's demand for jobs and equal opportunity—partly in an attempt to stem any further federal regulations and laws by showing that industry could resolve social and racial problems better than government. But NAM's support for equal employment rights was also in line with its developmental imperative to help employers negotiate labor markets. The push to hire beyond the traditional pool of white males was not new. NAM had long encouraged its members to use "nontraditional" labor sources, such as women and the handicapped (see chapter 4), but in the 1960s this project would finally gain traction, mostly because of new civil rights legislation.

Gullander called the Civil Rights Act of 1964 the most important legislation for industry since the Wagner Act.[3] But unlike the Wagner Act, the Civil Rights Act was accepted by NAM, which began organizing compliance seminars and materials even before the law was passed. Recall that it had done the opposite after the Wagner Act was passed in 1935, when it told members how to evade compliance (see chapter 5). Although NAM tried to weaken some of the Civil Rights Act's provisions, it did not lobby against it (as many of its members did), nor did it resist its passage. In 1972, it would oppose giving the Equal Employment Opportunity Commission (EEOC) cease-and-desist power (which liberals wanted), but it fully supported the 1972 Equal Opportunity Act, which gave courts power to adjudicate EEOC cases, a move that proved more effective in actually enforcing the new legislation.

At the same time, NAM continued its assault on organized labor, launching a well-coordinated campaign against an AFL-CIO-sponsored bill that would have repealed the Taft-Hartley Act's "right to work" provision. Also known as section 14(b), the "right to work" provision allowed states to ban union contracts that required workers to join unions or pay dues. NAM argued that requiring non-union workers to pay dues or join the union was "compulsory unionism," which undermined workers' "right to work." Unions argued that since all workers benefited from union contracts, all should be required to pay dues. Backed by a Democratic president and

---

2. On Gullander's campaign to embrace change, see his essay "NAM Meets the Challenge of Change," in *NAM Annual Report*, 1964.

3. "President's Report to the Board of Directors," July 17, 1964, series 1, box 45, NAMR.

Congress, the AFL-CIO pushed for a repeal of section 14(b) of the Taft-Hartley Act in 1965. NAM and allied organizations, such as the National Right to Work Committee, launched a successful campaign to stop them.

Recently historians have begun to pay attention to the overlap between African Americans' demands for jobs—a right to work, if you will—and conservatives' push for "right to work" laws.[4] While compulsory union dues were very different from unions' exclusion of blacks, both movements targeted historically white unions and shared a language of workplace "rights." Conservative "right to work" activists adopted the tactics of the civil rights movement and aligned themselves with blacks against exclusionary unions.[5] Although this strategy failed to attract African Americans, it called attention to unions' historic and ongoing racism in a way that eventually divided the labor-liberal coalition. This dynamic is key to understanding NAM's complicated support for civil rights, equal opportunity, and affirmative action.

Before the 1960s

NAM had begun supporting fair employment for black workers in the 1940s. In 1941, it pledged support for President Roosevelt's executive order 8802, prohibiting discrimination in the war industries. NAM's Industrial Relations Department followed the latest research on "Negro employment" and conducted surveys about employers' minority hiring practices, offering advice to members on how to comply with the wartime discrimination ban.[6] When talking to industry about hiring minorities in the 1950s, NAM used the phrase "full utilization of minority groups," which made it a practical labor supply issue, not a liberal cause. NAM also argued that unless African Americans could earn money and be independent, they would not only burden the welfare system but also be unable to participate in the free-market system as consumers. "A large untouched market" of minority groups could not be tapped unless those minority groups had a solid paycheck.[7] Prac-

4. See the essays in "Appropriating the Language of Civil Rights," part 3 in *The Right and Labor in America: Politics, Ideology, and Imagination*, edited by Nelson Lichtenstein and Elizabeth Tandy Shermer (Philadelphia: University of Pennsylvania Press, 2012).

5. Sophia Z. Lee, "Whose Rights? Litigating the Right to Work, 1940 to 1980," in Lichtenstein and Shermer, *The Right and Labor in America*; see also Reuel Schiller, "Singing the Right to Work Blues," in ibid.

6. "Data Sheet[s] for Occupational Survey Project," n.d. [1937], and "Problems of Racial Discrimination," August 5, 1942, series 7, box 136, NAMR.

7. "Suggested Outline for Booklet Implementing NAM's Position against Discrimination," September 27, 1950, series 7, box 135, NAMR.

ticing nondiscrimination in hiring and promotion was therefore "just good business," a slogan embraced by the civil rights community to push the case for fair employment and equal opportunity.[8]

The civil rights movement in the 1940s was focused on jobs and antidiscrimination legislation, with an emphasis on African Americans as rights-seeking individuals.[9] Led by the National Association for the Advancement of Colored People (NAACP) and the Urban League, the movement stressed access to jobs—the "right to work"—as essential to individual liberty and independence. One black fair employment activist testified that his right to work was essential not just to his own liberty but also to the health of his family and community.[10] In keeping with the antiracist philosophy of the day, which held that physical racial differences were meaningless, civil rights groups deemphasized "race" and group identity and promoted individual rights "regardless of race" as the politically correct position.[11] Unlike the philosophy of unionism, which emphasized collective identity, this was a position that NAM could embrace.

Speaking before black audiences, NAM leaders extolled the "right to work" as among the most sacred of individual rights and promised "full equality of employment opportunity" in industry.[12] The ultra-conservative NAM president William Grede, a member of the John Birch Society, told the audience at the historically black Lincoln College in 1953 that blacks' best

8. "Fair employment" referred to antidiscrimination policies and was the aim of civil rights activity in the 1940s and 1950s; "equal opportunity" (essentially the same thing) replaced "fair employment" in the early 1960s. On this and the idea that fair employment was good business, see Delton, *Racial Integration in Corporate America*, chaps. 2–3.

9. On the civil rights movements of this era, see Paul Moreno, *From Direct Action to Affirmative Action: Fair Employment Law and Policy in America, 1933–72* (Baton Rouge: Louisiana State University Press, 1997); Herbert Garfinkel, *When Negroes March: The March on Washington Movement and the Organizational Politics of the FEPC* (Glencoe, IL: Free Press, 1959); Anthony Chen, *The Fifth Freedom: Jobs, Politics, and Civil Rights in the United States* (Princeton, NJ: Princeton University Press, 2009); Nancy MacLean, *Freedom Is Not Enough: The Opening of the American Workplace* (New York and Cambridge, MA: Russell Sage Foundation and Harvard University Press, 2006).

10. David Grant, testimony before House Committee on Labor hearing, "To Prohibit Discrimination in Employment" (Washington, DC: US Government Printing Office, 1944), 53.

11. On the antiracist movement of the 1940s, see Ruth Benedict, *Race Science and Politics* (New York: Modern Age Books, 1940); Ashley Montagu, *Man's Most Dangerous Myth: The Fallacy of Race* (New York: Columbia University Press, 1942); Walter Jackson, *Gunnar Myrdal and America's Conscience: Social Engineering and Racial Liberalism, 1938–1987* (Chapel Hill: University of North Carolina Press, 1990).

12. "Fuller on Job Discrimination," *NAM Newsletter*, August 9, 1941; NAM press release, August 26, 1941; both in series 7, box 135, NAMR.

chance of success in America was the competitive free enterprise system, unhampered by government control and union racism, which impeded black workers' "right to work."[13]

NAM leaders equated unions' exclusion of blacks with the closed shop's exclusion of non-union workers, seeing both forms of exclusion as evidence of unions' restriction of the workplace, and hence of opportunity. There was a great deal of truth to NAM's take on how the closed shop operated to keep black workers out. Since blacks had historically been excluded from most unions, the closed shop automatically excluded blacks from attaining work.[14] Unions' progress in the 1930s was bad news for many black workers. The NAACP's Roy Wilkins reported that AFL unions were using the National Industrial Recovery Act (NIRA) protection of union rights to drive blacks out of certain occupations. Writing in *Crisis*, the NAACP's official journal, W. E. B. Du Bois likewise argued that union strategy in the New Deal era was to obtain the right to bargain collectively as the sole representative of labor and then close the union to black workers, cutting them off from employers.[15] There was a reason that African Americans referred to the NRA as the "Negro Removal Act."[16]

Employers had historically exploited this tension between black workers and white unions. Those firms that hired blacks often did so to avert unionization. A NAM survey interviewer in 1937 reported of one company: "Mr. Looney [personnel manager] felt that Negroes were not as susceptible to participating in unions as whites and since the personnel of the firm is as yet not unionized and as they are trying to keep it so, Negroes fit in nicely."[17] In addition, employers' use of black workers as scabs during strikes exacerbated racial hatreds and divided the working classes.

It is thus fair to say that historically black workers were pawns in the battle between industry and labor, and they continued to be, even in the civil rights

13. "NAM Speaks Out for Equal Opportunity," excerpts from a speech by William J. Grede, April 30, 1953, series 7, Box 135, NAMR.

14. The best analysis is Paul Moreno, *Black Americans and Organized Labor* (Baton Rouge: Louisiana State University Press, 2008). See also Oliver Ayers, *Laboured Protest: Black Civil Rights in New York City and Detroit during the New Deal and Second World War* (New York: Routledge, 2019); Robert Zieger, *For Jobs and Freedom: Race and Labor in America since 1865* (Lexington: University of Kentucky Press, 2007).

15. Cited in Moreno, *Black Americans and Organized Labor*, 167.

16. William Pickens, "NRA—Negro Removal Act?" *The World Tomorrow*, September 28, 1933, pp. 538–40.

17. American Maize Products Company, in "Data Sheet for Occupation Survey Project" [1937], series 7, box 136, NAMR.

era, as both organized industry and organized labor—or at least the CIO—tried to convince their members to be more inclusive.[18] Indeed, NAM and the CIO mirrored each other in their efforts to sell equal opportunity to their respective members. Both had practical reasons to promote integration and equal opportunity. Both were dealing with recalcitrant, racist members—companies in NAM's case, locals in the CIO's—who resisted the advice of leaders and experts. And each would use the issue to promote its agenda against the other. Just as NAM associated the closed shop with the restriction of opportunity, the CIO accused industry of being disingenuous in its support for equal opportunity, labeling its efforts "window dressing" and "tokenism."

In addition to scoring points against labor, NAM endorsed nondiscrimination policies as a way to avert further legislation. By 1959, eighteen states and thirty municipalities—mostly in industrial areas—were operating under some form of fair employment law.[19] The threat of federal legislation loomed large, and NAM felt that it might be avoided if all of industry voluntarily (or prompted by their trade associations) were to practice nondiscrimination in hiring and promotion above and beyond what state laws required. Just as NAM's employment stabilization drive had averted guaranteed wage legislation, it was hoped that "a positive NAM program which has as its purpose the elimination of discriminatory practices in industry" could, in the words of staff member Phyllis Moehrle, put NAM "on solid ground in questioning the necessity of fair employment practices legislation."[20] The aim was to "improve managerial performance to the point where it could be defended on the basis of factual achievement."[21] This was the message of NAM leaders like William Caples of Inland Steel, Ivan Willis of International Harvester, and Walter Wheeler of Pitney-Bowes, all of whom had hired black workers into "white" positions in their own plants.[22] NAM opposed federal fair employment legislation, which, it argued, would be ineffective, difficult to enforce, and more governmental overreach. But it did not oppose integration, the aim

---

18. The CIO worked to integrate its unions and promote equal opportunity beginning in the 1930s, while the AFL was less eager to take up this battle; see Zieger, *For Jobs and Freedom*, chap. 5.

19. See Delton, *Racial Integration in Corporate America*, 165–74; Moreno, *Black Americans and Organized Labor*, 109–33; Paul Norgren et al., *Employing the Negro in American Industry* (New York: Industrial Relations Counselors, 1959), 26–28; Theodore Kheel, *Guide to Fair Employment Practices* (Englewood Cliffs, NJ: Prentice-Hall, 1964), chap. 4.

20. Phyllis Moehrle, "Some Questions in Connection with Expansion of NAM Program re Discrimination," September 27, 1950, series 7, box 135, NAMR. Moehrle held a staff position in the Industrial Relations Department and was the point person on antidiscrimination issues.

21. Carrol French to Noel Sargent, April 5, 1948, series 7, box 135, NAMR.

22. See Delton, *Racial Integration in Corporate America*, 61–65.

of such laws. In the event that a federal law was passed, NAM said, industry would be in a better position to comply with it if it started now, voluntarily. This position was very different from NAM's position toward the Wagner Act, which was opposition to both the law and the law's aim.

There were businesses and employers whose opposition to fair employment laws reflected an antipathy to integration itself. The Minnesota Employers Association, for instance, stated that discrimination was "simply American freedom to do business free of government control."[23] And many businessmen would not accept that their own assumptions about the inadequacy of black labor might be discrimination.[24] However self-serving its anti-discrimination program, NAM was, unlike these business groups, sincerely interested in integration and hoped to convince recalcitrant employers to change their minds so as to avoid having the whole business community brought under legislative surveillance.

NAM's nondiscrimination program dealt only with African Americans. It did not address discrimination against women or the handicapped, probably because the potential laws that it was trying to avert would likewise have been geared to racial minorities. NAM continued to encourage the employment of the handicapped, as it had done since World War I. It was a member of the President's Committee on Employment of the Handicapped, founded by President Truman after World War II, and it worked to "create a climate of acceptance for physically handicapped, mentally retarded, and mentally restored workers" and eliminate barriers to their gainful employment. In 1952, NAM recommitted itself to this work, noting that "employers know from experience that the handicapped individual, when matched to the requirements of the job, is no longer handicapped."[25]

NAM's interest in women in industry, however, seemed to wane in the post–World War II years. The Women's Department was focused on free enterprise more than on bolstering women's rights in the workplace. Nonetheless, the NAM board adopted an "equal pay for equal work" resolution in 1942, declaring: "There is little difference between men and women as

23. Otto Christenson, "Fair Employment Act," 1949, cited in ibid., 31. On business opposition to fair employment, see Chen, *The Fifth Freedom*, chaps. 3–4; and MacLean, *Freedom Is Not Enough*.

24. Democratic congressman O. C. Davis from Texas, for instance, questioned denying the employer's freedom of choice "when he knows from his own experience that . . . he would get the best return on his investment by employing only white?" See Grant, "To Prohibit Discrimination in Employment," 60.

25. Harold Russell, "Government, Industry Help the Handicapped," *NAM Reports*, November 23, 1970, pp. 6–7.

regards their satisfactory performance in industry. . . . No emphasis should be placed on any distinction between them as workers."[26] In May 1955, NAM's Vada Horsch had organized a conference for French women industrial and business leaders that featured a healthy number of US business and professional women, including Grace Burns, the president of Grayborn Steel Company, as well as personnel managers and trade association heads.[27] Trade associations like NAM provided career opportunities for professional women. But judging from the shocked reactions to the "sex" component of Title VII, NAM members were poorly prepared for the prospect of actual increases in women's equality in the workplace.

Nonetheless, the organization had a well-established record of supporting antidiscrimination policies with regard to race and had long encouraged its members to overcome their prejudices to take advantage of "nontraditional" labor supplies. The civil rights movements, federal legislation, and the events of the 1960s would bring more urgency—and resistance—to this project, but NAM's previous policies prepared it to meet the challenge.

NAM and the Civil Rights Revolution

By 1960, much of American industry was operating under laws and regulations that prohibited discrimination. In addition to state and municipal antidiscrimination laws, the federal government required all contractors to practice nondiscrimination, a policy that began under President Roosevelt and was continued by Truman and Eisenhower, each of whom set up a committee to enforce the policy.[28] Despite these efforts, progress in black employment was slow. In 1960, for instance, black workers in Detroit made up less than 1 percent of skilled workers at Chrysler and General Motors, both of which were government contractors and operating under state fair employment laws.[29] Black unemployment in that year was twice that of whites (10.2 percent compared to 4.9 for whites), and black median

26. NAM, "Equal Pay for Equal Work in the United States," memo in series 1, box 187, "UNECOSOC" folder, NAMR.

27. "NAM Conference with French Women Industrialists and Business Leaders," May 2, 1955, series 1, box 76, "International Relations—Foreign Operations Admin" file, NAMR.

28. See Delton, *Racial Integration in Corporate America*, 175–91; and Timothy Thurber, "Racial Liberalism, Affirmative Action, and the Troubled History of the President's Committee on Government Contracts," *Journal of Policy History* 18, no. 4 (2006): 446–76.

29. See Sugrue, *The Origins of the Urban Crisis*, 105.

household income was 56 percent that of whites.[30] The problem was getting worse as automation squeezed out unskilled labor, the employment category to which most blacks were limited.

State laws and executive orders had proved to be largely ineffective. They targeted intentional discrimination, which was almost impossible to demonstrate, and did not address the way racism limited black workers' training and education opportunities, nor how past practices had created employment structures that ensured discriminatory practices. For instance, it was common practice to hire the friends and relatives of current employees; doing so saved time and money and helped produce a harmonious workplace. If employers were doing this to save time and money in hiring, state laws said, that was okay. If they were doing it to avoid hiring black workers, however, it was discrimination. But who could tell the difference? And what if it was both?[31] It turned out that most discrimination was not the result of intentional decisions, but the outcome of long-standing practices and customs that often (outside the South) were not explicitly about race but disproportionately penalized workers of color. Thus, just having a nondiscrimination policy and not considering race in employment decisions—the only requirements of state laws—did little to actually change the status quo that kept the labor market segregated.[32]

In 1961, the Kennedy administration tried to overcome these shortcomings by requiring government contractors to take "affirmative action" to make sure all applicants and employees were treated without regard to race or nationality. The goal was still color-blind nondiscrimination, but the means to that goal was color-conscious. "Affirmative action" at this point meant some indication that companies were seeking out black recruits, making connections to local black communities, attending fair employment conferences, offering special training opportunities, or otherwise going beyond a nondiscrimination policy and actually hiring and promoting black people into positions traditionally limited to whites.[33]

30. Unemployment rates are from George Thomas Kurian, ed., *Datapedia of the United States* (Lanham, MD: Bernan Press, 2004), table 8–3; median income data come from US Bureau of the Census, *Historical Statistics of the United States* (Washington, DC: US Government Printing Office, 1975), 303.

31. Delton, *Racial Integration in Corporate America*, 167.

32. On the inadequacy of nondiscrimination policies, see MacLean, *Freedom Is Not Enough*; Moreno, *Black Americans and Organized Labor*, chaps. 3 and 5; and Hugh Davis Graham, *The Civil Rights Era: Origins and Development of National Policy, 1960–1972* (New York: Oxford University Press, 1990), 9–24, and throughout.

33. This section draws heavily from Delton, *Racial Integration in Corporate America*, 177–91. On Kennedy's executive order 10925, see Graham, *The Civil Rights Era*, chaps. 1–2.

Initially, NAM was resistant to Kennedy's new requirements, as instituted in executive order 10925. In June 1961, NAM's Legal Department sent a statement to the President's Committee on Equal Employment Opportunity (PCEEO) detailing the burdens that those requirements placed on industry. Companies could be penalized for discrimination, the statement read, yet the term "discrimination" was undefined and subjective. No due process was provided for the contractor, who had no opportunity for rebuttal or witnesses. The executive order seemed to impugn contractors for the discriminatory actions of subcontractors and unions, even though contractors had no authority over these bodies. NAM acknowledged that the government had authority to set the terms of its contracts with private contractors, but Congress, not the executive branch, it argued, had customarily set those terms.[34] These complaints were not unreasonable, and indeed their substance would be the focus of much legal and administrative wrangling in the years ahead as the United States tried to correct the racial and economic injustices of American workplaces.

In 1961, the NAACP filed discrimination charges against Lockheed Aircraft Corporation, which had just won a new billion-dollar contract with the government. Alarmed, Lockheed executives met with the PCEEO and together they came up with a plan to end overt segregation, recruit qualified minority candidates, identify and train employees of color for advancement, and maintain statistics to keep track of Lockheed's progress. They called the deal a "Plan for Progress," and it was quickly embraced by other major defense contractors—many of them in NAM—who were looking for ways to comply with the administration's bold, but vague, new requirements. The Plans for Progress (PFP) program, in which participation was voluntary, provided guidance in putting one's company beyond what was required by executive order 10925 and thus avoid discrimination charges. NAM endorsed the program, which eventually became a quasi-governmental program in the PCEEO and would be endorsed by the head of PCEEO, Vice President Lyndon Johnson.[35]

In November 1962, Werner Gullander took the helm at NAM and declared his intention of putting industry ahead of the discrimination issue. Rather than just fighting the government over legal details, industry would exercise new leadership and take "affirmative action" in "making a reality of Equal

34. "Statement of the Law Department of the National Association of Manufacturers to the President's Committee on Equal Employment Opportunity Regarding Executive Order 10925 . . . ," June 30, 1961, series 7, box 135, NAMR.

35. On the PCEEO, see Graham, *The Civil Rights Era*, chaps. 1–2.

Employment Opportunity."[36] NAM assigned Charles Kothe, its vice president of industrial relations, to this task, which initially consisted mostly of publishing and distributing material about those companies that were taking actions to change the status quo, such as IBM and Lockheed. But Kothe also reached out to government and black community groups, both to let them know what NAM was doing and to ask for suggestions. The idea was to develop and advertise "free market solutions to the current Negro employment problem" and protect companies from boycotts and lawsuits.[37] From today's perspective, some of these efforts seem weak and extremely conservative. They allied with conservative African American leaders like black entrepreneur and NAM member S. B. Fuller, president of Fuller Products Company and publisher of the *Pittsburgh Courier* and *New York Age*, who spoke at NAM's annual 1963 meeting and blamed blacks for their plight. Laws would not help, said Fuller, voicing the opinion of many in the audience: "You can't legislate equality."[38]

But other parts of NAM's new "minority program" were more substantive. Kothe organized a series of seminars beginning in July 1963 to help employers prepare for the anticipated enactment of the Civil Rights Act. Gullander said that the seminars would "emphasize the positive techniques which management can use to adjust its procedures to the new law" and "assist industry in understanding Title VII before its provisions became mandatory."[39] This shows that NAM anticipated the bill's passage and had no plans to oppose it. The seminars were popular (or so NAM's publications said) and exemplified Gullander's new constructive approach.

Similarly, NAM sponsored a forum for member companies to meet with Plans for Progress companies to discuss the program. Although NAM assured members that it took no position on whether or not companies should participate, the invited PFP companies were clearly there to sell the program.[40] The PFP program was no walk in the sun. It required participating companies and their executives to submit to government oversight, attend what we today call diversity workshops, and come up with an actual plan for integration. There were benefits, however, and the PFP

36. NAM Industrial Relations Department, "Employment of Minorities," n.d. [February 1964], p. 2, series 7, box 135, NAMR.

37. "Minority Program," n.d., series 7, box 135, NAMR.

38. Quoted in Terry Smith, "Plight of Negroes Their Own Fault," *New York Herald-Tribune*, December 7, 1963. The following year NAM invited the Urban League's Whitney Young, a more forceful voice against white racism, to speak.

39. "Seminars to Help Members Deal with Civil Rights Act," *NAM Reports*, July 27, 1963, p. 1.

40. Charles Kothe to Bennett E. Kline, "Employment of Minorities," memo, January 20, 1964, series 7, box 135, NAMR.

reps highlighted them: (1) since the government advertised company participation, it offered "protection against pressure from the more militant minority organizations"; (2) PFP's industry-friendly "Advisory Council" helped member companies file the necessary reports; and (3) compliance inspections were "less frequent and bothersome."[41]

The forum got some takers. NAM member company Lukens Steel Company, a Pennsylvania company with about five thousand employees, signed up for PFP in June 1964. Lukens's head Charles Huston, a NAM member, sent his brother, Vice President Stewart Huston, to several EEO conferences; his careful notes suggest that Stewart Huston was taking the whole endeavor seriously.[42] What the very conservative Huston brothers liked best was that the program was voluntary. The heavy hand of the state was not compelling them to follow the law; instead, they had voluntarily signed up with a program that would help them take "affirmative action" to support equal opportunity. Some of the affirmative actions the company took included having departments submit progress reports and statistics, setting up goals for the number of black workers hired or promoted, recruiting at black colleges, desegregating locker rooms, and identifying workers of color for advancement.

For Kothe and NAM at this time, the term "affirmative action" signified a voluntary effort on the part of a company or organization to go beyond what state laws and executive orders required. It was a way for industry to show leadership on the issue. Although the term "affirmative action" would soon come to have a very different meaning, these kinds of policies would remain crucial to both the revised meaning of affirmative action and the implementation of the new Civil Rights Act.

TITLE VII

As various versions of the Civil Rights Act made their way through Congress, NAM's Legal Department kept members apprised of its progress and dangers. Legal Department staff disliked the bill and compared the proposed EEOC to the dreaded National Labor Relations Board (NLRB) in its ability to meddle in corporate employment decisions.[43] Members appreciated these

41. Ibid.

42. This information comes from Lukens Steel Company, Executive Office Files, 1903–1979, Hagley Museum and Library. See also Delton, *Racial Integration in Corporate America*, 184–86.

43. See especially NAM Legal Department, "Summary Analysis of EQUAL EMPLOYMENT PROVISIONS (Title VII)," 1964, a review of the House version of February 10, 1964, series 5, box 65, NAMR.

analyses, which provided the basis for their appeals to their congressional reps to amend or cut specific parts. Although it lobbied to restrain the scope and power of Title VII, NAM took no position on the bill as a whole, nor did it lobby against it. To oppose the bill "could be so easily misinterpreted," in the words of one businessman.[44] In all public pronouncements, NAM was neutral or positive about the bill.

Congress passed the Civil Rights Act in June 1964. Title VII of the act prohibited discrimination on the basis of race, national origin, religion, or sex in the hiring, firing, and promotion of employees, and it created the Equal Employment Opportunity Commission to receive and investigate individual complaints. Despite all of the evidence from state fair employment committees and presidents' committees that simply prohibiting discrimination was not enough to ensure workplace integration and advancement opportunities for people of color, Title VII used that same color-blind formula. One new addition, however, was "sex," meaning gender, as a category that could not be discriminated against.[45] The sex component caused consternation among the members who complained to NAM, but it was consistent with NAM's earlier positions on women workers and equal pay.[46]

Industry and business lobbying made Title VII weaker than civil rights activists wanted. Lacking enforcement or cease-and-desist powers, the new EEOC was punier even than some of the state-level enforcement agencies.[47] Moreover, Title VII specifically exempted accidental or inadvertent discrimination caused by, for instance, seniority, testing, or recruitment policies, all of which were permitted. Nor could anything in the new law be interpreted to require an employer to grant preferential treatment to any group to make up for a racial imbalance.[48] Finally, the new law gave no benchmarks for what compliance actually looked like, although that was not the wish of business and industry, which wanted clearer guidance.

---

44. C. E. Cunningham to Ted Compton, March 26, 1964, series 5, box 65, NAMR.

45. Democratic congressman Howard Smith from Virginia added this provision in an attempt to derail the whole law; see Graham, *The Civil Rights Era*, 134–39; Jo Freeman, "How 'Sex' Got into Title VII: Persistent Opportunism as a Maker of Public Policy," *Law and Inequality: A Journal of Theory and Practice* 9, no. 2 (March 1991): 163–84.

46. One NAM member wrote that "the seemingly innocent addition of that little word 'sex' in the employment section is the place where I anticipate the raising of some 'female hell' (if I know women)!" C. L. Irving to Lambert Miller, August 4, 1964, and similar letters, series 5, box 65, NAMR.

47. Graham, *The Civil Rights Era*, 156–61, 421–23.

48. EEOC, "Title VII of the Civil Rights Act of 1964," https://www.eeoc.gov/laws/statutes /titlevii.cfm; for discussion, see Graham, *The Civil Rights Era*, chap. 5.

Congress's failure to define discrimination or offer specific guidelines would create a space for industry to step up and shape Title VII.[49] NAM's compliance seminars and materials did just that, not only explaining what was no longer allowed under Title VII but also suggesting "affirmative actions" that employers could take to put themselves beyond compliance. Attended by over three thousand businessmen in 1964, the seminars featured panels of federal civil rights administrators, government compliance officers, and PCEEO representatives.[50] They told attendees that the law was "designed to give everyone an equal chance" at a desirable job.[51] They also assuaged businessmen's worst fears about the new law. In one session, a hypothetical employer was worried that if he was forced to hire a "Negro insurance man," he would lose customers and go broke. NAM's response: "There's nothing in the law that exempts you because you may go broke. But are you certain you'll go broke?" The law applied to everyone, including this employer's competitors: "You're going to be surprised at how fast the public's attitude will change." Also, the employer was free to fire the black salesman if he was in fact unable to sell, but odds were good that he would meet his sales goals. The law required only "that you at least give him the opportunity to demonstrate he can."[52] All of the typical concerns—from white workers' rioting to false accusations of discrimination—were similarly addressed in ways that allayed fears and offered simple solutions.[53]

The seminars also focused on how a company could take "affirmative action" to hire and promote black people. While liberals complained of the EEOC's weakness, NAM seminar leaders inflated its power to compel attendees to get their houses in order. As Professor Herbert Northrup bluntly put it at one seminar: "If you don't have any Negroes, you'd better get some."[54] The list of affirmative actions were those that had been tried successfully by other companies (mostly PFP companies), such as recruiting

49. This is the argument of Frank Dobbin, *Inventing Equal Opportunity* (Princeton, NJ: Princeton University Press, 2009).

50. See sample programs in series 7, box 135, NAMR.

51. "NAM Members Air Views on Civil Rights" *Daily Evening Item*, September 24, 1965, series 7, box 135, NAMR.

52. "Equal Opportunity Law Questions Answered by NAM Proponent," *Citizen Register*, October 5, 1964, in "Progress Report re Seminars on Title VII," December 1, 1964, series 7, box 135, NAMR.

53. See other articles in "Progress Report re Seminars on Title VII," December 1, 1964, series 7, box 135, NAMR.

54. Quoted in John Carberg, "NAM Seminar Sets Record Straight on Civil Rights Law," *Boston Herald*, September 24, 1964.

at black colleges, connecting to black community leaders, identifying and training people of color for advancement, attending EEO conferences, reassessing job qualifications, and the like.

One commonly asked question was whether the Civil Rights Act required affirmative action. The answer: "As a matter of legal, literal construction, the answer is No. However, positive action, which would be considered affirmative is being taken as a matter of common sense and in keeping with the practices of many companies who have government contracts with the scope of Executive Orders 10925 and 11114."[55] What if a company ended all of its discriminatory behavior and was still unable to hire very many black workers into traditionally white positions? Would that be cause for discrimination charges? In 1965, the answer was still no. But the EEOC, as state fair employment offices had done earlier, was using the number of black employees as a guideline to assess a company's compliance—even though Title VII prohibited hiring someone solely because of their race. Thus, NAM recommended that every company practice "affirmative action."

The point of all these endeavors was still to avoid the need for further legislation or amendments. Liberals almost immediately began to lobby for giving the EEOC more enforcement powers, and NAM was hoping to avoid this by encouraging industry to comply on its own. In addition, however, these efforts put NAM in a position to advise the government rather than oppose it. It had a constructive program that included not only the EEO seminars but also its STEP (Solutions to Employment Problems) program, and it had a new Urban Affairs Department, which worked with government agencies and community organizations to train and find jobs for underutilized or disadvantaged populations, such as high school dropouts and the "hardcore unemployed."[56] As a result, Gullander was invited to serve on a variety of government committees pertaining to "new issues," such as the Youth Task Force, the Minority Enterprise Council, and the Pollution Board.[57] Noting that "many of us were raised at a time when we were taught to have a different opinion about such organizations as the NAM," Vice President

55. "More on a Tale of 22 Cities," *NAM Reports*, February 15, 1965.

56. On the STEP program, see Charles Moore, "NAM Helping to Combat Social Evils," *Atlanta Constitution*, September 22, 1966, p. 61; Marie Smith, "Title VII Is Opening Doors but Not to Room at Top," *Washington Post*, July 14, 1965, p. B7; "Big Business Takes Big Step to Aid Unemployed," *Chicago Defender*, May 20, 1967, p. 14. On the Urban Affairs Department, see "NAM's Urban Affairs Dept. Is Expanded," *NAM Reports*, April 29, 1968, p. 1; special urban affairs section, *NAM Reports*, July 15, 1968.

57. See *NAM Reports*, June 14, 1965, September 29, 1969, and April 13, 1970.

FIGURE 9.1. Urban League head Whitney Young speaks before NAM, 1967. Copyright © National Association of Manufacturers; courtesy of Hagley Library and Museum.

Hubert Humphrey, a longtime civil rights liberal, marveled that this was no longer the case; the NAM was, at long last, "socially responsible."[58] In 1967, Whitney Young, civil rights activist and head of the National Urban League, addressed NAM's annual meeting.

A NEW KIND OF AFFIRMATIVE ACTION

NAM was able to use its newfound credibility with government agencies to help define a new results-oriented version of "affirmative action" that would require employers to hire a certain number of minorities according to the percentage of their local population. This version of affirmative action

58. *NAM Reports*, November 8, 1965.

emerged from the Office of Federal Contract Compliance (OFCC), which replaced the PCEEO in 1965. Located in the Labor Department, the OFCC was tasked with putting contractors in compliance with executive order 11246, which required government contractors to take "affirmative action" to ensure equal opportunity to all applicants and employees, and with the Civil Rights Act's Title VI, which prohibited discrimination in any project program or activity receiving federal funds. Not specifically banned from preferential hiring strategies (as the EEOC was), the OFCC had more leeway to try experimental programs, such as the Philadelphia Plan. The Philadelphia Plan, which initially targeted unions working on federal construction projects, required contractors to state in their bids how many minority group members they intended to have working in each craft position (plumbers, pipefitters, and so on); the idea was to attain some kind of racial balance in trade unions.[59] In 1967, the OFCC began to apply these requirements to projects in other cities and industries.[60] This created a furor on the part of both unions and industry over the use of quotas. The Johnson administration quickly abandoned the Philadelphia Plan, but the proposed "affirmative actions" and the idea of racial balance in the workplace would continue to be discussed and revised over the next three years and was eventually enacted by the Nixon administration.

NAM was nonplussed by the new "affirmative actions" and the idea of quotas, but it wanted to keep open its new contacts with the administration in hopes that it could have an impact on the enforcement process. In a meeting between NAM officials and the OFCC about the new directive, OFCC officials explained their expectations. According to NAM notes on the meeting, OFCC officials said that by "affirmative action" they meant "results." To get results, goals had to be set. To meet the goals, employers should revise their expectations of potential employees. Rather than looking for specific competencies and qualifications, employers needed to identify "apparent potential" in job candidates. Employers should also eliminate departmental seniority, which impeded black entrance into white positions, and consider giving back pay to black workers who had been denied promotion because of seniority policies. If employers ran into trouble with unions about these changes (seniority was a union policy), the OFCC would back the employer.

59. On the Philadelphia Plan, see Dean Kotlowski, *Nixon's Civil Rights* (Cambridge, MA: Harvard University Press, 2001), 99–115; David Hamilton Golland, *Constructing Affirmative Action: The Struggle for Equal Employment Opportunity* (Lexington: University of Kentucky Press, 2011), chap. 4.

60. Graham, *The Civil Rights Era*, 288–89; Kotlowski, *Nixon's Civil Rights*, 101–2.

Most importantly, however, and through informal negotiation with NAM officials, the OFCC understood that such efforts might fail to yield "results," but if a company could show that it had made a good-faith effort to set goals and try these new affirmative actions, the OFCC would not find it in violation.[61] Although the new "affirmative actions" relied on a standard of racial proportionalism that NAM opposed, NAM officials were satisfied that there was room for negotiation on a case-by-case basis. "It is clear that all demands made by OFCC or contracting agencies," it concluded, "are made for the purposes of negotiating equitable solutions."[62] "Equitable" here meant equitable for both employers and minorities.

NAM felt that negotiable requirements, setting "goals and timetables" (rather than quotas), and the OFCC's recognition of "good faith efforts" were workable for industry, although it still hoped to keep these new "color-conscious" kinds of affirmative action voluntary and not mandatory. In the fall of 1968, it cosponsored a series of conferences with Plans for Progress that featured a "dialogue" with EEOC and OFCC representatives. The idea was to review the new requirements in each agency, encourage the two agencies to coordinate with each other so as to avoid conflicting directives, and provide an opportunity to clarify what exactly would be expected from industry. NAM also tried to make it clear that "affirmative action" meant "industry action," not "compulsory and arbitrary action as imposed by the government."[63]

NAM officials were pleased with the first conference. The OFCC rep admitted that the government could not currently answer all of industry's questions and agreed to work with industry reps to come up with more concrete guidelines. Summing up the successful effort, NAM official Robert Godown noted that it provided aid to "member companies in an area of major importance," and that it "increased NAM acceptance at OFCC and EEOC and should help us in getting our voice heard in the future."[64] This was somewhat true, although NAM's influence was far less than it hoped and almost invisible to many of its members, who wished NAM would offer more resistance.

61. Delton, *Racial Integration in Corporate America*, 217–19, based on documents in series 5, box 64, "Philadelphia Plan" file, NAMR.

62. Quoted in Delton, *Racial Integration in Corporate America*, 219.

63. Quoted in NAM memo, H. deC. Williams to W. K. Zinke, August 21, 1968, series 5, box 64, "PFP" file, NAMR.

64. R. D. Godown to L. H. Miller, October 4, 1968, series 5, box 64, "PFP" file, NAMR.

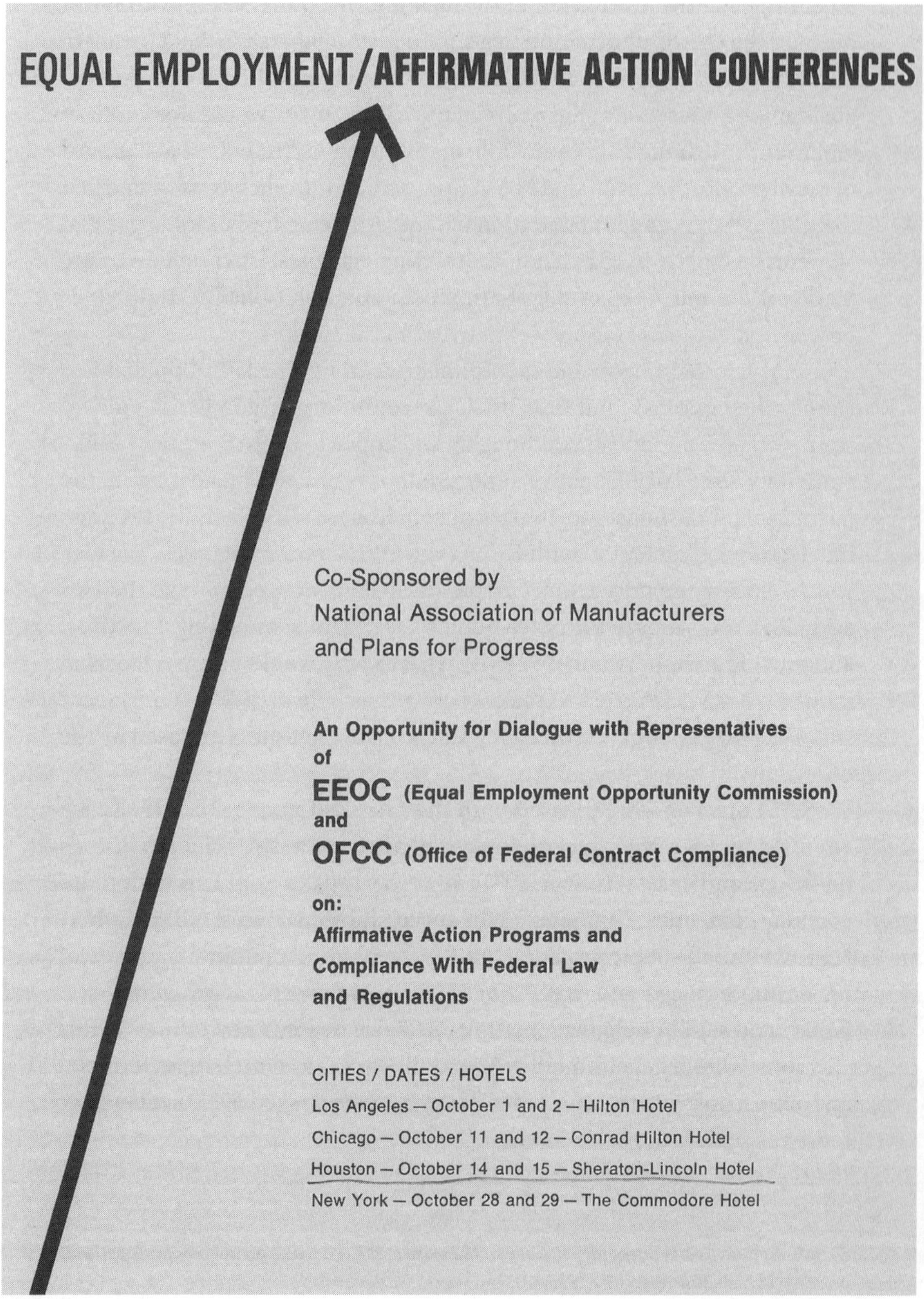

EQUAL EMPLOYMENT/AFFIRMATIVE ACTION CONFERENCES

Co-Sponsored by
National Association of Manufacturers
and Plans for Progress

**An Opportunity for Dialogue with Representatives
of
EEOC** (Equal Employment Opportunity Commission)
**and
OFCC** (Office of Federal Contract Compliance)

**on:
Affirmative Action Programs and
Compliance With Federal Law
and Regulations**

CITIES / DATES / HOTELS

Los Angeles — October 1 and 2 — Hilton Hotel

Chicago — October 11 and 12 — Conrad Hilton Hotel

Houston — October 14 and 15 — Sheraton-Lincoln Hotel

New York — October 28 and 29 — The Commodore Hotel

FIGURE 9.2. Flyer for NAM/PFP conferences. Copyright © National Association of Manufacturers; courtesy of Hagley Library and Museum.

The Nixon administration pushed ahead with government-mandated affirmative action. Unlike the Johnson administration, it was not beholden to unions and thus could crack down on union resistance. But it also cracked down on employers, instituting a revised Philadelphia Plan in November 1969 that required all government contractors to set goals and timetables to hire minority applicants in proportion to the minority population in their area.[65] In trying to calm the furor over order number 4 (as the directive was known), the OFCC explained that all it had done was make mandatory the voluntary affirmative action guidelines that had accompanied the NAM/ PFP conferences in the fall of 1968. Indeed, *Business Week* reported that the "unhappy parent" of the new hiring rules was none other than NAM itself.[66] Unamused, NAM officials snapped back that the whole point of their guidelines was that they were voluntary; many smaller companies did not have the resources to implement them.

The Labor Department revised order number 4 in ways that NAM presented to its membership as more flexible, implying that NAM itself had secured the "toned-down directive."[67] The new version added more flexibility to the process and recognized a company's good-faith effort as compliance, even if it failed to meet its specific goals. In assuring its members that the new version took a "softer approach," NAM was essentially saying that this was the best it could do.[68] But many members were angry at what they saw as NAM's capitulation to the government. A switchgear manufacturer from Fulton Missouri, for instance, wanted to know what NAM was doing "to stop this nonsense." Small companies like his were "helpless without an aggressive counterattack by NAM. Let's get to work!" he wrote.[69] All that the new NAM could say in response was that they had gotten a few details changed.

NAM leadership, however, could take some comfort in the fact that AFL members were likewise angry about government-mandated affirmative action—and that the issue weakened the liberal-labor coalition. In the years

65. Graham, *The Civil Rights Era*, 342–43; see also Kotlowski, *Nixon's Civil Rights*, 102–15.

66. Delton, *Racial Integration in Corporate America*, 221; "The Unhappy Parent of New Hiring Rules," *Business Week*, January 24, 1970.

67. "Toned-Down Directive Issued on Affirmative Action," *NAM Reports*, February 9, 1970, p. 1. Graham, *The Civil Rights Era*, 342–43, suggests that the revisions were minor.

68. See Delton, *Racial Integration in Corporate America*, 222.

69. Quoted in ibid. The exchange between Lambert Miller and M. E. DeNeui in March 1970 is found in series 5, box 64, "Philadelphia Plan" file, NAMR.

ahead, business would find that taking affirmative action was easier than fighting the EEOC or OFCC. It was actually clearer about what was expected of employers than the simple antidiscrimination directive had been.

When the Reagan administration attempted to eliminate affirmative action in 1985, NAM defended it. As one of its member companies put it, "We're accustomed to setting goals."[70] Plus, the government mandate ensured that all companies had to commit to the same expense, thereby removing the competitive advantage gained by slackers. Responding to a *New York Times* story on affirmative action, one reader wrote: "There is an important reason why affirmative action has so much industry support. It was developed originally in a cooperative venture by industry and government as an effective means of achieving equal opportunity after all previous methods had failed."[71]

DISCRIMINATION AGAINST WOMEN

NAM was less prepared for the prohibition of "sex" discrimination, which had not been part of government contract agreements or state-level antidiscrimination laws. The PFP program was focused solely on race, and the statistics, bibliographies, and case studies distributed by NAM and used in-house pertained to racial minorities. The factors behind racial discrimination were well documented, but there were fewer such studies of gender discrimination. Perhaps that is why Kothe, who led the EEO seminars and was usually very circumspect when speaking about race and racial discrimination, had this to say about the ban on gender discrimination: "When those women's magazines get hold of this law and start telling their readers about the 'new rights' of women, why the Emancipation Proclamation will be a pygmy by comparison."[72] In 1942, NAM had advocated equal pay for women and proclaimed that there were no differences between men and women that should lead to lower pay for women; it reaffirmed this principle again in 1957 for men and women doing the same job. In 1963, it testified to limit the application of the Equal Pay Act of 1963 (which prohibited wage differentials

70. Quoted in Delton, *Racial Integration in Corporate America*, 279.
71. Herbert Hammerman, letter to the editor, *New York Times*, November 8, 1985, p. A34. See also Tom Wicker, "A Deeper Division," *New York Times*, November 1, 1985; and Anthony Lewis, "The Party of Lincoln," *New York Times*, November 7, 1985, p. A35.
72. Arelo Sederberg, "Civil Rights for Women Pose Business Headache," *Los Angeles Times*, October 6, 1964, p. B8.

based on sex), but it had not formally opposed the act.[73] Nonetheless, NAM leaders and members—almost all men—seemed bewildered by the idea of equal opportunity for women.[74] Nor was this reaction limited to the business community. Democrats, the media, liberals, even the new EEOC director, Franklin Roosevelt Jr., were also flummoxed by the "sex" question.[75] But bewilderment was not resistance, and NAM added gender discrimination to the program, publishing and updating "sex discrimination" guidelines in *NAM Reports* and following court cases.

Just as it had done with regard to race, NAM's Legal Department expressed opposition to many of the OFCC and EEOC decisions and rules about gender. But whereas its complaints with regard to race usually focused on process issues, NAM's complaints concerning sex discrimination were based much more on employers' assumptions about women workers. NAM objected to being forced to hire women with children when "experience has shown that female employees who do not have facilities for supervisional [*sic*] care of their children soon become a problem in terms of absenteeism, tardiness, and partial work days."[76] Similarly, why put women in costly management trainee programs "when many recently trained women often leave the labor force for marriage and child rearing, with the result that their services are lost to the company which has underwritten training costs."[77] Although NAM officials encouraged employers to let go of their preconceived notions about African Americans, they did not do the same with regard to women. This was a reflection not just of sexism but also of the dearth of research and studies on sex discrimination.

Much like NAM officials, EEOC officials had not expected to deal with sex discrimination, which was a last-minute addition and had no organized constituency to recommend policies.[78] Thus, EEOC guidelines about sex discrimination were frustratingly unsettled. At first, the EEOC moved cautiously, saying that too literal an interpretation of Title VII might disrupt

73. "Equal Pay for Equal Work in the United States," 1948, series 1, box 187, "UNECOSOC" file, NAMR; resolution in support of equal pay for equal work, series 1, box 103, NAMR; Industrial Relations Committee meeting minutes, October 10, 1963, series 1, box 26, NAMR.

74. See Paul Gerhardt to Lambert Miller, June 8, 1964, and C. L. Irving to Lambert Miller, August 4, 1964, series 5, box 65, NAMR.

75. Graham, *The Civil Rights Era*, 205–11.

76. "NAM Raises Additional Questions on Sex Discrimination Guidelines," *NAM Reports*, August 18, 1969, pp. 28–29.

77. Ibid., 28.

78. On the divisions in the women's movements of the mid-1960s, see Graham, *The Civil Rights Era*, chap. 8.

long-established state statutes and collective bargaining agreements (which protected women's health and welfare) without achieving any compensating benefits.[79] But the EEOC began to equate gender discrimination with racial discrimination as the sex discrimination complaints poured in, and it sought to eliminate any distinctions based on gender, including protective legislation.

Unions supported protective laws and gender-segregated job categories, which were largely the fruit of their struggle to prevent industry from using women to undercut men's labor.[80] For this reason, NAM had historically opposed protective legislation for women (see chapter 4), arguing that women were individuals and equal to men in their ability to perform most jobs. One might think that NAM would have supported the EEOC's attempts to end such laws, which presented an opportunity to play unions against liberals. But it did not. Industry had adjusted well to protective laws and gender-segregated policies, and NAM's aim was to seek the least amount of disruption for member companies. Its civil rights seminars were designed precisely to prepare companies for the disruption of racial integration. No one had anticipated the addition of gender into the mix.

Gradually, however, NAM and industry adapted. NAM kept its members informed of what they needed to do to be in compliance and began to take more seriously the idea of women in the workplace. Articles about women and sex discrimination began to show up in the pages of *NAM Reports*, overturning old stereotypes and featuring professional women's experiences. In 1970, NAM cosponsored a conference with four corporations, a women's liberal arts college, and the head of the Labor Department's Women's Division. "Women in Industry: New Perspectives from Education, Industry, and Government" focused on how education could prepare women for leadership positions in business.[81] In 1973, NAM appointed its first-ever female vice president, Phyllis Moehrle, NAM's resident expert on African Americans in industry.[82]

---

79. "Sex Discrimination Guidelines Are Issued," *NAM Reports*, November 29, 1965, last page.

80. Unions continued to support such laws into the 1970s. See Graham, *The Civil Rights Era*, 208–9; and Dennis DesLippe, "Organized Labor, National Politics, and Second Wave Feminism in the United States, 1965–1975," *International Labor and Working-Class History* 49 (Spring 1996): 143–65.

81. Ralph Kittle, International Paper Company, "Women in Industry—New Perspectives," *NAM Reports*, January 18, 1971, p. 12.

82. *NAM Annual Report*, 1973; Moehrle biography found in *Enterprise* (March 1979): 31.

THE EQUAL EMPLOYMENT OPPORTUNITY ACT OF 1972

Almost immediately after the passage of the Civil Rights Act, liberals and civil rights activists attempted to secure cease-and-desist enforcement powers for the EEOC, along the lines of what the NLRB had. Business and NAM opposed this effort. The last thing they wanted was another NLRB-type agency surveilling their policies. The Nixon administration came up with a bill that authorized the EEOC to bring action in federal district courts, where employers would be given due process. The AFL-CIO backed the Democratic bill, and NAM predictably supported the Republican bill.

But it would be wrong to see the Nixon administration's bill as being less committed to the enforcement of Title VII. The Nixon administration had already proven its commitment to black civil rights by mandating that federal contractors set goals and timetables for hiring minorities—hardly a popular policy among Republicans, and one abandoned by Lyndon Johnson because of organized labor.[83] Moreover, even some civil rights activists preferred the courts option. Law professor Alfred Blumrosen, an architect of the EEOC and proponent of affirmative action, argued that the federal courts were more liberal than they had been in the early twentieth century, when liberals had turned to regulatory agencies to effect reform.[84] Regulatory agencies, on the other hand, were vulnerable to "capture" by those they were supposed to regulate. Blumrosen concluded that giving the EEOC additional power, as liberals sought to do, "would positively harm" the effort to end employment discrimination.[85]

NAM lobbied hard for the Republican version of enforcement, offering editorial comments on bills and decisions (rather than just reporting them) and urging members to contact their congressional representatives. As was the case so often in the past, old battles with labor guided their thinking. It was almost as though they were arguing against the NLRB all over again. NAM officials reminded themselves of Senator Taft's attempts to have the courts adjudicate labor cases (rather than the NLRB) and explained to members: "Like the National Labor Relations Board, whose many arbitrary decisions have stirred controversy over the years, the EEOC would have the power to serve complaints, hold hearings on them, and issue cease and

83. See Kotlowski, *Nixon's Civil Rights*, chaps. 4–5; Graham, *The Civil Rights Era*, chaps. 13 and 15.

84. Graham, *The Civil Rights Era*, 431. *NAM Reports* quotes Blumrosen to this effect in "The Argument over Power for the EEOC," *NAM Reports*, January 24, 1972.

85. Quoted in Graham, *The Civil Rights Era*, 431.

desist orders against companies, unions or whoever else was charged with discrimination in hiring and firing."[86] As they had argued with regard to the Wagner Act, NAM officials wanted employers to have the opportunity to defend themselves in an impartial court of law. It is unclear to what extent they understood that the courts were getting more liberal, though the evidence was all around them. The Supreme Court had just decreed in *Griggs vs. Duke Power Company* (1971) that policies leading to unequal results—disparate impact—were Title VII violations. NAM certainly reported on these cases with some degree of alarm. Its officials also made use of Blumrosen's argument about the federal courts' growing liberalism, suggesting that they knew that the courts would not necessarily offer industry an easier deal when it came to discrimination.

Years later, conservatives would blame liberals for "legislating from the bench," or using courts to legislate reform. But as this episode shows, Republicans and industry had a role to play in that development. One could even argue that it was Congress's refusal to define discrimination or the means by which it could be eliminated in its legislation that was responsible for the courts' role in defining those terms. But it was not just the courts that shaped how integration finally occurred in the United States—it was also the EEOC, civil rights activists, business and industry, and NAM. The affirmative action policies that ended up integrating employment in the United States—to the degree that it has been integrated—were to a large extent the product of employers' industrial relations offices trying to put firms in compliance with a vague law in negotiation with government offices and community organizers.[87]

Assessing NAM's Role

This chapter has shown that NAM did not oppose integration and that it proactively developed effective policies and persuaded its members to comply with new laws designed to integrate the US workplace. As we have seen, it did so for several reasons. Foremost among these reasons was a desire to avert or, later, to comply with legislation. But developing and utilizing

86. "Washington Outlook," *NAM Reports*, January 31, 1972.

87. As argued by Frank Dobbin, *Inventing Equal Opportunity* (Princeton, NJ: Princeton University Press, 2009); Pamela Walker Laird, "Entangled: Civil Rights in Corporate American since 1964," in *Capital Gains: Business and Politics in Twentieth-Century America*, ed. Richard John and Kim Phillips-Fein (Philadelphia: University of Pennsylvania Press, 2016), 217–34; and Delton, *Racial Integration in Corporate America*.

manpower was also a prerogative for industry during the Vietnam War. Indeed, the scarcity of construction workers in these years is what compelled Nixon to break unions' monopoly on the labor market, which is what the Philadelphia Plan did.[88] Although NAM celebrated the individualistic notion of equal opportunity, it nonetheless helped popularize and rationalize a more color-conscious standard of affirmative action. These actions helped NAM rehabilitate its reputation and get back in the game of influencing government rather than raging at it—all at little cost to industry. It was no skin off industry's back, and besides, NAM's actions contributed to weakening the liberal-labor coalition. It made economic sense, as both NAM and civil rights activists liked to say.

But just because its actions were self-serving to NAM and its members does not mean that they were disingenuous or ineffective. The job of a trade association is to serve its members. In this case, NAM served its members by helping them integrate their firms and factories, and in doing so it helped industry accept one of the most momentous reforms in US history.

88. Kotlowski, *Nixon's Civil Rights*, 103–5.

PART III

Decline and Recovery, 1960-2004

Manufacturing's growth rate began to decline in the 1960s, owing in part to rising international competition and increased imports. In 1971, the United States experienced its first merchandise trade deficit since 1893, beginning a trend that, in hindsight, signaled the decline of US-based manufacturing. The economic disasters of the 1970s—recession, inflation, and the oil embargo of the Organization of the Petroleum Exporting Countries (OPEC)—further eroded manufacturing. Nevertheless, it remained dominant and politically powerful. Manufacturing jobs in the United States reached an all-time absolute high in 1979, when 19.4 million Americans worked in manufacturing.

With the return of conservatism (or the rise of neoliberalism) and the decline of union power in the Reagan Era, one would have thought this would be a highpoint for NAM, which had long sought just this situation. But it was an era of plant closings and takeovers, and NAM's membership was devastated. Nor did Reagan's economic policies do much to help the manufacturing sector. Although NAM's multinational corporations profited from Reagan Era policies, US manufacturing suffered and, like labor, NAM lost much of its political influence in the 1980s.

Unlike labor, however, industry's fortunes would rebound in the 1990s through "just-in-time" production processes based on international supply chains, automated design, and electronic controls that cut human "man-hours" in half while increasing productivity and output. These new processes "dis-integrated" the vertical integration of the early twentieth century, creating opportunities for a new generation of small manufacturers. The North American Free Trade Agreement, the World Trade Organization, and the opening of China to US investment furthered the fortunes of large multinational companies, but these developments also eroded the manufacturing sector in the United States. NAM survived, but its influence was not what it was in the twentieth century.

10

Deindustrialization and the Global Imperative

On the surface, it seemed as though postwar tariff-cutting and liberal internationalist economic policies (chapter 7) had paid off. By exporting aid and new technologies to Europe and Japan, the United States had built up its allies' economies and staved off the communist threat. All well and good. But US allies had learned the lessons only too well, and by the mid-1960s, armed with dollars and know-how, they represented both a competitive and monetary challenge to the United States. Worse, rather than embracing the liberal internationalist free-trade position, they threw up barriers to their markets. The American share of world trade declined from 20 to 14 percent between 1950 and 1970. In 1964, the Johnson administration established a permanent federal task force to assist communities facing plant closings. In 1971, the United States saw its first merchandise trade deficit since 1893.[1]

The folks at NAM were just as baffled as US policymakers about this turn of events. But as it had in 1895 and, indeed, after both world wars,

---

1. Trade share and trade deficit figures from Thomas Ferguson and Joel Rogers, *Right Turn* (New York: Hill and Wang, 1986), 81; see also Stein, *Pivotal Decade*, chap. 1; Alfred Eckes Jr. and Thomas Zeiler, *Globalization and the American Century* (New York: Cambridge University Press, 2003), chap. 7; Bluestone and Harrison, *The Deindustrialization of America*, 140. On the administration's task force, see "LBJ Acts to Aid Jobless Areas," *Washington Post*, October 21, 1964, p. A1; *Public Papers of the Presidents of the United States: Lyndon B. Johnson*, Book 2 (Washington, DC: National Archives and Records Administration, Office of the Federal Register, November 22, 1963–June 30, 1964), entry 690, p. 691.

NAM believed that exports and foreign investment were the answer. Exports would help correct the trade deficit, while foreign direct investment (FDI)—building new factories abroad or attaining controlling shares of foreign plants—would provide markets for US exports and allow American multinationals to gain access to restricted markets in Europe and elsewhere. NAM member companies, like DuPont, had built new plants in Europe and elsewhere and had seen a corresponding rise in exports.[2] But FDI also built up foreign competition; indeed that was in many ways the point—to spur industrial development and create new markets. Moreover, companies were beginning to use FDI to engage in what later became known as "offshoring"—moving their plants to export platforms in developing areas with cheaper labor.

While organized labor was quick to recognize the dangers of cheap imports to its interests, organized manufacturing—that is, NAM—seemed belligerently oblivious, even as it was losing members at record rates. It is now widely accepted that imports, Cold War trade policies, and offshoring contributed to deindustrialization, which began in the 1960s. In promoting freer trade and FDI, NAM, despite its claims to the contrary, was working against the interests of small and midsized manufacturers, who were still the majority of its membership and the most vulnerable to imports. Together with a merger wave in the mid-1960s, deindustrialization eviscerated NAM's membership, which went from a high of 21,801 companies in 1957 to just under 12,000 by 1980. As its membership declined, NAM became even more dependent on large multinationals to meet the challenges of a global economy that it had helped create.

New Competition in the 1960s

By the late 1950s, US allies were emerging as major economic competitors. The European Economic Community (EEC), which formed in 1957, represented exactly the kind of multilateral "free trade" community advocated by liberal internationalists. Given Europe's history of war, cooperation among these nations was to be preferred to rivalries. But it also represented a concentration of economic power, and one that imposed tariffs and quotas on

---

2. DuPont reported $363 million in foreign business in 1960, an increase of 21 percent from 1959, and $218 million in its exports of US-made products, a 28 percent increase. See I. E. Du Pont de Nemours & Company annual report, 1960, pp. 16–18, available at Proquest Historical Annual Reports.

American goods.[3] The Japanese likewise imposed trade restrictions on the United States, while also benefiting from its most favored nation (MFN) status in terms of reduced tariffs to enter the US market. The United States tolerated these unfavorable trade conditions to keep its Cold War allies amenable in terms of foreign policy.[4] Nor did NAM object; after all, its leaders represented large multinational corporations that could build plants abroad to get around these restrictions. As a result, imports into the United States rose, which was good for foreign economies and American consumers but not, as it turns out, for US plants and their workers.

As early as 1960, NAM members wanted to know what NAM was doing to address the problem of foreign competition. The Economic Advisory Committee issued a report that slid around the problem. It provided no stats on foreign competition, but rather defended the "increased prosperity and productivity of other parts of the world" as good for the US economy. If there was a threat, it was to the US balance of payments, not to manufacturers. Yes, "old industries will disappear or decline," but new ones would take their place. That was capitalism. Companies facing competition needed to increase their productivity or find new "imaginative, hard-hitting sales tactics." The report reminded readers that NAM took no position on tariffs because of the diversity of interests it represented, but then it stated that the solution was not to isolate the US by reinstating tariffs. If members inquired as to how NAM was dealing with the problem, the proper response was to remind them that taxes and unions were the main impediments to US competitiveness and here NAM was, as ever, vigilant.[5] This document suggests either shortsightedness with regard to foreign competition or an intentional evasion of the threat posed by globalist interests to "old industries" and small firms.

President Kennedy attempted to deal with the new competition with the Trade Expansion Act of 1962, which replaced the old Reciprocal Trade Agreements Act (RTAA), giving the president greater powers to cut tariffs and negotiate multilateral deals and for the first time providing benefits and training to workers hurt by the policy.[6] As per the norm with tariff legislation, NAM took no official position, but quietly supported it by, for instance,

3. Stein, *Pivotal Decade*, 36.

4. This is Stein's argument. See also Eckes, *Opening America's Market*, chaps. 5–6.

5. NAM, "Foreign Competition: A Challenge for America," prepared by the Research Department and approved by the Economic Advisory Committee, September 13, 1960, series 1, box 76, NAMR.

6. Eckes, *Opening America's Market*, 179–89.

inviting President Kennedy to speak at its annual meeting. Kennedy was the first sitting US president to address NAM, and it is significant that this honor went to an internationalist, tariff-cutting Democrat. In his long and well-received address, Kennedy made the pitch for more liberal trade legislation, proposing across-the-board tariff reductions of 50 percent and stressing the benefit of imports to American consumers. Kennedy acknowledged the challenges that EEC competition posed to manufacturers and workers and argued that the new legislation would empower him to make the best deals.[7]

The following year the EEC head spoke to NAM, saying that the EEC represented not a barrier but rather an opportunity for American trade expansion. A representative from Japan also spoke, pleading for more American investment to help Asia "emerge from a stagnation of several centuries."[8] DuPont, for one, long a supplier of NAM directors, eagerly took advantage of opportunities in both Europe and Japan, noting in its 1960 annual report that the new markets being built in Europe by the removal of trade barriers and increases in the European standard of living presented "opportunities for construction of plants comparable in size and operating efficiency to those in the United States." In Japan, DuPont gained 50 percent ownership of two new companies formed to produce neoprene synthetic rubber and polythene, respectively.[9]

Once again, NAM unofficially supported a Democratic trade agenda, even as it became clearer that neither the Europeans nor the Japanese were going to reciprocate the reciprocity. Over the course of the 1960s, West German exports grew by 109 percent and Japan's by 333 percent, much of it coming into the United States or supporting US efforts in Vietnam.[10] At the same time, US FDI in manufacturing increased from $7.9 billion in 1957 to $24.1 billion by 1967 as those firms that could do so built or invested in factories inside those trade barriers.[11] US companies were investing more

7. Ibid., 186; "Text of the President's Address to NAM," *Washington Post*, December 8, 1961, p. A20.

8. Both quoted in "Common Market Held as US Outlet," *New York Times*, December 6, 1962, p. 28.

9. DuPont annual report, 1960, pp. 16, 18. At the end of 1960, DuPont had thirteen thousand employees in foreign plants and offices.

10. American exports grew by 67 percent. Numbers from John Judis, *Grand Illusion: Critics and Champions of the American Century* (New York: Farrar, Straus and Giroux, 1992), 208; see also Stein, *Pivotal Decade*, chap. 1.

11. "International Investment—Value of Direct Investments Abroad," in US Census Bureau, *Statistical Abstract of the United States* (Washington, DC: US Government Printing Office, 1959),

FIGURE 10.1. President Kennedy speaks before NAM, 1961. Copyright © National Association of Manufacturers; courtesy of Hagley Library and Museum.

resources at a greater rate in foreign countries (that is, in competitors) than they were in the United States. From 1958 to 1964, new jobs were created in the United States almost exclusively in the public sector. In 1964, Congress allowed multinationals to import goods assembled in their foreign

p. 871; and "Direct Investments Abroad," in US Census Bureau, *Statistical Abstract of the United States* (Washington, DC: US Government Printing Office,1969), p. 785.

factories back into the United States with only a value-added tax, leading to the development of export platform economies in Hong Kong, South Korea, and Taiwan.[12]

THE BALANCE-OF-PAYMENTS CRISIS

Although private investment abroad helped US corporations compete, it also exacerbated the balance-of-payments crisis. Ideally, all countries should have a balanced international account, with inflow and outflow of goods, services, and capital being about equal. US policymakers had set aside that conventional wisdom to spur economic recovery after the war. Huge US outflows in the form of military expenditures, foreign aid, and investment created a deficit, but one that US policymakers were comfortable with because they assumed that the Europeans would be returning those dollars by purchasing American goods. By the late 1950s, however, they had become uneasy. The US trade surplus was shrinking, and dollars were ending up in foreign banks or, worse, being exchanged for gold. This was alarming because the Bretton Woods system required the United States to underwrite the dollar with gold priced at $35 an ounce.[13] As Europeans cashed in dollars for gold, US gold reserves dwindled, putting the entire international monetary system in peril.

To balance the dollar outflow, US policymakers sought to attract dollars via increased exports. President Johnson created the Interagency Committee on Export Expansion to speed this along. NAM president Gullander happily sat on the National Export Expansion Council, which advised the new Interagency Committee. The State Department followed suit and made a pitch for the US Foreign Service as an export market for US manufacturers.[14] NAM set up programs encouraging small and midsized businesses "to learn about

12. Stein, *Pivotal Decade*, chap. 1; Bluestone and Harrison, *The Deindustrialization of America*, 142–43, Eckes, *Opening America's Market*, 217. Imports from US multinationals made up 34 percent of the import balance by 1970; see John Judis, *The Paradox of American Democracy: Elites, Special Interests, and the Betrayal of Public Trust* (New York: Pantheon, 2000), 114. For an overview of globalization in the 1970s, see the essays in *The Shock of the Global: The 1970s in Perspective*, edited by Niall Ferguson, Charles Maier, Erez Manela, and Daniel J. Sargent (Cambridge, MA: Harvard University Press, 2010).

13. On the balance of payments, see Stein, *Pivotal Decade*, chap. 1; Barry Eichengreen, *Globalizing Capital: A History of the International Monetary System* (Princeton, NJ: Princeton University Press, 1996), 113–20; Aaron Major, *Architects of Austerity: International Finance and the Politics of Growth* (Stanford, CA: Stanford University Press, 2014), chaps. 1–2.

14. Benjamin Weiner, "State Dept., Business Ties Are Strengthened," *NAM Reports*, March 15, 1965, p. 8.

the additional opportunities for trade inherent in foreign markets." By helping smaller companies enter the global marketplace, NAM also helped the
government "deal with the problem of deteriorating balance of international
payments."[15] As it had done in the early twentieth century, NAM organized
trade missions to Europe and elsewhere, introducing American businessmen
to their counterparts abroad.[16] It took out a special advertising section in
the *New York Times*, headlined "Export—The New Marketing Revolution,"
which declared that "Europe has never been in a better position to absorb
American products and shipping costs are low." It publicized something
called an "E award," for "enterprise in exporting." The 1968 recipient was
the Baltimore Air Coil Company, a NAM member, whose export sales rose
from 1 percent to 10 percent in just five years. NAM backed the expansion
of the Export-Import Bank, which provided loans to countries seeking to
contract with American companies.[17]

As in the past, NAM leaders felt that foreign investment abroad was key
to expanding America's export trade. They argued that US firms and investments abroad provided purchasing power to the people of the host country,
who could then purchase US exports. In addition, US-owned foreign firms
and subsidiaries were ready markets for US materials, parts and goods.[18]
Thus, in its effort to expand exports, NAM was also involved in numerous
ventures to increase FDI, such as the Asian Development Bank and the Private Investment Advisory Council (IPIAC), which was established by the
US Agency for International Development (USAID) to encourage private
investment.[19]

Even as government programs such as USAID were encouraging investment as part of US foreign policy, however, the Kennedy and Johnson
administrations were trying to *discourage* private investment abroad, which
they believed contributed to the balance-of-payments deficit. Foreign investment was just another case of dollars leaving the United States, and it should

---

15. *NAM Annual Report*, 1964, p. 8; "Pilot Program to Help Boston Raise Exports," *NAM Reports*, January 25, 1965.

16. *NAM Annual Report*, 1964, p. 8; see also "Gullander, Davis Well Received in S. America," *NAM Reports*, August 19, 1968, pp. 8–9.

17. "NAM Will Sponsor a Special Export Section in the Times," *NAM Reports*, July 12, 1965; "Honored with an E—Baltimore Air Coil Co.," *NAM Reports*, January 1, 1968; "NAM Backs Expansion of Import Export Bank," *NAM Reports*, April 24, 1967.

18. See, for example, "Investments Is Balance Key, Says Fenton," *NAM Reports*, October 18, 1965, p. 21.

19. "NAM Committee Backs Asian Development Bank," *NAM Reports*, January 1, 1966; "Gullander Named to Council for International Investment," *NAM Reports*, April 24, 1967.

FIGURE 10.2. Gullander with West Berlin's Mayor Willi Brandt, 1964. Copyright © National Association of Manufacturers; courtesy of Hagley Library and Museum.

be restrained until the deficit showed signs of abating. NAM officials and businessmen acquiesced in the Johnson administration's call for voluntary restraints on international investment, which they were told would be temporary.[20] But they continued to defend the idea that US investments abroad were the long-term answer to the balance-of-payments deficit.[21]

Aware that the onus for the balance-of-payments problem was being placed on multinational corporations, NAM leaders vigorously defended the contributions that multinationals made to US prosperity in general and to solving the balance-of-payments problem in particular. The president of Pfizer International assured NAM members that overseas manufacturing investments "used relatively few dollars in proportion to returns" and "returned dollars to the US more quickly and in greater volumes than any

20. See "To NAM Members," *NAM Reports*, March 8, 1965, p. 1.

21. See numerous George Hagedorn columns on this topic in *NAM Reports* during these years. Hagedorn was NAM's chief economist, and his columns were available for republication.

other phase of international business."[22] NAM gave extensive coverage to a program in which US multinationals such as IBM and the Singer Company (both NAM members) brought their European employees on vacation to the United States, where they could spend money and thereby help ease the balance-of-payments deficit.[23] Chrysler Corporation's president Lyn Townsend celebrated the billions of dollars that US auto companies had invested in foreign plants: "at last count, cars and trucks are now being manufactured by these American companies in ninety-eight plants in thirty-seven foreign countries." Although fewer than half of the total number of cars and autos were built in the United States, he crowed, "better than two-thirds were built by US companies or companies with which US companies are associated."[24] According to Townsend, this was a positive.

The worst thing the government could do was stifle the flow of capital and goods, which FDI defenders condemned as "economic nationalism." Speaking before NAM's annual meeting in 1965, General Electric president Fred Borch warned against "inhibiting world economic progress by resorting to economic nationalism" in attempting to "solve" the balance-of-payments problem.[25] Internationalists recognized the universal desirability of national sovereignty and self-sufficiency—indeed, wasn't the principle of self-determination why the United States was fighting communism? But then they held up an even greater ideal: international cooperation, which broke down the "artificial economic barriers between nations" and provided a countervailing force to political nationalism.[26]

In 1968, President Johnson placed mandatory restrictions on foreign investment. NAM strongly opposed these restrictions, which it felt would strengthen the hand of foreign competitors. It lobbied to get exceptions for its multinational members.[27] It also held a joint meeting of its committees

22. "Investments Is Balance Key, Says Fenton," *NAM Reports*, October 18, 1965, p. 21.

23. "Employers Pay Way to US," *NAM Reports*, September 19, 1966; "US Companies Build Good Will While Helping Ease Balance of Payments" ran the subheading. See also "White House Embraces NAM Groups' Travel Idea," *NAM Reports*, August 22, 1966. US tourists taking advantage of the strong dollar in Europe were cited as another factor in the balance-of-payments deficit and as an example of companies' attempts to turn around the "travel gap"; see Stein, *Pivotal Decade*, chap. 1.

24. Lyn Townsend, "Multinational Companies: Their Spread Benefits the World," *NAM Reports*, October 17, 1966, pp. 4–5, 5. This argument was made repeatedly.

25. "Avoid Economic Nationalism, Borch Tells NAM," *NAM Reports*, December 6, 1965, p. 1.

26. Townsend, "Multinational Companies," 4.

27. "Investment Control Change Asked by NAM," *NAM Reports*, May 27, 1968, p. 1; "Investment Control Change NAM Asked Is Made," *NAM Reports*, February 19, 1968. On the restrictions, see Joanne Gowa, *Closing the Gold Window* (Ithaca, NY: Cornell University Press, 1983), 57–59.

on International Economic Affairs and Money/Credit/Capital Formation for the purpose of taking a position on the crisis. Published as a booklet in 1968, the proceedings consisted of three speakers from such free-market globalists as Chase Manhattan Bank, the Organization for Economic Cooperation and Development, and the International Chamber of Commerce. The speakers had different perspectives about solutions, but all agreed that the US government could not sustain its military commitments (guns), while at the same time producing economic growth at home (butter). They identified government spending as the root of the $8 billion deficit, particularly the war in Vietnam. They conceded that the Bretton Woods arrangements— particularly the gold standard—"were not the wisest," but would have to be lived with.[28] Only one speaker brought up the idea of floating exchange rates, which he quickly dismissed as pure chaos. All were clear that the investment restrictions had not made a dent in the deficit and had contributed to widespread unemployment.[29] Sidney Rolf, from the OECD and ICC, recommended that the United States pull out of Vietnam and allocate some funds to "ease city and race problems."[30] The trio concluded that while private foreign investment was an outflow, it resulted in greater inflow, so it was not the cause of the problem and should not be restricted.

From this, NAM put together a statement that began by declaring that the objective of any solution should be to preserve and foster world trade. A monetary system that did not "facilitate the flow of investments, goods, and people" was not one worth preserving.[31] Their suggestions were to return to a balanced budget, end restrictions on foreign investment, and, going forward, limit the outflow of funds from the public sector, including military spending. Acknowledging the downward trend of commercial trade, they nonetheless blamed the government account for the deficit: "The private sector, through its great investment stake abroad, would be generating a net surplus on the balance of payments, if it were not for the extent of government expenditures abroad."[32] So trade would be the solution, even as

28. All saw the gold standard as a "barbarous relic."

29. The effectiveness of the controls is disputed. There is some evidence that they had restrained the deficit, as intended. See Gowa, *Closing the Gold Window*, 85–86; and Eckes and Zeiler, *Globalization and the American Century*, 182.

30. "Can We Muddle Through? Dollars, Gold, and the Payment Problem," proceedings of the Joint Meeting of the NAM International Economic Affairs and Money/Credit/Capital Formation Committees, 1968, pp. 17, 21.

31. Ibid., 33.

32. Ibid., 39. Despite the economic consequences of the Vietnam War for the payments crisis and the protests against the war industry, NAM never spoke out against the war, but rather offered tacit support for the military effort, which can be seen in the pages of *NAM Reports*.

many perceived it to be part of the problem, given the rapidly diminishing US trade surplus.

In 1971, President Nixon stopped the convertibility of dollars into gold, thereby averting the immediate monetary crisis, while also effectively ending the Bretton Woods Agreement. The currency crisis was resolved, but in its place there was a full-blown merchandise trade deficit, as well as runaway inflation, both of concern to NAM.

NIXON AND DÉTENTE

Nixon has been called "the last liberal president." His administration created the Environmental Protection Agency (EPA) and the Occupational Safety and Health Administration (OSHA), mandated affirmative action for government contractors, and imposed a Keynesian-style price and wage freeze to control inflation. But the new NAM loved him. True, NAM leaders opposed the EPA and OSHA, but they made peace with affirmative action (see chapter 9) and initially supported the price and wage controls, which were designed to stem inflation.[33] Moreover, Nixon proved interested in expanding export markets, including those in the communist "East," an area in which NAM globalists longed for a foothold. Nixon chose NAM director Maurice Stans as his commerce secretary, praised NAM's urban affairs and equal employment efforts, and appointed Gullander to a variety of government-industry committees.

In his 1970 speech before NAM, Nixon touted the free enterprise system, while at the same time proposing government policies to promote growth.[34] Whatever contradiction this might have presented at one time was lost on the new NAM, which under Gullander had all but erased the ideological enmity between government and industry. Indeed, NAM used its connections to the Nixon administration to sell its performance as a trade association to its members: "The value of the NAM to American industry in influencing events in Washington was never more evident than during the last months of 1971," began its annual report for that year. The leading example of this influence was, weirdly, Gullander's support for the wage and price freeze, "in spite of historical industrial opposition to economic controls." The president had assured Gullander that the sole purpose of the freeze was to stop inflation and had also pledged "to reduce government spending" and

33. "Report to Members—1971," *NAM Annual Report*, 1971, pp. 2–3.

34. "Here Is the Text of President Nixon's Address on the Economy," *Chicago Tribune*, December 5, 1970, p. 4.

"put business on a competitive basis with overseas competitors."[35] NAM chairman E. J. Dwyer was among the small group of businessmen whom Nixon consulted about phase 2 of the freeze. After hearing Dwyer's report, the NAM board temporarily suspended NAM's policy opposing wage and price controls.[36]

The Nixon administration was indeed friendly to overseas trade. It loosened the investment controls put in place by Johnson, eventually ending them in 1974. It pushed for new executive bargaining powers in the Trade Act of 1974, which focused on expanding exports, while also providing new ways for American companies to seek "import relief."[37] It created the Overseas Private Investment Corporation (OPIC), a government-created, privately managed corporation that encourages private investment in overseas development (and is still in operation today).[38]

Perhaps most thrillingly for NAM globalists, Nixon's détente policy created a space for US companies to finally get in on the Soviet market. The United States and the Soviet Union signed a trade agreement in 1972; despite complications, trade between the two countries steadily increased, and not just in grain exports (although that was the bulk of it).[39] In 1974, David Rockefeller of Chase Manhattan opened an office in Moscow, and soon enough executives from NAM members like General Electric and International Harvester followed suit. As in the 1920s, the Soviets were seeking technologically advanced factories, pipelines, and energy plants, and the opportunities seemed enormous.[40]

35. "Report to Members—1971," *NAM Annual Report*, 1971, 2.

36. By 1974, however, NAM would again oppose the controls. See Benjamin Waterhouse, *Lobbying America: The Politics of Business from Nixon to NAFTA* (Princeton, NJ: Princeton University Press, 2013), 113–23.

37. Dale Edwin Jr., "Nixon Seeks Sweeping New Power," *New York Times*, April 15, 1973, p. 211. Other historians say that Nixon was not helpful to globalists, such as those in the Trilateral Commission, founded by Chase Bank head David Rockefeller and internationalist policy wonks. See, for instance, Daniel Sargent, "The United States and Globalization in the 1970s," in Ferguson et al., *The Shock of the Global*, chap. 2. On the 1974 Trade Act, see Chorev, *Remaking US Trade Policy*, chap. 4.

38. "Private Overseas Aid Group Endorsed by Gullander," *NAM Reports*, June 2, 1969.

39. The complications were the Jackson-Vanik Amendment (1974), which denied MFN status to countries violating human or emigration rights, and another amendment that denied Soviet's access to Export-Import Bank funding. See Daniel Yergin, "Politics and Soviet-American Trade: Three Questions," *Foreign Affairs* (January 1977); Abraham S. Becker, "Main Features of United States–Soviet Trade," *Proceedings of the Academy of Political Science* 36, no. 4 (1987): 67–77.

40. For details on US business deals in the Soviet Union, see the very informative Harvey Shapiro, "Alexei Kosygin Has a Friend in Chase Manhattan," *New York Times*, February 24, 1974, p. 211.

NAM was very much a part of these efforts, despite conflicts within the organization concerning trade with communists. In 1964, anticommunist sentiment within NAM had prevented it from supporting legislation that loosened export controls against Rumania and Hungary. The commission it formed to study the issue discovered interest in Eastern trade, but recommended against such trade for the time being.[41] By 1972, however, NAM was singing a different tune. It set up a new East-West Trade Task Force, which held a series of conferences that eventually led to the formation of the Council for American-Soviet Trade (CAST) to provide an avenue for private-sector businesspeople to discuss business opportunities with state-controlled Soviet trade associations.[42] The inaugural meeting of CAST was held in Moscow and attended by a NAM delegation led by President E. Douglas Kenna. NAM also lobbied hard (if unsuccessfully) for MFN status for the Soviet Union.[43] In justifying its new position, it said that the traditional animosity of businesspeople toward the Soviet Union had been tempered by "curiosity regarding the Soviet Union's raw materials, markets, and purchasing power." NAM's new attitude, it said, simply "paralleled changes in American public opinion."[44] Thus did global trade continue to undermine NAM's traditional conservatism.

Fighting the New Protectionism

By abandoning the gold standard and putting a 10 percent surcharge on imports, the Nixon administration temporarily halted the rise in the trade deficit, but not before a new era of protectionism had set in. The impact of cheaper imports had already been felt by unions in lost jobs and membership, as well as by hundreds of communities across what would soon become known as the "Rust Belt."[45] Although actual union membership was at an all-time high, union members as a percentage of the workforce had

41. "NAM Won't Testify on Red Trade," *NAM Reports*, March 15, 1965, p. 2. The report, *East-West Trade and United States Policy* by Mose L. Harvey, was published by NAM as a book later in 1965.

42. See "An Old and a New Perspective on US-USSR Trade Relations," n.d., and other materials in in series 4, box 23, "East-West Trade" folder, NAMR.

43. See NAM news release, June 22, [1973], and other materials in series 4, box 23, "East-West Trade" folder, NAMR; see also Philip Shabecoff, "Talk by Brezhnev," *New York Times*, June 25, 1973.

44. NAM news release, June 22, [1973], and other materials in series 4, box 23, "East-West Trade" folder, NAMR; Philip Shabecoff, "Talk by Brezhnev," *New York Times*, June 25, 1973.

45. A study by Barry Bluestone and Bennett Harrison reported that 15 million jobs were lost in the United States between 1969 and 1976; see "Severe Impact Seen in Plant Closings," *New York Times*, April 13, 1980, p. 21.

been declining since the mid-1950s.[46] Meanwhile, multinationals' foreign employment had risen 26.5 percent from 1966 to 1970, while their domestic employment had increased only 7.6 percent. Their imports back to the United States in 1970 constituted 34 percent of all imports.[47]

The AFL-CIO, which had been so supportive of the postwar economic arrangement, would lead the charge against imports and foreign investment, which it believed had cost American workers "nearly one million job opportunities in the last six years." AFL-CIO head George Meany called on Congress to "stop the growing export of American jobs, capital, technology, production by multinational corporations based in the United States."[48] Two Democrats, one from Massachusetts, the other from Indiana, responded and sponsored the Burke-Hartke Act, which proposed to put quotas on imports, repeal tax credits and deferrals for corporations operating abroad (what NAM called "double-taxation"), and allow the president to regulate "transnational capital transactions."[49]

The business community as a whole opposed the Burke-Hartke Act, and NAM brought its full lobbying power against it beginning in 1971, when the bill was first introduced. NAM saw the Burke-Hartke Act as an attack on the multinational corporation and titled its strategy for combating the act "MNC Legislative Strategy" ("MNC" stood for multinational corporation). The strategy was familiar. NAM would educate the public and opinion-makers about the benefits of multinationals and US foreign investment and the "grave political threat to business" posed by the Burke-Hartke Act. It encouraged members to call on their representatives, provided sample op-eds for members to "write" for their local newspapers, distributed MNC-positive materials to the White House, members of Congress, and government agencies, and lined up NAM officials and experts to testify in hearings and talk up key politicians. The strategy also put forward a positive "world trade" campaign to address the root causes of the trade deficit and the declining competitiveness of US industry.[50]

46. The percentage of workers in unions peaked in 1954, when some 36 percent of private-sector workers were in a union; it would drop to 23 percent by 1980. See Jake Rosenfeld, *What Unions No Longer Do* (Cambridge, MA: Harvard University Press, 2014), 1–2.

47. Judis, *The Paradox of American Democracy*, 114.

48. Quoted in Marilyn Berger, "US-Japan Trade Dilemma," *Washington Post*, September 4, 1972, p. A1; see also Harry Ellis, "3M Adds to Tax Bill Outcry," *Christian Science Monitor*, April 5, 1973, p. 20.

49. "Progress Report on NAM's MNC Legislative Strategy," November 16, 1971, series 1, box 45, NAMR.

50. See Vernie Oliveiro, "The United States, Multinational Enterprises, and the Politics of Globalization," in Ferguson et al., *The Shock of the Global*, chap. 10, p. 146; "Progress Report on

Gangways to Progress

FIGURE 10.3. Part of NAM's world trade campaign, 1972. Copyright © 1972 National Association of Manufacturers.

Proclaimed in a flurry of press releases, the top priority for 1972 would be trade expansion: "The NAM Launches World Trade Campaign," announced the headline of *NAM Reports*' first newsletter of the year.[51] A major thrust of the campaign would be to "enlighten the public, government officials, and all businessmen regarding the social and economic benefits accruing from the

NAM's MNC Legislative Strategy," November 16, 1971, series 1, box 45, NAMR; Gullander's letter to NAM members about the campaign, n.d., series 1, box 45, NAMR; William Pollert, "Labor's Myths and the Facts about MNC," *NAM Reports*, March 6, 1972.

51. "The NAM Launches World Trade Campaign," *NAM Reports*, January 3, 1972, p. 1.

foreign operations of US firms."[52] Organized labor's attempt to have Congress control foreign investment would only lead to more closed plants at home, said Gullander. It would substantially increase the balance-of-payments deficit and reduce the demand for supplier parts—that is, US exports. Instead, NAM sought legislation that might include stronger provisions for employees whose jobs had been eliminated owing to imports or plant relocation, stronger anti-dumping laws to curtail cheap imports, the stimulation of US exports, and the modernization of US plants to make them more competitive (a goal that involved automation and layoffs).[53] Much of this proposal would end up in the Trade Act of 1974, which NAM fully supported.

Labor's critique of multinational corporations garnered sympathy in the press and among politicians concerned about high unemployment. Even the Republican Party condemned the "practice of locating plants in foreign countries solely to take advantage of low wages in order to produce goods primarily for sale in the US."[54] Thus, NAM kept the campaign positive. While emphasizing labor's backing of Burke-Hartke, its main talking point was that multinational corporations invested abroad to overcome trade barriers and take advantage of rising markets in Europe, which was a high-wage, high-tax region (contrary to labor's arguments about cheap labor). NAM's in-house analyses, however, clearly identified high wages at home as a factor in the decline of US competitiveness. The increasing productivity in developing nations at the same time created "increased foreign competition in labor-intensive industries."[55] Regrettably, the report noted, this problem would be obscured if tariffs were raised or foreign investment impeded.

NAM rarely, if ever, considered the harm that imports and FDI posed to small and midsized companies. But one member wrote to *NAM Reports* asking why the goods that US companies produced abroad had to be imported back into the United States. The writer was president of the L. S. Starrett Company in Athol, Massachusetts. He accepted the fact that US corporations had to build plants abroad to compete abroad, but he did not believe that capturing foreign markets meant that they had to sell their foreign-made

52. Ibid.

53. "Progress Report on NAM's MNC Legislative Strategy," November 16, 1971, series 1, box 45, NAMR; see also William R. Pollert, "The Multinational Corporation, *NAM Reports*, February 7, 1972, pp. 2–3.

54. From the 1972 Republican Party platform, quoted in Judis, *The Paradox of American Democracy*, 115.

55. Quote from "The Burke-Hartke Bill . . . Cyanamid Response," January 22, 1972, p. 2, series 1, box 45, NAMR. For an examination of this labor-blaming argument in the business community's stance toward inflation, see Waterhouse, *Lobbying America*, chap. 4.

goods in domestic markets. His solution was a border tax that would equalize the wage rates of foreign countries "with our own federal minimum wage rate," so that "no American jobs would be lost because of shipping back to this country." A border tax would be about "competition, not protection," the letter-writer said, and he faulted NAM for not supporting this. NAM published the letter, a rare acknowledgment that foreign investment hurt US domestic manufacturing.[56]

In the end, business opposition to the Burke-Hartke Act was effective. Although hearings were held, Burke-Hartke never came up for a vote. The issues it raised were resolved in the more business-friendly Trade Act of 1974.[57] The business community's three-year struggle against Burke-Hartke signified not just the global imperative of US business, but also a new kind of business unity delivered, in part, by the end of the post–World War II compact between labor and capital, in which large corporations had tolerated unions in exchange for economic stability.[58] NAM had helped bring about this accord with the Taft-Hartley Act, did not fully embrace it until Gullander, and then saw it collapse in the 1970s.

The end of this labor-management accord coincided, appropriately, with the end of that other postwar arrangement, the Bretton Woods fixed-currency international monetary system. The floating exchange rates that replaced Bretton Woods paved the way for even more global investment and currency speculation, enhancing the finance sector and leading multinational corporations to eventually shift their focus from actual production to investment opportunities, overseas ventures, and financial services.[59] Although labor militancy was on the rise in the 1970s, with 381 strikes and walkouts in 1970, there would be little need in the future for large multinationals to "cooperate" with organized labor, whose membership (and

56. "The Burke Hartke Bill," *NAM Reports*, May 12, 1972, p. 11.

57. Stein, *Pivotal Decade*, 49; Oliveiro, "The United States, Multinational Enterprises, and the Politics of Globalization," 147; "Trade Bill Is Due for Early Action," *New York Times*, May 24, 1974, p. 43.

58. The extent to which such a consensus ever existed has been much debated. For instance, Nelson Lichtenstein, in *State of the Union: A Century of American Labor*, rev. ed. (Princeton, NJ: Princeton University Press, 2013), chap. 3, argues against the idea of a labor-management accord. But others, particularly those trying to understand financialization or the transformation of corporate lobbying, have found it a useful way to explain a change in corporations' attitudes about working with organized labor, a transformation that had everything to do with labor's weakened position in the face of a more globalized economy. See Judis, *The Paradox of American Democracy*, 114–21; Harvey, *A Brief History of Neoliberalism*, chaps. 1–2; Davis, *Managed by the Markets*, chap. 1; Youn Ki, "Large Industrial Firms and the Rise of Finance in Late Twentieth-Century America."

59. See Davis, *Managed by the Markets*, 14–18.

power) in the private sector was in sharp decline. The long-standing divide between corporate liberals and labor-intensive conservatives, then, as well as the divide between industry and finance, began to shrink, and business was able to unite around a globalist agenda and shared concerns about taxation, inflation, and the runaway regulatory state.[60]

Membership Woes

The AFL-CIO was not alone in shedding members. NAM's membership had been in decline since 1958. Between 1957 and 1964, the peak years of loss, NAM lost members at an average rate of 14.25 percent a year. After 1958, resignations outnumbered new recruits (except for brief rallies in 1968 and 1974), with the result that by 1980 NAM membership had sunk below 12,000.[61] Whereas labor was quick to understand that cheaper imports and foreign investment abroad had devastated union membership, neither NAM's staff nor its leadership considered these as possible factors in the precipitous decline of membership between 1958 and 1973.

Membership losses were accompanied by some revenue loss, but this was insignificant, given the rate structure, wherein smaller companies paid only $100 annually in dues. And it was smaller companies NAM was losing. The losses were more than compensated for by the contributions of large multinational corporations, sixty-seven of which were paying $10,000 or more a year, including General Motors, US Steel, and DuPont, each of which was contributing $65,000 ($472,686 in 2018 dollars), and General Electric contributing $60,000, Bethlehem Steel $47,000, and Union Carbide and Eastman-Kodak $37,000.[62] If anything, membership revenue steadily increased, even as NAM lost members. It sustained losses in membership revenue from 1960 to 1964, when revenue fell from $5.9 million to $5.3 million, but thereafter it only increased, rising to $10.2 million in 1981.[63] That increase, however, would have just kept up with inflation. Moreover, NAM's costly new "positive" programs brought on a budget squeeze by 1976.[64]

60. See Waterhouse, *Lobbying America*.

61. Board of directors meeting minutes, February 9–11, 1984, series 13, box 246, NAMR.

62. "$10,000 and over Dues Paying Members," in board of directors meeting minutes, 1968, series 8, box 148, NAMR.

63. "Total Membership Billing" column in "Membership Change Summary, December 1983," in board of directors meeting minutes, February 9–11, 1984, series 13, box 246, NAMR.

64. Gene Hardy, memo to Larry Fox, July 15, 1976, and "Memorandum of Consideration Relating to . . . the Merger between the NAM and the Chamber," n.d. [c. 1976 or 1977], series 9, boxes 174 and 179, NAMR. The merger is discussed later in the chapter.

The main reason for membership losses was mergers, which were rampant in the 1960s as large diversified conglomerations bought up smaller companies.[65] Between 1965 and 1968, NAM lost 1,073 members owing to mergers, apparently 38 percent of its losses.[66] The procedure for recouping the loss was to ask the parent company to keep up the absorbed company's membership dues or increase its own. As a 1969 report on the problem noted, however, companies rarely agreed to this, sometimes responding that they "do not acquire companies to increase dues and contributions."[67] There was little that the Membership Department could do about mergers. The only way to deal with such losses was "through increased production," meaning recruitment of new members.[68]

In 1969, the Membership Department adopted a new sales approach that involved identifying the markets for NAM's "product" and figuring out their needs.[69] In-house research showed that NAM's main market was smaller companies, which were (still) the majority of manufacturers, but that it was having a hard time recruiting and retaining them. Although they provided little revenue, they were crucial to NAM's claims to represent all of industry. One analyst wondered if the problem was that the modern NAM was catering too much to the large companies, which accepted government spending and applauded NAM's positive problem-solving approach to national problems, whereas small manufacturers did not relate to these activities and resented government intervention and harassment. Indeed, during the 1970s, the National Federation of Independent Businesses (NFIB) would double its membership, suggesting that small manufacturers were recognizing that their interests differed from those of the large corporations that led NAM. The problem for NAM was figuring out how to attract these smaller, more conservative companies "without adversely affecting the Association's image as a positive problem-solving force."[70] Their answer was, in part,

65. On the rise of conglomerates, see Davis, *Managed by the Markets*, 77–81; Louis Hyman, *Temp: How American Work, American Business, and the American Dream Became Temporary* (New York: Viking, 2018), chap. 7.

66. "Mergers," in series, 8, box 148, "Board Meetings, 1969" folder, NAMR. Bluestone and Harrison, *The Deindustrialization of America*, 124, identify 1964–1968 as one of three post–World War II merger waves.

67. "Mergers," May 9, 1969, p. 1, in series, 8, box 148, "Board Meetings, 1969" folder, NAMR.

68. Ibid.

69. "To Members of the Membership Committee," n.d., series, 8, box 148, "Board Meetings, 1969" folder, NAMR.

70. Quoted in "NAM in Perspective," March 31, 1967, p. 2, in series, 8, box 148, "Board Meetings, 1969" folder, NAMR; on NFIB, see John J. Bean, *Big Government and Affirmative Action* (Lexington: University of Kentucky Press, 2001), 107.

developmental services, such as industrial relations clinics and civil rights seminars, which had gotten surprisingly good reviews in in-house polls.[71] The idea that membership losses might be due to foreign competition or increasing imports never came up.

Changes in NAM

Gullander stepped down as NAM president in 1973, after a decade of service in which he had softened NAM's reputation, expanded its legislative agenda, and developed "positive" alternatives to pollution control, packaging legislation, and further civil rights legislation. In his place, the NAM board chose E. Douglas Kenna, who was not a manufacturer but rather the president of an international financial services firm that had offices in New York, London, Beirut, Rome, Taiwan, and Belgrade and specialized in "the export-import business, venture capital situations, shipping, and oil and gas exploration."[72] Kenna's selection signaled a recognition of the importance of finance and global trade among NAM's multinational-dominated leadership.

Kenna moved NAM's headquarters from New York City to Washington, DC. NAM already had offices in Washington, of course, but, as Kenna noted, "government action affects business more and more." The move also offered a chance to consolidate the staff. There would be about two hundred staff members in the new Washington headquarters.[73] Other trade associations had made the same move, prompting one commentator to suggest that they recognized "the shots are being called by government now more so than by private enterprise."[74] That was certainly what NAM leaders were concerned about, and part of its reasoning was to strengthen the voice of private enterprise. In response, Common Cause, a self-styled "citizens' lobby," filed a suit charging NAM with failing to register as a lobbyist, alleging that NAM had moved its entire operation to Washington to "enhance the effectiveness of its lobbying efforts." As per the 1946 Lobby Act (see chapter 6), NAM had registered its individual lobbyists, but maintained that the main purpose of the organization was not lobbying per se.[75] Nothing came of the suit, but it speaks to increased concern about business lobbying in the 1970s.

---

71. "Your Opinion Please," survey, n.d., in series, 8, box 148, "Board Meetings, 1969" folder, NAMR.

72. "E. Douglas Kenna Elected New President of NAM," *NAM Reports*, December 11, 1972.

73. "NAM Plans Move Here," *Washington Post*, February 21, 1973, p. D11.

74. "Many Groups Quit NY for DC," *Christian Science Monitor*, January 11, 1974, p. 7.

75. "Suit Bids NAM File as a Lobbyist," *New York Times*, July 26, 1974, p. 43.

The social movements of the 1960s had resulted in new safety, environmental, and consumer-oriented regulations, as well as a compelling intellectual critique of corporate America and untrammeled growth.[76] In 1974, a group of young liberal Democrats, known as the "Watergate babies," won election to the House, promising yet more regulations. Combined with ongoing recession, inflation, and an energy crisis, the Democrats' win created a sense of urgency that unified the "old" business organizations, like NAM and the US Chamber of Commerce, and bolstered new conservative think tanks like the Heritage Foundation, the Cato Institute, and the American Enterprise Institute.[77] Together these organizations sought to salvage the reputation of free enterprise and pushed back against what they saw as a runaway liberal regulatory state.

Of note was the creation of the Business Roundtable in 1973 and the emergence of individual CEOs, such as DuPont's Irving Shapiro and General Electric's Reginald Jones, as prominent spokesmen for industry. Unlike NAM or the Chamber, which consisted of member companies, the Roundtable was a smaller group made up solely of the CEOs of America's largest multinational, mostly industrial, corporations. They represented what would soon be labeled the "smokestack industries," but they were also globalists, advocates of the free flow of capital and goods across borders that would one day reduce their companies' influence in America. In some ways, the new organization seemed redundant with NAM's leadership, whose company representation was almost identical to that of the Business Roundtable. But the new organization was unburdened by the responsibilities, services, and committee politics of NAM and the Chamber.[78]

A NAM/Chamber Merger?

One sign of the new business unity was that NAM and the US Chamber of Commerce seriously considered merging their organizations in 1976. The main reason for the proposal was the redundancy of the two organizations, which had overlapping memberships and virtually identical policy goals. Consolidating the two organizations would save valuable resources, increase the overall clout of business and industry, and more efficiently represent

---

76. See Waterhouse, *Lobbying America*, 31–45. NAM tried to stay on top of the cultural changes, and its newsletter featured articles about campus politics, today's youth, and intellectuals like Norman Mailer. See, for instance, "Message from Mailer," *NAM Reports*, June 17, 1968, p. 17.

77. Phillips-Fein *Invisible Hands*, 166–235.

78. Waterhouse, *Lobbying America*, chap. 3.

their interests in Washington. It was also true, however, that NAM was facing financial pressures. As their analysts saw it, the "explosion of government growth," new regulatory agencies, and the political influence of "special interest groups" had increased the complexity and scope of NAM's job, while revenue had stayed constant when adjusted for inflation.[79] Hence the proposed merger with the Chamber. Although NAM's Membership Department had boosted membership back up to thirteen thousand by 1976, the evidence of deindustrialization was all around them, and the trend could only mean fewer companies to recruit.

Meanwhile, the Chamber had a total and robust membership of sixty thousand companies and trade associations, the majority of them in the service industries. It is difficult not to see NAM's offer to merge with the Chamber as a symbol of manufacturing's decline in the United States. Here was the nation's foremost manufacturing organization literally asking to be absorbed by an organization representing the service and financial sectors that would soon replace manufacturing as the leading economic sectors.[80]

NAM and the Chamber agreed to pursue a merger in June 1976. The Chamber was ready to commit, but NAM wanted to explore the implications before agreeing to an actual merger. There was much support for the merger among NAM members for the reasons just stated. But many also opposed the merger. Some thought that two organizations would be better than one. Others questioned the anticipated savings. But most were concerned about being eaten up by the Chamber's huge membership, only a small percentage of which were manufacturers. Despite the dominance of large corporations in NAM, many of its smaller and midsized members had great fondness for their Association, particularly when compared to the Chamber, which, they felt, was too large and not as effective. They worried that NAM's "enthusiasm and dedication" would be lost and expressed dismay at combining with the Chamber's diverse membership, which included, as one Pittsburgh steel company head put it, "merchants of *all types and kinds,* as well as real estate people, insurance companies,

79. Quoted in untitled document headed "THE OBJECTIVE," pp. 3–4, series 9, box 174, NAMR. Information for this section was gleaned from the many letters, releases, and clippings found in series 9, box 179, "Merger" files, NAMR.

80. Included in the Chamber's membership were sixteen thousand manufacturing firms, which raises the question of why the Chamber represented more manufacturers than did NAM, an organization explicitly dedicated to manufacturers.

banks, etc., etc. [who] just do *not* have the industry point of view."[81] A textile factory owner from Chattanooga, Tennessee, concurred: "I cannot see how industry's position can be properly represented in Washington by an organization that has in its membership motels, filling stations, and other small retail establishments."[82]

Another source of negativity was that it seemed as though NAM leadership was trying to push the merger through. The board meeting at which the vote would happen was rushed, and previous engagements prevented many from attending. Alarmed NAM members felt that a decision such as this should be studied and discussed in an unrushed manner. The media was reporting the merger as if it had already happened, suggesting that NAM president Kenna assumed it was a done deal.

In September, the NAM board of directors voted down the merger, proposing instead a joint council between the two organizations to coordinate on common issues. The reason stated was concern about manufacturers' particular interests being lost in the shuffle. The NAM board at this time had two hundred members, including the president, the officers, the regional vice presidents, honorary members (retired vice presidents and presidents), and staff vice presidents. Of these, about 15 percent represented large multinational corporations, like US Steel, 3M, Dow, General Motors, Exxon, and Alcoa.[83] It is unclear who attended or voted at the meeting, but in general the board represented a wider swath of NAM than the top officials who had proposed the merger. Opposition to the merger had generally come from smaller companies, while those who supported the merger were companies of all sizes, large, small, and medium. Allied Chemical Corporation's Alexander Trowbridge, a former secretary of commerce and soon to be the new NAM president, was disappointed at the outcome, attributing it, as many did, to protective and parochial attitudes—a long-standing complaint from internationalists about small and midsized manufacturers.[84] Meanwhile, the number of retailers and

81. William Jackson to Richard Kautz, June 18, 1976, series 9, box 179, NAMR (emphasis in original). Jackson was chairman of the board of the Pittsburgh–Des Moines Steel Company in Pittsburgh.

82. Robert Davis to Doug Kenna, September 13, 1976, series 9, box 179, NAMR.

83. These figures are from my count of the 1977 listing of the board as found in the *NAM Annual Report*, 1977, in *NAM Reports*, January 1977. It may not include all of the multinational corporations listed, since it is unclear which of the listed companies were multinational.

84. Trowbridge to Kenna, September 28, 1976, series 9, box 179, NAMR.

finance companies among the Chamber's membership rose steadily in the late 1970s, soaring to 250,000 by 1982.[85]

Globalists

The new post–Bretton Woods system of floating exchange rates loosened up global financial markets and encouraged more foreign investment, which in turn required a certain amount of international cooperation to create a stable environment in which to conduct international business. In the past, the United Nations had been expected to do some of that work. But the world had changed with decolonization, which had not only resulted in a large number of independent developing nations, but also given rise to a critique of multinational corporations as perpetrators of a new kind of imperialism. Indeed, during the 1970s, the UN General Assembly had adopted resolutions critical of multinational corporations and supportive of state regulations to limit their influence.[86]

Nonetheless, the US government attempted to work with the UN-created Commission on Transnational Corporations to come up with a code of conduct that, ideally, would curb the abuses of multinational corporations while also providing stabilizing regulations for global trade.[87] The balance of power on the UN commission tilted toward the less developed nations trying to protect themselves from economic exploitation, and the United States made little headway in promoting liberal, free-trade principles or "fair treatment" for multinationals. It would have better luck working with the Organization for Economic Cooperation and Development, an intergovernmental economic organization created during the Kennedy administration to encourage a liberal democratic model of international trade. Consisting of a smaller number of industrialized countries, the OECD was able to come up with voluntary guidelines more amenable to the aspirations of the multinationalists, while also encouraging environmental protections, human rights, and social responsibility.[88]

NAM had long supported the OECD in an informal capacity and, as always, stood ready to help the US government attain a stable free-market,

---

85. Ann Crittenden, "A Stubborn Chamber of Commerce," *New York Times,* June 27, 1982, p. 107.

86. Oliveiro, "The United States, Multinational Enterprises, and the Politics of Globalization," 147.

87. Ibid., 148.

88. Ibid., 149.

free-trade international system that privileged private enterprises over state-controlled, highly regulated entities. NAM worked closely with the US State Department on the OECD "Guidelines for Multinational Corporations," reporting that it had "kept them voluntary" and made sure they applied equally to all countries.[89] In 1975, NAM's International Economic Affairs Department shifted its focus from helping small and midsized businesses export their goods to policy formulation and lobbying on such issues as multilateral trade, East-West normalization, international investment and MNCs, international monetary reform, and the like.[90] They were, of course, still interested in promoting exports among their membership, but the reorganized committee structure specifically pertained to the issues involved in creating a world safe for multinational trade. In 1974, it overcame conservative objections and supported a bilateral trade agreement with communist-controlled Romania. In 1979, it participated in a meeting of the State Department Advisory Committee on Transnational Enterprises in which "technology transfers, transborder data flows, and restrictive business practices" were discussed.[91]

The point is that NAM was fully committed and involved in setting up the global infrastructure of rules and regulations that would become known as neoliberalism. There is some debate among historians as to how calculated and coordinated the building of the neoliberal infrastructure was on the part of the United States; some suggest that external contingencies and unintended consequences were more of a factor than US hegemony in establishing the neoliberal globalism of the late twentieth century.[92] For historians looking for capitalist agency in US foreign and trade policy, there is plenty to find here, as there was back in 1895, when the brand-new NAM supported American imperial expansion.

These activities represent NAM's continuing support for an internationalist vision of freer trade, integrated economies, and world peace, as articulated by Woodrow Wilson, Cordell Hull, Franklin Roosevelt, and John F. Kennedy—liberal Democrats all. NAM's globalists had a tough time of it for

89. *NAM Annual Report*, 1976, in *NAM Reports*, January 1977.

90. Gene Hardy, memo to Larry Fox, July 15, 1976, series 9, box 174, NAMR.

91. "International Economic Affairs Committee Report," in *Business Activity Report*, May 8–September 22, 1979, series 13, box 246, NAMR.

92. See, for instance, Daniel Sargent, "The United States and Globalization in the 1970s," and other essays in Ferguson et al., *The Shock of the Global*, and Greta Krippner, *Capitalizing on Crisis: The Political Origins of the Rise of Finance* (Cambridge, MA: Harvard University Press, 2011), who argues that financialization was the result of attempts to deal with the balance-of-payments crisis. See also Slobodian, *Globalists*, on the intellectual and neocolonial roots of neoliberal policies.

most of the twentieth century, given NAM's staunch Republicanism and members' dependence on a protective tariff. But by the late 1970s, NAM's tariff battles seemed to have abated and a Republican president was leading the charge for international trade—even with communists. The arguments about trade and tariffs that had split the organization in the 1950s seemed over and done with. Organized labor embraced trade restrictions to stem the loss of jobs, but NAM and its majority of small and midsized manufacturers were quiet on the question. Surrounded by plant closings, NAM leadership promoted freer trade and foreign investment.

11

Nadir: The Reagan Era

Addressing NAM in 1982, President Ronald Reagan praised the organization for its lonely, valiant battle against "America's disastrous drift towards bigger and bigger government" in the 1950s. "We've come a long way together since those days," Reagan said, acknowledging NAM's role in the conservative movement.[1] But NAM had likewise come a long way from those days. For one thing, it was led by a Democrat. Alexander "Sandy" Trowbridge, an Allied Chemical Corporation executive and former commerce secretary under Lyndon Johnson, was president from 1980 to 1989 and brought in Jerry Jasinowski as chief economist in 1981. A policy wonk in President Carter's Commerce Department, Jasinowski was once an aide to the late Democratic senator Hubert Humphrey of Minnesota and helped author the Humphrey-Hawkins Full Employment Act of 1978 (which NAM opposed). It is safe to say that Jasinowski was the only NAM leader ever published in *The Nation*.[2] Though Democrats, Trowbridge and Jasinowski were fully committed to a free-market, globalist philosophy and the task of "revitalizing" American industry. But they were not always in lockstep with the Reagan administration.

The triumph of conservative ideas in Washington offered very little to old-line manufacturers, NAM's bread and butter. The pace of plant closings accelerated in the 1980s, while many of the largest NAM members fell victim to a hostile takeover wave. Trowbridge and crew would do their best

1. "Excerpts from the President's Speech to Business Executives," *New York Times*, March 19, 1982, p. D19.
2. "Mr. Nixon's Tax Mythology," *The Nation*, October 30, 1972, pp. 399–404.

to reignite manufacturing, but Reagan Era policies worked against them. As historian Judith Stein observed, Reagan's economic policies favored real estate, finance, and technology, "propping up nontrading sectors and hobbling the manufacturing ones."[3]

While Reagan's attacks on unions were ideologically satisfying, NAM's principal battle was no longer against labor, which had lost its bargaining power. Indeed, the NAM of the 1980s had much in common with its historical enemy as both sought to shore up "old" industries against new import-dependent retailers (like Wal-Mart) and non-unionized high-tech industries. Trowbridge even reached out to AFL-CIO head Lane Kirkland to see if they might be able to "bury the hatchet."[4] NAM and labor still skirmished, of course; it was in their DNA. But it is worth considering their common plight in the Reagan Era. Both had been losing both members and political clout. Both were part of the old "smokestack" industrial economy. And both were slowly being abandoned by the parties that had once fought their battles in Washington. Just as a new breed of Democrats were ignoring the demands of a shrinking union constituency, so too were Reagan Republicans less than thrilled about saving manufacturing.[5] Once at the forefront of shaping industrial capitalism, NAM and its union foes were now struggling to survive in a post-industrial economy.

There was one bright spot for NAM's multinational members, and that was globalization. But even that was fraught as NAM confronted a Reagan administration more concerned about fighting communism than opening markets. The Reagan Revolution was absolutely a victory for NAM's conservative vision and multinational leaders, but it also revealed industry's growing political impotence and furthered the manufacturing sector's decline.

A New Lobbying Landscape

The lobbying world changed considerably in the 1980s. New campaign finance laws and decisions in the 1970s led to the proliferation of corporate political action committees (PACs), consultants, law firms, and single-issue

3. Judith Stein, *Running Steel, Running America: Race, Economic Policy, and the Decline of Liberalism* (Chapel Hill: University of North Carolina Press, 1998), 273–74.

4. See Trowbridge to John Fisher, May 21, 1980, and Trowbridge to Kirkland, July 23, 1980, in series 14, box 201, NAMR. Both NAM and the AFL-CIO, for instance, opposed the Reagan administration's attempt to tax health care benefits; see "Groups Protest Tax on Health Benefits," *New York Times*, January 7, 1983, p. A15; and "Politics of Taxation Makes Strange Bedfellows," *New York Times*, December 6, 1984, p. B2.

5. Dubbed "neoliberals," new Democrats such as Gary Hart and Paul Tsongas were shifting the party away from unions and welfare to tech and trade; see Rothenberg, *The Neoliberals*.

interest groups, many of them representing the rising service and financial sectors. A dinosaur among these new, more nimble entities, NAM was no longer regarded as the quintessential business lobby. Indeed, a 1992 book on US lobbyists mentioned NAM only once: "The business world had grown too complex and too fragmented for huge umbrella organizations like the US Chamber of Commerce and the National Association of Manufacturers, to represent adequately."[6] Journalists still tapped NAM for "industry's view," of course, but NAM was forced to compete for members, dues, and political influence in an increasingly diversified lobbying market.

New smaller groups, such as the American Business Conference, which represented midsized, "new industry" entrepreneurs, and the Carleton Group, representing large multinationals, challenged the old trade association member-company model. Consisting of loosely connected executives, lawyers, and lobbyists, these groups cultivated the interests of their industries and clients while flying under the radar to avoid controversy— although public watchdog groups were very much aware of their growing influence. New consulting groups, law firms, and "hired guns," like Charls E. Walker, Inc., also offered lobbying services to both corporations and ailing trade associations, such as reframing legislation and arranging informal meetings with congressional reps. These groups networked and overlapped with each other, stoking fears of corruption but also offering a spectacle of Gucci-clad movers and shakers, to the delight of the journalists who covered them.[7]

There was also lobbying competition for NAM's smaller companies— the majority of its membership. The National Federation of Independent Businesses had doubled its membership to 600,000 companies in the 1970s, riding a wave of animosity toward both government and large corporations. Founded in 1943, the NFIB represented small businesses, mostly in the service industries, but about 12 to 14 percent of its members were manufacturing concerns. It would become one of the most influential business lobbies by the 1980s, surpassing both NAM and the Chamber in size and influence.[8]

6. Jeffrey Birnbaum, *The Lobbyists: How Influence Peddlers Get Their Way in Washington* (New York: Three Rivers Press, 1992).

7. See, for instance, Paul Taylor, "Gladiators for Hire," *Washington Post*, July 31, 1983, p. A1; Edward Cowan, "Carleton Group Spurns Limelight," *New York Times*, March 18, 1982, p. D1; Leslie Wayne, "The New Face of Business Leadership," *New York Times*, May 22, 1983, p. A1.

8. John J. Bean, *Big Government and Affirmative Action* (Lexington: University of Kentucky Press, 2001), 107; William C. Dunkelberg, "Small Business and the US Economy," *Business Economics* 30, no. 1 (January 1995): 13–18.

The major takeaway was that, unlike in the 1970s, when business interests were unified and articulated to the press by superstar CEOs like Irving Shapiro (DuPont) and Reginald Jones (GE), the new business lobbyists were diffuse and varied, and thus it was unclear how effective (or harmful) they really were. As NAM's Jasinowski put it in one of the many articles on the subject: "More lobbyists doesn't equal more influence. You get to the point where you start tripping over each other. You reach the point of diminishing returns."[9] Moreover, the increasing variety of organizations was due to the competing interests among them. The policy objectives of the American Business Conference's high-tech companies and junk bond dealers were different from those of the Carleton Group or NAM. So while business was riding high during the Reagan administration, it was no longer as organized and taut, nor did it privilege the interests of manufacturing.

While NAM's membership hovered around 13,000, the Chamber of Commerce had increased to 250,000 member companies and organizations by 1982; NAM had a $3 million budget, while the Chamber's stood at $60 million.[10] The competition for dues and influence required Trowbridge to update NAM's services. As he told journalists, "We're all going through a reexamination of what we do and how we can improve on that bottom-line value for our members."[11] Reaching out to its long-neglected base, NAM established a Small Manufacturers Council, whose chair would have a seat on the Executive Committee and whose members would sit on NAM policy committees to make sure their viewpoints were heard. NAM also issued a *Small Manufacturer* newsletter four times a year, as well as specific sections in its flashier monthly *Enterprise* for small and midsized members.[12] *Enterprise* reminded readers of what NAM was doing for them, while also offering quick tutorials on major economic issues and tips on public speaking, including an assortment of jokes and bon mots to work into speeches.

More seriously, NAM continued to promote minorities and women in business and the workplace, even highlighting the importance of government

9. Taylor, "Gladiators."

10. Ann Crittenden, "A Stubborn Chamber of Commerce Roils the Waters," *New York Times*, June 27, 1982, p. 107. NAM's budget information can be found in board of directors meeting minutes, January 24–25, 1985, series 13, box 247, NAMR.

11. Peter Prokesh, "A Time of Upheaval for Conference Board," *New York Times*, October 6, 1986, p. D1.

12. The creation of the council required an amendment to the NAM constitution; see board of directors meeting minutes, February 3–5, 1983, p. 15, series 13, box 246, NAMR. *Enterprise* began its twelve-year run in 1977 and received a slick upgrade in 1981.

training and diversity programs.[13] This would not have appealed to its traditional membership, but it was an effort to tap into a growing market of women- and minority-owned businesses. Indeed, the new head of its Small Business Committee was a woman named Patsy Williams, who also sat on the Executive Committee. Brenda McChriston, an African American woman who later founded her own human resources consulting company, headed NAM's new Human Resources and Equal Opportunity Committee.[14] As Williams and McChriston indicate, women's names were appearing more regularly on NAM rosters, and NAM chairman Robert Dee (head of Smith-Kline Beckman Corporation) chastised corporate leaders for creating a "glass ceiling," writing: "One-half of the population can't be frozen in place on the lower and middle rungs of American business if America is to face the enormous competitive challenges of the future."[15]

In 1985, the Reagan administration drafted a proposal to eliminate federal-mandated affirmative action programs. The business community, including NAM, pushed back. NAM testified in support of government affirmative action programs, including the goals and timetables, which Trowbridge stated were responsible for "dramatic progress" in "incorporating talented minorities and women into the workforce."[16] The NAM board adopted a resolution stating that affirmative action was "merely a recognition that ingrained prejudices remain in our society . . . we must be ever vigilant in facing these prejudices and overcoming them."[17] Such views were echoed by NAM's increasingly diverse staff, one of whom encouraged corporations to move beyond the old regulations and develop the talent and potential of minorities and women on their own, matching corporate goals to "the

13. Victor Rivera, "Make Way for Minority Business," *Enterprise* (September 1983): 22–23. See also Brenda McChriston, "Albert Angrisani on CETA, Jobs, and Training," *Enterprise* (September 1981): 22.

14. McChriston sits on the Maryland Commission for Women; see her biography at Maryland Department of Human Services, Maryland Commission for Women, http://dhr.maryland.gov /maryland-commission-women/commissioners-staff/brenda-mcchriston-ma-sphr-shrm-scp/. As NAM president in the 1990s, Jasinowski emphasized the entrepreneurial role of women and people of color in a speech before the Anti-Defamation League, "The Imperative of Diversity in the 21st Century"; see *Vital Speeches of the Day* 64, no. 3 (November 15, 1997): 92–95.

15. Robert Dee, "Antifreeze," *Enterprise* (July/August 1986): 3.

16. Quoted in "Business, Most Jews, and Senators Support Affirmative Action," *Atlantic Daily World*, December 31, 1986, p. 6; see also Herbert Hammerman, "Affirmative Action Happens to Be Working," *New York Times*, November 8, 1985, p. A34; and "Rethinking Weber: The Business Response to Affirmative Action," *Harvard Law Review* 102, no. 3 (January 1989): 658–71, 662.

17. Quoted in John Jacobs, "Why Business Backs Affirmative Action," *Afro-American*, November 2, 1985, p. 5.

quality that made our country great—human diversity."[18] From today's perspective, this seems like small potatoes, but these efforts normalized the idea of diversity, while also attempting to create growth and inclusion in a waning membership.

With its emphasis on development and efficiency, NAM's commitment to diversity hearkened back to its trade association roots. These Progressive Era ideas appeared as well in revived attempts to sell members on the trade association idea. In "Let a Trade Association Do It for You," the CEO of PPG Industries, Inc., Earl Burrell, sought to persuade readers that trade associations were worth their dues. Like reformers of old, Burrell emphasized that sharing information, developing industry standards, and acting on common problems helped individual companies—both large and small—navigate a rapidly changing world. Echoing Herbert Hoover, he reminded readers of the voluntarism at the core of the trade association ethos, which allows industry to improve itself and society without the heavy hand of state regulation. His own sprawling multinational paint and coating company paid over $600,000 a year to various associations at the local, state, and national levels. A company survey found that these memberships were worth every penny. They fulfilled a need that could not be met as effectively in any other way; moreover, "the relatively weak voice of one company could not match the collective power of a strong business association."[19] Indeed, the survey showed "that PPG as a company could neither afford to fund the level of effort attained by the associations surveyed, nor could we, by ourselves achieve their collective level of effectiveness."[20]

Finally, Trowbridge adopted a six-point "revitalization plan" for American industry, which focused on fiscal responsibility in government, capital formation, regulatory reform, energy policy, and international competitiveness.[21] This plan was based on ideas that Jasinowski had introduced to the NAM board in 1979, while he was still assistant secretary of commerce for policy. He told the NAM board that the nation's economic problems—inflation, waning productivity, and the loss of international markets—could not be resolved by 1960s-style economic policies that emphasized demand:

18. William McEwen, "EEO Wears a New Hat," *Enterprise* (March 1984). McEwen was vice chair of the NAM Human Resources and Equal Opportunity Committee. Employees of color typically worked in human resources and EEO offices, reflecting the corporate norm for this era.

19. J. Earl Burrell, "Let an Association Do It for You," *Enterprise* (April 1981): 12.

20. Ibid.

21. "Revitalization: NAM's Blueprint for Growth and National Strength," *Enterprise* (April 1981).

"The source of our problems lies not with our ability to consume but our capacity to produce." Thus, what was needed were policies that emphasized the "supply-side" of the equation.[22] By "supply-side" he meant tax policies that would recover capital for updating plants, equipment, transportation, and energy sources, which was not quite what Arthur Laffer's famous cocktail napkin "curve" meant. Unlike his predecessors, Jasinowski was not averse to pollution controls and energy efficiency, but he tied them to economic policies that would allow the renovation of outdated factories.[23] It was these ideas that NAM brought to the tax reform table in 1981.

Reaganomics

NAM could not have been more excited for Reagan's economic program, which promised tax cuts, fiscal responsibility, and a reduction in government regulations. Trowbridge urged NAM members to support proposed federal budget cuts—"including those that hurt"—so that the administration could move forward with the tax cuts intended to spark productivity and growth.[24] Tax-cutting, however, proved to be more complicated than anticipated.

In keeping with its capital formation agenda, NAM's tax plan was based on accelerated depreciation tax deductions. Known as the Accelerated Cost Recovery System (ACRS), NAM's plan featured a simplified "10-5-3" depreciation schedule (ten years for buildings, five for vehicles, and three for equipment). Corporations had long been able to deduct depreciation costs, but soaring inflation had distorted the schedules and, as Jasinowski explained, "resulted in higher effective tax rates on income from capital, a reduced rate of return to those who supply capital, and higher costs of capital for firms." All of which made it more difficult for manufacturers to invest in new energy-efficient, productivity-increasing equipment that would make US industry more competitive.[25] The 10-5-3 schedule would

22. Board of directors meeting minutes, September 21–22, 1979, p. 9, series 13, box 246, NAMR. On the basis of Jasinowski's performance at this meeting, Trowbridge offered him the position of chief economist with senior vice president status; Jerry Jasinowski, interview with the author, August 25, 2015.

23. Jerry Jasinowski, "Amend the Clean Air Act," *New York Times*, November 6, 1981, p. A31; "Business and the Reagan Tax Cuts," *Enterprise* (August 1981): 28.

24. See, for instance, "The President's Program for a New Beginning," *Enterprise* (March 1981).

25. Jasinowski, "Business and the Reagan Tax Cuts," *Enterprise* (August 1981): 28. On the tax reform battle, see Waterhouse, *Lobbying America*, chap. 5; and Stein, *Running Steel, Running America*, 374–76.

reverse these trends and allow large capital-intensive companies to recoup capital to update equipment and plants, making them more competitive and saving jobs. NAM had pushed a similar plan in 1979, and President Carter had initially supported it, until he found out how much it would cost in lost revenue. Critics called it a deficit-creating tax break for large corporations, and it died.[26] NAM hoped that Reagan would revive it.

Reagan was for tax cuts, of course, but he touted a much simpler and more politically savvy 30 percent "across-the-board" tax cut for all. Harnessing the populist energy from the tax revolts across the country, this plan was based on the supply-side idea that money freed from government coffers would be invested in the private sector, spurring economic growth and job creation. Although all brackets would be lowered, the target was the highest, investor class.[27] Initial deficits would be made up as anticipated growth led to more tax revenue—an idea, incidentally, that NAM president William Grede had preached in the 1950s.[28] But the Reagan Era NAM was wary of this plan. Trowbridge told the *New York Times* that it was too much of an economic stimulus and could contribute to inflation. The first priority, he said, should be "faster capital cost recovery" and the "promotion of savings and investment"—that is, targeted loopholes and deductions for manufacturers.[29] Left to their own devices, individual investors were more likely to invest in the industries of the future rather than those in the flailing manufacturing sector.

NAM was disappointed that the ACRS would not be the centerpiece of the new tax legislation, but it eventually agreed to a compromise that included a modified version of ACRS, along with the marginal tax rate cuts and an investment tax credit. Traditional conservatives, many of whom were business leaders, were concerned about deficits, but NAM, major business organizations, and the Republican Party all supported the bill, now called the Economic Recovery Tax Act (ERTA). Jasinowski declared the new bill a complete victory for NAM, assuring NAM members that the new (modified) depreciation schedule would bring growth and increase productivity.

26. Waterhouse, *Lobbying America*, 208; Stein, *Running Steel, Running America*, 274.

27. Also known as the Kemp-Roth plan, which called for a 30 percent cut in marginal tax rates for individuals over three years; see Stein, *Running Steel, Running America*, 274–75; Douglas Rossinow, *The Reagan Era* (New York: Columbia University Press, 2016), 61. On supply-siders, see Waterhouse, *Lobbying America*, 208–12; and Godfrey Hodgson, *The World Turned Right Side Up* (Boston: Houghton Mifflin, 1996), chap. 8.

28. On Grede's tax ideas, see Miner, *Grede of Milwaukee*, 113–14.

29. Clyde Farnsworth, "NAM President Urges Delay in Tax Cut Plans," *New York Times*, November 12, 1980, p. D24.

Chairman of the Board James Binns (Armstrong World Industries, Inc.), however, admitted that NAM did not get what it wanted, but that compromise was a crucial part of democracy and NAM should be proud to be a "positive, affirmative participant" in the historical coalition that Reagan had created.[30]

When the bill passed in August 1981, NAM jubilantly took credit for it. A reproduction of President Reagan's congratulatory letter graced *Enterprise*'s September cover; in it, the president himself acknowledged NAM's role in "marshalling public support" for the new law. Addressing NAM members, Trowbridge noted that the tax victory was the culmination "of a decade of demonstrable and constructive NAM leadership in pursuit of simpler and faster capital cost recovery provisions." NAM played a "vanguard role" made possible by the efforts of the board, the staff, the Tax Committee, and "effective grass-roots persuasion from member companies."[31] Credit for all. And when a compromise had to be made, NAM had the maturity and integrity to make it. It was a trade association proving itself effective.

But then came recession. In the month following the ERTA victory, 860,000 people lost their jobs, joining the 8.5 million people already out of work. The unemployment rate climbed to 8 percent. In the following two years, 100,000 steelworkers—one-quarter of all steelworkers—were let go.[32] On the verge of collapse, International Harvester, a NAM stalwart since the early twentieth century, closed nineteen plants, laying off 20,000 workers. Newspapers attributed the recession to a steep rise in interest rates beginning in 1979, which caused a slump in housing and cars; by 1981, the slump hit suppliers. By March 1982, the unemployment rate had risen to 9 percent, and by December, it was at 10.8 percent.[33]

Added to this dire situation was the 1983 budget with a projected $91.5 billion deficit. Typically conservatives, including those in NAM, opposed deficit spending. Alarmed economists and business leaders worried that this level of federal borrowing was contributing to high interest rates, slowing growth, and creating an overvalued dollar that disadvantaged US exports. Executives from the Business Roundtable met with Reagan to ask him to

30. Jerry Jasinowski, "Business and the Reagan Tax Cuts," *Enterprise* (August 1981): 28; James H. Binns, "The Reagan Tax Package: A NAM Compromise," *Enterprise* (August 1981): 31.

31. Alexander Trowbridge, "The Tax Breakthrough: NAM Leadership Pays Dividends," *Enterprise* (September 1981): 2.

32. Stein, *Running Steel, Running America*, 276; "Joblessness Grows as Slump Spreads," *New York Times*, November 14, 1981, p. 20.

33. For statistics on the recession of the early 1980s, see Richard C. Auxier, "Reagan's Recession," Pew Research Center, December 10, 2010, http://www.pewresearch.org/2010/12/14/reagans-recession/.

reduce military spending and entitlements, raise excise taxes, and delay the 10 percent income tax cut. NAM likewise called for defense cuts, but opposed raising taxes or delaying the tax cuts.[34] The deficit was projected to approach $300 billion by 1988. Trowbridge expressed concern about Reagan's call to increase defense spending over the next five years.[35] Reagan was eventually forced to raise taxes in 1982 and again in 1984, rescinding many of the gains that NAM and its allies had worked into the ERTA, including a significant part of the accelerated depreciation benefits.[36] Concerned about the deficit, NAM supported the Reagan tax hikes.

INDUSTRIAL POLICY?

Throughout this drama, the conflict between deficit hawks and supply-siders, between business leaders and cold warriors, NAM stood by Reagan, albeit uneasily. The organization had long touted the free enterprise ideas that Reagan embodied, and it was able to win some of its demands, particularly, as we will see, in trade. But Reaganomics was doing manufacturing no favors. What Trowbridge and Jasinowski really wanted was some kind of coherent "industrial policy" to revive industry.

There was a discussion at this time among economists, policy-types, and business leaders about how to deal with deindustrialization, the US trade deficit, and the ensuing dislocations. Should the government aid or protect failing and/or rising industries? A common argument was that other countries had national economic policies, such as government subsidies and tariffs that benefited key industries, while the United States had no such national policy and industry was thus disadvantaged. This was actually an old argument—one that NAM had been making since 1895 (see chapter 2)—but in the face of Japan's domination of the automobile, computer, and electronics markets, it gained new traction in the 1980s.[37] There was also interest in an industrial bank like Herbert Hoover's Reconstruction Finance Corporation (RFC) to provide low-interest loans for both rising tech industries and struggling industrial concerns.

34. Waterhouse, *Lobbying America*, 215–24; Judis, *The Paradox of American Democracy*, 182–83; "Manufacturers Criticize Budget," *Los Angeles Times*, March 12, 1982, p. A2; Howell Raines, "Executives Bid Reagan Cut Deficit," *New York Times*, March 13, 1982, p. 31.

35. Leslie Wayne, "Business Talks Back to Reagan," *New York Times*, January 30, 1983, p. A1.

36. Waterhouse, *Lobbying America*, 216.

37. Ibid., 241–42; Judis, *The Paradox of American Democracy*, 183–85; Peter Behr, "How to Recognize an Industrial Policy," *Washington Post*, July 10, 1983, p. G1; Otis Graham, *Losing Time: The Industrial Policy Debate* (Cambridge, MA: Harvard University Press, 1992).

Other ideas included government-business partnerships in research and development and the relaxation of antitrust laws to allow competing companies to pool knowledge or merge to conserve their strength.[38]

Democrats in particular sought a comprehensive industrial policy in response to the perceived failure of Reaganomics. Democrats were divided between "traditionalists," who supported tariffs and unions, and the new "Atari Democrats," or neoliberals, such as economist Robert Reich and Congressman Richard Gephardt of Missouri, who saw industrial policy as a way to smoothly transition the economy away from the smokestack industries and into the new information-, knowledge-, service-oriented—and mostly non-union—fields of the future.[39] As Gephardt put it, "The future of the American economy is in having the best thoughts, the best mental work, as opposed to having a work force that is particularly adept at making things."[40] There would still be a place for manufacturing in this new economy, but it would be streamlined and automated, not the employer of thousands.

Republicans steered clear of industrial policy, which they saw as a Democratic agenda item. But Trowbridge and Jasinowski embraced it. What was NAM's "revitalization plan" but an industrial policy?[41] Writing in *Enterprise* in 1979 (before he was with NAM), Jasinowski called for business to think more deliberately about policy solutions to make industry more competitive and productive, such as capital formation and automation. The status quo cannot be accepted, wrote Jasinowski: "We must as a nation define a new relationship, a new industrial policy," albeit one formulated by the business community.[42]

In 1983, Jasinowski, now with NAM, invited Robert Reich, then at the Kennedy School of Government at Harvard, and Bruce Scott of Harvard Business School to speak to the NAM board of directors about "Regaining America's Industrial Initiative." Both speakers assumed that government

38. Behr, "How to Recognize an Industrial Policy," G2.

39. Rothenberg, *The Neoliberals*, chap. 7.

40. Quoted in ibid., 85.

41. See Jasinowski's "industrial policy" speech in board of directors meeting minutes, September 21–22, 1979, series 13, box 246, NAMR; see also "Asst Commerce Sec Chosen by Manufacturers Group," *New York Times*, November 12, 1980. While he was still in Carter's Commerce Department, Jasinowski had cochaired a group reviewing the feasibility of industrial policy and potential approaches; see Graham, *Losing Time*, 40.

42. Jerry Jasinowski, "The Case for a New Industrial Policy," *Enterprise* (December 1979): 4–7. *Enterprise* also featured a whole issue on robots and automation in August 1982 that encouraged government research in the area; in March 1983, it published "Public Works: A Pivot for Economic Renewal," a plea for a government infrastructure program authored by Pat Choate and Susan Walter.

could be an ally in this project, but that it was up to business to send it in a forward-looking direction. As Reich explained, government could help industry maintain the status quo "with policies that don't improve our international competitive position," or it could work with industry to move US industry to "a higher value, more precision engineering with more high technology" and an upgraded, retrained workforce.[43] The problem was that corporations did not have the capital to do this and that the current solutions—loans, tariffs, tax breaks—tended to "preservationism" rather than innovation. Scott talked about Japan's economic strategy, which was brilliant, dynamic, and strategic compared to the approach in the United States, which had no strategy, only outdated hands-off practices. The United States, he said, must "begin to admit that an economic strategy is necessary," and that it should privilege job security as much as shareholder profits.[44] It is difficult to know how the NAM board actually responded to this session, but it was clear that these ideas were of little interest to Republicans. As Jasinowski noted, the main problem was political, not economic.

Dedicated to "industrial policy," *Enterprise*'s October 1983 issue featured articles both for and against the idea. The editors included die-hard opponents to any government-based policy, but they also gave a platform to proponents, including banker and Democratic Party adviser Felix Rohatyn, who contributed "The Free Market Is Not Always Adequate."[45] Jasinowski and Trowbridge were clear that they did not want more government regulations or policies, but that they did want an economic strategy to stem the decline of US manufacturing.

Reagan tossed them a bone in 1983, creating the President's Commission on Industrial Competitiveness, headed by Hewlett-Packard CEO John Young. A Republican, Young had concerns about Japan's competitive edge and wanted a genuinely nonpartisan group (that is, one including labor reps) to develop policy choices for the president. The resulting report, "Global Competition: The New Reality," called for government investment in worker retraining, education, and applied technology, as well as new cabinet-level positions in trade and technology. Reagan ignored the report.[46] But NAM endorsed it, and Trow-

---

43. Board of directors meeting minutes, February 3–5, 1983, p. 20, series 13, box 246, NAMR. The quotes are the minute-taker's paraphrases of what Reich and Scott said.

44. Ibid., p. 21.

45. Felix Rohatyn, "The Free Market Is Not Always Adequate," *Enterprise* (October 1983): 19; see also Jerry Jasinowski, "Strategy to Excel," *Enterprise* (October 1983): 6–7.

46. Judis, *The Paradox of American Democracy*, 183–84. Contrariwise, Stein, *Running Steel, Running America*, 285, says that the report "offered no specific advice."

bridge and other NAM leaders called for a Department of International Trade and Industry, along the lines of what the report had advocated.[47] Trowbridge also offered Young $75,000 to start a private competitiveness council, which would be composed of representatives from business, labor, academia, and the media. According to John Judis, the council publicized the need for "critical technologies" for US competitiveness in the world economy, but failed to make much headway with the Reagan or Bush administrations.[48] As we will see, the Clinton administration would be much friendlier to these ideas.

The point is that Trowbridge and Jasinowski were clearly interested in policy solutions, even though they tempered their public statements about them (which might be why some historians have argued that NAM rejected policy).[49] Like past NAM leaders, they supported Democratic approaches while presiding over a Republican membership. Their advocacy paid off in this case, as Congress and state governments adopted research and aid programs aimed at helping smaller companies adopt new technologies. These efforts included the expansion of the National Institute for Standards and Technology, originally founded in 1901 with NAM support.[50]

THE TAX REFORM ACT OF 1986

If further evidence is needed of how diminished NAM's political strength was in the Reagan Era, one can find it in the Tax Reform Act of 1986, which eliminated the investment tax credit, curtailed the depreciation deduction, and slapped an alternative minimum tax on corporations, *raising* the corporate tax bill by $140 billion.[51] Sponsored by two Democrats and signed

47. In fact, as early as 1983, Trowbridge was proposing such an office. See "Regaining the Competitive Edge" by the editors, *Enterprise* (March 1985): 5; and Alexander Trowbridge, "Needed: A Commitment to Competitiveness," *Enterprise* (March 1985): 6–7; see also Trowbridge, "Inside Industry," *Enterprise* (November/December 1985): 5; W. Paul Tibbetts, "Evening the Odds with Foreign Competitors," *Enterprise* (August 1983): 22–24; and Robert Dee, "Showdown," *Enterprise* (May/June 1986), also about industrial policy.

48. Judis, *The Paradox of American Democracy*, 184–85, based on Max Holland, *The CEO Goes to Washington* (Knoxville: Whittle Direct Books, 1994).

49. Both Stein, *Running Steel, Running America*, 284, and Waterhouse, *Lobbying America*, 242, say that NAM was not interested in "policy." One can see why NAM would downplay its interest in Walter Olson, "A Malleable Manufacturers Lobby," *Wall Street Journal*, October 10, 1984, p. 1, which disparages NAM's support for Democratic ideas.

50. John Holusha, "An Industrial Policy, Piece by Piece," *New York Times*, July 30, 1991, p. D3.

51. A conservative estimate that appears in "Taxation and Fiscal Policy," *Enterprise* (May/June 1986): 5; see also NAM's analysis in Paul Huard, "Tax Reform," insert in *Enterprise* (July/August 1985).

by Reagan in October 1986, the act erased the gains that large corporations and their lobbyists had succeeded in winning from Congress over the previous two decades. Public interest groups had explicitly targeted those gains. According to the liberal Citizens for Tax Justice, corporate taxes in 1984 were funding just 8.8 percent of public spending, whereas in the 1960s corporate taxes had funded one-quarter of public spending. Further, some of the largest, most profitable corporations were paying no taxes at all, even getting rebates. This was because of a jumble of corporate tax loopholes that had been in place since 1970; if eliminated, the deficit could be cut in half and interest rates lowered.[52] Conservatives concurred. Speaking before the Conservative Political Action Committee, Republican congressman Jack Kemp of New York said, "There is no reason conservatives should support tax breaks and subsidies for corporations. There's no reason for corporations to be subsidized by the government."[53]

The resulting bill shifted the tax burden from individuals to corporations. But not all corporations would be similarly burdened. Reagan had called for "a tax code stripped of favors for the few and offering lower rates for all," eliminating tax subsidies for *industry* (that is, large manufacturers), "and creating a freer market in which the old and new would compete on equal footing."[54] Treasury secretary Donald Regan specifically attacked accelerated depreciation and the investment tax credit as "industrial policy" that favored manufacturing over other sectors.[55] The resulting tax reform thus seemed engineered to benefit the rising financial and import-heavy service industries at the expense of manufacturing. Individual consumers would have more money to spend, which would enable them to buy more imported items, while manufacturers' higher tax bill would increase the cost of their products. As Jasinowski explained, greater consumer spending would be offset by a "contraction in investment and the increase in the trade deficit caused by the higher demand for imports."[56] The tax reform would devastate capital-intensive manufacturing, which, as Judith Stein noted, helped

52. Robert S. McIntyre, "Disarm the Deficit: End Corporate Tax Dodges," *Washington Post*, March 24, 1985, p. C1. In 1972, Jasinowski had made a similar argument in *The Nation*; see Jasinowski, "Mr. Nixon's Tax Mythology."

53. Quoted in McIntyre, "Disarm the Deficit: End Corporate Tax Dodges."

54. Dale Russakoff and Anne Swardson, "Drive to Simplify Taxes Runs into Complications," *Washington Post*, April 13, 1986, p. A1.

55. Quoted in Stein, *Running Steel, Running America*, 277.

56. Jane Seaberry, "More Imports, Less Investment Predicted at the End of the Tax Trail," *Washington Post*, August 18, 1986, p. A10.

accelerate the "shift from a manufacturing to a service economy."[57] Moreover, the freed-up money, now in the hands of individuals, would feed the demand for investment opportunities in the form of venture capital, junk bonds, real estate, and other Wall Street offerings.[58]

NAM followed, complained, and testified against the tax reform bill throughout 1985, but it kept a low lobbying profile as the law headed for a vote in the summer of 1986. "We're all resigned to it," said NAM spokesperson Sarah Ross in August 1986.[59] Economists predicted that the tax shake-up would lower interest rates and unemployment, while also being a boon for the service and tech industries—as indeed it was. Manufacturing and its lobbyists had thrived in an earlier era when large multidivisional corporations were a metaphor for a conforming social organization and when, in the words of General Motors CEO Charles E. Wilson, what was good for GM was good for the nation and vice versa.[60] In this new era of revived individualism and classical liberalism (sometimes called "neoliberalism"), economic and political power shifted to individuals, entrepreneurs, and venture capitalists. It marked as well the financialization of the US economy— the transformation into what Gerald Davis has called "shareholder capitalism," wherein corporate rule was transferred from professional managers concerned with "stakeholders" (employees, consumers, the community) to a new style of management that prioritized stock prices and shareholder value. This shift went hand in hand with the hostile takeover wave of the 1980s that began the dismantling of the multidivisional corporation that an earlier generation of NAM leaders had brought into being.

THE TAKEOVER WAVE

Mergers and takeovers were an intrinsic part of industrial capitalism from the start and had long affected NAM membership numbers. What was different in the 1980s and 1990s was the hostility of the takeovers, which led to a dismantling of the largest corporations, particularly those conglomerations

57. Quoted in Stein, *Running Steel, Running America*, 277.
58. Ibid., 277; see also Davis, *Managed by the Markets*, chap. 1.
59. Barbara Bradley, "Tax Lobbyists Waiting for Next Year," *Christian Science Monitor*, August 26, 1986, p. 1.
60. On "the age of organization," see Drucker, *The New Society*, and Whyte, *The Organization Man*. On this transformation, see Davis, *Managed by the Markets*; Louis R. Hyman, "Rethinking the Postwar Corporation: Management, Monopolies, and Markets," in *What's Good for Business: Business and Politics since World War II*, edited by Kim Phillips-Fein and Julian E. Zelizer (New York: Oxford University Press, 2012); and Lemann, *Transaction Man*.

that had been formed in the merger wave of the 1960s (see chapter 10). In part because of antitrust laws that prevented monopolies in single industries, corporations had expanded in the 1960s by acquiring companies from industries far afield from their own. Forming large diversified conglomerations, corporations such as LTV (electronics) and ITT (communications) acquired bakeries, auto parts, hotels, rental cars, sporting goods, steel, and various consumer products, with the aim of adding to their stock portfolios.[61] As it turned out, however, this led to a good deal of overhead and economic inefficiency that was eventually reflected, economists noted, in lower stock values.

Revised merger guidelines from the Justice Department's Antitrust Division in 1982 removed the prohibition against intra-industry mergers, leading, when combined with the low stock prices of the conglomerates, to what Gerald Davis has called a "bust-up merger wave": 28 percent of the largest Fortune 500 manufacturers faced hostile takeovers during the 1980s, most of them successful. By 1990, writes Davis, one-third of the largest corporations in the United States had disappeared as independent entities. The component divisions of the bought-up conglomerates were actually quite valuable, especially once liberated from the stranglehold of the inefficient conglomeration, and they were quickly sold at higher prices to firms in the same industry.[62] Such activity further fueled the rising financial industries.

As Davis shows—and Oliver Stone's film *Wall Street* (1987) captures so beautifully—this was an attack on the managerial class: the boards and governing structure of the Chandlerian corporation, with its long-term developmental outlook and governing managers who balanced the interests of "stakeholders" (consumers, labor, the community) rather than paying dividends to the "owners" (the shareholders). That is what Gordon Gecko rails against in the film's famous "greed is good" speech—the idea that the real owners of the company (the shareholders) are not getting their rightful return on investment because the bloated boards of directors are using that money to aggrandize their own positions and fiefdoms.[63]

This was a shock to corporate America and to NAM, whose most powerful members were targets of hostile takeovers (unlike in the 1960s, when its

---

61. See Davis, *Managed by the Markets*, 77–81; Hyman, "Rethinking the Postwar Corporation," 203–7.

62. Davis, *Managed by the Markets*, 84–85.

63. This scene from *Wall Street* is easily found via an internet search. Davis sees the attack on the top-heavy board structures as a factor in making "shareholder value" the measure of a company's success and investment payoff. Concurrently, he discusses new economic theories that saw the financial markets as the most reliable index of actual worth.

smaller, most vulnerable members were getting bought up). Armstrong World Industries, for instance, a multinational maker of floor coverings that had supplied NAM with several generation of leaders (indeed, Armstrong's chairman, James Binns, was NAM board chair in 1981), faced a takeover threat from an investment group led by the Belzberg family. When the Belzbergs made known their plan to sell off some of the company's subsidiaries, Armstrong said that it was not for sale and sought relief through new legislation restricting takeover bids.[64] NAM dedicated an entire issue of *Enterprise* to takeovers in October 1985. As the editors explained, there were a variety of views on the issue. Some saw the takeovers as corrections, a way to hold inefficient governing systems to account. Others believed that corporate raiders were turning acquired companies into "dustbowls," while undermining traditional business values. Either way, the takeovers were rewriting the "rules of the game," and NAM was pulling together what the savvy manufacturer needed to know.[65] NAM also compiled tips for combating attacks.[66] Reagan was not responsible for the takeover crisis, but the era that bears his name spelled the end of the kind of corporation and industrial capitalism that NAM had earlier brought to life.

International Trade

Underlying NAM's woes was the trade deficit. Ballooning to $159 billion in 1987, the trade deficit signified for many the end of US international economic dominance. Between 1981 and 1986, imports increased by $100 billion, a 73 percent increase, while US exports remained below their 1981 level. More than half of the deficit consisted of manufactured imports from Japan and Western Europe.[67] NAM officials felt that the trade deficit was a result of monetary policies that overvalued the dollar, making US exports expensive and imports cheap. They also felt that Japan and other countries restricted US goods while continuing to benefit from access to America's relatively unrestricted market.[68] Although NAM was feeling the pinch of full-on

---

64. Davis, *Managed by the Markets*, 56; Gregory Robb, "Belzberg Group May Bid for Armstrong World," *New York Times*, July 6, 1989, p. D4.

65. "A Blitz of Not So Tender Offers," *Enterprise* (October 1985): 5.

66. See, for instance, Paul Elicker, *Combating Takeover Attempts* (Washington, DC: NAM, 1985).

67. Judis, *The Paradox of American Democracy*, 181; trade section of *Enterprise* (May/June 1986); "Reagan's New Dollar Strategy," *New York Times*, March 3, 1985, p. F1; Chorev, *Remaking US Trade Policy*, 132.

68. Judis, *The Paradox of American Democracy*, 181–83; Eckes and Zeiler, *Globalization and the American Century*, 200–201; Jerry Jasinowski, "Let's Not Sell America's Industry's Short," *New*

globalization, it still saw exports as the solution to manufacturing's ills. In this regard, it found an inconsistent ally in Reagan. The Reagan administration's anticommunist policies and hostility to "corporate welfare" (such as the Export-Import Bank) made for a rocky start, but most historians recognize that Reagan ultimately loosened capital and trade constraints, thereby contributing to the free flow of money and goods across borders. This had always been NAM's goal—although NAM leaders may have miscalculated the extent to which it would benefit all manufacturers.

DOUBTS ABOUT FREE TRADE?

The 1980s saw a resurgence of protectionism and "buy American" campaigns, led in large part by labor.[69] But industry also sought to restrict imports through processes set up in the Trade Act of 1974, which allowed for retaliatory measures against unfair practices (such as dumping and subsidies), as well as an escape clause for those industries that presented evidence of import-caused damage. Steel, autos, textiles, shoes, and other NAM-represented industries (and their unions) applied for import relief, but with little success. Even when their requests were recommended by the International Trade Commission, the Carter and Reagan administrations turned down nearly half of all "escape clause" requests.[70] Aggrieved industries thus appealed to Congress, which saw 277 bills concerning import restrictions in 1985–1986 (of which six were enacted).[71]

Though shaken by the crisis and sympathetic to members' distress, NAM eschewed economic nationalism and import quota legislation. It blamed plant closings and the trade deficit on the overvalued dollar, budget excesses, and unfair trade practices—not on "free trade."[72] Nor did it support government aid to failing companies. In the wake of the Chrysler bailout in 1979, its board adopted a statement opposing "federal financial support for individual

---

York Times, October 29, 1982, p. A26. Irwin, Clashing over Commerce, chap. 12, takes the opposite position, arguing that trade played a "relatively small role" in the decline of manufacturing and that a trade deficit presented no economic crisis.

69. Dana Frank, Buy American: The Untold Story of Economic Nationalism (Boston: Beacon Press, 1999), chaps. 6–7.

70. Eckes and Zeiler, Globalization and the American Century, 200, 209; Chorev, Remaking US Trade Policy, 117–28; see also Stein, Running Steel, Running America, 281–83.

71. Chorev, Remaking US Trade Policy, 134.

72. The July 1983 issue of Enterprise is dedicated to the dislocated worker and the "National Conference on the Dislocated Worker," cosponsored by the National Alliance of Business (NAB), NAM, and other groups.

private enterprises unless the support is based on laws which have general applicability to comparable enterprises." The debate and vote on this resolution was reminiscent of the old tariff arguments. President Heath Larry (formerly of US Steel) had to calm an angry Lee Iacocca, assuring him that the resolution was not about Chrysler specifically; he certainly understood the challenges of regulations and imports, he told the Chrysler chairman, but NAM also represented small and midsized businesses that were also suffering from regulations and imports and that resented government bailouts of large concerns.[73]

Nonetheless, NAM leaders of the 1980s were more open to the idea of retaliatory trade restrictions and tough negotiations than they had been in the past. They now regularly called for the government to stand up to unfair trade barriers abroad and update GATT agreements to reflect Japan's and Germany's new economic power. "Tough negotiations do not necessarily move us to protectionism," NAM board chair Stanley Pace (of TRW, Inc.) wrote, but could lead to freer trade by reducing trade barriers.[74] While import restrictions in the United States should be limited and temporary, there were three conditions that warranted them: for purposes of national defense, in response to other countries' unfair use of them, and "to ease the trauma of an industry, including its workers and communities," devastated by international competition.[75] NAM director W. Paul Tibbett (American Motor Company) dismissed conservative attacks on regulation as "shopworn" and called for government oversight of trade relations, including the deployment of retaliatory import restrictions: "It is suicidal to follow a turn-the-other-cheek, free-trade ideology when every other industrial nation has promoted and protected its basic industries."[76] In 1984, NAM passed a resolution calling for the government to take coordinated action with other nations to "reduce dollar exchange rate misalignment." Trowbridge called on the government to "cap" the dollar and prevent any further rise in its value, citing the overvalued dollar as the cause of "at least half" the trade deficit.[77]

---

73. Heath Larry to Lee Iacocca, October 10, 1979, in board of director meeting minutes, September 21–22, 1979, series 13, box 246, NAMR. On the actual resolution vote, see pp. 8–9 of the minutes.

74. Stanley Pace, "Fixing the Trade Deficit," *Enterprise* (March 1985): 3; see also Bernard O'Keefe, "Equal Rights for US Trade," *Enterprise* (February 1983): 3.

75. Pace, "Fixing the Trade Deficit"; O'Keefe, "Equal Rights for US Trade."

76. W. Paul Tibbetts, "Evening the Odds with Foreign Competitors, *Enterprise* (August 1983): 24.

77. Neil Murphy, "Beyond the Declining Dollar," *Enterprise* (May/June 1986): 16; Clyde Farnsworth, "Debate on Trade Affecting Parties," *New York Times*, April 11, 1985, p. A1.

The *Wall Street Journal* lambasted these calls as "protectionist," akin to labor's nationalist call for tariffs.[78] NAM disagreed. Industry did not seek to protect uncompetitive industries, it said, but rather to ensure "fair trade" by enforcing GATT agreements and the 1974 Trade Act, both of which allowed sanctions for dumping and other unfair practices.[79] In the face of mounting discontent from industry, labor, and farmers, Reagan finally took action along the lines that NAM leaders had called for. In 1985, he took steps to devalue the dollar, particularly against the yen.[80] He also took retaliatory measures against Brazil and South Korea, while with Japan he arranged and enforced "voluntary export restraints."[81] Practicing what some called an "aggressive reciprocity," Reagan sought to open markets abroad, while also appeasing protectionists at home. This was exactly what NAM wanted.

In 1988, Reagan signed a toned-down Omnibus Trade and Competitiveness Act, which made it easier for the government to retaliate against unfair trading practices and protect intellectual property, while also providing programs for dislocated workers. NAM supported the bill (after the removal of a provision requiring companies to give sixty days' notice of plant closings). Critics condemned the law as protectionist and worried that it would start a trade war.[82] Again, NAM argued that, far from being "protectionist," the bill's intent "was to maintain respect for the rules of the trading system," that is, to strengthen international trade.[83]

78. See Walter Olson, "A Malleable Manufacturers' Lobby," *Wall Street Journal*, October 10, 1984, p. 1.

79. For NAM Trade Committee recommendations, see Donald Davis, "Trade Policy Pivot," *Enterprise* (May/June 1986): 17.

80. Eckes and Zeiler, *Globalization and the American Century*, 200; Pater Kilborn, "Reagan's New Dollar Strategy," *New York Times*, March 3, 1985, p. F1.

81. Chorev, *Remaking US Trade Policy*, 134–35. In a footnote, Judis, *The Paradox of American Democracy*, 182–83, suggests that Reagan was soft on Japan because it used its surplus exports to invest in US real estate, factories, and the like, which funded the US deficit, saving the United States from having to borrow at double-digit interest rates. This is confirmed by Robert Brenner, *The Economics of Global Turbulence: The Advanced Capitalist Economies from Long Boom to Long Downturn, 1945–2005* (New York: Verso, 2006), 189, who argues further that the US deficit, which he calls "Keynesian," saved the world economy by creating demand for Japan's exports; the US treasury needed Japanese lenders, while Japanese manufacturers needed US borrowers—that is, the demand created by the tax cuts.

82. See "Wrong Direction on Trade," *Los Angeles Times*, April 27, 1988, p. C6; "1930 Protectionist Law Colors Trade Bill Debate," *The Tennessean*, November 15, 1987, p. 3-G.

83. NAM rep quoted in "1930 Protectionist Law Colors Trade Bill Debate," *The Tennessean*, November 15, 1987.

Much has been made of Reagan's "free trade" rhetoric contradicting what many saw as his protectionist actions.[84] But from NAM's perspective, there was no contradiction. Indeed, this was one issue on which NAM and Reagan were in complete agreement—enforcing established trade policies made international trade safer, sounder, and stronger. More recently, sociologist Nitsan Chorev has likewise argued that this approach contributed to overall trade liberalization by opening markets, while placating protectionist energy.[85] The question is, did these moves benefit manufacturing? Historians Alfred Eckes and Thomas Zeiler suggest not. They agree with Chorev that Reagan's policies led to trade liberalization and a more integrated global economy—but one that would benefit the service and financial industries more than manufacturing.[86]

EXPORTS AND FOREIGN INVESTMENT

As in the past, NAM continued to see exports and foreign investment as key to manufacturing success. It continued to fight for and tout the benefits of the Export-Import Bank (EXIM), which NAM had supported since its creation in the 1930s (chapter 5). Funded by the government, the EXIM supplied long-term loans and credits to buyers of American goods in foreign countries; it also assumed risk so as to draw private-sector funding into export financing.[87] Critics said that it represented a subsidy to large multinational corporations, like Boeing. The Reagan administration agreed and, in keeping with its free-market principles, proposed to cut funding for it in 1983 and 1985.[88]

Used to such criticisms, NAM argued that the EXIM was necessary to counter government subsidies given to US international competitors, that it was no cost to the US taxpayers, and that it actually turned a profit for the government. It was too bad that such a program was needed, but as long as other countries subsidized their exports, the market was already skewed.

---

84. See William Niskinen, *Reaganomics: An Insider's Account of the Policies and the People* (New York: Oxford University Press, 1988); Richard Cooper, "An Appraisal of Trade Policy during the Reagan Administration," *Harvard International Review* 11, no. 3 (1989): 90–94; more recently, see Irwin, *Clashing over Commerce*, chap. 12. Judith Stein, on the other hand, is critical of Reagan for not being protectionist enough.

85. Chorev, *Remaking US Trade Policy*, 135.

86. Eckes and Zeiler, *Globalization and the American Century*, chap. 9.

87. Jordan Jay Hillman, "EXIM Bank as a Private Enterprise," *Northwestern Journal of International Law and Business* 4, no. 2 (Fall 1982): 374–421.

88. Ibid., 412; "Export-Import Bank Faces Stiff Cut in 1983," *New York Times*, February 7, 1982, p. 28.

"Free enterprise can do wonders," wrote NAM chair Bernard O'Keefe in defense of the EXIM, "but it cannot compete against cartels such as OPEC or protectionist governments such as Japan."[89]

Sensitive to its membership demographic, NAM also stressed that the EXIM was a resource for small and midsized businesses. "Do you have a product you think you might sell on the overseas market?" asked one *Enterprise* article about the new EXIM hotline, which was "designed to encourage small and medium sized businesses to export their products—and help reduce our huge trade deficit." With this help, a Florida businessman sold eels to Japan and a North Carolina nozzle-maker was able to find markets in Holland. In combination with the Small Business Administration (SBA), the Commerce Department, and the Overseas Private Investment Corporation (OPIC), the EXIM was also organizing conferences and radio shows to get the word out to small businesses about the opportunities abroad.[90] NAM leaders hoped that the EXIM would benefit smaller manufacturers and thus help close the trade deficit, but these efforts also legitimated its mission in an anti–big corporation climate.

Reagan himself was torn between the free-market ideologues at the CATO Institute, who hated the EXIM, and pragmatic businessmen at NAM who made a commonsense argument about American competitiveness.[91] He twice signed a budget that reduced EXIM appropriations, only to praise the EXIM in his State of the Union Address.[92] NAM was frustrated with Reagan's flip-flopping on the issue, but in the end the EXIM escaped unscathed and, in the opinion of Reagan's trade representative and labor secretary, William Brock, emerged stronger owing to reforms that made it more transparent and fiscally responsible.[93]

Another clash with the Reagan administration concerned its tightening of trade sanctions against the Soviet Union. As we saw in the previous chapter, NAM had successfully pursued new trade protocols with the Soviet Union

89. Bernard O'Keefe, "Equal Rights for US Trade, *Enterprise* (February 1983): 3; see also "America Can Compete in World Markets," and interview with Stanley C. Gault, both by Alexander Trowbridge, *Enterprise* (Winter 1987): 12–13.

90. "Want to Export? Dial EXIM Hotline," *Enterprise* (December 1979): 16; Craig Nalen, "Your 'In' to Overseas Opportunities," *Enterprise* (March 1985): 19–21.

91. Reagan appointed Simon Fireman, a Massachusetts boating industry supplier, to head the EXIM in 1987; see "A Businessman Takes Control of the Exim Bank," *Boston Globe*, November 2, 1987, p. 51.

92. Stuart Auerbach, "Ex-Im on the Block Again," *Washington Post*, February 5, 1985, p. C1.

93. See William Brock III, "Don't Kill the Export-Import Bank," *New York Times*, July 28, 2014. Brock was a member of the Reagan administration who worked on reforming the EXIM.

in the 1970s. In Reagan's revival of the Cold War, however, trade with "the enemy" was discouraged in the name of national security, trade sanctions were tightened in response to martial law in Poland, and American firms and European allies were warned not to contribute to a pipeline being built from the Soviet Union to West Germany. The Reagan administration said that the pipeline not only handed over technological secrets to the Soviets, but also gave them economic leverage over West Germany. Experts disputed this, as well as the effectiveness of trade sanctions on political matters. Tension developed between the anticommunist Defense Department and the protrade Commerce Department, headed by NAM ally Malcolm Baldridge.[94]

NAM had long opposed—albeit quietly—the excessive export controls demanded by Cold War policies (see chapters 7 and 10). Its leaders always acknowledged that military weapons and technology should not be traded (obviously), but argued that controls on other exports seemed random and impeded US export opportunities. NAM was dismayed by Reagan's sanctions against the Soviet pipeline, but initially accepted them as a foreign policy prerogative. "We're not keen to see foreign goods replace ours in trade," NAM's Lawrence Fox said, "but this has to be seen in [a foreign policy] context." By August, however, as the Reagan administration attempted to enforce sanctions in Europe, Trowbridge wrote to Reagan to express NAM's "exasperation and concerns" over the export control regulations, which "cast a long shadow over US commercial transactions, especially in Western Europe."[95] A frustrated Jasinowski told the *New York Times*, "It makes little sense for the government to penalize a foreign subsidiary of an American company for obeying the laws of a nation in which that subsidiary is incorporated and operates."[96]

In 1987, Reagan finally lifted the ban. A jubilant Trowbridge credited the turnaround to "a few corporations" (TRW, Inc., and Halliburton), the Petroleum Equipment Suppliers Association, and NAM, which together were able to convince the administration of the "folly of export controls." Here was another example of trade associations in action—and another step forward for multinational corporations.[97]

94. Becker, *The Dynamics of Business and Government Relations, Industry, and Exports*, 74.

95. Clyde Farnsworth, "Collision Is Near on Soviet Pipeline," *New York Times*, August 2, 1982, p. D1.

96. Clyde Farnsworth, "Government Puts Two French Concerns under Trade Curb," *New York Times*, August 27, 1982, p. A1.

97. Alexander Trowbridge, "One That Worked!" *Enterprise* (Spring 1987): 3.

In other ways, the Reagan administration was more helpful. In 1982, Reagan endorsed and signed the Export Trading Company Act, designed to address the trade deficit by encouraging the development of trading companies that would help small and midsized businesses export their products. The new law suspended antitrust and banking regulations to allow cooperation between trading companies, manufacturers, and private bankers.[98] A trading company would arrange financing, research markets, fill out paperwork, secure transportation and warehousing, and help a potential exporter navigate foreign laws. As you may recall from chapter 2, these were the kind of services that NAM offered its members in the early twentieth century. Indeed, the ill-fated NAMUSA Corporation performed exactly these functions, likewise requiring changes in antitrust regulations (Webb-Pomerene Act of 1918) and financing (Edge Act of 1919). Of note in this 1982 version was the amendment of banking laws to allow for "meaningful and effective" bank participation in the financing and development of the new trading companies, which was, one expert noted, "a significant breach in the wall that has separated banking and commerce since the 1930s."[99] The new law allowed exemptions from laws like the Glass-Steagall Act (1933) and the Bank Holding Company Act (1956), so that approved banks with expertise and interests in overseas markets could make equity investments in the new trading companies.[100] This was intended to encourage exports, but by loosening up bank regulations, it also boosted the finance sector.

NAM helped spread the word about the new opportunities. Even before the law passed, NAM was promoting the trading company in the pages of *Enterprise*: "Exporting, importing, bartering—these are just some of the functions of the trading company," which might be the "next great growth industry if America is to prosper in world markets." And in keeping with the spirit of globalism: "a trading company is a mechanism for facilitating the flow of goods and services across international boundaries."[101] In 1984, Honeywell, a Minnesota-based multinational corporation and NAM member, founded Honeywell High-Tech Trading, Inc., which provided services to aspiring small and midsized tech exporters, using Honeywell's offices in twenty-nine countries "to simplify distribution" and "its expertise in

98. Donna M. Petkanics, "The Export Trading Company Act of 1982: Are Banks the Answer to Our Export Trading Problems?" *Berkeley Journal of International Law* 1, no. 1 (1983): 197–217.

99. Ibid., 200.

100. Ibid., 206.

101. John Boles, "An Industry Born of Necessity," *Enterprise* (April 1982): 19–21.

international legal requirements, communications, and taxation" to help client companies export their goods.[102]

Another program that NAM promoted to help smaller businesses' exports was the Overseas Private Investment Corporation. Developed by NAM in 1969, OPIC was a government corporation, similar to the EXIM, but it used private funds to provide loans and insurance for those seeking to invest in developing "third world" markets. As the OPIC director explained to NAM readers, many of these developing markets "are simply too small to support a huge multinational operation, unlike smaller enterprises that are better geared to the markets' economic capacity."[103] Many of these countries required manufacturers seeking access to their markets to set up factories in their country. Featuring photographs of softball and chocolate factories in Haiti and Jamaica, the story seems like an invitation for smaller businesses to get in on offshoring.

In combination with the cheaper dollar, the new trading companies and OPIC helped increase exports. Indeed, US export growth exceeded Germany's and Japan's between 1985 and 1997 (although imports grew even faster).[104] But such exports offered limited help to NAM's older manufacturers. As the examples given here indicate, they bolstered the service components of multinationals (in the case of Honeywell) and encouraged smaller companies to offshore their production (softballs in Haiti). Foreign direct investment increased, but investment in banking, finance, real estate, and services doubled between 1982 and 1990, while manufacturing remained about the same.[105] McDonald's, Visa, Disney, and the like contributed to a trade surplus in services that helped offset the ever-expanding merchandise deficit.[106] By 2000, finance and services would represent almost half of FDI, surpassing manufacturing, which would make up only 27 percent.[107] So the very thing that NAM had always counted on to revive manufacturing—the

102. "Doing Business Abroad," *Enterprise* (December 1983/January 1984): 10.

103. Nalen, "Your 'In' to Overseas Opportunities," 20.

104. During these years, the US growth rate in exports was 9.3 percent, compared to Germany's 5.7 percent and Japan's 4.1 percent. See Brenner, *The Economics of Global Turbulence* 215; and Peter Drucker, *Managing for the Future* (1992; New York: Routledge, 2011), chap. 5.

105. In 1982, America had $207.8 billion invested abroad—27.8 percent of which was invested in petroleum; 40.2 percent in manufacturing; and 15.8 percent in banking, finance, insurance, and real estate (FIRE), and other services. By 1990, the United States had $430.5 billion invested abroad—12.3 percent in petroleum; 39.5 percent in manufacturing; and 33.4 percent in FIRE and services. See Eckes and Zeiler, *Globalization and the American Century*, 213.

106. Ibid., 210.

107. Ibid., 213.

more open exchange of goods and capital—actually helped competing sectors surpass it.

One can follow the corresponding decline of NAM through its journal *Enterprise*. At the start of the 1980s, it was a full and strapping monthly. In 1985, there were ten issues. In 1986, it was a thin bimonthly. By 1987, it had been reduced to a quarterly. Then it ended. In 1987, NAM also reduced its staff from 215 to 185.[108] But all was not lost. Due to plant closings, downsizing, and automation, the manufacturing sector was becoming more productive and, wonder of wonders, actually increasing exports. Jasinowski took the NAM helm in 1990. Full of ideas and energy, he would increase membership, restore NAM influence, and reimagine manufacturing's role in the new economy.

108. "Shaken by Downsizing the Groups Regroup," *New York Times*, May 1, 1988, p. F13.

12

Back on Track?

NAM celebrated its one-hundredth anniversary in 1995 amid vastly improved conditions. Both exports and productivity were up. American manufacturing companies had regained a competitive edge in world markets. Blasting premature claims about manufacturing's death, NAM president Jerry Jasinowski declared that American industry was back on track, continuing "its historical role as the primary engine for economic progress."[1] Manufacturing had transformed itself to meet the global future. Granted, it did so through downsizing, automating, and relocating production abroad. But, Jasinowski insisted, it was still a generator of jobs—better jobs, smarter jobs, and jobs in which workers' input and empowerment were crucial to success. Speaking at the World Economic Forum in Davos, Switzerland, Jasinowski painted a picture of US economic resurgence led not by Reagan-era policies or the service sector, but by a revolution in American manufacturing.[2]

There was no bigger champion of manufacturing than Jerry Jasinowski, the first NAM president who was neither a manufacturer nor a businessman. He grew up in a union family, was a Democrat, and came to NAM after working for the government—or the "dark side," from most NAM members' perspective. But Jasinowski's dedication to and optimism about

1. Jerry Jasinowski and Robert Hamrin, *Making It in America: Proven Paths to Success from 50 Top Companies* (New York: Simon & Schuster/Fireside, 1995), 32. See also Drucker, *Managing for the Future*, chap. 5.
2. Jerry Jasinowski, "America's Manufacturing Revolution," in *Vital Speeches of the Day* 61, no. 11 (March 15, 1995): 348–52.

manufacturing served NAM well, as did his ties to the Democratic Party. "NAM has access to the White House," he reported in a February 1993 meeting, explaining how to best use it.[3] It should come as no surprise that NAM in the 1990s would move closer to the Democratic Party, which had kept its liberal internationalism while jettisoning its New Dealism. Presidential candidate Bill Clinton promised "a national strategy to compete and win in the global economy," something NAM had been asking for since the 1980s.[4] As president, Clinton delivered the North American Free Trade Agreement (NAFTA) and the World Trade Organization (WTO), both culminations of NAM's hundred-year quest for global integration. At this point, NAM was perceived as somewhat less conservative than other business groups. But it was still a conservative and largely Republican organization, and still opposed to new human resource, labor, and environmental legislation.

Like past NAM leaders, Jasinowski placed enormous importance on "getting out the story," but the story was no longer about "free enterprise." It was about the manufacturing sector's contribution to economic growth and global competitiveness. He was the first NAM president to speak of manufacturing as an economic "sector"—those before him had always been able to equate manufacturing with the economy as a whole. Despite these changes, however, there remained continuity in NAM's lobbying and membership concerns, its vision of management-labor relations, and its commitment to globalism.

Lobbying and Membership in the 1990s

Jasinowski's energy helped revive NAM's reputation. *Business Week* reported that he'd "turned the NAM into a lobbying powerhouse."[5] On just about every major economic issue of the day, journalists still consulted NAM to speak for industry. But NAM was absent from the top ten of *Fortune* magazine's list of most influential pressure groups in the 1990s, even as its various rivals were listed, including the US Chamber of Commerce, the AFL-CIO, and the National Federation of Independent Businesses (NFIB).[6] NFIB

3. See Executive Committee meeting minutes, February 12, 1993, series 13, box 251, NAMR.

4. Stephen Smith, ed., *Preface to Presidency: Selected Speeches of Bill Clinton, 1974–1992* (Fayetteville: University of Arkansas Press, 1996), 108.

5. "This Feisty Democrat Has a Business Lobby Fired Up," *Business Week*, December 26, 1994, p. 72A.

6. In fairness, NAM was still number nine among Republican lobbies. Judy Sarasohn, "Fortune Cookie," *Washington Post*, November 25, 1999, p. A41; "Clout, a Lot Like Beauty," *Washington Post*, July 5, 2001, p. A11; Jeff Nirnbaum, "Follow the Money," *Fortune*, December 6, 1999.

seemed to take on the role that NAM had held in the 1950s, in terms of its connections to the conservative movements of the day.

NAM membership had fallen to 12,179 in 1992, the lowest since 1982. The organization claimed that its member companies employed 85 percent of all manufacturing workers and produced more than 80 percent of US manufactured goods, but its membership had not kept pace with changes in the field. As president, Jasinowski reached out to newer tech and communication companies not only to bolster membership but also "to upgrade the representation of manufacturers in the NAM" in ways that reflected the technological and global changes of the age.[7] Producers of semiconductors, routers, and microprocessors joined the automakers and floor-covering magnates. Jasinowski recruited tech giants Hewlett-Packard, Oracle, and Intel. He also targeted foreign companies with plants in the United States, such as Toyota and Siemens.

Nothing reflected the new global reality of manufacturing better than NAM's recruitment of foreign-based companies. From Jasinowski's perspective, the decision was about adapting NAM to the new realities—and welcome opportunities—of a global economy. A world with softer borders was, after all, the promise of internationalists since the days of Woodrow Wilson. But a significant number of members opposed the decision; they still viewed NAM as first and foremost a *national* trade association and feared that foreign companies would corrupt the policymaking processes in ways that benefited their home countries.[8] Foreign-based companies made up only a small percentage of the membership, but given their size and the dues structure, they may have contributed more in revenue than most NAM members. Through such tactics, NAM would succeed in pushing membership back up to 13,623 by its centennial, and to 14,000 by the end of the century.[9]

Like the Chamber and the NFIB, NAM opposed new government regulations. According to an in-house survey conducted in 1993, over half of

7. Jerry Jasinowski, phone interview with the author, October 1, 2015. Further evidence of these membership campaigns and targets can be found in Executive Committee meeting minutes, series 13, box 251, "1993–1998" folder, NAMR.

8. Jerry Jasinowski, phone interview with the author, October 1, 2015.

9. The 13,623 figure is from NAMR. The figure 14,000 is from "Baroody's Bottom Line," *National Journal* 31, no. 11 (March 13, 1999): 700–701. The *Wall Street Journal* reports 16,000, which seems unlikely; see Rodney Ho and Dan Morse, "Update on Small Business," *Wall Street Journal*, October 27, 1998, pp. B2–3.

NAM board members surveyed thought that government mandates and regulations harmed US manufacturing, with environmental regulations at the top of the list.[10] NAM reliably lobbied against environmental regulations, including the Kyoto Protocol on climate change of 1997—one of the few international treaties it openly opposed. It even joined forces with the United Mine Workers of America to lobby against US participation in the Kyoto Treaty.[11] Despite its opposition to the treaty, however, NAM encouraged its members to voluntarily set pollution reduction goals and "achieve environmental excellence."[12] Just as it had done with civil rights, it argued that environmental protection "makes good business sense." It reminded members that their performance in this area could affect their "ability to build new facilities, renew permits, manufacture new products. . . . and ultimately compete in a global marketplace," and it touted the success of those member companies that had modified products to be more environmentally friendly or invested in environmental research and development.[13] Although NAM's efforts were intended in part to combat environmental legislation, they were consistent with its longtime mission of keeping members abreast of the latest industrial innovations and trends. It also bolstered members who made products that helped companies conform to changing environmental standards.

HEALTH CARE REFORM

Large manufacturers had offered workers lifelong health care benefits beginning in the 1940s, as a way to mollify unions and deter Democrats' efforts to enact universal health care.[14] But health care costs had risen dra-

10. "A Survey of NAM Board Members," conducted by Peter D. Hart Research Associates, February 1993, series 13, box 248, NAMR. Environmental regulations cut both ways, however: there were manufacturers who produced goods to help companies comply with them. See quote from Donaldson Company in "A Survey of NAM Board Members," p. 10.

11. See Jerry Jasinowski, "Bust—US Jobs and Industry Lost," *Christian Science Monitor*, December 12, 1997, p. 18; John Cushman Jr., "Intense Lobbying against Global Warming Treaty," *New York Times*, December 7, 1997, p. 28.

12. Phrase from Jasinowski and Hamrin, *Making It in America*, 235. Achieving "environmental excellence" was actually one of the book's "proven paths to success."

13. Ibid., 235–47.

14. Cathy Jo Martin, *Stuck in Neutral: Business and the Politics of Human Capital Investment Policy* (Princeton, NJ: Princeton University Press, 2000), 74–80. On business offering health insurance, see Christy Ford Chapin, *Ensuring America's Health: The Public Creation of the Corporate Health Care System* (New York: Cambridge University Press, 2017), chap. 2.

matically in the 1980s, creating crippling outlays for corporations.[15] A NAM health care task force that studied the issue in 1990 recommended a "pay or play" policy, which would have capped costs, regulated rates, and mandated that employers either offer health insurance or pay a fee to fund a public insurance plan.[16] NAM's Tax Committee, however, viewed the plan as a corporate tax and opposed it, and the NAM board voted the proposal down.[17]

Given the health care burden on major corporations, the Clinton administration was hopeful that it could get buy-in for reform from the major business groups, including NAM. Jasinowski liked the idea of reduced costs, but knew it would be tough to persuade the organization. The small manufacturers—the majority in NAM—"were pretty universally opposed to any kind of federal healthcare."[18] Nor were pharmaceutical companies fans of reform. But from the perspective of policy, Jasinowski thought that it would be an interesting challenge to work with the administration to craft a bill that both reduced costs *and* expanded coverage. For six months, he worked with student-radical-turned-business-consultant and Clinton appointee Ira Magaziner, whom Jasinowski described as a "mad genius in terms of having a grasp of the details of policy issues," and as someone who had "an enormous grasp of every detail of our healthcare system."[19] While Jasinowski enjoyed working with Magaziner, he quickly realized that it would be hard to rein in his ambitious desire for immediate universal coverage.[20]

Unhappy with the way the plan was developing, NAM publicly criticized its scope and cost. Jasinowski felt that the Clinton plan was becoming too ambitious in what it proposed to cover (mental health, prescriptions, and long-term care) and too bureaucratically complex: "The scope of the benefits package . . . must be reduced to basic and affordable core benefits. In the future we can choose to add benefits as it becomes clear we can afford to pay for them." In the end, the NAM board of directors voted to oppose the plan, as did other major business groups.[21] But NAM had stuck out

15. Martin, *Stuck in Neutral*, 175.

16. Ibid., 100, 175.

17. Nevertheless, a survey of NAM members showed that 55 percent (of those surveyed) favored a "pay or play" approach as part of a comprehensive health care reform. See ibid., 176.

18. Jerry Jasinowski, interview with the author, October 8, 2015.

19. Ibid.

20. Ibid.

21. Quoted in Robert Pear, "Business Group Assails Scope and Cost of Clinton Health Plan," *New York Times*, October 21, 1993, p. A1; see also Steve Pearlstein, "National Manufacturers Group Joins Opposition to Clinton Plan," *Washington Post*, February 6, 1994, p. A7.

its neck the furthest, and the debacle soured relations with the Clinton administration.

THE MANUFACTURING CAMPAIGN AND INSTITUTE

On the brighter side, a big NAM initiative—the "Manufacturing Campaign"—was proceeding apace. Tied to NAM's centennial, it was another in a long line of public relations efforts geared toward educating the public. This one was focused on "Manufacturing's New Era" and specifically targeted congressional representatives and their staffs. Manufacturing had changed—it was automated and high-tech, lean and flexible. It was producing exports that made up 30 to 40 percent of the GNP, and its productivity rates were on par with Japan's and Germany's.[22] The problem was that Capitol Hill policymakers held an outdated image of manufacturing as "old factories, old workers, old technology, and old management style," in Jasinowski's words.[23] None of them had visited a plant for decades. The Manufacturing Campaign sought to convince Congress and its staff that manufacturing had fundamentally changed and was still crucial to economic growth and well-being—something that had once just been assumed. The goal was to get them to enact "pro-manufacturing agenda items," such as workforce training and capital cost reduction.[24] Jasinowski urged NAM directors to open their plants, get involved, and donate money to get the message out. Maytag made the first $100,000 contribution, followed by NAM stalwarts Armstrong World Industries, Boeing, Rubbermaid, and Emerson Electric.

Part of the campaign's efforts would fund a new Manufacturing Institute, a nonlobbying think tank that would conduct research and publish reports about manufacturing and manufacturing employment. The Institute provided fact-based information—such as *The Facts about Modern Manufacturing*[25]—that could be used and distributed by NAM to "get the message out." The Manufacturing Institute would become NAM's research

---

22. See Jerry Jasinowski, interview with the author, October 8, 2015; Sylvia Nasar, "American Revival in Manufacturing Seen in US Report," *New York Times*, February 5, 1991, p. A1; "Americans Lazy? Not So, Says Japanese Study," *Los Angeles Times*, February 4, 1992, p. WA4; and *Economic Report of the President* (Washington, DC: US Government Printing Office, 1996), chap. 8.

23. "National Association of Manufacturers President Jerry Jasinowski's Report on the Manufacturing Campaign," October 19, 1991, p. 10, series 13, box 248, NAMR.

24. Ibid., 18.

25. Manufacturing Institute, *The Facts about Modern Manufacturing*, 8th ed., 2009, http://www.themanufacturinginstitute.org/~/media/D45D1F9EE65C45B7BD17A8DB15AC00EC/2009_Facts_About_Modern_Manufacturing.pdf.

arm, focusing particularly on training, education, and the skill shortage crisis.[26]

The Manufacturing Campaign was tied to NAM's centennial in 1995. Though cause for celebration, the centennial was also an uncomfortable reminder of NAM's "age of industry" roots. To combat this image problem, NAM commissioned psychedelic pop-artist Peter Max to design a series of posters highlighting the dynamism of American manufacturing. As NAM chairman J. Tracy O'Rourke (of Varian Associates, medical equipment and semiconductors, Palo Alto, California) put it, "[We need] something that depicts our industry as the key to our future, not a quaint relic of our past. Something that demonstrates our pride, our excitement and our new emphasis on brains over brawn."[27] Called "100 Years of Manufacturing Excellence," the poster series captured the themes of NAM's evolving manufacturing campaign: quality products, innovation, creativity, and employee teamwork.

To mark the centennial further, Jasinowski coauthored a book called *Making It in America: Proven Paths to Success from 50 Top Companies*, which examined how fifty successful companies (many of them NAM members) had met a specific challenge and turned themselves around. Offering lessons to others, it was the quintessential developmental project, advising manufacturers on how to manage their workers, streamline their processes, and export their goods—just as NAM had been doing for a hundred years. Its particular emphasis on employee teamwork, worker training, and "smarter jobs" put a positive spin on one of the main consequences of the new productivity, which was the decline of manufacturing jobs.

Employee Empowerment in the Age of Lean Industry

While manufacturing as a sector of the US economy was enjoying a revival, labor-intensive industry continued its exodus to other countries. As historians Alfred Eckes and Thomas Zeiler noted, US companies that had once manufactured appliances, machine tools, and apparel were now more like "marketing organizations for foreign producers."[28] Manufacturing still

26. Jerry Jasinowski, interview with the author, October 1, 2015; board of directors meeting minutes, February 9–11, 1995, p. 20, series 13, box 248, NAMR.

27. "Peter Max and the 100 Years of Manufacturing Excellence," Hagley Library and Research Center, September 15, 2017, https://www.hagley.org/research/programs/nam-project-news /peter-max-and-100-years-manufacturing-excellence.

28. Eckes and Zeiler, *Globalization and the American Century*, 211; see also Geoffrey Jones, *Multinationals and Global Capitalism* (New York: Oxford University Press, 2005), 102–5.

occurred in the United States—as evidenced by the 365,000 manufacturing companies with fewer than 500 employees, which supplied parts and components to downsized larger companies.[29] Indeed, the United States still led the world in manufacturing added-value. But manufacturing jobs were in steady decline both in absolute numbers and as a percentage of the workforce.[30]

US industry regained high rates of productivity by disintegrating the vertical integration that had once made it a symbol of American power. Rather than transforming raw materials into finished products in a single, multidivisional, Chandlerian production unit, large companies in the 1990s assembled products from supplies and parts manufactured by smaller plants elsewhere, either at home or abroad.[31] Thus, for instance, autoworkers assembled cars and trucks from contracted components rather than manufacturing them in-house. Likewise, new steel mini-mills produced specialized steel parts rather than finished steel sheets from iron ore. Sometimes called "lean production" or "post-Fordist," the new production systems allowed manufacturers to cut their labor force, while creating opportunities for smaller, more efficient companies in an increasingly global supply chain. Established companies such as Hewlett-Packard, IBM, and Sony eventually sold their production facilities to new generic electronics manufacturing firms and then contracted with them for routers, cable modems, and other products "produced" under their auspices, but no longer in their plants.[32]

Advances in technology and communications enabled and encouraged this process, allowing companies to coordinate and track production

---

29. Data from John Holusha, "An Industrial Policy Piece by Piece," *New York Times*, July 30, 1991, p. D1. For an overview of manufacturing employment and productivity, see Martin Neil Baily and Barry P. Bosworth, "US Manufacturing: Understanding Its Past and Its Potential Future," *Journal of Economic Perspectives* 28, no. 1 (Winter 2014): 3–26.

30. From a high of 19.5 million in 1979, manufacturing jobs had declined to 17.2 million by 2000; Vaclav Smil, *Made in the USA: The Rise and Retreat of American Manufacturing* (Cambridge, MA: MIT Press, 2013), x. In 1947, the manufacturing sector employed 25.8 percent of the workforce, more than any other sector (if one separates out retail, education, professional, health, and the various other service sector categories); by the 1990s, manufacturing employed around 15 percent of the workforce. See Baily and Bosworth, "US Manufacturing," 4; Derek Thompson, "Where Did All the Workers Go? 60 Years of Economic Change in 1 Graph," *Atlantic*, January 26, 2012, https://www.theatlantic.com/business/archive/2012/01/where-did-all-the-workers-go-60 -years-of-economic-change-in-1-graph/252018/.

31. As Gerald Davis, *Managed by the Markets*, 12, put it, "Transactions that would have been protected within a single organizational boundary in the industrial era are more cheaply outsourced across organizational and national borders today."

32. Ibid.

in other locations and countries.[33] While some companies sold off their production facilities, others updated their machines, automating processes once performed by workers.[34] With such organizational and technological innovations, the "man-hours" per ton of US steel production dropped from eleven to four, below the average of Japan and Germany.[35]

Reducing man-hours reduced the need for large numbers of employees. As a result, private-sector unions never recouped their membership numbers, nor their power. Private-sector unionization fell by two-thirds from 1973 to 2009, dipping below 10 percent of the labor force in the 1990s.[36] The AFL-CIO was still around, but its resources were directed to public-sector unions, which still constituted a healthy 35 percent of the public-sector workforce. Remnants of the old industrial unions held on in steel and autos, for example, but their bargaining power had vanished. Unable to resist the speedups, automation, and temporary workers that were making industry more productive, unions and the government infrastructure that supported them became increasingly irrelevant.[37]

But workers and employees were still very much relevant, and how to retain and train them continued to be the focus of NAM efforts. As it had done in the 1920s (chapter 4), NAM focused on worker empowerment and training as ways to increase productivity. Jasinowski's book *Making It in America* identified the first "path to success" as "Releasing the Creativity and Power of Workers." The manufacturing renaissance, wrote Jasinowski, was "about respecting the individual and unleashing the full creative power of people," especially the workers on the production floor: "They are the ones who

33. The best description of this is Nelson Lichtenstein, *The Retail Revolution: How Wal-Mart Created a Brave New World of Business* (New York: Picador, 2010), chaps. 2 and 6. See also Davis, *Managed by the Markets*, chap. 1.

34. See, for instance, "At Ingersoll, Flexibility, Change, Are a Way of Life," *Chicago Tribune*, November 5, 199, p. D12.

35. Jasinowski and Hamrin, *Making It in America*, 28. On these new processes, see Jones, *Multinationals and Global Capitalism*, 96–97; and Barry C. Lynn, *End of the Line: The Rise and Coming Fall of the Global Corporation* (New York: Doubleday, 2005), chaps. 3–7.

36. Rosenfeld, *What Unions No Longer Do*, 3–4; see also Kimberly Phillips-Fein, "Why Workers Won't Unite," *Atlantic* (April 2015), https://www.theatlantic.com/magazine/archive/2015/04/why-workers-wont-unite/386228/.

37. On the obsolescence of the National Labor Relations Board, see Thomas Geoghagen, *Only One Thing Can Save Us: Why Our Country Needs a New Kind of Labor Movement* (New York: New Press, 2015); and Jonathan Rauch, "The Conservative Case for Unions," *Atlantic*, July/August 2017, https://www.theatlantic.com/magazine/archive/2017/07/the-conservative-case-for-unions/528708/.

FIGURE 12.1. Labor Union Membership as a Percentage of the Non-agricultural Workforce, 1930–2010. After 1980, the data on union density are from private-sector unions. *Sources*: US Census Bureau, *Historical Statistics of the United States, Colonial Times to 1970*, bicentennial edition (Washington, DC: US Government Printing Office, 1975); US Census Bureau, *Statistical Abstract of the United States* (Washington, DC: US Government Printing Office, 1980, 1990, 2019).

must take full advantage of today's sophisticated and expensive machines."[38] Reflecting the resurgence of individualism, the goal of empowerment was "to make every employee an entrepreneur," which was (re)defined as "motivated to do their job in the best manner possible."[39] Bolstered by rewards and incentives, the goal was to create "high-performance workplaces" with motivated workers fully committed to efficiency and quality.

Unions could be a part of this strategy, and indeed several unionized companies are featured in the book. But as Jasinowski said elsewhere, "The bulk of the success stories are clearly in the nonunion camp. That is just the facts."[40] Industrial unions had historically opposed such gambits, which they regarded as manipulative anti-union claptrap.[41] Indeed, NAM's program of "positive employee relations" included a session called "Union Avoidance

38. Jasinowski and Hamrin, *Making It in America*, 51.

39. Ibid., 51. On how the "rights revolution" of the 1960s and the revival of "individualism" in the 1980s undermined unionism, see Lichtenstein, *State of the Union*, chaps. 5–6.

40. Louis Uchitelle, "Defining New Role for Unions of Future," *New York Times*, August 8, 1993, p. A1, 32.

41. On labor's view of these changes, see Lichtenstein, *State of the Union*, 238–45. For the debate on "democratic" management methods, see Bruce Kaufman, *Managing the Human Factor: The Early Years of Human Resource Management in American Industry* (Ithaca, NY: Cornell University Press, 2008), chaps. 1–2; and Sanford Jacoby, *Modern Manors: Welfare Capitalism since the New Deal* (Princeton, NJ: Princeton University Press, 1997).

Training for Supervisors and Managers."[42] In their weakened state, however, unions could offer little resistance. Plus, there was a whole new generation of workers who were willing to give strategies like NAM's a try.

There was no denying the power of the rhetoric. Worker "empowerment" required that bosses and managers "let go" and trust their workers' own initiative and know-how. Hierarchy in the form of a looming boss or stringent rules and regulations impeded workers' ability to take ownership of their work. "Empowerment produces excited and committed workers," wrote Jasinowski. A female worker from an Ohio-based engine mount manufacturing company testified: "I like coming to work because I know that I'm important. I matter."[43] Also part of the package was teamwork, which created a sense of "belonging" (long a concern of management experts), while also privileging the wisdom of the work group or "hive-mind." Cooperation and teamwork sat easily beside empowerment and individualism; what is the group, readers were reminded, but a collection of striving individuals?

Trusting one's workers required a lot of training, another twentieth-century managerial chestnut. Training was necessary not just to keep workers up to date with rapidly changing technology but also to inculcate worker loyalty and productivity. Training was the second "proven path to success" (after worker empowerment) in Jasinowski and Hamrin's book, but it had always been part of streamlining and rationalizing industry. As in the past, companies weren't doing nearly enough of it. Jasinowski praised Chaparrel Steel Company for its policy of having 85 percent of its 950 employees enrolled in training programs at any one time.[44] Successful companies understood training as an investment, not a cost. It boosted productivity, lowered costs, and was necessary if companies wanted to introduce advanced manufacturing technologies or restructure work around self-managed teams.[45] The language of "worker empowerment" thus went hand in hand with the creation of "high-performance workplaces," which required "continuous improvement" and "increased speed and agility," with an emphasis on total quality control. Again, though couched here in the language of empowerment and "change," these were basically speedups, long resisted by industrial unions.

The final proven path to success was to "shake up the organization." "If it's not broken, break it," quipped the authors. The lesson from NAM member

42. Board of directors meeting minutes, February 7–11, 1991, p. 7, series 13, box 248, NAMR.
43. Jasinowski and Hamrin, *Making It in America*, 55.
44. Ibid., 90.
45. Ibid., 81.

Varian Associates was "perpetual revolution"—an expression most associated with Lenin, but also in keeping with the "creative destruction" that these successful companies were engaged in as they radically transformed production floors and fifty years of labor relations.[46]

The Clinton administration's Labor Department, headed by Robert Reich, embraced these ideas about "high-performance workplaces" and training. As discussed in the previous chapter, Jasinowski had invited Reich to NAM in 1983 to discuss industry's future. Even then, Reich had been interested in helping to transition the old industrial economy into a more high-tech, efficient, non-union industrial economy.[47] Now the head of a Democratic administration's Labor Department, Reich had to take unions more seriously, which he did by pushing for a minimum wage hike, parental leave, and a law prohibiting employers from replacing striking workers—all measures strenuously opposed by NAM.

But in terms of rationalizing industry, worker empowerment, and training, Reich was on the same page as NAM. In his memoir *Locked in the Cabinet*, Reich describes visiting the LS Electro-Galvanizing Corporation in Ohio, which, he was pleased to see, spent more than 10 percent of payroll on training and used worker committees to do hiring and set production. In referring to the company in terms of "we and us" rather than "they and them," the workers revealed, he believed, that they had a stake in the company. In a paragraph that could have come right out of Jasinowski and Hamrin's book, Reich writes:

> Eventually places like this will replace factories and offices where Americans used to work, where decisions were made at the top and employees merely followed instructions. That's because the old competitive advantage—depending on large scale and specialized machines doing the same operations over and over—is being eroded by global competition and new technologies capable of performing many different operations.[48]

One problem with the employee participation model, however, was that the National Labor Relation Board deemed the new worker committees or

46. The quoted material in this paragraph are headings from the final section of Jasinowski and Hamrin, *Making It in America*, called "Focusing on Continuous Improvement," pp. 205–325. For a smart analysis of how the "neoliberals" co-opted the language of revolution from the left, see Lichtenstein, *State of the Union*, 219–20.

47. On Reich's views, see chapter 11; see also Rothenberg, *The Neoliberals*; Lichtenstein, *State of the Union*, 215–18; and Robert Reich, *The Next American Frontier* (New York: Penguin, 1983).

48. Robert Reich, *Locked in the Cabinet* (New York: Alfred A. Knopf, 1997), 112; see also Lichtenstein, *State of the Union*, 217–18.

groups to be company unions, which were prohibited by the National Labor Relations Act. Indeed, the NAM Legal Department fought NLRB rulings that deemed workplace "action committees" at Electromation, Inc., and DuPont to be "illegal company dominated labor organizations" according to the NLRA.[49]

In an effort to address just such anachronisms, Reich and Commerce Secretary Ronald Brown formed the Commission on the Future of Worker-Management Relations in March 1993, with the additional aim of improving both labor-management relations and productivity. Headed by labor economist and former labor secretary John Dunlop, the Dunlop Commission (as it was called) consisted of three former labor secretaries, one former commerce secretary, three academic experts, two former union leaders, and two corporate heads.[50] They took testimony from interested parties, including NAM.

NAM witnesses testified to the importance of employee involvement programs. NAM lawyer Rosemary Collyer agreed that company unions should be prohibited, but argued that the experimental employee involvement programs were not company unions.[51] A worker from a "self-directed team" at NAM member company Universal Dynamics, Inc., said that workers wanted to "participate in the decision-making process at work," but that this was not happening because of the NLRB. As a result, "management groups that are genuinely trying to bring about positive changes in their labor management relationships" were hindered, while others were given "an excuse not to even try to change."[52] Universal Dynamics CEO and NAM director John C. Read summed it up by saying that while work processes and roles had changed, "our industrial relations system remains intact," to

49. See board of directors meeting minutes, February 11–13, 1993, p. 26, series 13, box 248, NAMR.

50. "Contact Information for the Members of the Commission on the Future of Worker-Management Relations," January 1994, retrieved January 10, 2019, from Cornell University, School of Industrial and Labor Relations, http://digitalcommons.ilr.cornell.edu/key_workplace/414/.

51. "Issues of Employee Participation in the Workplace: Statement of Rosemary M. Collyer on Behalf of the National Association of Manufacturers before the Commission on the Future of Worker-Management Relations," August 10, 1994, Cornell University, School of Industrial and Labor Relations, *Federal Publications: Key Workplace Documents*, https://digitalcommons.ilr .cornell.edu/cgi/viewcontent.cgi?article=1338&context=key_workplace.

52. "Statement of Chester McCammon on Behalf of the National Association of Manufacturers before the Commission on the Future of Worker-Management Relations," August 1994, from Cornell University, School of Industrial and Labor Relations, *Federal Publications: Key Workplace Documents*, https://digitalcommons.ilr.cornell.edu/cgi/viewcontent.cgi?article=1366&context =key_workplace.

the detriment of all.[53] Jasinowski also testified in favor of "alternative dispute resolution," which used peer-reviewed arbitration panels and the like to resolve labor-management problems, rather than the NLRB. This would save companies millions of dollars in legal fees, while also, in theory, fostering a more cooperative and congenial workplace.[54]

The Dunlop Commission's final recommendations endorsed both labor's desire for simplified union formation and management's hope for NLRB revision. The Clinton administration sought a compromise between labor and management on these issues, but none was forthcoming.[55] NAM opposed the recommendations favoring labor, but it praised the Dunlop Commission's call for "properly organized nonunion employee participation programs," which were, said Jasinowski, "the cornerstone of the new smart workplace."[56] The Commission disbanded and faded from public memory; Reich does not even mention it in his memoir. But it captured the Clinton administration's attempts to guide this economic transformation.

NAM's commitment to worker training and education in the 1990s recalls its efforts on behalf of compulsory high school education in the 1910s (chapter 1). Given that the new manufacturing jobs required more skills and education, NAM lobbied the government to support educational reform and workforce readiness. Its work in this area resulted in the bipartisan-supported Goals 2000: Educate America Act (1994), which set educational goals and provided resources for schools to update their curricula and technology to prepare students for twenty-first-century jobs, and the School-to-Work Opportunities Act (1994), which provided funding for schools to make education relevant to students' future careers, ensuring that "students learn the habits and skills that employers value" and increasing their chances of

53. "Statement of John C. Read on Behalf of the National Association of Manufacturers before the Commission on the Future of Worker-Management Relations," September 8, 1994, from Cornell University, School of Industrial and Labor Relations, *Federal Publications: Key Workplace Documents*, https://digitalcommons.ilr.cornell.edu/cgi/viewcontent.cgi?article=1378&context=key_workplace.

54. "Testimony of Jerry J. Jasinowski before the Commission on the Future of Labor-Management Relations," November 1993, p. 11, from Cornell University, School of Industrial and Labor Relations, *Federal Publications*, http://digitalcommons.ilr.cornell.edu/key_workplace/346/.

55. Lichtenstein, *State of the Union*, 245.

56. See "Blueprint for Labor Peace Feeds Fires of Contention," *Chicago Tribune*, January 10, 1995, p. C1; and Monica Gliva and Pete Lunnie, "Dunlop Commission Report Acknowledges Importance of Employee Involvement Says NAM," press release, January 9, 1995, retrieved from Cornell University, School of Industrial and Labor Relations, http://digitalcommons.ilr.cornell.edu/key_workplace/467.

finding "high-skill, high-wage employment."[57] As Cathy Jo Martin discusses in more detail, these education and training bills represented one of the few areas of domestic bipartisan agreement and government-industry cooperation during this time.[58]

Global NAM

NAM's hundred-year commitment to exports and economic internationalism paid off in the 1990s. The end of the Cold War, improvements in transportation and communication, and the loosening of currency controls sped up globalists' dreams of an economically integrated world. These same factors, however, also sparked greater resistance to economic globalism, particularly from parts of the Democratic Party. With the Cold War ended, national security could no longer justify cultivating trade relations with erstwhile competitors. Then, too, many Americans and workers blamed globalization for the death of manufacturing jobs. Nonetheless, a preponderance of thought-leaders, intellectuals, media commentators, bankers, and business leaders welcomed the possibilities of more fluid borders and assured naysayers that global integration would bring progress, peace, and prosperity, not just to Americans, but also to the rest of the world. NAM led the chorus, continuing its export campaigns, but also lobbying hard for NAFTA, the General Agreement on Tariffs and Trade, and trade with China.

THE NORTH AMERICAN FREE TRADE AGREEMENT

The North American Free Trade Agreement of 1994 was a regional trade agreement that removed barriers to trade and investment between Canada, Mexico, and the United States, while also providing intellectual property protections, investment safeguards, and dispute resolution guidelines. Negotiated in 1991–1992 under the George H. W. Bush administration, the final agreement was passed by a Democratic Congress and signed into law by Clinton in 1993. It took effect in January 1994. The new North American market was a counter to the European Union, which had united the European

---

57. Quoted in "School to Work Opportunities Act," https://www2.ed.gov/pubs/Biennial/95 -96/eval/410-97.pdf. On NAM support for these acts, see board of directors meeting minutes, February 8–10, 1996, pp. 4–7, series 13, box 248, NAMR. On the history of business support for education and training reform, see Martin, *Stuck in Neutral*, chap. 6.

58. Martin, *Stuck in Neutral*, chap. 6.

market during the same years; these new economic blocs quickly became the world's two largest.

NAFTA had bipartisan support in the United States, but it also faced fierce, organized opposition. The AFL-CIO, environmentalists, and other parts of the Democratic Party saw it as a way for corporations to escape environmental and labor regulations and exploit low-wage labor. These critics claimed that it would destroy American manufacturing jobs and contribute to further environmental degradation. Republican-oriented nationalist types, such as businessman Ross Perot and textile manufacturer (and former NAM member) Roger Milliken, also feared the further decline of American manufacturing and the loss of US sovereignty.[59]

Corporations, however, were united behind NAFTA. The major business organizations—NAM, the US Chamber of Commerce, the Business Roundtable, and various coalitions made up of their members—worked together to lobby Congress and spread the message that trade creates jobs. They argued that NAFTA would not only create jobs but also lower prices for consumer goods and strengthen American firms' competitiveness at home and abroad. US companies, of course, *already* built plants in Mexico (*maquiladoras*) that imported duty-free goods back into the United States. They did not need NAFTA to do that. What NAFTA would do was remove Mexican and Canadian import barriers so that US companies could sell more goods in those markets. Those exports would create jobs for Americans. As Jasinowski noted, "Mexico may be a poor country, but it's a good customer, a better customer than Japan for manufactured goods."[60] The financial sector argued further that the agreement would create a safe and open investment environment free from distortions caused by subsidies and trade barriers.[61]

NAM worked hard for NAFTA, and its meetings hummed with reports of NAFTA-related activities. It turned out to be a relatively easy win. As Jasinowski recalled, "It's not like we were in World War I and in the trenches."[62] NAFTA had broad support among the media, intellectuals,

59. On the NAFTA debates, see Irwin, *Clashing over Commerce*, chap. 13. For a more critical perspective, see Eckes and Zeiler, *Globalization and the American Century*, 231–43; and John R. MacArthur, *The Selling of "Free Trade": NAFTA, Washington, and the Subversion of American Democracy* (New York: Hill and Wang, 2000).

60. "Business Leaders Say Compete Don't Retreat," *Washington Post*, October 26, 1993, p. B1; Irwin, *Clashing over Commerce*, chap. 13.

61. Eckes and Zeiler, *Globalization and the American Century*, 232.

62. Jerry Jasinowski, interview with the author, September 22, 2015. Jasinowski's observation is interesting because, in subsequent accounts, those who were favorable to NAFTA tend to emphasize the ferocity of the opposition and the closeness of the congressional vote (Irwin,

and people in power. Writers such as Thomas Friedman and Francis Fukuyama viewed globalization as inevitable, the direction of history. Even at this late date, however, there were still NAM members who quit the organization because of its support for freer trade. Of note here was Roger Milliken, the CEO of the privately held Milliken & Company, a textile and floor-covering corporation based in South Carolina. Part of the old Manion Forum crowd, Milliken was a longtime conservative activist who had helped fund William Buckley's *National Review* and Barry Goldwater's 1964 campaign. But he wanted no part of the Clinton era global free trade agenda. One wonders why he stayed in NAM as long as he did.[63]

As promised, NAFTA increased US exports to both Mexico and Canada.[64] This was great for many NAM member companies. As Jasinowski explained, "The real cutting edge from a revenue point of view was exports."[65] On the other hand, imports increased even more, leaving the United States with ever-widening trade deficits with its North American partners.[66] The results of NAFTA are still being contested, although focus has shifted to the massive trade deficits that the United States has racked up with China, which dwarf whatever effects NAFTA had.[67]

THE GENERAL AGREEMENT ON TARIFFS AND TRADE

Concurrent with the NAFTA negotiations, the United States was also engaged in negotiating the latest round of GATT agreements. The Uruguay Round (as it was called) lasted from 1986 to 1994 and included 123

Clashing over Commerce, chap. 13), while those who were more critical of it point, as Jasinowski did, to its easy passage (Eckes and Zeiler, *Globalization and the American Century*, 225–42).

63. Jasinowski recalled that he and Milliken argued several times about NAM's support for NAFTA, and that Milliken finally took his company out. Inside the used copy of John McArthur's *The Selling of "Free Trade"* that I ordered online was a notecard from Milliken touting the book as "important reading!" On Milliken's protectionism, see Patrick J. Buchanan's eulogy, "Requiem for a Patriot," *American Conservative*, January 3, 2011, https://www.theamericanconservative.com /2011/01/03/requiem-for-a-patriot/.

64. US exports to Mexico went from $51 billion in 1994 to $164 billion in 2010. Exports to Canada went from $114 billion to $249 billion in the same years. See US Census Bureau, "Trade in Goods with Mexico," https://www.census.gov/foreign-trade/balance/c2010.html#1994; and US Census Bureau, "Trade in Goods with Canada," https://www.census.gov/foreign-trade/balance/c1220.html.

65. Jerry Jasinowski, interview with the author, September 22, 2015.

66. With regard to Mexico, the United States went from a $1 billion trade surplus, to a $66 billion deficit, while the Canada deficit went from $13 billion in 1994 to $28 billion in 2010. See US Census Bureau tables cited in note 64.

67. On the impact of NAFTA, see Lynn, *End of the Line*, 40–41.

contracting nations. It revised agricultural and textile agreements, while also developing new policies on intellectual property rights, financial services, telecommunications, and a host of other issues concerning the service industries, which were heavily regulated in most nations. The United States was interested in eliminating these regulations, which its negotiators called "trade barriers," in order to bolster the international expansion of the service and finance sectors in a way that would balance the US trade deficit in goods.[68]

The Uruguay Round created the World Trade Organization, a more palatable version of the ill-fated International Trade Organization from 1947 (see chapter 7). The WTO was conceived as a supranational arbiter for "free trade" that would create regulations, enforce them, and settle disputes among signatories. Its rulings, for instance, would replace the unilateral sanctions allowed in the 1974 Trade Act, which Reagan had used to handle unfair practices (see chapter 11). The net result and intent was to shift trade regulation from nations to the international trade community, leaving less powerful nations with less control over their environment, working conditions, and economic fate. The WTO was the culmination of a search on the part of international capitalists, including those in NAM, for a way to protect international economic investments from national laws and regulations.[69] It makes sense that NAM, which had been fighting against its own government's regulations for a hundred years, would resist other countries' regulations as the international economy became more integrated.

NAM worked hard to shape the negotiations. NAM's International Economic Affairs Committee regularly reported on GATT progress over the seven years, while its Public Affairs Committee helped mobilize regional organizations to lobby for it.[70] As it had done with NAFTA, NAM worked with the other major business organizations to ensure congressional approval of the new GATT agreement in 1994.[71] There was some opposition, but in another victory for global capitalism, the bill passed handily.

---

68. Chorev, *Remaking US Trade Policy*, 149–59; Irwin, *Clashing over Commerce*, chap. 13.

69. As such, these efforts represented an affront to national sovereignty, in the way that right-wingers like Milliken and Patrick Buchanan believed it did. The idea of the WTO as an attempt to avoid national laws and regulations is explored in Slobodian, *Globalists*, introduction.

70. See, for example, board of directors meeting minutes, January 30–February 2, 1992, p. 6, series 13, box 248, NAMR.

71. See their full-page ad in the *New York Times*, April 15, 1994, p. A26.

TRADE WITH CHINA

Back in the 1890s, the young NAM, enthralled by the potential size of the Chinese market, had lobbied the US government to keep an "open door" to China. A hundred years later, still dazzled by export prospects, it was still lobbying the government to promote trade with China. As NAM-friendly Democratic senator Lloyd Bentsen saw it, "In Asia . . . they will spend a trillion dollars in infrastructure of all types in the next decade. . . . I'm from Texas. I'm used to big. But it is difficult to comprehend how big that market is and how those economies are transforming."[72] It was not just Chinese markets that American business was interested in, but also Chinese labor. By the early 1990s, more and more American businesses and brands were having their goods manufactured in "special economic zones" set up in China. Most famously, Wal-Mart had a string of suppliers in Guangdong Province.[73] Motorola, a producer of advanced electronics and semiconductors (and a NAM member), began to produce some of its products in China in the early 1990s.[74] No longer were Chinese factories simply churning out undifferentiated cheaper goods; now they were manufacturing more advanced electronics. By 1993, China was the tenth-largest trading nation in the world, with 35 percent of its exports going to the United States.[75]

But China was still a long way from being welcomed into the world economic community. The United States and Europe were concerned about its human rights record, its mostly communist economy, its piracy, and its other violations of intellectual property rights. The United States offered China provisional most favored nation status beginning in 1979, but it had to be renewed regularly, and each time it came up for renewal there was debate in Congress about its worthiness.[76] And then, in 1989, China brutally suppressed protesters at Tiananmen Square, killing hundreds of

---

72. Quoted in Thomas Friedman, "Looking to Asia, Bentsen Sees History in the Making," *New York Times*, March 19, 1994, p. 39.

73. On how China became part of the supply chain of American retailers like Wal-Mart, see Lichtenstein's excellent book *The Retail Revolution*. On China's opening in the 1990s, see Lynn, *End of the Line*, chap. 2; and Appleby, *The Relentless Revolution*, 374–84.

74. Lynn, *End of the Line*, 45–48.

75. Kim Changsoo, "Terms of Endearment: The United States' China Policy and China's Accession to the World Trade Organization," *Journal of East Asian Affairs* 10, no. 1 (Winter/ Spring 1996): 74–100, 85.

76. Changsoo, "Terms of Endearment," 84–85.

students.[77] Expressing outrage, Congress passed a flurry of bills putting trade sanctions on China. While critical of the Chinese government, President Bush did not want to threaten US-China trade relations and worked to quiet the situation, eventually waiving sanctions and renewing China's MFN status. This gave presidential candidate Bill Clinton the opportunity to attack Bush for his "indifference to democracy."[78]

As president, Clinton himself renewed China's MFN status. To the alarm of the business community, however, he added conditions that China would have to meet in order for its MFN status to be renewed again the following year. Immediately, NAM, the Chamber, the Emergency Committee for American Trade, and others sprang into action with a yearlong media blitz. In letters to the president, on TV talk shows, in newspapers, and with charts, NAM and its allies argued that true progress in human rights would come, as it always had, with economic prosperity and modernization—not by isolating nations. The only nation hurt by these kinds of unilateral moral policies was the United States, which felt the loss of jobs and growth as other nations— our competitors—were quick to scoop up the opportunities left on the table by our moral outrage.[79] Responding to this pressure, Clinton backtracked, delinking human rights from MFN renewal in 1994 and renewing China's MFN status. After this victory, NAM and its allies turned their attention to getting China into the new WTO.[80]

CONSEQUENCES OF NAM'S INTERNATIONAL ACTIVITIES

As a result of these activities, exports of US-made goods increased, from $585 billion in 1995 to $1,279 billion in 2010. US exports to China rose from $12 billion to $92 billion during those same years. At the same time, as per

77. The number of deaths remains uncertain and has been exaggerated. The Tiananmen Mothers Organization has concretely identified 202 victims, whose names are listed at http:// www.tiananmenmother.org/index_files/Page480.htm (in Chinese). I thank my colleague Jenny Day for this reference.

78. See David M. Lampton, "America's China Policy in the Age of the Finance Minister," *China Quarterly* 139 (September 1994): 597–621.

79. For a summary of these arguments, see Lampton, "America's China Policy in the Age of the Finance Minister," 604–7. On NAM's role, see board of directors meeting minutes, February 8–11, 1996, p. 4, series 13, box 248, NAMR; see also numerous newspaper articles citing NAM as a leading manufacturers' group seeking China's MFN renewal, such as Daniel Southerland, "Business Leaders to Urge Clinton to Reverse His Stance on China Trade," *Washington Post*, October 23, 1992, p. B1A.

80. For the factors behind Clinton's actions, see Lampton, "America's China Policy in the Age of the Finance Minister"; and Peter Behr, "US Business Waged Year Long Lobbying Effort on China Trade," *Washington Post*, May 27, 1994, p. A28. On the WTO campaign, see Changsoo, "Terms of Endearment," 93–100.

usual, imports also increased. The US trade deficit in goods went from $101 billion in 1990 to $635 billion in 2010.[81] A trade deficit is not necessarily a bad thing, especially for those US corporations producing goods in China. Nor is it clear that a trade deficit is economically detrimental, or even a sign of economic weakness, given the increasing interconnectedness of supply chains and production systems. Nonetheless, there remains concern about the effect of trade deficits on US manufacturing and employment.

Scientist and policy analyst Vaclav Smil, for one, sees the merchandise trade deficits as a sign of the ongoing devastation of US manufacturing. Like Jasinowski, Smil sees a healthy manufacturing sector as fundamental to economic growth. Manufacturing is the principal driver of technical innovation, which has been the source of growth in all modern societies. Moreover, the dependence of much of the service industry on manufacturing creates demand for jobs in accounting, legal, education, transportation, and so on. So the idea that a nation could survive in the world on merchandise imports strikes Smil as absurd.[82] In his view, the number-one threat to US manufacturing and jobs has not been globalization per se, but the uneven trade arrangements that have resulted in these gigantic and growing trade deficits. In 2000, the US trade deficit with China was $83.3 billion, which surpassed the long-standing deficit with Japan, but in four short years even that would double to $162 billion.[83]

Smil attributes these deficits mostly to China's manipulation of its currency exchange rate and its low wages. But he also faults US companies' obsessive pursuit of China's market. Other countries offer even cheaper labor, but not the promise of the largest new market in the world, which was what led US companies to produce their goods there, despite having to endure forced technology transfers and intellectual property theft.[84] He concludes: "There can be no doubt that many American companies became active participants in the deindustrialization of the US economy as they went out of their way to kowtow to China in order to maximize their profits."[85]

Smil's concerns are validated by the greatest loss of US manufacturing jobs since before World War II that occurred between 2000 and 2010, when

81. The US trade deficit with China rose from $34 billion in 1995 to $273 billion in 2010. Figures from US Census Bureau, "Trade in Goods with China," https://www.census.gov/foreign-trade/balance/c5700.html#1995. See also Smil, *Made in the USA*, 147–56, for the effects of China trade.

82. Smil, *Made in the USA*, 12–14.

83. Ibid., 147. Smil discusses at some length the problems with trade data and competing models.

84. Ibid., 150.

85. Ibid., 150, citing various studies.

US manufacturing lost 5.7 million jobs. In the auto industry, jobs declined from 1.3 million workers in 2000 to 624,000 in 2009. Part of this decline was due to the 2008 recession; nevertheless, despite the recovery of 800,000 jobs by 2014, that still left a net loss of 4.3 million jobs.[86]

There is lively debate about how much of this decline was due to the trade deficit and China's economic rise, and how much was due to other structural and economic factors, such as automation.[87] Smil, however, makes the case (via Labor Department algorithms) that the majority of these job losses were due specifically to trade with China.[88] These declines in employment were accompanied by (temporary) declines in productivity and output as well.[89]

Like Smil, Jasinowski saw manufacturing as essential to economic growth. He lectured politicians about manufacturing's "multiplier" effect in creating jobs, education, and opportunities, which was why the government needed to support the manufacturing sector. Smil and Jasinowski even agree that exports were key to bolstering manufacturing. In retrospect, Jasinowski admits, "we were too easy on a number of these trade agreements and the NAM would better have served manufacturers if it had taken a somewhat harder line" with regard to trade abuses, currency devaluation, and subsidies.[90] When it came to relocating production to China, however, there was no way that American companies, or NAM, would have stood by and let others get into that market. Even back in 1900, NAM had worried that American manufacturers were being kept out of China. The United States could not have survived with exports if other countries (its competitors) had set up shop in China and secured that market for themselves. As Jasinowski said, "If you were genuinely a global player, you had to talk like a global player. So you couldn't just pretend that being global meant exporting only."[91] In other words, to *not* have pursued trade in and with China would not have been in manufacturing's interest either.

86. See Robert E. Scott, "Manufacturing Job Loss: Trade, Not Productivity, Is the Culprit," Economic Policy Institute Issue Brief 402, August 11, 2015, p. 3. On auto jobs and decline in 2000–2010, see Smil, *Made in the USA*, x, 109–11.

87. Baily and Bosworth, "US Manufacturing," 3–26, try to parse out various explanations for manufacturing's decline in the first decade of the twenty-first century.

88. Smil, *Made in the USA*, 149.

89. Scott, "Manufacturing Job Loss," 2. Productivity has risen steadily since 2010, even as manufacturing employment remains flat. See charts in Sarah Chaney and Anthony DeBarros, "Many Manufacturers' Ups and Downs Have Little to Do with Trump," *Wall Street Journal*, September 26, 2019, https://www.wsj.com/articles/many-manufacturers-ups-and-downs-have-little-to-do-with-trump-11569490204?mod=hp_major_pos3.

90. Jerry Jasinowski, interview with the author, September 22, 2015.

91. Ibid.

While the manufacturing sector suffered as a whole, the largest NAM corporations continued to prosper, at least in the short term. The question of whether the trade association acts in the interests of all manufacturers or only in the interests of the largest has dogged NAM its entire history. It was a common charge lodged against NAM throughout the Progressive Era, the New Deal, and the early Cold War eras, although it was mainly a dig, a way to call out the rich and powerful. NAM did serve its smaller members in many ways, and not just by schooling them in how to act more like large corporations. It also provided them with access to resources, information, networking connections, and potential business opportunities. As it reminded them regularly, it kept unions at bay and fought back the federal government. And of course members were always free to leave, as many did.

But it is hard to look back at NAM's constant push for lower tariffs, foreign investment, and trade expansion and not wonder if its leaders ever hesitated about the threat that imports posed for NAM members. As long as large corporations like Monsanto were defending tariffs, NAM internationalists were hemmed in, forced to negotiate safety nets and redress for those harmed by imports and forced to be sensitive to the consequences of freer trade. By the 1990s, however, the world they had worked to bring about was upon them. But now NAM, which had begun its existence rationalizing and organizing industrial capitalism, found itself beginning the twenty-first century swept up in a new version of capitalism that it had helped create but could not control.

Epilogue

NAM is still a going concern. It has survived and adapted to new circumstances, and it has a purported membership of 14,000.[1] It keeps a lower profile. It is no longer the go-to "voice of business," but it still partners up with the US Chamber of Commerce and the Business Roundtable. No longer separating employers from workers, today's NAM says that it represents "more than 12 million men and women who make things in America."[2] This claim boosts its numbers, but also suggests a post-union world in which NAM is no longer an employers' association per se, but rather presides over a specific economic sector. The current NAM president is Jay Timmons, a former chief of staff for Virginia Republican George Allen. Another non-manufacturer, Timmons has been NAM president since 2011. He lives with his husband and three children in a DC suburb.

In other ways, the current NAM resembles its old historic self, despite the drastically different economic and political climate of the twenty-first century. It continues to promote development, offering seminars, data, and other resources to help new manufacturers navigate the new economy. It continues to promote exports and international cooperation, even as a new Republican administration has brought back the tariff. It is still fighting international cartels and defending the Export-Import Bank. As in the past, NAM has its critics, which include not just organized labor and the left but

1. NAM, "Jay Timmons," https://www.nam.org/Contact/Staff/Jay-Timmons/.
2. Ibid.

also smaller manufacturers, who view it as representing large firms at the expense of innovation and smaller firms.[3]

NAM today walks a fine line with regard to President Donald Trump. On the one hand, it has applauded Trump's specific recognition of manufacturing as key to America's past and future "greatness," as well as the tax cuts and his "tough on China" stance. If *Business Insider* is to be believed, NAM has "unfettered access" to the Trump White House and is "making a killing."[4] On the other hand, Trump's revival of economic nationalism and tariffs presents a problem to a new generation of smaller, domestic manufacturers who have come to depend on imported parts and components.[5] NAM supports "a smart strategic approach" to China's "market-distorting behaviors," but warns about the damage that tariffs can do to manufacturers and workers in the United States.[6] NAM offers its criticisms carefully because it sees an ally in Trump.

On immigration, NAM has been somewhat bolder in speaking for its interests. Anti-immigrant policies have rarely served the interests of US manufacturers, especially in a tight labor market. Even before Trump became president, NAM was calling for bipartisan comprehensive immigration reform, uniting with other business and education groups to make it easier for high-skilled workers, especially in the STEM fields, to work in the United States. In June 2018, NAM demanded an end to the policy of separating parents and children at the border with Mexico.[7] Timmons has used the Trump-inspired immigration "conversation"/crisis to renew calls for reform and has shared NAM's immigration plan with FoxBusiness.com.

3. "An Open Letter to Jay Timmons, President and CEO of the National Association of Manufacturers," *The Belden Blog*, September 26, 2013, http://beldenblog.com/an-open-letter-to-jay-timmons-president-and-ceo-of-the-national-association-of-manufacturers/.

4. Joe Perticone, "The Manufacturing Sector Suddenly Has Unfettered Access to the White House under Trump, and It's Making a Killing," *Business Insider*, May 7, 2018, https://www.businessinsider.com/national-association-of-manufacturers-have-exploded-in-the-trump-era-2018-4.

5. NAM, "NAM Statement on Implementation of New China Tariffs," press release, August 7, 2018, https://www.nam.org/Newsroom/Press-Releases/2018/08/NAM-Statement-on-Implementation-of-New-China-Tariffs/.

6. Keith Laing, "Tariff Turmoil 'Cuts Legs Off' Manufacturers," *Detroit News*, June 18, 2019, https://www.detroitnews.com/story/business/autos/2019/06/18/manufacturers-warn-trump-chinese-tariffs-will-hurt-bottom-line/1477267001/.

7. NAM, "Manufacturers Demand End to Immigration Policy of Separating Children from Parents," press release, June 18, 2018, https://www.nam.org/Newsroom/Press-Releases/2018/06/Timmons--Manufacturers-Demand-End-to-Immigration-Policy-of-Separating-Children-from-Parents/.

Titled "A Way Forward," the plan includes physical barriers to "strengthen border security," but then seeks more humane, compassionate, and permanent solutions for those populations seeking to remain in or gain entrance into the United States.[8] The plan resembles the Immigration Reform and Control Act of 1986, which allowed those who had entered the United States illegally to stay and be granted amnesty, while putting in place new, enforceable legal restrictions, a law that NAM had supported.[9]

In some ways, the Trump phenomenon is a reprisal of the old protectionist, economic nationalist wing of NAM, the conservative John Bricker, *Manion Forum* devotees who eschewed international cooperation. The internationalists' vision had triumphed in NAM, but weirdly in 2016, the ghosts of nationalist conservatives came back to needle the globalists. And not just in the United States. Around the world, nationalists are striking back at the globalist agenda and its mores. We see it in Brexit, in Marine Le Pen and the Yellow Vest movement in France, in Orbán's Hungary, and elsewhere. But one place you don't see the nationalist agenda is in today's NAM, whose members have adjusted to the opportunities and challenges of the global supply chain and do not want it disrupted.

Having tied its fortunes to economic globalization, having welcomed into its fold companies from other countries, having shared its know-how over the decades with foreign manufacturers, NAM constantly pushed beyond the "National" in its name and eventually created a world where it no longer makes sense to talk about US manufacturing, or any other nation's manufacturing, as distinct from the supply chains and international finance markets that support it. NAM and the capitalism it upheld may have proved Marx wrong about the world historical role of the working class, but they validated his contention that "all old-established national industries have been destroyed or are daily being destroyed." As it turned out, it was the capitalists of the world who united, and it is their world we live in. For now.

---

8. Timmons writes about his plan in "The Immigration Plan America Needs," *FoxBusiness*, February 13, 2019, https://www.foxbusiness.com/politics/the-immigration-plan-america-needs.

9. Although NAM always opposed punitive regulations against employers. See William Carris (head of NAM's Human Resources and Equal Opportunity Committee), "In Search of Reasonable Immigration Reform," *Enterprise* (May/June 1986): 12; and "Immigration," *Enterprise* (April 1983): 28.

ACKNOWLEDGMENTS

This book has been a challenging project, but I feel fortunate to have been supported in this endeavor by Skidmore College and would like to acknowledge specifically the generosity of the Judith Johnson Carrico '65 Fund for Faculty Support and the Douglas Family Chair in American Culture, History, and Literary and Interdisciplinary Studies. Thanks as well to former dean of the faculty Beau Breslin and History Department chair Tillman Nechtman, who both encouraged me to take a leave to finish this book, the hardworking interlibrary loan staff of Scribner Library, and history students George Pisano, MacKenzie Little, and Mariana Toro, who compiled an excellent database of NAM companies in 1906, using data from *Moody's*.

A huge thank-you to former NAM president Jerry Jasinowski, who gave generously of his time and whose interviews provided some of the most illuminating insights in the book (in my opinion).

The Business History Conference has been a source of intellectual comradeship and encouragement over the past decade, and for this I would like to express my gratitude to Pamela Walker Laird, Roger Horowitz, Andrew Popp, Ben Waterhouse, Christy Ford Chapin, Laura Sawyer, and Richard John. At Hagley, I benefited from the help of Lucas Clawson and Angela Schad in finding materials. I would also like to acknowledge the efforts and inspiring energy of Lynn Cantanese, who is no longer with us. Thanks also to Janick Marina Schaufelbuehl, who shared with me some wonderful sources from her own research on international trade.

Thanks as well to those who generously read parts of this book and offered incisive comments that helped me think more clearly about what I was trying to say; they are Kim Phillips-Fein, Aaron Major, Vince DiGirolamo, Tillman Nechtman, and the two anonymous readers for the press. I would also like to express appreciation to Eric Crahan and the very efficient editorial team at Princeton University Press for all of their hard work bringing this book to market.

317

Finally, I would like to thank my friends and colleagues who have over the past six years indulged my many anecdotes and constant references to NAM, even though, let's face it, NAM is not everyone's cup of tea. You know who you are. In this regard, special thanks go to Ed McGill, a man whose love of history surpasses even mine, and who now asks whenever we happen upon an old factory or some decaying industrial structure, "I wonder if they were in the NAM?"

SELECTED BIBLIOGRAPHY

Books

Jerold Auerbach, *Labor and Liberty: The La Follette Committee and the New Deal* (Indianapolis: Bobbs-Merrill, 1966).

Raymond Bauer, Ithiel de Sola Pool, and Louis Anthony Dexter, *American Business and Public Policy: The Politics of Foreign Trade* (New York: Atherton Press, 1963).

William H. Becker, *The Dynamics of Business and Government Relations, Industry, and Exports, 1893–1921* (Chicago: University of Chicago Press, 1981).

Bernard Bellush, *The Failure of the NRA* (New York: W. W. Norton, 1975).

Gerald Berk, *Louis D. Brandeis and the Making of Regulated Competition, 1900–1932* (New York: Cambridge University Press, 2009).

Barry Bluestone and Bennett Harrison, *The Deindustrialization of America: Plant Closings, Community Abandonment, and the Dismantling of Basic Industry* (New York: Basic Books, 1982).

Clarence Elmore Bonnett, *Employers' Associations in the United States: A Study of Typical Associations* (New York: Macmillan, 1922).

Alfred Chandler Jr., *The Visible Hand: The Managerial Revolution in American Business* (Cambridge, MA: Harvard University Press, 1977).

Nitsan Chorev, *Remaking US Trade Policy: From Protectionism to Globalization* (Ithaca, NY: Cornell University Press, 2007).

Gerald F. Davis, *Managed by the Markets: How Finance Reshaped America* (New York: Oxford University Press, 2009).

Brian Doherty, *Radicals for Capitalism: A Freewheeling History of the Modern American Libertarian Movement* (New York: PublicAffairs, 2007).

Peter Drucker, *The New Society* (1950; New York: Harper & Row, 1962).

Alfred E. Eckes Jr., *Opening America's Market: US Foreign Trade Policy since 1776* (Chapel Hill: University of North Carolina Press, 1995).

Alfred E. Eckes Jr. and Thomas Zeiler, *Globalization and the American Century* (New York: Cambridge University Press, 2003).

Arthur Jerome Eddy, *The New Competition: An Examination of the Conditions Underlying the Radical Change That Is Taking Place in the Commercial and Industrial World—The Change from a Competitive to a Cooperative Basis* (Chicago: McClurg & Co., 1914).

Edmund Fawcett, *Liberalism: The Life of an Idea* (Princeton, NJ: Princeton University Press, 2014).

Niall Ferguson, Charles Maier, Erez Manela, and Daniel J. Sargent, eds., *The Shock of the Global: The 1970s in Perspective* (Cambridge, MA: Harvard University Press, 2010).

Dana Frank, *Buy American: The Untold Story of Economic Nationalism* (Boston: Beacon Press, 1999).

Elizabeth Fones-Wolf, *Selling Free Enterprise: The Business Assault on Labor and Liberalism, 1945–1960* (Champaign: University of Illinois Press, 1994).

Louis Galambos, *Cooperation and Competition: The Emergence of a National Trade Organization* (Baltimore: Johns Hopkins University Press, 1966).

Julie Greene, *Pure and Simple Politics: The American Federation of Labor and Political Activism, 1881–1917* (New York: Cambridge University Press, 1994).emery

Howell John Harris, *The Right to Manage: Industrial Relations Policies of American Business in the 1940s* (Madison: University of Wisconsin Press, 1982).

David Harvey, *A Brief History of Neoliberalism* (New York: Oxford University Press, 2005).

Patrick Hearden, *Architects of Globalism: Building a New World Order during World War II* (Fayetteville: University of Arkansas Press, 2002).

Mark Hendrickson, *American Labor and Economic Citizenship* (New York: Cambridge University Press, 2013).

Robert F. Himmelberg, *The Origins of the National Recovery Administration: Business, Government, and the Trade Association Issue* (New York: Fordham University Press, 1993).

Louis Hyman, *Debtor Nation: The History of America in Red Ink* (Princeton, NJ: Princeton University Press, 2011).

Doug Irwin, *Clashing over Commerce: A History of US Trade Policy* (Chicago: University of Chicago Press, 2017).

Jerry Jasinowski and Robert Hamrin, *Making It in America: Proven Paths to Success from 50 Top Companies* (New York: Simon & Schuster/Fireside, 1995).

John Judis, *The Paradox of American Democracy: Elites, Special Interests, and the Betrayal of Public Trust* (New York: Pantheon, 2000).

Edward Kaplan, *American Trade Policy, 1923–1995* (Westport, CT: Greenwood Press, 1996).

Gabriel Kolko, *The Triumph of Conservatism* (1961; Chicago: Quadrangle, 1967).

Greta Krippner, *Capitalizing on Crisis: The Political Origins of the Rise of Finance* (Cambridge, MA: Harvard University Press, 2011).

Naomi Lamoreaux, *The Great Merger Movement in American Business, 1895–1904* (New York: Cambridge University Press, 1985).

Nelson Lichtenstein, *State of the Union: A Century of American Labor*, rev. ed. (2002; Princeton, NJ: Princeton University Press, 2013).

Nelson Lichtenstein and Elizabeth Tandy Shermer, eds., *The Right and Labor in America* (Philadelphia: University of Pennsylvania Press, 2012).

Kim McQuaid, *Uneasy Partners: Big Business in American Politics, 1945–1990* (Baltimore: Johns Hopkins University Press, 1994).

Cathie Jo Martin and Duane Swank, *The Political Construction of Business Interests: Coordination, Growth, and Equality* (New York: Cambridge University Press, 2012).

Mark Mazower, *Governing the World: The History of an Idea* (New York: Penguin, 2012).

David Brian Peterson, *Capital, Labor, and State: The Battle for American Labor Markets from the Civil War to the New Deal* (Lanham, MD: Rowman and Littlefield, 2000).

Kim Phillips-Fein, *Invisible Hands: The Making of the Conservative Movement from the New Deal to Reagan* (New York: W. W. Norton, 2009).

Kim Phillips-Fein and Julian E. Zelizer, eds., *What's Good for Business: Business and Politics Since World War II* (New York: Oxford University Press, 2012).

Randall Rothenberg, *The Neoliberals: Creating the New American Politics* (New York: Simon & Schuster, 1984).

Karl Schriftgiesser, *The Lobbyists: The Art and Business of Influencing Lawmakers* (Boston: Little, Brown, 1951).

John Scoville and Noel Sargent, *Fact and Fancy in the TNEC Monographs* (New York: NAM, 1942).

Albert K. Steigerwalt, *The National Association of Manufacturers: A Study in Business Leadership* (Ann Arbor: University of Michigan, Graduate School of Business Administration, Bureau of Business Research, 1964).

Martin Sklar, *The Corporate Reconstruction of Capitalism, 1890–1916* (New York: Cambridge University Press, 1988).

Stephen Skowronek, *Building a New American State* (New York: Cambridge University Press, 1983).

Quinn Slobodian, *Globalists: The End of Empire and the Birth of Neoliberalism* (Cambridge, MA: Harvard University Press, 2018).

Vaclav Smil, *Made in the USA: The Rise and Retreat of American Manufacturing* (MIT Press, 2013)

Judith Stein, *Pivotal Decade: How the United States Traded Factories for Finance in the Seventies* (New Haven, CT: Yale University Press, 2010).

Judith Stein, *Running Steel, Running America: Race, Economic Policy, and the Decline of Liberalism* (Chapel Hill: University of North Carolina Press, 1998).

Peter Swenson, *Capitalists against Markets: The Making of Labor Markets and Welfare States in the United States and Sweden* (New York: Oxford University Press, 2002).

Benjamin Waterhouse, *Lobbying America: The Politics of Business from Nixon to NAFTA* (Princeton, NJ: Princeton University Press, 2013).

Robert Wiebe, *Businessmen and Reform* (Cambridge, MA: Harvard University Press, 1962).

Mira Wilkins, *The Maturing of Multinational Enterprise: American Business Abroad from 1914 to 1970* (Cambridge, MA: Harvard University Press, 1975).

William Appleman Williams, *The Contours of American History* (New York: World Publishing, 1961).

Articles

Philip H. Burch Jr., "The NAM as an Interest Group," *Politics and Society* 4, no. 1 (1973): 97–130.

Alfred Cleveland, "NAM: Spokesman for Industry?" *Harvard Business Review* (May 1948): 353–71.

Malcolm Forbes, "The NAM Would Do Better Dead," *Forbes*, August 15, 1951, p. 10.

Richard Gable, "NAM: Influential Lobby or Kiss of Death?" *Journal of Politics* (May 1953): 254–73.

Richard Gable, "Birth of an Employers' Association," *Business History Review* 33 (Winter 1959): 535–45.

Youn Ki, "Large Industrial Firms and the Rise of Finance in Late Twentieth-Century America," *Enterprise and Society* 19, no. 4 (2018): 903–45.

Jonathan Soffer, "The National Association of Manufacturers and the Militarization of American Conservatism," *Business History Review* 75 (Winter 2001): 775–805.

Richard S. Tedlow, "The National Association of Manufacturers and Public Relations during the New Deal," *Business History Review* 50, no. 1 (Spring 1976): 25–45.

Allen Wakstein, "The National Association of Manufacturers and Labor Relations in the 1920s," *Labor History* 10 (1969): 163–76.

Andrew Workman, "Manufacturing Power: The Organizational Revival of the National Association of Manufacturers, 1941–45," *Business History Review* 72, no. 2 (Summer 1998): 279–317.

Primary Sources

US Senate Judiciary Committee, *Maintenance of a Lobby to Influence Legislation*, 4 vols. (Washington, DC: US Government Printing Office, 1913).

Archives

National Association of Manufacturers Records (NAMR), accession 1411, Hagley Library and Museum, Wilmington, Delaware.

William J. Grede Papers (WJGP), 1909–1979, MSS 341, Wisconsin State Historical Society, Madison, Wisconsin.

Robert F. Kelley Papers, Georgetown University Library, Washington, DC.

J. Howard Pew Personal Papers, accession 1634, Hagley Library and Museum, Wilmington, Delaware.

Journals of Clarence B. Randall on Foreign Economic Policy, Clarence B. Randall Papers, MC109, Public Policy Papers, Department of Rare Books and Special Collections, Princeton University, Princeton, New Jersey.

INDEX

Italic page numbers refer to figures and tables.

"100 Years of Manufacturing Excellence" (poster series), 297
3M, 261

Accelerated Cost Recovery System (ACRS), 271–72
Accident Prevention and Relief (Schwedtman and Emery), 35
Acheson, Dean, 159, 172
affirmative action, 2; changing workforce and, 211–12, 217–30, 233–35; executive order 10925 and, 218n33, 219, 224; executive order 11114 and, 224; new kind of, 225–30; Nixon and, 229, 249; Office of Federal Contract Compliance (OFCC) and, 226–31; Philadelphia Plan and, 226, 229, 235; quotas and, 226–27; Reagan Era and, 230, 269
AFL (American Federation of Labor), 17; employee representation plan (ERP) and, 91; Gompers and, 63–70, 73–74, 77, 79, 87–89, 92, 157; growth of, 63, 65; improving industry and, 29, 34, 36–37; individualism and, 63; Eric Johnston and, 139; labor policies and, 83, 85, 87, 91, 93–96, 101; lobbyists and, 37, 62, 74–75, 80, 151, 202, 292; NAM's opposition to, 62–76, 80; public opinion and, 72; standardization and, 62; strikes and, 64–66, 93, 112, 143; structure of, 63; Wagner Act and, 111–12; workforce changes and, 215n18, 229, 233
AFL-CIO: *America at Work* and, 205; conservatives and, 202, 205; declining membership of, 256, 299; Equal Employment Opportunity Act and, 233; lobbyists and, 202, 292; NAFTA and, 306; postwar economic order and, 180, 186n110, 252; protectionism and, 252; Reagan Era and, 266; Taft-Hartley Act and, 212;

Trowbridge and, 266; workforce changes and, 211–14
African Americans, 97n50, 102, 210, 216; affirmative action and, 2, 211–12, 217–30, 233–35, 249, 269; discrimination and, 212–19, 222–24, 226, 230–34; NAACP and, 213–14, 219; Reagan Era and, 269; Title VII and, 217, 220–25, 231–34; Urban League and, 213, 220n38, 225
Agricultural Adjustment Administration (AAA), 119, 125
Alcoa, 261
Aldrich, Nelson, 162
Alexander, Magnus, 85
Allied Chemical Corporation, *9*, 261, 265
Allis-Chalmers, 127, 182
Alsop, Joseph, 180
Alsop, Stewart, 180
American Anti-Boycott Association (AABA), 65, 68, 73
American Business Conference, 267–68
American Creosoting Corporation, 206, 209
American Cyanamid Company, 127, 207
American Enterprise Association, 189–90
American Enterprise Institute (AEI), 190, 259
American Farm Bureau Federation, 147
American Federation of Labor. *See* AFL
American Individual Enterprise System, The (NAM), 140–43
American Industries journal: expanding trade and, 42, 47, *48*, 51, 56, 58, 60; improving industry and, 33, 35, 38; labor management and, 88–92, 99, 103–4; unions and, 73, 75
American Iron and Steel Institute, 24, 114
Americanization, 98, 100–101
American Management Association, 86, 199
American Manufacturers' Export Association (AMEA), 50–51

A NOTE ON THE TYPE

This book has been composed in Adobe Text and Gotham.
Adobe Text, designed by Robert Slimbach for Adobe,
bridges the gap between fifteenth- and sixteenth-century
calligraphic and eighteenth-century Modern styles.
Gotham, inspired by New York street signs, was designed
by Tobias Frere-Jones for Hoefler & Co.